WHO SPEAKS
FOR THE CHILDREN?
The Handbook of Individual
and Class Child Advocacy

Edited by
Jack C. Westman, MD

Professional Resource Exchange, Inc.
Sarasota, FL

To receive the latest catalog from
Professional Resource Press, please call 1-800-443-3364,
fax (941-366-7971), or write to the address below.

Printed in the United States of America

Hardbound Edition ISBN: 0-943158-48-6
Library of Congress Catalog Card Number: 90-52847

The copy editor for this book was Patricia Hammond, the managing editor was Debbie Fink, the graphics coordinator was Laurie Girsch, and the cover designer was Bill Tabler.

DEDICATION

To the parents, professionals, and politicians who have found the rewards of personal sacrifice for the next generation.

ABOUT THE EDITOR

Jack C. Westman, MD, is Professor of Psychiatry at the University of Wisconsin Medical School at Madison, Wisconsin. He brings 30 years of experience to the problems children face in the legal, human service, and educational systems. He has authored numerous professional articles and books and is the editor of *Child Psychiatry and Human Development.* Dr. Westman was the President of the American Association of Psychiatric Services for Children and is the President of the Multidisciplinary Academy of Clinical Education. He has been honored with the Award for Service to Children and the Citizen of the Year Award of the Wisconsin Association for Mental Health and the Distinguished Teaching Award of the Wisconsin Law College.

LIST OF CONTRIBUTORS

Ann R. Bailey, University of Wisconsin Continuing Education - Outreach, Madison, WI.

Carol E. Behm, Public Relations Director, Wisconsin Federation of Foster Parent Organizations, Lomira, WI.

Edith D. Bek-Gran, MSW, Community Support and Health Services Department, Madison, WI.

Beverly B. Bliss, PhD, Affiliated Psychological Resources, Madison, WI.

Janet L. Breidel, MSW, Child Protective Services Planner, Wisconsin Department of Health and Social Services, Madison, WI.

Rosemarie Carbino, MSW, Clinical Associate Professor of Social Work, University of Wisconsin, Madison, WI.

Ellen Wright Clayton, JD, MD, Assistant Professor of Pediatrics, School of Medicine, Vanderbilt University, Nashville, TN.

Thomas J. Corbett, PhD, Institute for Research on Poverty, University of Wisconsin, Madison, WI.

Martha L. Fineman, JD, Professor of Law, University of Wisconsin, Madison, WI.

James Garbarino, PhD, President, Erikson Institute for Advanced Study of Child Development, Chicago, IL.

Gail Goodman, PhD, Associate Professor of Psychology, State University of New York, Buffalo, NY.

Lynn Green, MSW, Social Services Program Manager, Dane County Department of Social Services, Madison, WI.

Stanley S. Herr, JD, DPhil, Associate Professor of Law, University of Maryland School of Law, College Park, MD.

David L. Kaye, MD, Clinical Assistant Professor of Psychiatry, State University of New York, Buffalo, NY.

Marygold S. Melli, JD, Professor of Law, University of Wisconsin, Madison, WI.

Gary B. Melton, PhD, Professor of Psychology and Law, University of Nebraska, Lincoln, NE.

Valerie Polakow, PhD, Associate Professor, College of Education, Eastern Michigan University, Ypsilanti, MI.

David A. Riley, PhD, Assistant Professor of Child and Family Studies, University of Wisconsin, Madison, WI.

Patricia A. Schene, Director, Children's Division, American Humane Association, Denver, CO.

Stephen A. Small, PhD, Assistant Professor of Child and Family Studies, University of Wisconsin, Madison, WI.

Laurence Steinberg, PhD, Professor of Psychology, Temple University, Philadelphia, PA.

Sara G. Tarver, PhD, Professor of Rehabilitation Psychology and Special Education, University of Wisconsin, Madison, WI.

Judith H. Weitz, The Center for the Study of Social Policy, Washington, DC.

Jack C. Westman, MD, Professor of Psychiatry, University of Wisconsin, Madison, WI.

ACKNOWLEDGEMENTS

In an effort to draw upon the expertise of a wide range of professionals in preparing the manuscripts for this book, a number of people were asked to comment on early drafts of the chapters. I am particularly grateful to Rosemarie Carbino of the University of Wisconsin School of Social Work, Marygold Melli of the University of Wisconsin Law School, and Ann Bailey of the University of Wisconsin Continuing Medical Education Department for their assistance in arranging for the cooperation of laypersons and community, state, and university professionals.

The comments of Carol Behm from the perspective of foster parents were incorporated in Chapter 1, "The Principles and Techniques of Individual Child Advocacy." As an attorney and pediatrician, Ellen Clayton contributed substantially to Chapter 3, "The Legal Rights of Parents and Children." Edith Bek-Gran provided the perspective of a county social service department for Chapter 5, "The Role of Guardians *Ad Litem* in Custody Contests." The research on children as witnesses by Gail Goodman was the stimulus for preparing Chapter 6, "The Protection and Reliability of Children as Witnesses." The perspective of Stephen Small as a child development specialist was helpful in preparing Chapter 7, "Child Advocacy in Day Care." Sara Tarver commented as an educator and Beverly Bliss as a clinical psychologist on Chapter 8, "Child Advocacy in Special Education." From the perspectives of a state department, Janet Breidel, and of a county department of social services, Lynn Green reviewed Chapter 9, "The Context of Child Abuse and Neglect Assessment." Rosemarie Carbino reviewed Chapter 10, "Interventions in Child Abuse and Neglect," from the point of view of social workers. Robert Callahan assisted in the preparation of Chapter 12, "The Termination of Parental Rights as a Therapeutic Option." David Riley commented as a child development specialist on Chapter 13, "Selling Adults on Children's Issues." Stephen Small reviewed Chapter 14, "Workplace Dilemmas for Mothers and Their Children." Thomas Corbett of the Institute for Research on Poverty commented on Chapter 15, "Public Policies for Disadvantaged Children and Their Families."

Chapter 7 is an abridged version of "The Risks of Day Care for Children, Parents, and Society" as it appeared in B. J. Christensen (Ed.), *Day Care: Child Psychology and Adult Economics.* Rockford, IL: The Rockford Institute.

Most of all, I am indebted to my wife, Nancy Baehre Westman, for her forbearance and for typing and editing much of the manuscript.

PREFACE

For most children, life unfolds without the need for special professional or public concern. For many, however, the intricate and fragmented legal, health, education, and welfare systems are their only hopes for a reasonable chance to succeed in life. Unfortunately, these systems lack coherent means for applying the principles of child advocacy to the lives of these vulnerable children.

For two decades, child advocates have been working to advance the causes of children in the midst of widespread public apathy. Recently, however, that mood has shifted. More Americans are coming to recognize that most social problems have their roots in the life experiences of the young. Of particular significance in our society is the realization that economic productivity depends upon strong families.

For many professionals child advocacy means only lobbying for children in legislative halls. They do not realize that it is an important, and in some instances essential, aspect of their work with individual children and their families. Both individual and class child advocacy offer organizing concepts and procedures for helping them find, understand, and serve children at risk and for generally focusing attention on the needs and rights of children.

The purpose of this book is to bring the concepts of child advocacy to the professional management of children who are caught in the webs of family, legal, educational, social service, and political systems. When the perspective of child advocacy is omitted from actions affecting them, children often are harmed even as adults think they are helping them.

The most important characteristic of professional child advocacy is that it requires the collaboration of different disciplines and interest groups. Seldom can it be carried out effectively by a single person or discipline. The key word is teamwork.

Jack C. Westman, MD
Madison, Wisconsin

TABLE OF CONTENTS

PART II.
THE LEGAL SYSTEM

PART III.
THE EDUCATIONAL SYSTEM

INTRODUCTION

Youth comes to us wanting to know what we propose to do about a society that hurts so many of them.

Franklin Delano Roosevelt, 1936

For American children and youth, growing up today is difficult in unprecedented ways. Perplexed parents seem to be treating childhood and adolescence as an experiment as the roles of mothers and fathers are being revised. Although middle- and upper-class children are acquiring more performance skills at early ages with the encouragement of their parents, a motif of absence - physical, emotional, and moral - runs through the lives of many young people who lack adult models of competence, commitment, and compassion.

Instead, our society presents young people with adults who model greed on Wall Street, deceit in government, and hypocrisy in the pulpit. The media offer a backdrop of sex, violence, hot cars, and fast foods. Commercial interests view the young as prime targets for exploitation. Adults who are not personally affected parents protest the costs of public education and child health programs, the location of children's group homes in their neighborhoods, and workplace accommodations to parents and young children. Nowhere does there seem to be a political or economic motive for presenting children with models of trustworthy adults.

As an extreme symptom of this combination of stimulation, neglect, and exploitation, urban ghetto youths now resemble the wild children of post-World War I Russia. The products of fragmented families and sensual overstimulation, many ghetto youths are members of gangs at war over the profits of addicting drugs. Now comprising some 20% of the school-age children and youth in this nation, those living in poverty are growing in numbers at a faster rate than the general population due to the higher birth rates of teenagers who drop out of school. Contributing to this situation are immigrations that have added families who lack the background and language to help their children in school (Hodgkinson, 1985).

Still, without question, children in the United States fare better today than in previous generations when extreme discrimination against them in the form of "ageism" prevailed. This was illustrated dramatically by a 1646 Massachusetts Bay Colony statute that decreed "if a man had a stubborn or rebellious son" of at least 16 years of age, he could bring him to the magistrate's court where "such a son shall be put to death." On the other hand, even in pre-Crusade Europe, some parents made substantial efforts to secure the health and well-being of sick and damaged children (Kroll & Bachrach, 1986).

From earlier times in which children were barely recognized as more than miniature adults, we have come to appreciate childhood as a period of growth during which personalities and abilities are shaped. Beginning in the last century with the efforts of "child savers" to free children from oppressive labor, we now have reached a time in which we are contemplating ways of assuring them fulfilling childhoods.

At the same time, children pose both overt and covert threats to adult control, so that adults harbor an ambivalent attitude toward children expressed in the form of the prejudice of ageism, akin to racism and sexism. Early in this century, Maria Montessori called attention to what she called universal prejudices against children (Montessori, 1974). Most important was the belief that adults know what is best for children and always "act for their good." As examples, she cited the assumptions that children must be taught to learn, overlooking their inherent, insatiable curiosity; that children's minds are empty, overlooking their rich imaginations; and that children do not work, overlooking their creative play.

Along with Montessori in Italy a few pediatricians, psychiatrists, and psychologists in the United States became involved with neglected, delinquent, and orphaned youths brought to juvenile courts and social agencies. Under the influence of psychoanalysis, these unfortunate young people came to be viewed as acting out neurotic conflicts rather than as simply incorrigible. As a result, community child-guidance clinics were spawned by the Commonwealth Fund in the 1930s. At the end of that decade the first pediatricians-turned-child psychiatrists were appointed to full-time medical school faculties. Not until 1953, however, did efforts to develop child psychiatry as a clinical specialty culminate in the founding of the American Academy of Child and Adolescent Psychiatry.

After World War II, the "Baby Boom" led to widespread concern about education and parenthood. In the wake of population shifts, rural-urban mobility, and technological advances, a great deal of unrest developed throughout large segments of the population. These feelings were accentuated by the pervasive influence of television, which exposed many of the economically and educationally disadvantaged members of society to a better quality of life. In consequent efforts to achieve medical, welfare, and educational benefits, consumer and civil-rights advocates were in the forefront. A flood of "Great Society" legislation to benefit the economically disadvantaged was enacted during the Johnson administration. Much of it was patterned after the New Deal, which had been created in response to the depression of the 1930s.

One goal of the consumerism and civil-rights movements was representation of racial, ethnic, and sexual minorities on governing bodies. A variety of forms of injustice were attacked, including racial, ethnic, sexual, and religious discrimination, and discrimination against the aged and the physically and mentally handicapped.

In this context, the impetus for child advocacy as a means of rectifying discrimination against children came in 1969 in the report of the Joint Commission on the Mental Health of Children with the support of the 1970 White House Conference on Children. A confluence of currents led to the subsequent endorsement of child advocacy (Westman, 1979). First were the efforts of child mental health workers to focus public attention on the shortage of children's mental health services. Second was the growing use of self-help and advocacy techniques by minority groups. Third was the activity of state governors' committees on children and youth. Fourth were campaigns by community action groups to improve living conditions generally. Finally, there was growing interest in the prevention of mental illness, which was seen as extending beyond the boundaries of health care to penetrate the very fabric of society and as involving a range of ecological, sociological, cultural, psychological, and biological factors.

The Joint Commission on the Mental Health of Children recommended a hierarchical federal child advocacy system with child development authorities and councils at the local and state levels. In 1973, Kahn, Kamerman, and McGowan reviewed the status of child advocacy efforts throughout the United States and concluded that such a hierarchical system was not feasible because of the lack of clarity of the concept and the pragmatic failure to distinguish services from political lobbying.

During the later 1970s and the 1980s a number of factors sidetracked development of the concept of child advocacy. The first was a misapplied emphasis on the rights of children without recognizing their inherent dependency on their parents. As a result, many child advocates became immersed in dead-end pursuits, such as abolishing minority status completely and assuming antiparental stances. This led to inappropriately granting adult rights to adolescents, as in right-to-refuse-treatment legislation that resulted in greater problems for troubled youths. The second was a general reduction in federal funding for programs that benefited children. This retrenchment was based upon disillusionment with the Great Society programs and the belief that children were the responsibilities of parents and not society. The third was the replacement of community child guidance centers by adult-oriented mental health centers. The fourth was the misconstruing of the discoveries of the neural sciences to mean that behavior and mental disorders were mostly caused by brain disorders and not by environmental and interpersonal factors. All of these elements eclipsed awareness of the importance of parent-child relationships and family and community life in the development of children.

Today one reason for the present focus on children's issues is that over 60% of the electorate is of parenting age. Many parents express anxiety about the impact of changes in the modern family and the economy on their children. They believe too little is being spent on education. They know that they have difficulty finding the kind of day care they desire at a price they can afford. They are concerned about latchkey children who are left alone part of each work day. They believe that parents should be able to take time off from work to care for their newborn or newly adopted children without fear of losing their jobs. They believe that babies fare better if they are cared for by their parents.

Beyond the concern of parents is growing public awareness of the child-development process. People recognize that children are not simply passive recipients of adult socialization, and that the parent-child unit, not the individual child, is the centerpiece of child development. We know that the child-parent unit is influenced by the interacting temperamental and cognitive endowments of each child and parent. We also know that children both legitimately and illegitimately place demands on adults, and that they subtly, but inexorably, change the society in which they become the succeeding generation (Gideonse, 1982).

Although parents are the natural advocates of children, our thesis is that all professionals who work with children have an ethical responsibility to learn individual and class advocacy skills and, in concert with others, influence child-caring systems to serve children more effectively. Without an advocacy stance, professionals tend to concentrate only on symptom-focused diagnostic and treatment procedures for children and overlook the influences of the families and environments in which they live. Because children comprise a permanent minority group, advocacy for them must be an enduring component of both professional practice and political systems.

Child advocacy is a state of mind that guides action. It is consciousness raising, so that professionals and policy makers alike think about the places and families in which children live. It should be a natural part of all long-range planning and of assessing the future consequences of present actions. It is not a megaphone for children's wishes but a method for determining and furthering their developmental needs. It can aid parents in negotiating the often bewildering paths to clinical and educational assistance for their children. It can help agencies identify as-yet-untapped needs for their services and find new ways to reduce redundancy of efforts through interdisciplinary cooperation. It emphasizes strengthening existing caregivers rather than removing children from them to impersonal institutions.

The experience of the last two decades has revealed that freestanding child advocates seldom can effectively meet the needs of individual children. As a result, multidisciplinary teams are employed in the schools to help children with specialized educational needs. Child-abuse teams have been formed to deal with abused and neglected children in hospitals. Special teams handle sexual-child-abuse cases in law-enforcement agencies.

However, these efforts are limited to either the educational, health, or law-enforcement systems and address only a part of each child's problem. They also tend to be oriented toward symptoms rather than causes. Their existence substantiates the fact that no single professional discipline is in a position to design and implement a viable plan that will make a substantial difference in the life of a troubled child. They point to the need to mobilize necessary knowledge, skills, and power through the collaboration of a variety of disciplines that cross professional systems. Rather than deal only with a particular symptom or crisis, the goal is to design and implement a life plan for a child. The system-bridging child advocacy team can fill this need more effectively than single-system teams by bringing professionals from different systems together around a particular child and family regardless of the presenting problems. It can fill the gap created by the legal system's shift away from juvenile and family courts by combining legal and mental health resources to deal with troubled children and their families.

Participation in advocacy for individual children places professionals in a position to appreciate the need for, and to contribute to, class advocacy. When professionals experience success in managing difficult cases, they can help to focus the efforts of class advocates. Individual and class advocacy are interdependent. Neither is complete without the other. Both offer adults opportunities to demonstrate their trustworthiness to the young.

REFERENCES

Gideonse, H. D. (1982). The politics of childhood. In K. M. Bowman (Ed.), *The Social Life of Children in a Changing Society* (pp. 276-277). Hillsdale, NJ: Lawrence Erlbaum.

Hodgkinson, H. (1985). *All One System: Demographics of Education, Kindergarten Through Graduate School.* Washington, DC: Institute for Educational Leadership.

Kahn, A. J., Kamerman, S. B., & McGowan, B. J. (1973). *Child Advocacy: Report of National Baseline.* New York: Columbia University School of Social Work.

Kroll, J., & Bachrach, B. (1986). Child care and child abuse in early medieval Europe. *Journal of the American Academy of Child Psychiatry, 25,* 562-568.

Montessori, M. (1974). *Childhood Education.* Chicago, IL: Regnery.

Westman, J. C. (1979). *Child Advocacy.* New York: Free Press.

Part I

THE FAMILY SYSTEM

INTRODUCTION

Children are potentially free . . . they are not things and cannot be the property either of their parents or others.

Georg W. F. Hegel, 1831

The tendency to limit the concept of child advocacy to lobbying for children in governmental circles has led professionals who deal with children to assume that someone else - usually a few class child advocates - is representing the needs of children. For this reason, the distinction between class and individual advocacy is important. Both are devoted to creating and providing opportunities and resources for children and their families who need them. But class advocacy does that for children in general or for specific groups of children, whereas individual advocacy identifies a specific child, determines that child's needs, and insures that those needs are met.

The traditional roles of clinicians as diagnosticians, therapists, and consultants usually are sufficient for professional work with adults. However, in order to help many children the additional role of advocate is necessary. Although professionals are neither qualified nor authorized to act as parents, they can help when parents are not able to fully provide sustenance, nurturance, and advocacy for their children.

Competent professional practice necessitates weighing, balancing, and resolving conflicting demands, expectations, and pressures. For this reason, individual child advocacy cannot focus

3

simply on a child, because the child is part of a child-parent unit, and the needs of the child and the parent must be considered simultaneously. Thus, advocacy for a particular child means family advocacy by supporting whenever possible the advocacy functions of that child's parent.

In addition to families, communities benefit from individual child advocacy. Professionals who assume an advocacy role with children and youth model community involvement in the lives of its young people. In communities where parents, teachers, and other adults take an active responsibility and express consistent values and expectations, most youths weather the storms of adolescence and pass into adulthood successfully (Ianni, 1989). But in communities riddled by conflict, isolation, and despair, where institutions and people do not offer cogent and consistent direction or hope for a brighter future, many young people become discouraged, confused, and cynical and drift into delinquency, truancy, unemployment, unwed pregnancy, and suicide. Confronted with the often conflicting demands of homes, peers, schools, and the job market, young people look to adults for guidance on major questions of values and future direction. To reclaim these youths, we must become actively involved in their lives as advocates.

Coons and Sugarman (1977) suggested three qualities of an ideal child advocate: (a) the advocate truly incorporates the voice of the child in decision making; (b) the advocate really cares about the child; and (c) what happens to the child directly affects the advocate. Professionals do not meet all of these criteria, but most parents do. This favors a basic presumption in favor of parents with interventions that support families. Conversely, it points to the importance of terminating parental rights over children when parents are demonstrably unwilling or unable to function as such and obtaining parents who can do so.

Even the most experienced and competent professionals risk allowing personal attitudes to distort professional decisions, and they may be unable to perform more than one role with reference to a particular child. One way of guarding against biases is by sharing responsibilities with colleagues, agreeing on the task each will undertake, and helping each other to keep each respective role clearly defined (Provence, 1986). The child advocacy team provides a vehicle for doing this.

An underlying social attitude contributes to the problems of adolescents and the special considerations involved in advocacy for them. It is the fact that our society does not accept the adolescent years as a legitimate period of life. Teenagers cannot wait to "grow up," and many adults would abolish adolescence, if it were possible to do so. This lack of understanding and acceptance of adolescents as a permanent segment of a community is reflected in the public school's view of secondary education as preparatory for college or vocations rather than as an important phase of life in itself. This view is illustrated by the statement on the death of an adolescent that "she had not yet begun to live." It is no wonder that adolescents are impatient and bored with a society that views them as transitional objects on their way from carefree childhood to adult maturity at some later date. It is the fortunate adolescent and family who find the teenage years to be special and who treasure the freshness and vitality of youth. Paradoxically American society, which seemingly tries to recapture its youthfulness, robs those living through adolescence of the dignity and respect due anyone at any age. For this reason, in addition to the capability of adolescents to contribute to the process themselves, it is useful to distinguish youth advocacy as a special form of child advocacy.

Both individual and class child and youth advocacy can help protect future generations by increasing the number of adults who are competent parents. They offer opportunities for breaking the family cycle of disadvantage passed from one generation to the next by adults who themselves had detrimental childhoods.

REFERENCES

Coons, J. E., & Sugarman, S. (1977). *Parents, Teachers, and Children: Prospects for Choice in American Education.* San Francisco, CA: Institute for Contemporary Studies.

Ianni, F. A. J. (1989). *The Search for Structure: A Report on American Youth Today.* New York: Free Press.

Provence, S. (1986). Preface. In J. Goldstein, A. Freud, A. J. Solnit, & S. Goldstein, *In the Best Interests of the Child: Professional Boundaries.* New York: Free Press.

5

1

THE PRINCIPLES AND TECHNIQUES OF INDIVIDUAL CHILD ADVOCACY

Jack C. Westman

The social role of parenting includes sustenance functions that provide food, shelter, and clothing; developmental functions that offer affection and restraint; and advocacy functions that introduce and maintain children as members of their communities. This chapter defines individual child advocacy as an extension of parental advocacy.

The techniques of individual child advocacy are devoted to finding, evaluating, and obtaining help for vulnerable children. They depend upon the cooperation and integration of a variety of professional disciplines, as can be accomplished by a child advocacy team.

In 1800, a naked boy was captured in the woods of central France. He was mute, shameless, and interested only in eating, sleeping, and escaping. Named Victor, he was housebroken and trained like a dog with a leash. He ultimately came to the attention of a speech pathologist, Jean Itard, who provided foster care and special training for Victor, but fell exasperatingly short of helping him become a fully human person (Lane, 1975).

Itard established a model for child advocacy by assuming complete responsibility for a young person for whom he had therapeutic objectives. His work could not have been done simply through conventional treatment methods. His concern for Victor, the "Wild Boy of Aveyron," was an unusual example of

7

interest in a child two centuries ago. Victor received attention because of his dramatic situation at a time when children were regarded as the possessions of their parents; many were mistreated by modern standards while discrimination against them in the form of "ageism" prevailed. Without question, children fare better today.

In the affluent United States, one may question why child advocacy is needed at all. From earlier times in which children were regarded as miniature adults, we have come to appreciate childhood as a period of growth during which personalities and abilities are shaped. In some ways we worry too much about our children. Although conflicts between older and younger generations still reflect adult ambivalence toward children in society, it seems clear that our society's will is to promote the healthy development of children. The problem lies less in the lack of desire than in finding practical ways to do so.

That we have good reasons to be concerned about our children is illustrated by the fact that, in comparison with other technologically developed nations, the United States has fallen behind in the indicators of the quality of life. It has a lower rate of growth in gross national product and profit rate in manufacturing. It has the highest levels of infant mortality, divorce, teenage pregnancy, and homicide. Most significantly, it allows one-fourth of all its young children to live in poverty (Bronfenbrenner, 1986).

Another reflection of the distress of young people in the United States is a characteristic pattern, described by Urie Bronfenbrenner, of progressive alienation of young people from affluent as well as disadvantaged families. The principal elements in this "syndrome of alienation" emerge in chronological order: lack of attentiveness in school; academic underachievement; misbehavior in school; smoking and drinking; sexual promiscuity; substance abuse; cynicism toward work; teenage pregnancy; dropping out of school; and ultimately vandalism, violence, criminal acts, or suicide.

Research on the origins of this pattern of progressive social alienation reveals causal factors at two successive levels. The principal one is family stress and disorganization. The second is the absence of significant models in the lives of young people for the development of competence and the capacity for making commitments. The most important deterrents to social alienation and an adult criminal life are a fortunate biological endowment, secure parental attachments, and consistent discipline - the central features of family life (Wilson & Herrnstein, 1986).

The evidence is clear that strengthening relationships between adults and children, most critically in families, is needed to insure the healthy development of children, reduce society's problems, and increase both the economic productivity and the moral stature of later generations (Edelman, 1987; Yogman & Brazelton, 1987). The family is the most humane, powerful, and efficient system for producing competent human beings. There are other ways, but they are far less dependable and so much more expensive that no society, however prosperous, can afford them. Previous efforts in communist countries and in Israel to replace the family failed (Westman, 1989, pp. 18-20).

FUNCTIONS OF THE FAMILY

An appreciation of the functions of the family is helpful in understanding child advocacy. The heart of the family is the parent-child unit. The social role of parenting includes three basic sets of functions: (a) *sustenance functions* through providing food, shelter, and clothing; (b) *developmental functions* through affectionate and restraining caregiving and parental modeling of coping skills and values; and (c) *advocacy functions* through planning for, making decisions about, and negotiating a child's sustenance and developmental needs in the community by arranging for housing; child care; health care; education; social, organizational, and recreational activities; and by intervening when a child has problems in the community. Parents vary in the ways they perform these functions and the degrees to which they meet the corresponding needs of their children.

Theoretically, when adults function in parenting roles their interests and the interests of their children are congruent. In reality, the interests of adults in roles apart from their parenting roles frequently conflict with the interests of their children. When this happens, and when parental advocacy is insufficient, professional child advocacy is needed.

PRINCIPLES OF CHILD ADVOCACY

In England and the United States professional child advocacy is an extension of parental advocacy based upon the traditional *parens patriae* and *in loco parentis* doctrines, both of which traditionally lodge responsibility for children with the state. It is assuming responsibility in varying degrees and ways for meeting the sustenance and developmental needs of children through both class and individual advocacy. Class child advocacy aims to represent the interests of children in society and is discussed in Chapter 13. The aim of individual child advocacy is to support, restore, or replace parental advocacy.

The methods of individual child advocacy are interdisciplinary; professional coordination and continuity are stressed because of the prevalent fragmentation and discontinuity of services for children (Young, 1990). The objectives of child advocacy are based upon value judgments related to furthering the development of personal competence in children. Important ingredients of personal competence are social skills, self-control, the ability to learn, prosocial values, decision-making ability, a coherent self-identity, and self-esteem. In order to develop these qualities, children need dependable, intimate relationships with adults who model competent living and with peers with whom they learn social skills.

The nature of child advocacy can be clarified by making a semantic distinction between the legal concepts of acting *in behalf* and *on behalf* of a person. Acting in behalf is acting in the place of a person with no obligation to consult with or abide by the wishes of that person. Acting on behalf of a person is acting as an extension of that person. With mentally incompetent adults, legal advocacy is acting in behalf of an adult. With mentally competent adults, legal advocacy is acting on behalf of an adult. Because of the varying degrees of decision-making competence inherent in childhood, child advocacy is acting both in behalf and on behalf of a child. It involves judgments on the part of the advocate regarding the interests of a child and incorporating the child in that process. At the same time the challenge is to make the advocacy process a constructive developmental experience for the child. In itself, the problem-solving nature of child advocacy offers a model of competence for children who have experienced incomplete or ineffective parenting.

PROFESSIONAL RESISTANCES
TO CHILD ADVOCACY

There is a pressing need to sensitize and prepare professionals for advocacy roles. Many parents also need help in more effectively carrying out their advocacy functions with their children. In spite of legislative efforts to recognize the interests and rights of children, practical and effective means of doing so have been slow in coming.

Unfortunately, professional systems that deal with children have built-in mechanisms that make it possible for professionals to insulate themselves from awareness of the need for child advocacy. As a means of warding off the helpless anxiety and uncertainty generated by seemingly overwhelming family problems, the health worker is preoccupied with the treatment of disease, the lawyer with legal procedures, the social worker with administrative policies and paperwork, and the educator with the mechanics of teaching. All professionals can claim that advocacy is not their responsibility and that, even if it were, it is too time-consuming and difficult.

These defenses allay the anxiety of professionals but also interfere with their empathic involvement in children's lives and are antithetical to the interests of children. The need for these defenses can be reduced by professional knowledge of advocacy techniques that surmounts uncertainty about whether or not one should intervene, and how to do so.

THE TECHNIQUES OF
INDIVIDUAL ADVOCACY

The techniques of professional individual child advocacy can be described as: (a) *case finding* to identify vulnerable parent-child units; (b) *system bridging* to coordinate pertinent child-caring systems; (c) *fact finding* to determine the needs of a child and the capacities of a parent to meet them; (d) *communication with the child* to involve the child directly in the advocacy process; (e) *defining objectives* of supporting, strengthening, or replacing parental sustenance, developmental, or advocacy roles; (f) *conflict resolution* between individuals and between child-caring systems; (g) *formulating and implementing a life plan* for the child based upon knowledge of child development; and (h) *protecting and promoting the legal rights* of children.

CASE FINDING

The first technique of *case finding* involves sensitivity to the emotional, behavioral, and situational manifestations of vulnerability in child-parent units. Knowledge of the ways in which children and parents directly and indirectly signal their needs for help provides cues for expanding one's professional role in a child or parent's life beyond the usual responsibilities of one's discipline. These signals of parent-child unit vulnerability exist when a child's emotional, behavioral, or educational problems occur in the setting of disruption or disturbance of the parent-child unit.

Disruptions of parent-child units include separation, divorce, bereavement, and unwed teenage parenting. Disturbed parent-child units include child abuse and neglect, alcoholic and drug-addicted parents, and mentally ill parents. In 1979 in the United States, an estimated 20% of all children lived in disrupted parent-child units, and 21% of all children lived in disturbed parent-child units (Westman, 1979, pp. 18-21). Those percentages probably are higher today.

SYSTEM BRIDGING

The second technique is *system bridging,* which means inquiring beyond the usual purview of one's discipline into the status of a child's family. At the least, it means communication between teachers, children, and parents (Rutherford & Edgar, 1979). At the most, it means bringing together professionals from all relevant disciplines to exchange knowledge about a child's life situation. A planning conference, which precludes thinking of any part of a child's life as separate from other parts, is essential for beginning the advocacy process. Establishing a foundation for effective advocacy depends upon awareness of the importance of time, place, and interpersonal context for each child. The time in the child's life in which vulnerability of the parent-child unit takes place is important. A child's reactions are determined by the place in which events occur, because the nature of the setting determines the attitude and behavior of a child. Gathering information from other observers helps determine the significance of a child's behavior. The interpersonal context also is important, because a child may act one way with one person and another way with another person.

FACT FINDING

The third technique is *fact finding,* which means determining a child's sustenance, developmental, and advocacy needs and the capacities of a parent to meet them. At the least, this process involves assembling information about a particular need on the part of the child, such as special educational placement. At the most, it involves interdisciplinary diagnostic procedures. Because advocacy interventions can be drastic, they should not be based upon superficial assumptions. Child advocacy draws upon the diagnostic and investigative procedures of the social service, health, and legal systems because of their individual person focus. Specific knowledge about a particular parent-child unit is essential for informed child advocacy.

COMMUNICATION WITH THE CHILD

The fourth technique is *communication with the child* in order to gain access to the child's experience of the family, school, and community. It also enables interpretation of ongoing events to the child and participation of the child in the advocacy process. Many children do not understand why their parents divorced, why they were placed in special education classes, or why they were placed in foster homes. The failure to emphasize communication with a child can lead to investigative and placement interventions without a child's understanding of why they are taking place, leaving explanations to the child's imagination. Depending upon the age, attitude, and circumstances of a child, special techniques may be required to facilitate communication. At the least, establishing rapport is vital in order to enlist a child's cooperation. Play techniques, structured interviews, as in instances of possible sexual abuse, and projective psychological testing may be required to ascertain a child's perceptions and reactions.

DEFINING OBJECTIVES

The fifth technique is *defining objectives* as an advocate. The objectives depend upon the extent to which parenting capacities can potentially meet the developmental needs of a child. For example, the primary objective for a handicapped child might be supporting parental advocacy by finding appropriate resources and insuring that the child benefits from them. At the next level, the objective might be strengthening parenting capacities through therapy, training, or education, as with physically abusive parents. At a more intrusive level, the objective might initially, or ultimately, be replacing neglectful parents temporarily through foster care or permanently through termination of parental rights and adoption. Tentatively setting objectives at the outset, progressing from the least to the most intrusive, frequently is not done. The consequence is that crisis situations often are handled with the most drastic interventions without an assessment of the individual circumstances and the feasibility of less intrusive possibilities. For this reason early attention to determining the least detrimental alternative for the child is imperative (Goldstein, Freud, & Solnit, 1973; Goldstein et al., 1986).

CONFLICT RESOLUTION

The sixth technique is *conflict resolution*, or mediation. Whether conflicts exist between children, parents, schools, neighbors, or institutions, their resolution comprises much of the work of individual advocacy. Most adults think that they know what is best for a child. Furthermore, under stressful circumstances, adults often behave like children with rivalries, envies, and competition. There also is a strong tendency to handle embarrassment, shame, and guilt by projecting blame onto others and denying personal responsibility. Identifying these sources of anxiety and empathically dealing with them by employing mediation techniques can convert a stormy course of advocacy to a relatively harmonious one.

Conflicts often revolve around a child's role in decision making. Three factors should be taken into account in assessing a child's capacity to assume responsibility for personal decision making. The first is that the parent bears responsibility for the care and support of the child and the consequences of the child's actions or inactions. A child, in turn, is responsible to the parent, who bears societal responsibility for the child. A young person's decision-making capacity, therefore, must be seen in the context of the parent's responsibility for the child. The second is the child's cognitive capacity and wisdom to appreciate the nature, extent, and probable consequences of a specific decision. The third is the extent to which decision making can be a joint undertaking by child and parent as a part of the developmental process and as an experience that will facilitate learning for the child.

In actual practice, the issue of a child's ability to make decisions usually arises only when a conflicted child-parent relationship exists. This is precisely when the child or youth is most likely to seek independence as a means of rebelling against authority. Because the parents have not fostered self-determination, that same young person lacks preparation for independent decision making. The young person may have the cognitive capacity to make decisions but lacks wisdom and is driven by impulsive motives. Thus, the real question is less when a young person is ready to assume responsibility for autonomous decision making and more how to mediate between parent and child in order to facilitate joint decision making.

FORMULATING AND IMPLEMENTING A LIFE PLAN

The seventh technique is *formulating and implementing a life plan* to facilitate a child's growth, personality development, social adaptation, and education. The life plan, or permanency plan, is handled by an interdisciplinary advocacy team, as described more fully in Chapter 4. This usually is a complicated process that extends over years of a child's life, because it involves coordination and continuity over time, as does the usual advocacy of a parent for a child. At the least, it is helping parents arrange for the specialized health care or education of children with handicaps. At the most, it involves the interdisciplinary coordination of multiple systems over an extended period of a child's life.

Unfortunately, the usual fragmentation of services and lack of continuity of care prevents the appropriate and expeditious formulation of a life plan and its implementation in harmony with a child's changing developmental course with family and peer relationships and with the school calendar. For this reason, the long-term monitoring and updating of a child's life plan is important.

PROTECTING AND PROMOTING LEGAL RIGHTS

The eighth technique is *protecting and promoting the legal rights* of a child. Child advocacy sets up a useful tension between the rights of children and the rights of people who influence their lives. The rights to counsel, due process, and to equal protection apply to both children and their parents. The rights to an education and to appropriate care and treatment apply in varying degrees to children. A guardian *ad litem* in legal matters that affect children can handle legal advocacy for a specific child.

CASE EXAMPLES

The application of all of these techniques of individual child advocacy can be illustrated by two cases: one involving a custody and visitation dispute and the other the management of child abuse and neglect. These cases were selected to illustrate the

15

incredible circumstances experienced by children who need effective, interdisciplinary advocacy.

A CUSTODY AND VISITATION DISPUTE

The case of 10-year-old Kathy illustrates the practice of child advocacy by a teacher, pediatrician, social worker, child psychiatrist, and attorney in a custody dispute.

Kathy's parents were married 1 year before she was born. Her father had a history of episodic alcoholism and violent behavior. When Kathy was 3 years old her parents divorced after several separations and reconciliations. Three months after the divorce, her father murdered her mother. She was taken in by her mother's adoptive parents, who were granted guardianship. Over the subsequent 6 years Kathy was exposed to repeated litigation between her father and maternal grandparents over her custody and his visitation rights. After he was granted visitation privileges with Kathy, her grandparents tried to have them suspended. The father's relatives intervened on his behalf. By the age of 7, Kathy was showing behavior problems surrounding visits with her father in the state penitentiary to which she was driven by social workers under court order.

Kathy's school teacher expressed concern to her grandparents and the school psychologist about the effects of visiting her father. Her pediatrician related her headaches to the visits and urged the grandparents to seek psychiatric advice. Her social workers documented the behavioral upsets seen around the paternal visitations and the lack of interaction between father and daughter on those occasions. The grandparents were encouraged to seek elimination of paternal visitation, and a guardian *ad litem* was appointed for Kathy.

Subsequent investigation by a forensic child psychiatry service revealed that Kathy was bonded to her maternal grandparents and that the father's motivation for visitation was to enhance his chances of parole from prison on the grounds of being needed by his daughter. The court then affirmed the grandparents' full legal custody of Kathy and ordered that paternal visitation would be at their discretion.

A CASE OF CHILD ABUSE AND NEGLECT

The Smith family, consisting of two parents, an infant son, 2- and 4-year-old girls, and a 6-year-old boy, illustrates the application of child advocacy principles to a situation of child abuse and neglect.

The Smiths initially lived in a neighboring state where repeated reports of child neglect were made by neighbors to the county department of social services. An investigation was not initiated, however, until a physician reported concern about the survival of their infant son, who was manifesting the failure-to-thrive syndrome. When the investigation began, the family moved to stay with a relative in another state. Several weeks later the relative reported that the parents were beating the older children and ignoring their baby.

Investigation by the county department of social services revealed a malnourished 5-month-old boy, who immediately was hospitalized, in addition to unkempt, ill-fed older children with bruises on their bodies. The children were found to be in need of protective services. Their guardianship was assumed by the county, and they were placed in foster care. The guardian *ad litem* referred the case to a forensic child psychiatry service for assistance in determining the children's needs and the parent's capacities to meet them in order to design a dispositional plan. At that point a child advocacy team was convened consisting of the guardian *ad litem*, the county social workers, the county attorney, and the child psychiatrist. Necessary interviews, data collection, investigations, and testing were planned and carried out.

The children were found to show evidence of varying degrees of neglect as reflected in developmental delays and behavior problems. The mother was found to be of borderline intelligence with a major auditory memory deficit and a dependent personality disorder. The father was found to have an antisocial personality disorder. He had periodically left the family, and his motive for returning to them was presumed to be to receive the social security benefits of the two older children (whose father was deceased) and the Aid to Families with Dependent Children benefits for the two younger children. The findings were discussed at a conference of the child advocacy team and the attorneys for the parents. Return conditions were established at the dispositional hearing on the Child in Need of Protective Services petition, and a termination of parental rights warning was given and acknowledged by the parents in the court record.

One year later the child advocacy team reviewed the parent's compliance with the treatment plan and found it to be marginal. Although they had maintained a stable marriage and residence without responsibility for the care of their children, they had participated in only half of the scheduled counseling and parent training sessions. They had not recognized their children's birthdays nor kept regular visitation with the children; when they did, there was little parent-child interaction. The three younger children were thriving in foster care, but the 7-year-old required placement in a child-caring institution. Re-evaluation of the parents and children by the child advocacy team did not reveal significant change in the parents and confirmed the progress in the children.

The county attorney initiated a termination of parental rights action. At the jury trial the parents alleged mismanagement by the county department of social services and denied their neglect. They introduced a mental health professional who, on the basis of a 2-hour interview with the parents, testified that the parents should have another chance. The judge did not permit the guardian *ad litem* to participate in the summation to the jury. The jury found that parental rights should be terminated, but also found that the county department of social services had not been diligent in trying to help the parents. The judge, therefore, dismissed the case. An appeal by the county attorney resulted in an appellate court ruling that the case be retried. During the intervening year, the parents left the state, and their rights were ultimately terminated on the grounds of abandonment. The three younger children were adopted by their foster parents. The oldest child left residential care and was placed in permanent subsidized foster care.

This case illustrates the need for the sustained pursuit of advocacy for a child over a period of several years to cope with the points at which the vagaries of the mental health and legal systems can subvert it.

THE CHILD ADVOCACY TEAM

In general, when children need professional advocacy, the efforts of a single discipline are insufficient, and the formation of an interdisciplinary child advocacy team is indicated. In child abuse and neglect matters the initial stage is case finding, usually carried out in the educational, health, mental health, law enforcement, or social service systems. The signs that help is needed appear in the behavior or condition of a child and in events that occur in or outside the home. Although physical abuse is more easily detected, emotional abuse and neglect are more damaging to children. The professional contacted or making direct observations bridges systems by extending the inquiry beyond the immediate condition, such as injury to or neglect of a child, to gathering information about the child's life situation.

The next stage is intervention by the social services, legal, and mental health systems. This can be done in response to parental request or by involuntary legal actions, such as through invoking protective services for a child by court action. The formation of a child advocacy team is helpful at this point. A fact-finding investigative process then can determine the child's sustenance, developmental, and advocacy needs and the parents' capacity to meet them. The extent of disorganization or disturbance of the child-parent unit can be assessed. Communication with the child can insure that the child's perspective is taken into account and that the child understands the events that are transpiring. A tentative determination can then be made as to whether the objective is to support, strengthen, or replace parenting roles. The existence of the child advocacy team averts or minimizes conflicts between professionals.

A life plan for the child then can be formulated so that elements to support, strengthen, or replace parent roles can be defined and provided. The design of the life plan can be most appropriately carried out by the social services system in collaboration with the mental health system. The structuring, monitoring, and modification of the life plan is most effectively handled by the legal system. Treatment can be carried out by the mental health system in collaboration with the social service system. Throughout these procedures, the rights of the child and parents to due process and equal protection can be insured by the legal system.

An essential element in a child's life plan is to establish the conditions under which parents can resume full responsibility for the care of their children. Expectations of the parents should be clearly stated with criteria for ascertaining whether or not they have been met. Because of the importance of time in the development of a child, the statutory time limits should be rigorously observed so that time is not lost due to clinical and procedural delays. If parents are unable to meet the criteria for resuming care of their children, either voluntary or involuntary termination of their parental rights should be expeditiously sought so that a permanent home can be provided through adoption or subsidized permanent foster care.

SUMMARY

Child advocacy is a parental role through which parents plan, make decisions about, and negotiate their children's sustenance and developmental needs in their communities. Consequently, professional individual child advocacy is an extension of parental advocacy that supports, restores, or replaces parental advocacy.

The techniques of individual child advocacy are case finding, system bridging, fact finding, communicating with the child, objective defining, conflict resolving, formulating and implementing a life plan for the child, and protecting and promoting the legal rights of the child.

The application of child advocacy techniques can be most effectively carried out by an interdisciplinary child advocacy team composed of representatives of the social service, legal, and mental health systems in collaboration with the health, education, and law enforcement systems.

The complicated, time-consuming, and costly process of professional child advocacy and the even greater cost of omitting it highlight the importance of developing social and public policies that promote and support competent parenting.

REFERENCES

Bronfenbrenner, U. (1986, July 23). *A Generation in Jeopardy: American's Hidden Family Policy.* Senate Committee on Rules and Administration Testimony, Washington, DC.

Edelman, M. W. (1987). *Families in Peril.* Cambridge, MA: Harvard University Press.

Goldstein, J., Freud, A., & Solnit, A. J. (1973). *Beyond the Best Interests of the Child.* New York: Free Press.

Goldstein, J., Freud, A., Solnit, A. J., & Goldstein, S. (1986). *In the Best Interests of the Child: Professional Boundaries.* London: Collier-Macmillan.

Lane, H. (1975). *The Wild Boy of Aveyron.* Cambridge, MA: Harvard University Press.

Rutherford, R. B., & Edgar, E. (1979). *Teachers and Parents: A Guide to Interaction and Cooperation.* Boston, MA: Allyn & Bacon.

Westman, J. C. (1979). *Child Advocacy: A New Professional Role for Helping Families.* New York: Free Press.

Westman, J. C. (1989). The risks of day care for children, parents and society. In B. J. Christensen (Ed.), *Day Care: Child Psychology and Adult Economics*. Rockford, IL: The Rockford Institute.

Wilson, J. Q., & Herrnstein, R. J. (1986). *Criminals Born and Bred: Crime and Human Nature*. New York: Simon & Schuster.

Yogman, M. W., & Brazelton, T. B. (1987). *In Support of Families*. Cambridge, MA: Harvard University Press.

Young, T. M. (1990). Therapeutic case advocacy. *American Journal of Orthopsychiatry, 60*, 118-124.

2

DEVELOPMENTAL CONSIDERATIONS IN YOUTH ADVOCACY

Laurence Steinberg

The need to think in terms of youth advocacy as a form of child advocacy signals the special nature of adolescence as a permanent minority status through which each young person must pass. Professor Steinberg points out that there is no cultural or societal precedent for the inaccurate assumption that puberty accords adult status. The maturation of most of the brain at about the age of eighteen with continued growth of some parts into the twenties adds a confirmatory biological foundation for this fact. Furthermore, the evidence is that the judgment of young persons between eleven and fifteen years of age is particularly vulnerable. Even tenth grade students may not seriously consider the consequences of their actions or value the advice of others.

Most young people do communicate with their parents on critical issues, so that the "generation gap" is not inevitable. However, when they do not, there often are family problems and varying degrees of immaturity, irresponsibility, and rigidity in both the parents and teenagers. This means that young persons involved in clinical and legal situations may not be as competent to make decisions as comparable youths with positive parental relationships. Therefore, there is great danger in assuming that all sixteen-year-olds, or adults for that matter, are equally mature and wise. The essential point is that individual differences make generalizations of little value in specific cases.

There are a variety of peer groups. Those composed of young people with solid parental identifications often are quite prosocial. At the same time, there are antisocial peer groups that exert strong, often decisive, influences on young people with varying degrees of alienation from prosocial parental influence. Some are influenced by antisocial parents and adults.

Because it operates from statutory and common-law foundations, the legal system has limitations in providing the protection and support of autonomy needed by youth. When legal, health, educational, and social service professionals find themselves dealing with what appear to be hopeless impasses between youth and parents, the mental health system can play an important role. Family counseling and psychotherapy are the treatments of choice for communication problems in families. Such interventions are not always successful, but they should be drawn upon before concluding that parents and young people are irreconcilable.

Professor Steinberg concludes that our society has tipped the balance between protection and preparation for adulthood too far toward the side of preparation by confronting youths with too many adult responsibilities and temptations. Young people still need and desire protection, not only by their parents but by society and their communities as well.

This chapter examines the interface between adolescent and parental responsibility from the perspective of a developmental psychologist with interests in psychological growth during the second decade of the life span. I begin with two straightforward questions: What is the developmental course of independence during the second decade of life, and how does the development of independence affect transformations in the adolescent's relationships in the family? In the pages that follow, I shall discuss what recent research on adolescent development suggests in regard to these questions, and examine how this knowledge applies to the issues facing professionals interested in youth advocacy.

The study of independence and family relations during adolescence has a longstanding history among developmentalists for several reasons. First, because of the inherent transitional nature of adolescence as a period in the life span, scholars have long been interested in the ways in which young people are prepared (or are left ill-prepared) to assume adult responsibilities as they mature toward majority status. This issue, restated in terms of the interests of youth advocates, might be this: How should societal institutions be structured to insure that young people grow up to be competent, responsible adults?

Second, because industrialized society is both highly age-graded and highly age-segregated (and appears unlikely to change in either regard), social scientists concerned with adolescence have been interested in the impact on the development of responsibility of young people spending so much time in the company of their agemates, and so little time in the company of adults. Youth advocates may wonder whether peer pressure has become so substantial in contemporary society that it is useless to try to involve parents in decisions concerning teenagers.

Finally, because adolescence, and early adolescence in particular, is a time of significant and dramatic biological, cognitive, and psychological changes, it is important to ask how, and along what developmental timetable, adolescents become psychologically and behaviorally capable of responsible independence. Professionals working with young people want to know at what age adolescents are capable of making decisions independently. I hope to shed light on each of these questions in this chapter.

ADOLESCENT RESPONSIBILITY
ACROSS TIME AND SPACE

Let me begin with the first one: What do we know about the ways in which young people are, and should be, readied for adult responsibilities? Most of our knowledge in this area comes from the historical, sociological, and anthropological literatures on adolescence. The literature from these disciplines contrasts, across time and space, the various approaches to managing adolescent passage.

We now have reasonably good data on how the adolescent transition has been managed in so-called "primitive," or nonindustrialized, societies, and we have increasingly better information on how the transition was managed in our own society during the 18th and 19th centuries. The picture to emerge of adolescence in these other contexts generally comes as a surprise to many who are unfamiliar with these data. Typically, the naïve presumption is that, in comparison with their earlier counterparts (or with young people living under less industrialized conditions), many adolescents in our society live under circumstances of prolonged dependence upon their elders. This dependence allegedly has created autonomy-related difficulties among contemporary young people, who are seen as immature, irresponsible, and juvenile. This reasoning has been used repeatedly to justify allowing young people to have more autonomy over decision making at an earlier age than they presently do. After all, the argument goes, if adolescents of yesterday were capable of supporting themselves and raising a family by the time they were 15 or 16, why can't young people today be expected to behave responsibly and make decisions without parental input?

The data on adolescence in this country before the Industrial Revolution, and data on adolescence in nonindustrialized societies, however, cast doubt on the notion that young people in these social ecologies lived more autonomous lives than young people do today. In contrast to the widely held image of young people in the 19th century in this country - living on their own and raising a family at a relatively young age, for example - careful studies now indicate that the second decade of life (and indeed a good part of the third decade of life) was spent in a state of "semi-autonomy," in which adolescents and young adults held jobs, but did not marry, and, more importantly, lived under the close supervision of adults in their community (Katz, 1975; Kett, 1977). Although they worked and earned income, the behavior of 19th century teenagers was regulated and carefully monitored by parents or other adults. Contrary to popular belief, individuals were older when they married during that epoch than generally has been the case in the 20th century, and the age at which young people established an independent residence from their family of origin was considerably later 100 years ago than it is today (Modell, Furstenberg, & Hershberg, 1976).

A similar picture emerges when we look at adolescence in nonindustrialized societies. The prevailing image - again, a misinformed one - is that in these societies the young person passes through a formal initiation ceremony sometime around puberty, and is then accorded adult status and privileges by his or her community. This clearly has not been the case, however, in most parts of the world. Rather, most adolescents in primitive societies undergo *two* rites of passage: the first, around puberty, marks the individual's readiness for entering into a period of training for adulthood; and the second, occurring sometime during late adolescence, marks the individual's formal entrance into adult status. During the transitional period between the two ceremonies, the supervision of the adolescent is the responsibility of the community, and the training of the young person is the responsibility of the adults designated as teachers and socializers of the young (Mead, 1928). In most cases, the initiate does not live with his or her parents during this transitional period but, rather, is separated from the family of origin (a practice known as *extrusion*), and lives under the supervision of nonfamilial adults (Cohen, 1964). Adolescence in nonindustrialized society therefore is, as it was in preindustrialized society, a period of semi-autonomy. Not until the individual has proven himself or herself capable of handling adult responsibilities is he or she treated as an adult.

Nineteenth century America and the beaches of Samoa seem far removed from the world of today's teenager. But a close look at the structure and function of this period of adolescent semi-autonomy is informative to the present discussion in several respects.

First, it is important to note that the period of semi-autonomy allowed for a more gradual, more protected transition into adulthood. Additionally, the extended period of partial dependence ensured that a youngster's behavioral emancipation from his or her parents was delayed beyond the point of the individual having established both psychological and economic autonomy. (It is impossible, of course, to determine whether young people of previous eras were, in fact, psychologically "mature" when they became behaviorally independent, but it seems a reasonable enough assumption, given that behavioral emancipation did not occur until relatively late in adolescence or early in adulthood.) In other words, structuring the adolescent passage in this fashion helped to mitigate against young people having behavioral independence before they were emotionally and economically ready for it.

Second, it is important to point out that the individual's movement along the road of responsibility - from the dependence of childhood, to the semi-autonomy of adolescence, to the independence of adulthood - was accompanied by a change in the agent designated as responsible for monitoring the individual's behavior. In preindustrialized and nonindustrialized societies, the responsibility for monitoring the adolescent's partial independence is not limited to the adolescent's parents, but is shared between the parents and the community's adults. In preindustrialized Europe, for instance, a youngster was "placed out" at puberty from the parents' home into the household of another family in the community (Katz, 1975). The adults of this family were expected to act *in loco parentis*. In nonindustrialized societies, similarly, young people leave home at puberty and live with other members of the community, or in an area of the community designated for young people in training for adulthood. In other words, the young person entering adolescence not only moves from the dependence of childhood to the partial independence of adulthood, but also moves from fairly exclusive parental supervision to joint supervision shared between the parents and the community.

Several inferences derived from these data are relevant to the present discussion. The first is that, prior to industrialization, adolescence was structured as a transitional period both with regard to independence, and with regard to responsibility. A second inference is that the transitions that characterized the growth of independence and the transfer of responsibility were relatively gradual, or "continuous," as anthropologist Ruth Benedict described them (Benedict, 1934). Also, the period of semi-autonomy occurred within the context of an age-integrated social context in which adolescents of different ages mixed with each other and with nonfamilial adults. Finally, the assumption of adult responsibilities and the attainment of adult privileges occurred relatively late during the adolescent period and likely followed, rather than preceded, the development of psychological maturity.

It does not take much scrutiny to see that we find ourselves in quite a different position today. Although we tend to think of ourselves as more enlightened in our treatment of young people than our predecessors were, in many regards adolescents were treated more protectively previously than they are today. Adolescence in contemporary society is a murky, unstructured period, with cloudy boundaries separating it from childhood and from adulthood. Not only are young people cut off from contact with nonfamilial adults, but, increasingly, neither do they have a great deal of meaningful contact with their parents. It is a time of tremendous discontinuity, when young people must make decisions and take responsibility for behaviors about which they have had little formal schooling or informal counsel. It is a period during which it is not at all clear how responsibilities are to be divided among the adolescent, his or her parents, and the community. And it has become a period in which youth are pushed to engage in adult-like behavior and make adult-like decisions - pushed by the media, by their friends, and by their parents - at an age that is, in my view, simply too young.

Journalist Marie Winn, in her engaging book, *Children Without Childhood* (1983), draws our attention to an interesting distinction that bears on many of the issues before us in this chapter. She notes that we have moved from an "Age of Protection," to an "Age of Preparation," in our approach to rearing young adolescents. During an age of protection, adults attempt to protect youngsters from the "realities" of adulthood, because many of these realities, in the eyes of a 13-year-old, are potentially dangerous, unsettling, or corrupting. During an age of preparation, adults attempt to prepare youngsters for the realities of adulthood - even realities that *are* dangerous, unsettling, or corrupting - through exposure. We Americans think of ourselves as more protective than we are, but deep down, many adults believe in the "school of hard knocks" approach to adolescent-rearing. For example, my colleague Ellen Greenberger and I (1986), in our studies of teenagers who worked, found that many working youngsters were jaded and cynical about work, used drugs and alcohol to relieve job stress, and winked at such behaviors as stealing from an employer or overstating one's hours on a timecard. We found these patterns disturbing. Many of our colleagues and many parents who were angered by our book took issue with us, however, insisting that because most adults were cynical about their jobs, unwound from work with drugs and alcohol, and engaged in minor forms of occupational deviance, the adolescent workplace was providing a training ground of sorts for adulthood.

The distinction between preparation and protection is an important one. Obviously, there is a point in the individual's development when he or she is more in need of preparation than protection (for the sake of argument, let us say sometime in late adolescence) but in many ways, our current stance toward young adolescents suggests that we are overly concerned with their preparation and insufficiently concerned with their protection. I believe that adolescents are being harmed, not well-served, by this orientation, for it provides a rationale for the abdication of parental and societal authority, concern, and vigilance during a time when the youngsters may profit from all three. I believe, further, that we are seeing over and over again the unfortunate results of this orientation.

ADOLESCENT RESPONSIBILITY
AND THE PEER GROUP

Let me turn now to the issue of age-segregation and adolescent independence in the peer group. It is often observed that adolescents in this country have little contact with nonfamilial adults and spend much of their day in the company of peers. As psychologist Urie Bronfenbrenner (1974) has pointed out, this state of affairs has likely contributed to the alienation of young people from society, an estrangement manifested in high rates of teenage suicide and depression, drug and alcohol problems, academic malaise, and delinquency. If we chart rates of these disturbances over time, we find steady increases in virtually all problem areas from 1950 onward.

Increases in many of these adolescent maladies have been attributed over the years to the breakdown of the family and the rise of age-segregated peer groups. Many authorities have portrayed the peer group as a solely negative influence on the development of responsibility among young people, suggesting that peers influence adolescents in ways that are antithetical to the values held by adults. This view was set forth initially by James Coleman some 25 years ago in *The Adolescent Society* (1961), and has been raised repeatedly whenever the problems of young people have received national attention (see, for example, the President's Science Advisory Committee, 1973). The evidence for this position, however, despite its simplicity and intuitive attractiveness (i.e., parents are good; peers are bad), is very slim. Indeed, most studies of adolescent peer group value systems suggest (a) that the adolescent peer culture is as heterogeneous as is the adult culture (Brown, Lohr, & McClenahan, 1986), and (b) that the values held by a youngster's friends are generally concordant with those held by his or her family (Hill, 1980). It is true that there are adolescent peer groups, as well as adult groups, that condone or even encourage deviant behavior. However, while much of the misbehavior adolescents engage in takes place in the *company* of peers, we should not assume that peers necessarily are the *cause* of the misbehavior. Indeed, one might argue that the high rates of adolescent misbehavior and the prevalence of age-segregated peer groups are both manifestations of the same fundamental problem: the failure of the community to protect, as well as prepare, young people.

A balance between protection and preparation was achieved in previous eras through such mechanisms as "placing out" and extrusion. The adolescent was *prepared* for independent adulthood through his or her separation from parents, but *protected* from precocious independence by the vigilance and concern of other adults. For this reason, I find it difficult to discuss the interface between parent and adolescent responsibility without considering society's responsibility at the same time. At the heart of the interface between parent and adolescent responsibility is the interface between society's responsibility for families and families' responsibility for youngsters. One fundamental role that the youth advocate can play is to make sure that society does not shirk its responsibility to protect youngsters until they are psychologically ready to protect themselves. One very important way that this can be achieved is by making sure that families are sufficiently well-protected themselves.

In answer to a question posed earlier - Does the apparent strength of today's peer group suggest that it is futile to try to engage parents and teenagers together in joint decision making? - the answer derived from studies of adolescents and their families is clearly "No." For one thing, studies show that adolescents who are close to their parents are less susceptible to peer pressure, and more likely to select friends whose values are in line with their parents' (Hill, 1980; Steinberg & Silverberg, 1986). For another, recent intervention studies indicate that it is possible to increase parental involvement in adolescent rearing even in families that would appear to be beyond hope (e.g., Patterson, 1982). These intervention studies also suggest, however, that the earlier the intervention is, the more likely it is to be successful.

THE DEVELOPMENT OF RESPONSIBILITY IN ADOLESCENCE

This then leads me to the final issue studied by scholars interested in the development of independence during adolescence: age-related changes in youngsters' capacities to act responsibly, monitor themselves, and make independent decisions. The question I raised earlier concerned the age at which youngsters appear to be capable of making independent decisions. I want to focus on three studies in particular that bear on this, because they illustrate that, from a developmental perspective, the transition between early and middle adolescence, around age 15, seems to be an important turning point both in the growth of independence and in the transformation of family relationships.

The first study examines conformity and social influence in adolescence, and was conducted by Thomas Berndt several years ago (Berndt, 1979). It since has been replicated twice in Madison, Wisconsin; once by my research staff (Steinberg & Silverberg, 1986) and once by Bradford Brown and his colleagues (Brown, Clasen, & Eicher, 1986). In these studies, youngsters are presented with a series of hypothetical dilemmas in which they are pressured to engage in a given behavior (some are antisocial behaviors, some are not) by either parents or peers, and then asked whether they would go along with what the others want them to do, or if they would follow their own inclinations. When susceptibility to pressure is plotted out developmentally, an interesting pattern emerges. From elementary school onward, susceptibility to *parental* pressure declines steadily and linearly: 3rd graders are more likely to be influenced by their parents than 6th graders, who are more likely to be influenced by 9th graders, who, in turn, are more likely to be influenced by 12th graders.

Susceptibility to *peer* pressure follows a different pattern, however: Here we find an inverted U-shaped curve, with peer pressure susceptibility increasing from 3rd to 9th grade, and decreasing thereafter. This is especially true when susceptibility in antisocial situations is studied. In other words, elementary school students are basically "good" boys and girls who follow their parents' wishes and resist the influence of their friends to behave in ways that are contrary to what they know are correct. Junior high school students, however, have begun to distance themselves from their parents, but have not yet developed the internal wherewithal to go against the crown when they are with their friends. Not until high school does it appear that youngsters develop true behavior autonomy, which is the ability to make their own decisions in the face of parental *or* peer pressure to do otherwise.

The second relevant study was conducted by Catherine Lewis in 1981. She presented adolescents of different ages with a series of problems that they were to help another teenager solve. The adolescents were asked to suggest the things that the other teenager should think about in making a decision of what to do. Lewis then coded their responses along several dimensions and examined the prevalence of the different sorts of suggestions as a function of the advice-giver's age. She found that quite dramatic increases occurred in the sophistication of decision making over the course of the adolescent years. For example, only 10% of the young adolescents (12- and 13-year-olds) considered the future consequences of following different courses of action, and only 20% of these youngsters suggested that an independent specialist be consulted in instances where expert advice would have been helpful. By 10th grade, these percentages had risen to 20% and 45%, respectively. By 12th grade, a third of the students advised considering the future consequences of decisions, and half advised seeking independent consultation. In other words, there is evidence that young people become better decision makers as well as more autonomous individuals during the secondary school years. Of course, it is important to note that even by 12th grade, two-thirds of all adolescents did *not* suggest that it was important to consider the future consequences of their decisions, and one-half did not advise seeking independent consultation. Thus, although decision-making abilities improve over the course of adolescence, they are far from perfect by the end of high school.

The third study was conducted by my staff on a sample of 900 Madison, Wisconsin youngsters (Steinberg & Silverberg, 1986). In this study, we examined youngsters' emotional autonomy from their parents (the extent to which they de-idealized their parents and saw themselves as independent individuals) alongside their susceptibility to peer pressure. We found that the junior high years are a time of considerable emotional autonomy, but also a time of considerable susceptibility to peer pressure. Young adolescents appear to detach themselves from their parents before they establish a genuine sense of self-direction. We also found that youngsters who were likely to describe themselves as relatively more autonomous from their parents were more easily swayed by the influence of their friends.

Taken together, these three studies suggest that responsible independence has an interesting developmental timetable in adolescence. Pre-adolescents (for my purposes, 10 years of age and younger) are not yet capable of responsible independence or sophisticated decision making, but they do not really need to be, because they are still very much under parental control emotionally and behaviorally. Many, but not all, older adolescents (15 years of age and older) appear to be reasonably competent at decision making and at resisting the influence of their agemates to go against what they think is right, so they are less of a worry for this reason. But early adolescents (from the ages of 11 to 14) would seem to be at greatest risk, because they have distanced themselves from their parents but do not yet have the cognitive or emotional skills necessary to handle their independence. It is for this reason that young adolescents - and their parents - need a good deal of protection by society.

The psychological immaturity of today's young adolescents, however, is camouflaged by their superficial signs of adulthood: their clothing and make-up, their blasé attitude, their consumerism, and their early involvement in such "forbiddens" as sex, alcohol, and drugs. As adults and parents, we are easily fooled by their outward appearance and may attribute more emotional and cognitive sophistication to these youngsters than they actually possess. Yet, under the mask of apparent adult sophistication, are youngsters who are "pseudomature" - easily influenced by others around them, quick to reject their parents' advice, too often left unsupervised, and therefore unprotected.

Where does this view of adolescent independence leave us as far as youth advocacy is concerned, at least from the perspective of an adolescent developmentalist? I would like to make three points in conclusion. First, I think it is clear that we need to differentiate between young adolescents - those between the ages of 10 and 14 - and their older counterparts. The evidence is quite persuasive that there are many important cognitive and emotional changes during this time which bear on the young person's decision-making abilities and sense of responsibility. I, for one, would feel uncomfortable with policies that treated young adolescents as if they had the developmental competence of older ones, and would advocate drawing a rather firm boundary between youngsters 15 years old and older (i.e., of high school age), and those 14 years old and younger (i.e., of junior high school age or younger). For example, while I feel fairly confident that a 16-year-old is capable of making decisions concerning the use of contraception without discussing it with parents, I am less confident that a 13-year-old is capable of exercising the proper judgment on the same issue. This does not mean that we should encourage older adolescents to make important decisions without consulting their parents, nor does it mean that we should forbid younger adolescents from acting on their own behalf when their parents have forsaken their responsibility. It does suggest, however, that professionals working with young people should be aware of the potential pitfalls of encouraging independent decision making before an adolescent becomes psychologically capable of such action.

It is imperative to note, however, that individual differences among adolescents (and among families, for that matter) make generalizations difficult solely on the basis of chronological age. Surely there are young adolescents who are psychologically capable of mature decision making before the age of 14, and older adolescents who, even at the age of 17, are in need of adult guidance and counsel. Unfortunately, those adolescents who do not have positive family relations (and hence, are not likely to turn to their parents for advice) are probably the most in need of adult guidance. Research has indicated that responsible autonomy is facilitated by close, rather than distant, relations with parents (Hill & Holmbeck, 1986).

A second point is that professionals working with young people need to know that the early adolescent population is likely at special risk, and in need of more guidance and counsel than they presently receive. Joan Lipsitz, some 10 years ago, published a book called *Growing Up Forgotten* (1977), which details the ways that young adolescents are ill-served by society. Unfortunately, little has changed since that time. An especially pressing problem concerns the millions of young adolescents who are left on their own during after-school hours, which may place them at great risk for involvement in deviant and problem behavior. A recent Ford Foundation study demonstrates, for instance, that many adolescent pregnancies were conceived not on Saturday nights in the back seats of cars, but on weekday afternoons in the privacy of the adolescent's own home ("Fathers, Earnest and Pathetic," 1985). One suspects that the same pattern holds true for experimentation with drugs, alcohol, and delinquent activity.

Finally, it is important to point out that, in our concern with getting young people socially prepared for adulthood, we seem to have tipped the balance between protection and preparation too far toward the side of preparation. Young people still are in need of protection - not only by their parents, but by society and their communities as well. Youth advocates can play a critical role in making sure that we do not lose sight of this protective function. I agree with others that the likely place to look for the protection of young people is their family; indeed, most studies of intergenerational relations suggest that the majority of adolescents enjoy close, rather than contentious, relations with their parents. However, given the historical evidence I presented earlier, it may be unrealistic to expect that parents can play a protective role throughout the adolescent years without the support of other societal and community institutions. Historically, we encouraged adolescents to separate from their parents once they reached puberty, but we provided a protective environment for them to separate into. Today, we still encourage the separation, but seem to have forgotten the other part of the package. While we need to find ways to strengthen parents' ability to protect as well as prepare their youngsters, we also need to think of ways in which society's institutions can serve and assist in these functions, as they have in other eras. Although societal institutions cannot replace the family in its many functions, these institutions can support families through such means as therapy, parent education, and family enhancement programs.

Understanding the interface between parent and adolescent responsibility is not simply a matter of deciding at what age a parent's responsibility ends and an adolescent's begins. This view leads us down the wrong path, for it implies that when the adolescent is developmentally capable of making decisions, the parent can cease to be responsible. But the task facing the parent of a teenager is not deciding when to abdicate responsibility; it is, rather, determining how to make the transition from a relationship characterized by unilateral authority to one characterized by mutual respect, compromise, and dialog. The issue facing all of us concerned with the well-being of parents and teenagers is how we, as youth advocates, can help both parties, in conjunction with society, behave responsibly together.

REFERENCES

Benedict, R. (1934). *Patterns of Culture.* Boston: Houghton Mifflin.

Berndt, T. (1979). Developmental changes in conformity to peers and parents. *Developmental Psychology, 15,* 608-615.

Bronfenbrenner, U. (1974). The origins of alienation. *Scientific American, 231,* 53-61.

Brown, B. B., Clasen, D. R., & Eicher, S. A. (1986). Perceptions of peer pressure, peer conformity dispositions, and self-reported behavior among adolescents. *Developmental Psychology, 22,* 521-530.

Brown, B., Lohr, M., & McClenahan, E. (1986). Early adolescents' perceptions of peer pressure. *Journal of Early Adolescence, 6,* 139-154.

Cohen, Y. (1964). *The Transition from Childhood to Adolescence.* Chicago: Aldine.

Coleman, J. (1961). *The Adolescent Society.* New York: Free Press.

Fathers, earnest and pathetic [Editorial]. (1985, June 16). *The New York Times*, p. 20.

Greenberger, E., & Steinberg, L. (1986). *When Teenagers Work: The Psychological and Social Costs of Adolescent Employment*. New York: Basic Books.

Hill, J. (1980). The family. In M. Johnson (Ed.), *Toward Adolescence: The Middle School Years* (Seventy-ninth yearbook of the National Society for the Study of Education, pp. 32-55). Chicago: University of Chicago Press.

Hill, J., & Holmbeck, G. (1986). Attachment and autonomy during adolescence. In G. Whitehurst (Ed.), *Annals of Child Development*. Greenwich, CT: JAI Press.

Katz, M. B. (1975). *The People of Hamilton, Canada West: Family and Class in a Mid-Nineteenth-Century City*. Cambridge: Harvard University Press.

Kett, J. F. (1977). *Rites of Passage: Adolescents in America 1790 to the Present*. New York: Basic Books.

Lewis, C. C. (1981, June). How adolescents approach decisions: Changes over grades seven to twelve and policy implications. *Child Development, 52,* 538-544.

Lipsitz, J. (1977). *Growing Up Forgotten*. Lexington: Lexington Books.

Mead, M. (1928). *Coming of Age in Samoa: A Psychological Study of Primitive Years for Western Civilization*. New York: Morrow.

Modell, J., Furstenberg, F., Jr., & Hershberg, T. (1976). Social change and transitions to adulthood in historical perspective. *Journal of Family History, 1,* 7-32.

Patterson, G. (1982). A comparative evaluation of parent training programs. *Behavior Therapy, 13,* 638-650.

President's Science Advisory Committee. (1973). *Youth: Transition to Adulthood*. Chicago: University of Chicago Press.

Steinberg, L., & Silverberg, S. B. (1986, August). The vicissitudes of autonomy in early adolescence. *Child Development, 57,* 841-851.

Winn, M. (1983). *Children Without Childhood*. New York: Penguin.

Part II

THE LEGAL SYSTEM

INTRODUCTION

*In the little world in which children have their existence . . .
there is nothing so finely perceived and so finely felt as
injustice.*

Charles Dickens, 1852

The law originated as a civilized effort to deal with conflicts between people without bloodshed. In the tradition of Hebrew, Roman, and English common law, the American legal system has become an established mechanism for dealing with interpersonal relations in general. In contrast, only during this century have mental health professionals begun to deal with conflicts between people. For even less time in recent decades have the legal and mental health systems been defining their differences and finding common ground.

Originally based upon the conception that God would strengthen the hand of the righteous, whether in a duel or in arguments before a judge, the legal format involves the vigorous advocacy of opposing points of view in order to permit an impartial judge or jury to accomplish justice. Although useful in criminal and tort cases, in matters of domestic relations adversarial procedures polarize and heighten the disparate interests of the individual members of families rather than mediating their conflicting interests. Adversarial techniques cannot take into account the fact that the rights of children, parents, and society are interdependent. Fortunately, in

41

actual practice the counseling roles of attorneys foster compromise and negotiation as ways of resolving conflicts outside of the adversarial courtroom format.

In the past, courts in the United States were specialized to accommodate the special requirements of youths and families. Juvenile courts were established early in this century in order to adapt the legal system to the rehabilitation of young offenders. They usually were devoted to delinquency and child abuse and neglect matters. With a similar adaptive purpose, family courts were established to deal with marital, divorce, domestic violence, domestic tort, and adoption matters (Freed & Walker, 1988). Over the last two decades the separate juvenile and family court systems have given way to general courts (McNally, 1982). This resulted from the belief that juvenile courts were not successful and that the emphasis of the legal system should be on the procedural protection of constitutional rights. Actually, the juvenile courts did not fail because their purposes were inappropriate, but because they did not function as the legal arms of community networks of services and as mediators between offenders and the offended.

In theory, the need for family courts has decreased because of the trend toward no-fault divorce. The principles underlying this trend are reflected in a shift from fault to need, from reactive punishment to problem solving, from a focus on the individual to the family, from adversarial competition to conciliatory cooperation, and from gender-specific rights to nongender-linked responsibilities (Koopman & Hunt, 1988). As a result, nonmonetary contributions, such as homemaking and child rearing, generally are considered as contributions to the economic assets of marriage. The ownership of property is determined by equitable division rather than title. Child custody is not to be based on parent gender, and joint custody is an available option. Child support is an obligation for both parents, and grandparent visitation rights increasingly have been acknowledged.

Rather than becoming simplified, however, contested custody in divorce is a complex dilemma involving individual, family, social, cultural, and legal factors. Strained family relationships often block the constructive resolution of conflicts. In these contests, justice for the children means meeting their needs, not prematurely burdening them with adult responsibilities, and fairness and reciprocity between generations. Injustice, on the other hand, means using children as pawns in marital conflicts, seeking their custody for personal gain, and neglecting children's needs in favor of the personal desires of their parents (Musetto, 1982).

As the legal system has shifted away from a treatment orientation toward juveniles and families in order to concentrate on procedural and decision-making functions, the need for social service and mental health collaboration has become more evident. The legal system can provide the authority required to insure implementation and monitoring of reasonable life plans for children; however, the social service and mental health systems are needed in order to determine what those life plans should be. Child advocacy teams can provide this integration on a case-by-case basis and fill the gap in general courts created by the shift away from juvenile and family courts.

REFERENCES

Freed, D. J., & Walker, T. B. (1988). Family law in the fifty states: An overview. *Family Law Quarterly, 21,* 417-571.

Koopman, E. J., & Hunt, E. J. (1988). Child custody mediation: An interdisciplinary synthesis. *American Journal of Orthopsychiatry, 58,* 379-386.

McNally, R. B. (1982). Nearly a century later: The child-savers, child advocates and the juvenile justice system. *Juvenile and Family Court Journal, 33,* 47-52.

Musetto, A. P. (1982). *Dilemmas in Child Custody.* Chicago, IL: Nelson-Hall.

3

THE LEGAL RIGHTS OF PARENTS AND CHILDREN

Jack C. Westman

The law presumes that natural bonds of affection lead parents to act in the interests of their children. It also presumes that parents possess what children lack in experience and judgment.

Moreover, for most children and their parents, the question of the legal rights of either does not arise. It is only when family conflicts enter the legal arena, or when legislative issues involve general considerations of age of eligibility, consent, or responsibility that attention is focused on the duties and privileges accorded parents and their daughters and sons.

The powers that parents wield over their children have been limited by statutes, such as those defining child abuse and neglect. In counterpoint to this negative view is a growing trend to define the rights and responsibilities of children in positive terms. This has led to a clearer definition of the rights and responsibilities of parents. The perspective gained from considering the interdependent roles of parents and their offspring in times of crisis can contribute to our understanding of family life in general.

This chapter deals with the legal rights of both parents and children. It also considers society's responses to minority status and the ways in which the legal rights of minors can be represented in the courts.

There is no question that all persons are entitled to fair treatment in a just society. Therefore, as members of society, children are entitled to the same rights as adults to the extent that they are able to assume the responsibilities accompanying each right.

Under 18th-century English common law, children were regarded as chattels of their parents and wards of the state with no recognized legal rights. Still, Blackstone's *Commentaries on the Laws of England*, first published in 1765, revealed that criminal law then regarded minority as a special period of life before the age of 25 having four stages (Blackstone, 1982). *Infantia* was from birth until 7 years of age. *Infantial proxima* was from 7 to 10-1/2 years. During these first two stages, children were not punishable for any crime. *Pubertati proxima* was from 10-1/2 to 14, followed by *pubertas* from 14 upward. During these latter stages, children were punishable if found to be "capable of mischief" but with mitigations and not with the utmost rigors of the law. During the last stage, however, minors could be punished as adults.

Over the years, the law's concern with children has added protection to considerations of punishment by intervening in family life. The gradual emergence of children's rights is an outgrowth of the protective doctrine of *parens patriae*, which has justified state intervention with parental prerogatives and even the termination of parental rights in certain circumstances. The doctrine, literally interpreted as "father of his country," stems from early English common law in which the king had a general duty to protect all citizens, especially those incapable of protecting themselves. It placed the ultimate authority of the state over parental rights. Accordingly, it could deny parents' freedom to act, in addition to taking liberty from children. Furthermore, the doctrine permits the state to compel children and their parents to act in ways beneficial to society. However, the doctrine never implied that the state could assume parenting functions and was limited to influencing parent-child relationships.

From this background it is evident that the legal rights of children cannot be considered apart from the rights of their parents and the state. Their rights involve power over and decision making in their own lives. When children do not have certain rights, someone else, either their parents or the state, exercises those rights for them (Davis & Schwartz, 1987). At the same time, the power of children, parents, and the state is strongly influenced by the right of families to privacy. Because providing children with rights detracts from the power of parents and the state, it is likely that a latent fear of the rebellion of children has been, and still is, one of the deterrents to the full recognition of the rights of children. Thus, the tendency of the law to cast the interaction of children, parents, and society in adversarial power terms is simultaneously an advantage and a disadvantage for children, because it threatens parental and state authority.

In this ambiguous context, a body of law that can be described as children's law has emerged in recent decades. It balances a desire to accord children a greater degree of control over their lives against a desire to protect them from their own immaturity. The law grants a measure of autonomy to minors in certain areas, such as abortion decisions, torts, and non-life-threatening medical decision making, and by ultimate emancipation that grants full autonomy (Davis & Schwartz, 1987, p. 201). At the same time, the law protects children from responsibility in the areas of contracts, employment, and to a great extent, medical decision making in life-threatening cases. This balance between autonomy and protection occurs in the larger context of the autonomy of the family. Intervention by the state in parental functions challenges the right of the family to be left alone, and it raises the question of whether an intervention will do more harm than good (p. 206).

In practice, the legal adjudication of parent-child rights occurs largely when protection of a child's interests is an issue. The state has the power to intervene and assume temporary custody or guardianship of children when neglect, abuse, or parental incompetence exist. Children can be placed in foster care, and parental rights can be permanently terminated. The state exercises responsibility for determining custody in divorce cases and for establishing a legal parent-child relationship through adoption. Unfortunately, criteria for making these decisions are not well-defined, so that the general practice is to exercise judicial restraint and perpetuate the status quo rather than resolve issues in a timely and definitive manner for a child's benefit. For example, many youngsters spend years in foster care, because no one has assumed the responsibility for making the definitive decisions that are necessary in the legal pursuit of their interests.

THE LEGAL RIGHTS OF PARENTS

Parents are the primary spokespersons for, and protectors of, the young, but often there are conflicts of interest between parents and their children, some of which are subtle. For example, in 1972 the U.S. Supreme Court in *Wisconsin v. Yoder* held that Amish parents could remove their children from public school at the age of 14. The teenagers in that case apparently did not object to leaving public school, but one could argue that their interests might have been better served by exposure to a broader education.

There is a fundamental reason why separating parents' and children's rights is difficult. It is because the basic unit of a family is neither child nor parent but child-parent. Consequently, the relationship between child and parent should be the focus of attention, not what a child or a parent does as a separate entity. The welfare of a child and an adult as a parent are inseparable. There is a difference in power, however. The parent as an adult can act independently, whereas the child inherently is dependent. An important distinction exists, therefore, between the interests of a person as an adult and that same person as a parent. This divergence of interests between different roles in life is the source of internal conflict and tension for every parent.

Theoretically, the interests of adults who are parents and the interests of their children are complementary. By definition, parenting is nurturing and protecting a child. Confusion arises over the term "parent," because some adults or teenagers conceive and give birth to children but do not function as parents. A more precise definition of what parent means would help to clarify what appear to be conflicts between parents' rights and children's rights. On close scrutiny, these conflicts usually are based upon the personal wishes or needs of a person apart from that person's role as the child's parent. That person may not be considering, as a parent, the child's interests at all. Consequently, it is important to recognize that parenthood is an earned state of reciprocal attachment between an adult and a child rather than being accorded by simply conceiving or giving birth to a child. For example, the real parents of an adopted child are the adoptive parents who have reared the child, not the persons who conceived and gave birth to the child.

Parental authority generally is honored because it is presumed to be based upon wisdom and love for a child. Prevalent legal theory holds that parental duties toward children are accompanied by the inherent powers necessary to carry out those duties. Thus the consent of children is not required for the exercise of parental power. Because they are entitled to parental support, children must follow the directions of their parents. Parents may act as they wish with their children, except as the state imposes standards of conduct and duties upon them. Some traditional categories of this broad parental power are rights to name a child, to custody, to service and earnings, to control religion and education, and to discipline; the power to make decisions about where children will live, what they will eat, and how they will dress; and the power to censor the books read and movies seen by the child. For these reasons, it is in the privacy of their homes that the rights of children are the least protected.

The law is moving in the direction of defining the limits of parental power, as illustrated by denying parent-invited state intervention against children who are disobedient or "incorrigible." The informal sanctions available to parents for obtaining obedience and the disadvantages of running away are so strong that, when children do engage in chronic disobedience or run away, quite likely their behaviors are symptoms of family problems that state intervention through action directed solely against the children will not address. In these situations the legal presumption is becoming that either parental authority has not been used effectively or has been abused.

Still, the state has been reluctant to intervene in family affairs, because its power can undermine the attractiveness to adults of assuming parental responsibilities. Parenthood is a sacrificial burden and is becoming more of a voluntary option than an expected role in life. The prospect of state intervention could negatively influence whether or not adults choose to become parents. In actuality, this concern is not realistic, because parents who are likely to invite state intervention are rarely those who exercise thoughtful decision making over whether or not to become parents. A more realistic consideration is that parental authority can be undermined, if it is not supported by society. The potential for tyranny of children over adults is one of the hazards of family life.

While authority usually is more effectively exercised through persuasion than through force, the security, role modeling, leadership, and limit setting essential for child development are less likely to be provided by a *laissez-faire* family than one that is based upon ultimate parental authority. To the extent that government policies foster noncommittal attitudes on the parts of parents, either because parents believe they have no right to give direction to their children or because they fear that the state will not support them, both the children of those families and society as a whole will suffer. Therefore, social policies that encourage and support parental responsibility for children are in the interests of children and society.

THE LEGAL RIGHTS OF MINORS

Clearly, children must have legal rights to protection. The development of the capacity for autonomous decision making, however, is a learning process that can be stunted, if unlimited freedom and responsibility are thrust too soon upon the young. Moreover, the lifelong effects of unwise choices with binding consequences, such as marrying and choosing whether to seek education, can create permanent effects far more detrimental than the temporary limitations upon freedom inherent in the child-rearing process. Children will outgrow their immature state, but the important question is whether they will outgrow it with the capacity to function as mature, independent members of society. Precisely because they lack this capacity, minors need legally protected rights to special treatment, including protection against their own immaturity so that they will have the opportunity to develop the capacity to make mature choices.

As more attention is paid to the legal rights of children in the United States, a useful distinction can be made between rights to nurturance, to protection, and to make choices. The law has recognized the right of children to food, shelter, clothing, and medical care through statutory definitions of child neglect. It also has recognized the right of children to be protected from harmful acts of others and themselves, as defined by child abuse statutes. These rights are dealt with in other chapters of this book. The right to make choices has been defined more or less clearly in age-grading statutes and legal policies that award responsibilities and privileges at certain ages, such as expressing choices in post-divorce custody, driver's licenses, and voting eligibility.

Obviously, sheer physical size, knowledge, and skill give adults power over children. This is necessary because the ability of the young to accurately perceive circumstances and to make choices is heavily colored by egocentricity from infancy through early adolescence. Before the onset of formal operational thinking, children cannot view their parental relationships abstractly. The ability to realistically evaluate circumstances once they are accurately perceived is a later acquisition which, even then, is biased by egocentricity and loyalty conflicts. Furthermore, a young child's verbal expressions are largely based on the child's wishes and emotions. Only later are they intended to enhance a listener's understanding. For example, children frequently capitalize on hostilities between their divorced parents by making statements about one parent to the other based on their own anger, and thus fuel discord between their parents.

It is during adolescence that the conflict between the rights of adults and of minors to make choices usually arises. One of the developmental hazards for adolescents is their capacity to act in ways that pose long-range deleterious effects. The stakes are too high to ignore the fact that an adolescent's actions can lead to self-defeating consequences. Yet the matter is complicated, because adolescents need to psychologically and emotionally detach themselves from adults. The testing and depreciation of parents aids the definition of their own strengths. Part of this process is their newly found ability to recognize discrepancies and inconsistencies in adults. During this period, they find that their parents are not as good or as bad, and not as powerful or as weak as previously believed.

Ordinarily, adolescent testing of parental authority is contained within the family unit, and the community is unaware of the struggle. However, when parents are unable to fill a youngster's need for a limit-setting foil, the adolescent conflict extends outside of the family, usually first to the school and then to the community. As a result, most adolescents who come to the attention of the legal system have not had the opportunity to learn how to modulate their own impulses, ideas, and attitudes. Thus family problems come to the attention of society in the form of teenage antisocial behavior or running away. At this time, sufficient knowledge of the adolescent's family must be obtained to evaluate whether or not taking the adolescent's side in a dispute is in the young person's interests. There are always two sides to each story. Unless parents truly are unable to meet their teenager's needs, family therapy can help to resolve these family conflicts.

Another fundamental aspect of adolescent personality development is experimentation through which teenagers learn about themselves and the range of life's opportunities and hazards. This means that adolescents have developmental license to be impulsive, idealistic, and changeable. Preoccupied with establishing themselves as persons with unique qualities, they are necessarily limited in objectivity. Therefore, they require limit setting and guidance in order to place their actions and ideas in perspective. This does not mean that adolescents should be protected from making mistakes and from the consequences. Deprived of

51

these self-learning corrective experiences, they cannot fully develop their decision-making capacities. In fact, one of the unfortunate aspects of the juvenile court system was a tendency to protect adolescents from full realization of the gravity of their offenses and an appreciation of the consequences of their actions. Law enforcement officers are well aware of juvenile offenders returned to the streets with the sense that they have conned the system, only to act more provocatively and provoke intervention again. Unfortunately, the legal system's responses often are either too lenient or too severe. An intermediate balance of consequences appropriately related to actions can be facilitated by the premise of the U.S. Supreme Court in the Gault decision: that offenses should be clearly defined and consequences appropriately selected (*In re Gault,* 1967).

Adolescents often aspire to adult privileges and responsibilities, but these require wisdom resulting from life experience beyond the maturation of their mental equipment for important decision making. Although it is evident that anyone requires orientation, training, and experience to become capable of decision making in a new job, it is often difficult for adolescents to recognize that assuming specific adult responsibilities is of the same order. Furthermore, there are wide individual differences in adolescents of the same age in physical growth, emotional maturity, and social judgment. Some teenagers possess maturity in all of these areas at the age of 15, while others still are emotionally and socially immature at the age of 25.

The wide range of individual differences in maturity points up the problems in arbitrarily selecting a chronological age at which adult responsibilities are awarded. For global privileges, such as voting, responsibility has been established by age for reasons of practicality. However, past experience in the screening of 18-year-olds for military service has repeatedly disclosed that a significant number have not attained sufficient maturity to function in military life, leading to a surprisingly high rejection rate. Still, ages are established for nonhazardous rights that involve all young people, because the immense numbers preclude individual screening. In contrast, when risk to society exists, there is little question about individual screening, such as in obtaining an automobile driver's license.

There is an answer to the question of what rights are appropriate for an adolescent at a particular age. Individual variations can be accounted for by offering graduated steps for demonstrating skill or decision-making responsibility before a particular right is assumed. The principle is simple enough: In questionable instances a test of responsibility can determine an individual's readiness to acquire a right. The reluctance of many parents to permit adolescents to test their capacities for responsibility only delays maturity and ultimately breeds rebellion. The essential point is that adolescents need early graduated pathways to self-responsibility, so that they are not confronted with later wrenching and overwhelming shifts into adult autonomy.

SOCIAL RESPONSES
TO MINORITY STATUS

There is growing statutory recognition that children's interests should be paramount when they conflict with the personal interests of their parents, while safeguarding the legitimate rights of parents to raise their children as they see fit. For example, in recent years legislatures have acted to allow minors to consent to their own medical treatment for venereal disease, drug and alcohol dependency, abortion, and contraception.

Unfortunately legislation that affects children and youth often is motivated by special interest groups, such as merchants, ideologues, industrialists, and parent organizations, none of whom necessarily represent the interests of teenagers. This lack of representation was seen dramatically in the class action suits and legislation of the 1970s. Those cases were pursued almost exclusively by lawyers with a libertarian agenda with little input from the named parties or other class members.

The legislative responses to minors can be divided into two categories: those that restrict and those that award privileges. In the first, society acts to protect teenagers by proscribing or requiring certain activities, such as alcohol consumption or school attendance. These age-based restrictions on the liberties of young people are intended to protect the parent-child relationship and to protect minors and society from their immature judgment and lack of skill (Dodson, 1984, pp. 118-120).

The proscription of adolescent behavior is in laws that ban drinking under a certain age, that prevent the sale of obscene material to minors, that impose penalties upon those who provide drugs to minors, and that forbid the sale of cigarettes to minors. Many of these laws have been upheld in the face of challenges. In *New York v. Ferber (1982)*, the U.S. Supreme Court decision to uphold a statute banning the distribution of child pornography was unchallenged even by strident civil libertarians. The U.S.

Supreme Court also ruled that adolescents can be denied access to materials that were not obscene enough to be outlawed outright (*Ginsberg v. New York*, 1968) or even that were merely vulgar (*Board of Education v. Pico*, 1982).

The flaw in these prohibitive laws is that they usually do not work. All of these "forbidden fruits" are easily and increasingly available to teenagers. For instance, in a study in Massachusetts where the sale of cigarettes to minors is forbidden, an 11-year-old girl was able to buy cigarettes in 75 out of 100 stores (DiFranza et al., 1987). When asked subsequently, 73% of the vendors knew about the law and nonetheless sold cigarettes to the girl. This pervasive disregard of the law is engendered by the economic gain of providing these products to teenagers and by a generally cynical public attitude toward authority. When laws are enacted but not enforced, the benefits of the statutorial disapproval of certain activities must be weighed against the risks of hypocrisy.

The second way in which the law responds to teenagers is by awarding privileges and attempting to encourage dialogue between adolescents and their parents. This approach is epitomized by legislation regarding parental and minor consent in health matters. Parental permission generally signifies informed consent for health care involving young persons below the age of majority, now 18. However, parental permission and the sole consent of minors overlap on a gradient that ranges from complete reliance upon parental permission at one end, to only the consent of the minor nearing the age of majority at the other end.

The dilemma of minor versus parental consent surfaces dramatically in the question of parental consent and notification for a minor's abortion. Although in *Planned Parenthood v. Danforth* in 1976 the U.S. Supreme Court ruled that a state may not impose a blanket requirement that minors procure the consent of others to obtain an abortion, the question of parental notification about an abortion remains unsettled (Kfoury, 1987).

There is little question that pregnant teenagers need to be able to discuss their predicaments with sympathetic adults. The problem with laws that mandate parental notification, however, is that they are brought to bear only upon girls who perceive, rightly or wrongly, that their parents are not sympathetic. For them, the parental roles of protection and nurturance already appear to have failed, and it is disingenuous to suggest that forcing this confrontation between parents and daughters will be beneficial. The U.S. Supreme Court has stated that even "immature minors" must be given the option of avoiding this potential conflict by appealing to judges, who then decide whether the minors are mature enough to make the decision themselves, and if not, to decide for them whether abortions are in their best interests (*Akron v. Akron Center*, 1983; et al.). It is by no means obvious, however, that brief discussions with judges will provide the guidance that these teenagers need. Controversies about whether adolescents ought to have access to contraceptives, rehabilitation for substance abuse, and treatment for sexually transmitted diseases without parental knowledge or consent raise similar questions. The confusion, intensity of emotions, and communication problems underlying these situations point to the need for mental health rather than legal remedies.

The controversy over dispensing contraceptives in school-based clinics epitomizes the conflict between the desires of teenagers and what adults might think is in their long-range interests. Teenage pregnancy is a major personal and social issue. Every year almost 1 million teenagers become pregnant; over 40% of them obtain abortions, and almost 47% give birth (Hayes, 1987; Moore, 1989). A Planned Parenthood Federation of America poll of teenagers conducted by Louis Harris and Associates in 1986 revealed that 57% used no birth control during their first intercourse, and 27% were not using it at the time of the interview. Asked why they did not use birth control, 39% answered that they just did not want to or that they wanted to get pregnant. Fifty-nine percent had sex education classes at school, and 39% had classes that included birth control information. Seventy-eight percent thought that they should have access to birth control measures without anyone else finding out.

Contraceptive-dispensing clinics in schools are advocated by those who support the desires of teenagers and hold that family planning is the best way to reduce pregnancy. They also point out that public health principles dictate that clinics should be as near to the patients as possible, in this case in schools or accessible to them. They would have such clinics invite initial contacts, because adolescents often seek health care only during crises. They would have the clinic staff encourage teenagers to communicate with their parents. They conclude that parents already in communication with their teenagers have nothing to fear, and that parents who are not should welcome such a clinic, because it could open up that communication.

The opposite point of view does not accept the inevitability of adolescent copulation and holds that providing contraception- and abortion-counseling clinics tacitly encourages children to act promiscuously. Those who hold this view believe that the presence of these clinics in schools undermines the rights of parents and weakens self-discipline among teenagers. They see self-indulgence as the message conveyed to teenagers. Instead, they hold that schools should join parents in promoting virtue and deferral of gratification among young people. They would have schools use educational methods to reduce pregnancies, abortion, and venereal disease. They point out that teenagers need realistic guidance in understanding that sexual intercourse outside of committed relationships is exploitative and that teenagers are better off refraining from sexual intercourse altogether (Joffee, 1986). They are critical of family-planning counselors who try to maintain value neutrality and miss the opportunity to help their clients cope with a society that entices them into irresponsible sexual behavior. Because of these conflicting views about the role of schools in teenage sexuality, professional youth advocacy is needed in order to separate the long-range interests from the short-range desires of teenagers in managing their sexual behavior.

In actuality, the statutes that permit minors to consent to their own health care enable, rather than require, physicians to provide treatment. It is important, therefore, that an effort be made to assist teenagers to involve their parents in all matters affecting their health. Health professionals can serve as intermediaries in restoring interrupted intrafamily communication that could not have come about otherwise. Withholding information from parents inherently further jeopardizes parent-child relationships. Therefore, the existence of communication problems between youths and parents on health matters is in itself a reason for therapeutic intervention.

There are even greater hazards in a parent's or a minor's right to refuse treatment. Adults may refuse treatment for illnesses as long as the public interest is not endangered by an untreated condition. However, the legal presumption is that minors should receive necessary health and mental health care so as to enter adulthood in a healthy state. For this reason, parental refusal of treatment for children can be judicially overridden. However, in the instance of mental illness parental consent may exist, but adequate treatment may or may not be available. Youths should not be able to refuse necessary, adequate psychiatric treatment, but they also should not be required to submit to inadequate or potentially harmful procedures or confinement.

In practice, the question of refusing treatment arises with adolescents from troubled families, so that objectivity is clouded in all quarters. In these instances, the adversarial legal process only heightens conflict between parent and child, and doctor and patient. The state, however well motivated, should show that it can commit resources to treat a child properly before it can override parental authority and medical opinion and permit a minor to refuse necessary and adequate treatment.

THE REPRESENTATION OF MINORS IN COURT

Children depend upon the courts to define their rights and protect their interests, not simply to administer justice as in adult criminal and civil matters. Because each child is part of a psychological, emotional, and physical child-parent unit, the child should not be dealt with apart from the child-parent relationship. The dependent nature of the child-parent unit gradually diminishes until the emancipation of passing from minority to adult status. In recent years the statutory definition of emancipation as attaining the age of 18 has been broadened to allow minors to petition courts prior to that age for a declaration of emancipation based upon their independent living status (Davis & Schwartz, 1987, p. 40).

Litigation involving minors really should not be balancing power between children, parents, and the state but should be directed toward insuring a favorable future outcome in a child's life. Unlike criminal and civil law, which are devoted to protecting the rights of defendants when issues of whether or not alleged events occurred, litigation involving children should be based on determining and furthering a child's interests. Given the adversarial nature of the legal and political systems, however, ascribing rights to children is the most practical means of bringing children's points of view into the courts and legislatures.

The law presumes that parents are generally best suited to represent and safeguard their children's interests. That presumption, however, should not prevail once a child's living arrangements become the subject of a parental dispute that cannot be resolved without resort to the courts, as a custody or visitation contest in a divorce or separation proceeding, or when the state challenges the fitness of adults to remain parents. Nor should it be presumed, as it often is, that the state represents the interests of the child. Its policies or practices may conflict with those of the child. Nor should it be presumed that a child's interests are represented by child-caring agencies that can have conflicts of interest between safeguarding agency policies and the needs of a specific child. In none of these instances does anyone have a conflict-free interest in representing the child.

For this reason, accommodations that address the interests and special needs of minors have been made in the legal system through special procedures, the appointment of guardians *ad litem*, and the use of legal standards for determining the interests of children.

SPECIAL PROCEDURES

Over the last decade the special procedures of separate juvenile courts have been replaced by incorporating juvenile cases into general adult court systems, in part as a result of the U.S. Supreme Court *In re Gault* decision in 1967. The Gault decision often was construed to have abolished the unique privacy and treatment orientation of juvenile courts and to apply adult criminal procedures to juvenile offenders, such as the routine Miranda warning at the point of first contact with a youngster, together with advice of the right to avoid self-incrimination and to have the representation of counsel.

The widespread influence of the Gault decision on the legal management of juveniles has dramatically highlighted the dilemmas posed in defining the legal rights of teenagers. On the one hand, the protective, presumably helpful, shield of parents and juvenile courts has been relied upon to guide adolescents through transient antisocial behavior resulting from the dependent, still immature side of their development. On the other hand, it has been clear that all parents and all court practices cannot be relied upon to be benign and helpful.

In the Gault decision, the Supreme Court actually recognized the value of the juvenile court system as a means of processing juveniles separately from adults, of insuring the confidentiality of police and court actions involving minors, and of implementing the treatment of juvenile offenders. To these ends, the Gault decision ordered the implementation of due process only during the adjudicatory phase of juvenile court proceedings, the steps taking place in the courtroom. The Supreme Court specifically recognized the need to preserve informality and confidentiality during the prejudicial interviewing and post-judicial dispositional phases. In fact, it was the harshness of the disposition of the

Gault case that led the Supreme Court to link the need for due process to the potentially drastic interventions available to the juvenile court rather than the court's abstract concern for observing due process with juveniles.

The Gault decision, then, required juvenile courts to adhere to the following procedures during formal adjudication: Juveniles and their parents must receive written notice of formal court proceedings; juveniles and their parents must be informed of their rights to counsel; the literal confessions and testimony of juveniles should be evaluated with great care; and juveniles and their parents must be afforded the rights of confrontation and sworn testimony of witnesses available for cross-examination. These modifications of juvenile court procedures were intended to reinforce the helping role of the courts by insuring more knowledgeable processing of juveniles and by protecting juveniles from abuse by courts.

The Gault decision did not award adult rights to juveniles except as they contribute to fairness in the courtroom management of their problems. The Supreme Court, in effect, upheld the uniqueness of adolescence as a developmental period characterized by special needs and behavior problems. From the law-enforcement point of view, there are offenses peculiar to adolescents, such as running away, incorrigibility, delinquency, and truancy. From the psychiatric standpoint, school phobias, suicide attempts, and identity crises with the need for treatment of an adolescent with parental consent, or at times without it, are encountered. The health problems of adolescents also pose unique issues related to parental knowledge and consent. Venereal disease, abortion, accidental injuries, drug abuse, and teenage pregnancy are examples. In the area of family law, there are special considerations surrounding child custody, visitation rights, foster home and child-caring institutional placement, parental fitness, and child abuse. Juveniles do pose issues and situations not encountered with adults. The legal system is struggling with finding ways to adapt general court procedures to these unique issues posed by minors, as discussed in the following chapters.

THE GUARDIAN AD LITEM

Crucial to determining a minor's interests in court is provision for personal representation of that young person. Most states mandate that a guardian *ad litem* or counsel be appointed for a child in civil judicial proceedings arising from reports of abuse or neglect. The enabling language usually is sufficiently broad to include the right to a guardian *ad litem* or counsel from the first hearing until the final case outcome, which may include the termination of parental rights (Davidson & Horowitz, 1984, pp. 296-299). In many states this policy also applies to contested divorce custody and visitation matters.

By definition, the roles of a guardian *ad litem* and a counsel are different. The former is charged to advocate the client's interests, whereas the latter is obligated to represent the client's expressed desires. Dual representation of the child can occur in some states; however, the American Bar Association's Model Code of Professional Responsibility suggests that guardians *ad litem* should obtain all possible aid from clients who are capable of understanding the matters in question and of contributing to the advancement of their own interests.

A guardian *ad litem* usually investigates a case, represents the child in all court proceedings, develops dispositional plans, and lessens the trauma of legal intervention for the child. The guardian *ad litem* also may be an officer of the court and thereby entitled to make recommendations to the court.

LEGAL STANDARDS FOR DETERMINING A CHILD'S INTERESTS

If the interests of children are to be represented in court, legal standards are needed for determining those interests. This is particularly important when decisions that affect the course of a child's life must be made. The standards in general usage are the "best interests," "the least detrimental available alternative," and the "primary caregiver" described in Chapter 5. Because no definitive answers lie in these, or other, standards, the legal principle of "indeterminacy" applies to them, and, therefore, they remain crude guidelines rather than definable tests (Mnookin, 1985, p. 24.)

The "Best Interests" Standard. The "best interests" of the child standard appears to have emerged around the middle of this century from child-custody litigation incident to divorce, and later was applied to child abuse and neglect cases. However, it has never been construed to mean that children should be removed from their parents to be placed in more affluent or educated families. Still, idealistic interventions on the basis of middle-class conceptions of a child's best interests frequently arise in child abuse and neglect matters. On the other hand, the "best interests" standard does convey to decision makers that the child in question is a victim of environmental circumstances, is at risk, and needs better alternatives in life.

How to determine the "best interests" of a child is an exceedingly difficult matter (Mnookin, 1985, p. 42). For this reason, a child's "best interests" often are fashioned primarily to meet the needs of competing adult claimants or to protect the general policies of agencies (Goldstein, Freud, & Solnit, 1973, p. 54). The indeterminacy of the "best interests" standard results in an ambivalence reflected in either woefully treating children or glorifying their interests. Because neither approach is realistic, the end result often is either frustrated withdrawal or inaction on the part of legal professionals.

The "Least Detrimental Available Alternative" Standard. In order to help courts reasonably determine the way and extent to which children's developmental needs are assessed and met, the focus can be shifted from an ideal standard to the "least detrimental of the available alternatives" standard (Goldstein et al., p. 53). This standard realistically examines the available alternatives in a child's life and favors the one that offers the prospect of being the least harmful to the child. It offers the prospect for a child of maintaining a relationship with at least one adult who is or will become the child's psychological parent.

In another vein, efforts to give adolescents access to abortion and birth control can be construed as applying the "least worse" or "least detrimental" alternative (Zimring, 1982). Even though teenagers should receive guidance about sexuality from parents or other adults, often this does not occur. Given the extraordinary social costs of teenage pregnancy, its prevention by contraception can be seen simply as a lesser evil than that of being trapped by a pregnancy as a consequence of experimentation with drugs and sexuality. As it now stands, teenagers can consent legally to abortions but not to plastic surgery, and they can obtain contraceptives but not alcohol or vulgar reading material. The concept of the "least detrimental alternative" provides a more rational ground for these distinctions than does according teenagers the constitutional right of adults to privacy and personal choice. The teenager's progress toward adulthood is not hindered by being prohibited access to cosmetic surgery, drugs, or obscenity, but a pregnant teenager's decision to have an abortion or to keep her child affects the rest of her life.

The challenge for judges and child advocates is to apply interest standards to individual cases with an awareness of their indeterminacy and the long-range repercussions of current decision making.

SUMMARY

Children are entitled to rights simply because they are members of society. Because they comprise a permanent minority, institutionalized mechanisms are needed to insure that their interests are protected in society and in legal matters. By virtue of their immaturity and lack of political enfranchisement, the young cannot do so for themselves.

The legal rights of minors cluster around rights to nurturance, to protection, and to make autonomous choices. There is a developmental gradient in minors' capacities to perceive, to understand, and to express their views of life circumstances. The authority of their parents generally is honored because of the presumption that it is based upon love and wisdom. It is based also upon the awareness that parenthood involves sacrificial duties that, in turn, require the cooperation and obedience of children. Theoretically, the interests of parents and children are congruent when an adult is functioning competently in the parenting role. When conflicts arise between the rights of parents and children, they usually are based upon the personal interests of a person outside of the parenting role.

Through legislation, society restricts and awards privileges to minors by age-grading principles while protecting the parent-child relationship. The restrictions are related to what are regarded as harmful activities. They articulate social values that are useful for most young people but that do not prevent others from tasting "forbidden fruit." The privileges usually pertain to health matters when communication barriers between young persons and their parents are perceived as insurmountable or when parents are suspected of denying treatment or forcing an inadequate or harmful treatment on minors.

The recognition that conflicts between the rights of parents and children are based upon conflicts between family members highlights the need for providing counseling and support for children, youths, and their families. To deal with minors as free-standing individuals often aggravates alienation within families and misses an opportunity to heal wounds and improve lifetime relationships. The most commonly encountered example is revealed in the myth that children and youths cannot profit from counseling or psychotherapy unless they initially say they want to participate. In fact the authority of the courts is frequently required to insure that minors and their families participate in and benefit from treatment.

The nature of juvenile and family law differs from adult criminal and civil law because, in addition to the administration of justice, the courts have an obligation to define and protect the interests of minors. This can take place through due process safeguards during adjudicatory hearings and the presence of legal representation, usually in the form of guardians *ad litem*, to advocate the interests of minors.

The determination and implementation of the interests of minors is "indeterminate" from the legal standpoint because of the lack of definitive and reliable standards. The "best interests of the child" standard is too vague and idealistic to be of practical value in courts. The "primary caregiver" standard, described in Chapter 5, has value in contested custody cases, because it is based upon demonstrable historical facts. In general, however, the "least detrimental available alternative" standard has the greatest value, because it evaluates practical alternatives in terms of which would be the least harmful to the child.

The law would profit, as would society, from recognizing childhood and adolescence as legitimate phases of life during which developmental issues of dependence and independence are worked through with great variation from one individual to another.

REFERENCES

Akron v. Akron Center for Reproductive Health, 426 U.S. 416 (1983); *Planned Parenthood v. Ashcroft,* 462 U.S. 476 (1983); *H. L. v. Matheson,* 450 U.S. 398 (1981); *Bellotti v. Baird,* 443 U.S. 622 (1979); *Bellotti v. Baird,* 428 U.S. 132 (1976); *Planned Parenthood of Central Missouri v. Danforth,* 428 U.S. 52 (1976).

Blackstone, W. (1982). *Commentaries on the Laws of England. Volume IV of Public Wrongs.* Boston: Beacon Press.

Board of Education v. Pico, 457 U.S. 853, 871 (1982). See *FCC v. Pacifica Foundation,* 438 U.S. 726 (1978).

Davidson, H. A., & Horowitz, R. M. (1984). Protection of children from family maltreatment. In R. M. Horowitz & H. A. Davidson (Eds.), *Legal Rights of Children*. Colorado Springs, CO: Shepard's/McGraw-Hill.

Davis, S. M., & Schwartz, M. D. (1987). *Children's Rights and the Law*. Lexington, MA: Lexington Books.

DiFranza, J. R., Norwood, B. D., Garner, D. W., & Tye, J. B. (1987). Legislative efforts to protect children from tobacco. *Journal of the American Medical Association, 257,* 3387-3389.

Dodson, G. D. (1984). Legal rights of adolescents: Restrictions on liberty, emancipation, and status offenses. In R. M. Horowitz & H. A. Davidson (Eds.), *Legal Rights of Children*. Colorado Springs, CO: Shepard's/McGraw-Hill.

In re Gault, 387 U.S. 1 (1967, May 15).

Ginsberg v. New York, 390 U.S. 629 (1968).

Goldstein, J., Freud, A., & Solnit, A. J. (1973). *Beyond the Best Interests of the Child*. New York: Free Press.

Hayes, C. D. (Ed.). (1987). *Risking the Future: Adolescent Sexuality, Pregnancy, and Childbearing*. Washington, DC: National Academy Press.

Horowitz, R. M., & Davidson, H. A. (1984). *Legal Rights of Children*. Colorado Springs, CO: Shepard's/McGraw-Hill.

Joffee, C. (1986). *The Regulation of Sexuality: Experiences of Family Planning Workers*. Philadelphia, PA: Temple University Press.

Kfoury, P. R. (1987). *Children Before the Court: Reflections on Legal Issues Affecting Minors*. Stoneham, MA: Butterworth Legal Publishing.

Mnookin, R. H. (1985). *In the Interest of Children: Advocacy, Law Reform, and Public Policy*. New York: W. H. Freeman.

Moore, K. A. (1989). *Facts at a Glance*. Washington, DC: Child Trends.

New York v. Ferber, 458 U.S. 747 (1982).

Planned Parenthood v. Danforth, 428 U.S. 52, 96 S.Ct. 2831, 49 L.Ed 2d 788 (1976).

Wisconsin v. Yoder, 406 U.S. 205 (1972).

Zimring, F. E. (1982). *The Changing Legal World of Adolescence* (pp. 61-67). New York: Free Press.

4

THE PURPOSE AND OPERATION OF THE CHILD ADVOCACY TEAM

Jack C. Westman

Mental health professionals generally are held in low regard in courts of law because of their ambiguous and divergent viewpoints. In fact the "hired gun" image frequently is applied to them.

Reasons for this credibility problem range from reliance upon speculation to drawing conclusions from inadequate and incomplete data. Of greatest importance is the inappropriate use of mental health professionals outside of their usual helping context. Mental health professionals alone cannot effectively help children who are caught in the adversarial format of the legal system just as they have been in their troubled families.

With the demise of treatment-oriented juvenile and family court systems, a new model is needed to appropriately deal with family law matters as qualitatively distinct from criminal and civil law issues. The child advocacy team offers a means of adapting court procedures to the circumstances of individual cases and combining the decision-making power of the courts with the healing processes of the mental health system.

An appreciation of the differences between the *modi operandi* of the legal and the mental health systems is essential for both attorneys and mental health professionals, if they are to serve

65

their clients and patients constructively. This particularly is the case in family law matters, because they involve interpersonal disputes rather than detecting and punishing wrongdoing (Schetky & Benedek, 1980). The legal and mental health systems can either aggravate or help to heal the pain and frustration of the parents and children involved. Unfortunately, as it now stands the harm often outweighs the help to affected children.

The legal system operates on the adversary principle by which conflicts are resolved by pitting opposing viewpoints against each other with resulting negotiation between them or prevailing of one position. It also takes as much time as is needed to consummate that process. Its tactics selectively present information in order to favor a party's point of view in bargaining and litigation. George Bernard Shaw once said, "The theory of the adversary system is that if you set two liars to exposing each other, eventually the truth will out."

In contrast, the mental health system operates on the principle that conflicts are resolved by finding the truth and by teamwork. It is aware of the importance of time in the lives of children and the need for the speedy resolution of conflict. Its tactics depend upon open access to all information pertinent to a given case. However, it lacks mechanisms for insuring that the information is accurate.

The legal and mental health systems share a commitment to individual case study. In fact, legal fact-finding techniques can be invaluable for mental health professionals. Both the legal and mental health systems seek just solutions to problems in human relationships. Both employ mediation techniques. Because there is an undercurrent of guilt and retribution in the litigation of family law and an emphasis on allegations rather than fact finding, the combined resources of the mental health and legal systems can keep the legal focus on decision making regarding the welfare of affected children and the mental health focus on absorbing and mediating accusations and rebuttals.

INTEGRATING THE LEGAL
AND MENTAL HEALTH SYSTEMS

The challenge is to integrate the decision-making powers of the legal system with the conflict-resolving powers of the mental health system. The involvement of the legal system in family matters usually results from the inability of parents to maturely and reasonably manage family affairs. The court is brought in as a parent surrogate, *in loco parentis*, to make decisions ordinarily within the province of parents. The wisdom of the court can be enhanced by knowledge gained from consultation with mental health professionals, who also can assist family members to more realistically and effectively face and cope with their specific problems. In so doing neither the legal system nor the mental health system should compromise its basic ethical principles in dealing with family problems. The legal system should not deviate from the pursuit of justice nor the mental health system from its obligation to heal and not harm.

In practice, both legal and mental health professionals often do compromise their standards. Lawyers seek, and mental health professionals provide, information that will not bear up under the scrutiny of the courtroom. The results are a low regard for mental health testimony by judges (Faust & Ziskin, 1988) and an avoidance by mental health professionals of frustrating legal interactions. Both may rationalize their antipathy on the grounds that no one has the knowledge needed to make crucial decisions in the lives of children. However, mental health professionals are better equipped to help in decision making regarding human relationships than are judges and attorneys, who are not trained in child development, family dynamics, and human motivation (Gardner, 1982). Most importantly, children cannot wait for research in child development to answer questions of immediate impact in their lives.

Neither the legal nor mental health systems can conscientiously be indifferent to the human distress evident in family legal matters. The statutory commitment of the legal system usually is to further the interests of the affected children, however painful this may be for the adults involved. Mental health professionals naturally wish to help distressed children and parents. If unable to help, the most important decision for the mental health professional is whether to become involved in a legal matter involving a family at all. If one is inexperienced or uncertain, the prudent decision is to decline. It is better for the professional to "do it right" or not at all. Attorneys are accustomed to the adversarial format and have mechanisms for collecting their fees. However, the time-consuming details of telephone calls, correspondence, scheduling, vagaries of legal schedules, subpoenas, waiting for and postponement of hearings, hostile responses from offended parties, and the failure to pay fees all combine to create an untenable form of practice for mental health professionals unless the process can be structured according to a logical model.

A "no" at the outset can save grief and spare the court and family what will be a fruitless experience.

The financial cost of multiple, contradictory expert witnesses in extended litigation and the emotional cost to the children and parents, who are buffeted by the adversarial format, justify turning to the healing potential of combined forces. Knowledgeable collaboration between the legal and mental health systems can enhance the possibility of stipulated agreements that offer not only less cost but greater long-range benefit for the affected parties.

In order to insure that both legal and mental health standards of practice are maintained, a model is needed to distinguish the role of the mental health expert in family legal matters from the usual employment of experts in criminal and civil actions. In such actions, the expert ordinarily provides information about a specific point, such as the cause of death or the tensile strength of a steel beam. In family law the mental health expert is asked to provide more extensive information that bears upon the life course of a child. In addition, the expert is asked to do so through highly personal interchanges with children and their parents, who are struggling through crises of varying degrees.

In order to serve their clients and patients constructively, attorneys and mental health professionals can adapt their usual procedures, so that a useful interface between the legal and mental health approaches can be created. Both need to educate each other in their operational policies. This can be done by employing the principles of mental health consultation (Steinberg & Yule, 1985) and child advocacy (Westman, 1979). In this way the mental health professional acts as a consultant to an attorney and both, together with other professionals, act as advocates for a child.

Mental health consultation is designed to help other professionals use their knowledge, skills, and resources more effectively. It is a process that respects the autonomy of the consultee in both solving specific problems and gaining new knowledge. It is ideally suited to the needs of attorneys whose investigative style is to become informed in all aspects of a particular client's case. The aim of the attorney is to become the "expert" for the client by drawing upon pertinent aspects of all relevant disciplines. In contrast with the circumscribed evaluation of a child by a clinician in response to an ambiguous question, consultation is an active interaction with another professional, the child, and the family in order to meet the needs of the consultee and the child.

As a consultant, the first responsibility of the clinician is to help attorneys ask appropriate questions and to know what procedures are required in order to answer them. It makes no more sense for a clinician to be asked to perform a specific psychological technique than for a physician to be asked to perform a specific laboratory test. For example, an expert witness should not be asked to employ specific techniques to gain information, such as by a doll interview with a child. Clinical procedures are not intended to be taken out of a professional context. It is the interpretation of procedures that reveals useful information, not the procedures themselves. McDermott, Tseng, and Char (1978) found this to be the case when they furnished videotapes of interviews in child custody matters for use in the courtroom. Laypersons were unable to interpret the videotape data accurately; they required professional assistance in doing so. There are circumstances in the physical sciences and technologies when raw data can be provided appropriately by an expert witness for interpretation by laypersons, but this rarely is the case in the clinical professions.

Thus attorneys have specific questions and needs that can or cannot be answered by mental health professionals (Duquette, 1990). They also can have preferences about the way that the mental health professional is involved that are incompatible with the latter's professional policies and procedures. For example, an attorney may want a clinician to evaluate a child without interviewing the parents and having access to additional information, in order to obtain an "objective" assessment. Or a clinician may be expected to carry out an evaluation without access to previous evaluations, or on the basis of written reports only, in order to insure an "unbiased" opinion. In each of these instances, the attorney prescribes the means for the clinician to carry out an "objective" study and arrive at "unbiased" conclusions. The actual intent usually is to obtain opinions favorable to a particular litigant's point of view by selecting the information available to the clinician.

THE CHILD ADVOCACY TEAM

A more reliable assurance that the clinician will be as objective and unbiased as possible is for the clinician to take the initiative in forming a child advocacy team. The aim of the child advocacy team is to assist the legal system to achieve its goal of justice through legal and clinical collaboration. Legal procedures can be used in a constructive manner. Questions can be framed in answerable terms, and clinical procedures can be carried out to answer them. At the same time, the clinician can employ therapeutic skills. It makes no sense to deprive the family of the opportunity for constructive change and conflict resolution during the evaluation process. In fact to do so conflicts with the clinician's ethical obligation to help and not to harm clients or patients.

The goal of the child advocacy team is not simply to assist the court in decision making but to assist the litigating parties to do so through stipulated agreements as well. The mental health system is a logical support for the legal remedies of out-of-court settlements, because of its primary human-relations focus. The spectacle of an array of conflicting psychiatric and psychological experts retained by each parent has become all too familiar. Although the child advocacy team model does not eliminate that possibility, it enters the legal arena in a manner that maximizes the possibility of cooperation between the litigating parties.

Although a child advocacy team can be organized in a variety of ways, the essential first step is initiation of the request for a child advocacy team to the court by the guardian *ad litem* or by both counselors for the litigating parties. The second step is appointment of the convener of the team by the judge, so that the accountability of the team is to the court and so that the cooperation of all parties is insured. The University of Wisconsin Forensic Child Psychiatry Service, for example, accepts referrals only when the child psychiatrist is appointed by a judge at the request of a guardian *ad litem* to serve as a consultant to the court on custody and visitation, child witness, or child abuse and neglect matters. The guardian *ad litem* and the child psychiatrist then select other relevant members of the child advocacy team.

The interdisciplinary model of the child advocacy team composed of the guardian *ad litem*, mental health clinician, social services personnel, and other relevant professionals under appointment by a judge provides an interface between the legal and mental health systems that can be used for both obtaining information and assisting in conflict resolution. If a child does not have legal representation in court, the opposing attorneys can agree to participate in the child advocacy team. The legal professionals can then act as counselors rather than simply advocating a particular client's point of view.

The child advocacy team also relieves clinicians who are treating involved persons from untenable roles as participants in litigation in which they cannot be expected to be impartial because of the limitations of their perspectives and their confidential treatment relationships with the affected persons. When contacted by parents or attorneys, those clinicians can assist in routing a request for a child advocacy team through the judge or the guardian *ad litem* of the child.

PLANNING CONFERENCE

The first step is a planning conference to form a child advocacy team in order to apply the advocacy techniques as described in Chapter 1. The composition and functions of the team vary depending upon whether the legal matter is a child in need of protective services, a divorce custody or visitation contest, or a child as a witness in criminal or civil actions. The purpose of the conference is to orient professionals to the concept of child advocacy, assemble existing information, plan for interviews and testing, obtain authorizations for the release of additional reports, assign tasks to team members, and define the specific legal issues and procedures to be followed. The team's activities should not be restricted by deadlines, so that reasonable time for unexpected developments is allowed.

At the outset it is important to determine how the fees will be paid. The referring parties should be informed of the likely time and cost involved in the clinical aspect of the process. The court should establish responsibility for the payment of fees, whether by the litigating parties or public sources. When payment is assigned to the parties, a retainer to be directly used in payment or a trust deposit to be used by the clinician in the event funds from other sources do not materialize should be obtained. The clinician should have protection from the failure to pay by disappointed parties, who are confronted with unusual expenses relating to their family situations and legal costs. Billing should be on a time basis and include record review, interviewing, conferences, report preparation, travel time, and court appearances.

CLINICAL INTERVIEWS

The next phase is meeting with the persons involved and conducting required interviews. The authority of the court can be used to insure the participation of all relevant parties.

Because of the court mandate, the issue of confidentiality throughout all of the clinical interactions bears special consideration. An environment in which free communication can take place is important for effective interviewing and obtaining information necessary to carry out clinical evaluations. Parties are understandably reluctant to disclose information that may be introduced into courtroom proceedings. At the same time the nature of the study necessitates the disclosure of personal information to the court. Actually, the problem is not as complicated as it may seem. All information communicated in confidence to any mental health professional is subject to judicial summons. Even when statutes grant privilege to psychiatrists, the ultimate privacy of that relationship is determined by the courts.

The confidentiality of the professional-patient-client relationship is defined variously by state statutes (Barnum, Silverberg, & Nied, 1987). Many interests are in tension with each other in determining what kinds of procedural protections make sense. Among them are the individual's rights to privacy and against self-incrimination; the state's interest in furthering trust within a patient-psychotherapist relationship; and the state's interest in furthering family autonomy, protecting children, and protecting public safety. The guiding principle for protecting or divulging information involves balancing these interests. If information is generated improperly by a court-ordered clinical examination not preceded by a warning, then it may not be usable. On the other hand, if too much effort is formally devoted to protecting confidentiality, clinical rapport is inhibited, and needed information will not be generated.

The involved parties should be informed at the start that the interviews are court ordered and that the clinician's primary obligation is to assist the court in making a decision that will further the interests of the child. At the same time, the need for free disclosure on their parts should be acknowledged. They should know that findings and recommendations will be shared with them before they are reported to the attorneys and the court, if that is the case. They can be given the option for individually designating specific communications made privately to the clinician as confidential. In those instances the judge will determine whether or not disclosure of that information is necessary in court. An effort should be made to insure that the parties understand this information. Documentation should be made of this exchange in the clinical record and in the clinician's report.

The matter of confidentiality is especially critical for children. Recognizing the undesirability of forcing a child to disclose preferences that could jeopardize a relationship if made known to a parent, the child should be informed that communications can be made *in camera* to the judge who will decide whether or not disclosure will be made in the courtroom. A case example illustrates this point:

> An 8-year-old boy indirectly expressed to the psychiatrist his wish to live with his father. He did not want to offend his mother, however, and was reluctant to make this disclosure openly in court. When it was explained that he could invoke confidentiality and that the judge would be informed of his dilemma, he agreed to make that communication with the understanding that it would be information to be used at the judge's discretion. In the courtroom proceedings that followed, the judge ruled that the communication was made to him through the boy's confidential relationship with his psychiatrist and was not essential to the conduct of the adversarial proceedings, because the child was not old enough to be a material witness, and the expert's interpretation of his statements was sufficient.

When therapeutically desirable, parents and children can be assisted to share information previously regarded as secret. They also may well find that the interviews will be useful to them in their own decision making. For example, parents can decide to arrive at a stipulated custody agreement or a parent can decide to voluntarily terminate parental rights as a result of the evaluation process.

In our practice we usually include the guardian *ad litem* for the child in our clinical interviews. In abuse and neglect matters social workers may be included as well in order to verify the accuracy of a parent's statement to us. Our intent is to provide the guardian *ad litem* with first-hand experiences in a clinical setting with the involved parties. We also wish to insure that the information we obtain from often defensive and guarded adults is accurate and to observe their responses to confrontations with reality. This also facilitates the child's perception of the guardian *ad litem* as the child's attorney.

Special attention should be devoted to preparing children for their interviews. After eliciting their fears, they often need explanations of what is happening both in the larger picture and at the moment. Younger children need to understand that they are not expected to make choices or decisions regarding their situations and that other adults will be doing that. Children should be seen both alone and with their parents in order to assess their behavior under each circumstance and to make direct observations that bear on parent-child relationships.

REPORTING CONFERENCE

The next phase is meeting with the team members and the parties concerned in order to verify the accuracy of critical information and share preliminary findings and recommendations. This may be followed by additional meetings with the parties to assist with out-of-court settlements. This phase provides an opportunity for working through feelings and clarifying observations so that fine tuning of decisions can take place.

REPORT PREPARATION

The next phase is preparing the clinician's report to the court. In general, the purpose of the report is to assist the court in deciding specific legal issues at hand. In order to insure that the findings are accurate and as complete as possible, the clinician should review all relevant clinical, social service, law enforcement, and legal documents. The material included in the report, however, should be limited to that which is necessary to demonstrate the validity of the findings, the thoroughness of the evaluation process, and the bases for conclusions and recommendations. The report should be written with the expectation that it will be read and criticized by all parties as a semi-public document. For this reason, professional jargon and pejorative language should be avoided. Tentative findings and conclusions should be so designated as should those formed to a reasonable degree of professional certainty. The latter are usually defined as being of sufficient certainty so that a treatment plan would be based upon them. The phrasing of findings and conclusions that would be perceived as painful by one or more parties should be as humane as possible in order to facilitate their acceptance and understanding. Generalizations from research should be avoided unless they are used to support specific findings in the case.

A detailed description of the evaluation process and the information available to the clinician is helpful. The referral source; the reports provided; the dates, places, and people involved in interviews; and missed or cancelled appointments should be noted. Quotations should be used whenever possible to support findings. Psychiatric diagnoses should be made according to the current *Diagnostic and Statistical Manual* of the American Psychiatric Association with the expectation that cross-examination will take place on the data supporting each of the criteria cited in the *Manual* to support a specific diagnosis (American Psychiatric Association, 1987). Projective psychological testing should be used only to corroborate findings and not as a primary source of information.

The recommendations carry more weight if they are made after evaluating the possible dispositional alternatives and selecting the one that the clinician believes is the least detrimental to the child. The assumption that the past is the best predictor of the future when nothing has occurred to give evidence of a change in pattern is reasonable.

DEPOSITIONS

In civil cases it is customary to depose the expert prior to trial. This permits the opposing attorney to question the expert in preparation for the trial. The attorney by whom the expert is retained is present and may be consulted during the proceedings. A copy of the deposition should be requested by the clinician and should be reviewed for errors prior to trial. It also can be used as a reminder of what was said, since reference will be made to the deposition during the trial.

COURTROOM TESTIMONY

The next phase is providing courtroom testimony. The expert clinical witness should insist upon scheduling a convenient date for appearance and advance briefing on both the questions that will be asked on direct examination and the probable questions that will be asked on cross-examination. The time of the courtroom appearances should be scheduled so that the expert is the first witness of the morning or afternoon, in order to avoid waiting in court. When served with ill-conceived subpoenas without previous agreement outside of the context of a child advocacy team, the clinician often can avoid appearing completely by informing the summoning attorney of the nature of one's testimony that will not be favorable to the attorney's position.

In facing what can be a trying experience, especially if the clinician's position is perceived as hostile by one of the parties, it is helpful to be aware of the attorneys' expectations (Foster,

1983). Generally speaking, the expert is expected to offer opinions with reasonable medical certainty about data that are not within the realm of a layperson's knowledge and common sense. For this reason, the expert witness is permitted to draw upon any pertinent information including hearsay evidence. The expert is expected to be able to evaluate the pertinence and reliability of information and, therefore, may express opinions. The facts upon which an expert's opinion are based may be challenged but not the opinion, which involves the professional judgment of the expert.

Most U.S. courts apply the "Frye Test," named for a 1923 decision which allows scientific evidence to be admitted if it has gained "general acceptance" among specialists in a given field. Judges often view testimony from experimental psychologists as suspect because specialists in the field argue about the data and findings. But testimony from mental health professionals based on intuitive assumptions rather than on rigorous research is seldom ruled out. Apparently, the less evidently controversial though weaker the information is, the more readily it is accepted (Saks, 1987).

The expert's credibility usually is questioned in contested matters. The credibility of an expert witness is based upon credentials in the particular area at issue. In family law, it involves knowledge of child development and family dynamics in addition to psychiatric diagnostic, treatment, and prognostic knowledge of adults and children. Special training and experience in forensic matters also are relevant. State licensure, board certification, and membership in professional organizations are appropriate credentials in addition to the number of similar cases included in one's professional experience.

In challenging witness credibility, the argument has been advanced that mental health expert witnesses should not be advocates for the child in order to maintain unbiased scientific testimony. This is based upon the model of the objective expert witness in criminal and civil proceedings. However, family law involves much more than the determination of facts. It is a complicated process of determining dimensions of a child's developmental welfare that should be assessed and weighting these dimensions to reach a decision that is the least detrimental for the child. Family litigation involves allegations, legal guidelines, and judicial decisions that are more blatantly value laden and subjective than in criminal and civil litigation (Wittman, 1985). Without the expression of opinion and the weighting and interpretation of data by the clinical expert witness, the court is left to do what the clinicians are needed for in the first place: to help interpret situations to assist the court in determining the child's interests.

Witness credibility can be challenged further on the grounds of how the referral was made, who paid the fees, and knowledge of the literature. These factors are irrelevant when the expert functions as a member of a child advocacy team, and the procedures followed bear that out.

In the courtroom, the expert witness should avoid fencing with lawyers who are on their own turf. Badgering of the witness will be apparent to the judge and jury, if the witness remains aloof from it. When needed, the attorney who called the witness has an opportunity to clarify and defend the expert's testimony.

Expert witnesses are well advised to recognize that they bring a level of knowledge and experience to the courtroom that exceeds that of other participants. If this were not the case, they would not be there. In order to generate an appropriate level of self-confidence, it is helpful to review the record immediately before the courtroom appearance so as to be familiar with names, ages, dates, and numbers that can be used without reference to the record. This eliminates the need to bring the complete record to the courtroom, where it can be introduced as evidence and used as a basis for diversionary inquiries.

In the courtroom, direct examination is followed by cross-examination, during which the opposing attorney will attempt to discredit the expert witness' testimony or credibility. It is important for the expert to answer briefly. If a yes or no is inappropriate, this should be pointed out. If questions are confusing, the expert should ask that they be repeated or clarified. Pausing before answering a misleading question may give a cue and time for the other attorney to raise an objection. Hypothetical questions can be answered at the expert's discretion, but their lack of relevance to the present case also can be pointed out. When new information is introduced or a citation quoted, the expert should ask to review it and can choose to alter an opinion.

The redirect examination is an opportunity for both attorneys to clarify what has been said or inquire about new information introduced during testimony. The judge then may ask questions.

Simple answers to questions are preferable to complicated explanations and can be made with confidence, if the criterion of professional certainty is borne in mind. Acknowledging misstatements and the existence of differences in opinions is important. Hedging or equivocating on the grounds of intellectual or scientific precision are not needed and can be harmful, when one considers the fact that a judge or jury will make decisions based upon lesser levels of knowledge. The expert should be in a better position to speak with conviction than are they. The courtroom is the legal workplace in which decisions for better or worse must be made, not a research laboratory or a scientific meeting.

In the courtroom it is helpful for the expert witness to speak directly to the judge or the jury when possible, even though the questions are directed by a particular attorney. The principles of persuasion apply in the courtroom as in any other setting. If a hostile attorney is on the wrong track, that will be evident to others and will be obscured if the expert witness becomes defensive or rattled.

SUMMARY

The decision-making powers of the legal system can be integrated with the conflict-resolving powers of the mental health system through the activation and operation of child advocacy teams.

Composed of attorneys, mental health clinicians, social workers, and other relevant professionals, interdisciplinary child advocacy teams can assist parents in forging settlements and courts in adjudicating litigated family issues. The operations of the team include a planning conference, clinical interviews, the collation of information, reporting to the concerned parties, report preparation, and courtroom testimony.

When called as an expert witness in court, the clinician is well advised to become familiar with legal procedures. Attention to pre-trial briefing with the summoning attorney, the latitude of the expert in expressing opinions, the buttressing of opinions with supporting data, and the expression of opinions with warranted conviction are the most important factors in providing credible testimony in a courtroom.

REFERENCES

American Psychiatric Association. (1987). *Diagnostic and Statistical Manual of Mental Disorders* (3rd ed. rev.). Washington, DC: Author.

Barnum, R., Silverberg, J., & Nied, D. (1987). Patient warnings in court-ordered evaluations of children and families. *Bulletin of the Academy of Psychiatry and Law, 15,* 283-300.

Duquette, D. N. (1990). *Advocating for the Child in Protection Proceedings. A Handbook for Lawyers and Court Appointed Special Advocates.* Lexington, MA: Lexington Books.

Faust, D., & Ziskin, J. (1988). The expert witness in psychology and psychiatry. *Science, 241,* 31-35.

Foster, H. H. (1983). Child custody and divorce: A lawyer's view. *Journal of the American Academy of Child Psychiatry, 22,* 392-398.

Gardner, R. A. (1982). *Family Evaluation in Child Custody Litigation.* Cresskill, NJ: Creative Therapeutics.

McDermott, J. F., Tseng, W. S., & Char, W. F. (1978). Child custody decision making. *Journal of the American Academy of Child Psychiatry, 17,* 104-116.

Saks, M. J. (1987). Accuracy v. advocacy: Expert testimony before the bench. *Technology Review, August-September.*

Schetky, D. H., & Benedek, E. P. (1980). *Child Psychiatry and the Law.* New York: Brunner/Mazel.

Steinberg, D., & Yule, W. (1985). Consultative work. In M. Rutter & L. Hersov (Eds.), *Child and Adolescent Psychiatry* (pp. 914-926). Oxford, England: Blackwell Scientific Publications.

Westman, J. C. (1979). *Child Advocacy.* New York: Free Press.

Wittman, J. J. (1985). Child advocacy and the scientific model in family court: A theory for pretrial self- assessment. *Journal of Psychiatry and Law, 13,* 61-82.

5

THE ROLE OF
GUARDIANS AD LITEM
IN CUSTODY CONTESTS

Martha L. Fineman

This chapter reveals the difficulties experienced by guardians ad litem *and mental health professionals in divorce custody cases, leading some to question the need to represent the children's interests in contested divorce custody actions at all. However, the inadequacies of current practices can be stimuli to improve the system rather than indications that the conceptual basis for representing children in court is unsound.*

The mandatory appointment of guardians ad litem *in divorce cases in which custody is contested is due in part to the shift from "innocence versus guilt" to "no-fault" divorces. No longer is it possible to identify one parent as blameworthy and by implication less fit to be a parent. It also reflects the progressive movement of the legal system toward recognizing that children have legal rights in decision making that substantially affects the courses of their lives. This is a departure from the view of children as the property of their parents and of the absolute authority of parents over children. The need for this has been amply demonstrated in child abuse and neglect matters, but it also exists in many contested divorce custody cases as well.*

This chapter identifies the key issue underlying the representation of children separately from their parents in court: When are parents likely to be unable to represent the interests of their children through their attorneys? The presumption that parents are likely to be unable to do so in all divorces is unreasonable. The time for legal representation of the child should be when parents disagree. Contesting parents cannot be relied upon to present all of the pertinent information to the court, so that the judge can make a decision with the interests of the child in mind.

Professor Fineman argues that guardians ad litem *are not needed if their only role is that of reviewing the evidence and formulating recommendations for decision making regarding a child's custody. These are the responsibilities of judges. She sees advocacy for public policies as consonant with the interests of children, and the guardian* ad litem's *role in organizing and participating in child advocacy teams as contributing substantively to the legal process. As the legal component of a child advocacy team, the guardian* ad litem *can orchestrate an objective and definitive evaluation of the child's interests and legal principles, such as due process, adherence to definable standards, and cross-examination.*

Professor Fineman proposes that the "primary caretaker" standard be employed to determine the interests of a child, because it relies upon demonstrated performance rather than opinions about future possibilities. It does not rely on generalizations and encourages study of each case on its own merits. It can be addressed within both the medical and legal models, because they are based upon the principle of understanding each case in the light of its facts.

Contrary to their image as combatants in the adversarial format of the courtroom, attorneys actually function in mediating and negotiating roles in most divorce actions. For this reason, attorneys and mental health professionals have a common basis for helping, rather than polarizing, parents in custody contests. Without a more formalized structure for teamwork, however, this potential is seldom realized.

INTRODUCTION

Several years ago I received a phone call from a Wisconsin state legislator's assistant who asked me to comment on the legislator's idea that a guardian *ad litem* should be appointed in all divorce litigation involving children, whether custody was an issue or not. She was interested in how this reform might be best implemented, and what I thought might be its positive impact. I asked her who was to pay for these expensive additions to the divorce process, and she responded that, of course, the parents would bear the additional cost. I immediately replied that, in that case, I thought it was a "terrible idea," and furthermore, I was not sure what a guardian *ad litem* added, besides expense and time, even in contested cases.

I also stated that, as a general rule, I felt if the state was not willing to bear even a part of the cost of proposed reforms, she and her legislator should think long and hard before adopting and imposing them on a process which already was emotionally and financially burdensome for a large number of persons who had no choice but to resort to it for legal redress. To this she replied that it was *not* for *me* to conclude whether or not the mandatory appointment of a guardian *ad litem* in all divorce cases was a *good* idea, as that called for a *political* judgment; I was only being asked to comment on the proposal. She obviously did not like my response, and I wondered why I had been asked to make one.

I begin with this story because it contains the essential elements of the critique this chapter will make of guardians *ad litem* in divorce actions. Guardians *ad litem* are politically appealing, both because we can feel we are doing something for children, and because it is a reform which costs the system very little while allowing it to continue to limp along with no significant improvements. As a reform, guardians *ad litem* are justified by resort to asserted benefits of child advocacy on the part of a variety of professionals, often grouped together in a child advocacy team (Westman, 1979). I should also disclose that I am skeptical of many of the claims touting the benefits of involvement by nonlegal professionals in divorce custody decision making and have questions about the legal professional as a child advocate.

I proceed with the assumption that the guardian *ad litem* is an attorney. If this is not the case, then there is no creation of a child-client; rather, the guardian *ad litem* is a substitute for, or an addition to, the mental health or social work professionals involved in divorce contests. I have addressed the problems I see with these professionals' involvement in the divorce process elsewhere (Fineman, 1988). The presence of an attorney as the guardian *ad litem* creates problems that transcend and complicate the problems associated with the involvement of mental health professionals who perform court evaluations. This is particularly true because of role confusion of these professionals, coupled with uncertainty as to who and what is represented, as will be illustrated below.

I will begin with a description of the nature of legal proceedings in divorce actions and then explore two major points before I conclude with suggestions for the optimal role of the guardian *ad litem*. The first is the creation of the child as a separable "client" in need of advocacy services. The second is the attempt to articulate and define the difficult task the advocate faces in determining the child's best interests. I will conclude this chapter with the suggestion that the guardian *ad litem*, as part of a custody evaluation team, not try to be a mental health professional, but bring legal expertise to bear on the process.

THE PROCESS OF DIVORCE CUSTODY DECISION MAKING

Nonlawyers often have distorted views of the process whereby issues involved at divorce are resolved. The images generated by references to the "adversarial" system are really not appropriate in most instances. Divorce and custody disputes rarely are fought out in true adversarial style. Instead, the system should be described as one that encourages negotiation of issues by divorcing parties utilizing lawyers as both their go-betweens and advisors on legal rights and obligations (Mnookin & Kornhauser, 1979). In this regard, court personnel often encourage settlement.

In this negotiation process, the lawyers often barter certain things for others. For example, spousal support may be offered in the form of a lump sum property division or monthly payments, depending on tax circumstances or employment prospects. One person may accept less property than might otherwise be expected in order to induce the other party to be more lenient with visitation arrangements. The point is that the negotiation is a complex process in which all aspects of the divorce are considered. Economic and custody issues are inseparably intertwined. Having custody means little if you do not have the economic resources to care for the child.

In the few cases that actually do proceed to trial, all issues potentially involved in the divorce are seldom litigated. Rather, there typically is one major sticking point about which the couple cannot agree. Such disagreements occur even after months of negotiations, often under the guidance of a court commissioner or magistrate. In such cases, the parties seem committed to protracted, hurtful proceedings, and I doubt that any process would make them less hostile and adversarial.

In spite of the negotiated nature of the ordinary divorce action, the process continues to be labeled as adversarial. The use of various personnel to supplement or to supplant judges and divorce lawyers is often suggested as a remedy for hostility engendered by a legalized process (Stone, 1982). Additional personnel from both the helping professions and the legal profession are proposed because of the "neutral," nonadversarial nature of the information or expertise they supposedly can supply. The call for guardians *ad litem* is part of this pattern.

THE CREATION OF THE CHILD-CLIENT

A serious historical look at the academic literature that underlies the notion of a guardian *ad litem* for children in divorce cases reveals the striking fact that neither the arguments for nor against the institution have changed much over the past 25 years. There also has been little progress in the development of consensus about the functions of a guardian *ad litem*. One study revealed that attorneys who act as either an advocate for the child or a guardian *ad litem* in custody proceedings have different perceptions as to their role (Note, 1978). The basic divergence is that many attorneys see their role as merely "fact finder," or assistant to the judge, while others see their role as an "advocate" for the child as an independent party in the divorce proceeding. Under each of these two categories, there are numerous definitions of the proper duties of a fact finder or advocate in representing the child.

In practice, the guardian *ad litem* is an institution that continues to be ill-defined, idiosyncratically implemented and, for these reasons alone, ineffectively criticized or controlled. One might ask how such an institution can, nonetheless, have strong support among judges, lawyers, and mental health professionals. If I am right about the lack of structure and definition in the role, why is it that legal professionals, at least, are not more critical?

One obvious reason is that the guardian *ad litem* was the creation of the legal profession. The potent idea of a legal advocate for children in divorce actions can be traced back to a series of articles, beginning in 1966, by Judge Robert Hansen of Milwaukee, Wisconsin. In part, the creation of the guardian *ad litem* for children resulted from the recognition by judges and family court personnel that the "child's best interests" test was not functioning well in the courts.

The creation of a child's legal advocate like the guardian *ad litem* was an inevitable product of the general unease generated by the widespread acceptance of no-fault divorce, and by the breakdown of the "best interests of the child" test. This test became unworkable when the old rules of thumb that were used to implement it, such as a maternal preference, became unacceptable in custody decision making. With the emphasis on gender neutrality, which occurred as a result of feminist agitation during the 1960s and 1970s, the presumption that children belonged with their mothers unless the mothers were unfit began to fade from favor as a way to make custody decisions. In addition to genderized presumptions, fault also had earlier provided a way to resolve custody issues. Adulterers and others found to be at fault in a divorce lost custody of their children.

The best interests test had worked, in part, because these other references had served to resolve most cases. In the 1970s, the best interests of the child test, degendered and free from fault, began to be viewed as unworkable in *any* context by the judges who had to employ it (Chambers, 1984). The best interests test has tremendous symbolic appeal, however, focusing as it does on the child. Attempts to change the test are met with charges that parents' interests are being substituted for those of children.

Continued adherence to the best interests test has necessitated a consistent search for alternatives to the court as the legal decision maker in custody cases as judges became more uncomfortable with the demands of the test. As a result the resort to the helping professions as alternative assessors of the best interests of a child has become widespread (Okpaku, 1976). The guardian *ad litem* is part of this process. A central problem is that the resort to these nonjudicial decision makers masks the severe problems with the best interests test and, in fact, supports its use.

For the purpose of this discussion, the significance of the continued use of the best interests test, post-maternal-preference and post-fault, is found in its theoretical separation of the child from the family. When the maternal preference was viable, the child was conceptually aligned with the mother, who, absent compelling evidence to the contrary, was presumed to be acting in her child's interest. The designation of the "innocent," not at fault, spouse functioned in the same way as an allocation device. The process of removing these easy indicators meant we began to focus on the child as an independent individual with interests that differed from both parents. It is this development that clearly created the need for an advocate for the child as distinct from those who represented the parents or family.

The child is now viewed as an independent entity who is the focus of the custody proceeding. Like all language of rights, the language used in advancing the arguments for the necessity of a guardian *ad litem* is symbolically powerful and compelling, particularly since the term "child" is highly sentimentalized in our culture. For example, the Family Court of Milwaukee County's "Bill of Rights for Children in Divorce Actions," a document publicized in Judge Hansen's 1966 article, was picked up and used by other guardian *ad litem* proponents (Foster & Freed, 1972). Proposition 1 in that Bill of Rights is: "the right [of the child] to be treated as an interested and affected person and not as a pawn, possession or chattel of either or both parents" (p. 5). Proposition 10 states that there is "the right to recognition that children involved in a divorce are always disadvantaged parties and that the law must take affirmative steps to protect their welfare, including the appointment of a guardian ad litem to protect their interests" (p. 6).

Note that this emphasis on children's need for, and right to, protection is to be implemented through a legal advocate, and is built upon the unquestioned assertion that children were being used as "pawns," or were viewed as "property" by their parents. Characterization of children as innocent victims in need of protection from their parents' self-centered ways is typical of this viewpoint in this era of no-fault divorce.

In fact, there is a strong antidivorce aspect to much of this rhetoric and the reforms it supports. Thus, even though access to divorce was eased as a result of no-fault legislation, the state's role in the termination of this relationship increased through the imposition of substantive standards regulating divorce and custody. In fact, at least one commentator has suggested that an important function of the guardian *ad litem* in some cases could be to prevent the divorce in the interests of the child by an extension of provisions for conciliation between spouses. Such provisions focus on children but in fact establish compulsory nonjudicial conciliation (Stone, 1982).

A significant component of the modern regulatory, interventionist view of divorce is the notion that the state's historic interest in protecting children establishes a legitimate avenue for the exercise of state control through judgments at the time of divorce about parenting behavior (Grossberg, 1983). If judges need to make decisions based on the best interests of the child, but feel unprepared to do so, they must look elsewhere for answers. For the most part, they have looked to members of the helping professions, but legal specialists acting in the child's interests, such as the guardian *ad litem*, also have been employed (Levy, 1985). The acceptance of children as victims, which is evidenced by the rhetoric surrounding discussions of divorce and is manifest in the interpretation of the best interests test, is the ideological basis upon which the arguments for increased state involvement implemented through extra-judicial actors was constructed.

I characterize this decision-making trend as constituting increased state involvement because the result of adding this battery of experts who are presumed to act in the best interests of children means that both the questions and their answers concerning any individual child are developed *independent of parental decisions or initiative.* The description and characterization of the problems facing the child, the important judgments that must be made, and the suggested solutions, are all in the hands of the professionals. If a child's future cannot be entrusted to his or her parents, then a child advocate is essential. The rationale for this is that parents experiencing divorce can no longer be trusted to act in their child's interests. The fact that they are enmeshed in an adversarial contest alone is deemed sufficient to find them incapable of acting in their child's best interests. They are assumed to be concerned only with their own self-serving ends.

It is not surprising that because this conceptual separation of the child occurs in the context of divorce, which is always a legal proceeding, child advocacy in the divorce context has increasingly become understood to require separate legal representation. The best interests of the child test, therefore, is a substantive rule which, in order to be appropriately implemented, has the effect of creating a client, the child, for the legal advocate. At the same time, the designation of a child's advocate allows the best interests test to remain the substantive standard. In this way, the procedural innovation of establishing guardians *ad litem* masks the inadequacies of the substantive test and allows it to continue to be the law.

The first question that we should have asked (and it may be too late now to do so) is whether or not it is really accurate to cast children as "victims" of divorce. Even if it is, does this necessitate the establishment of separate, independent legal advocacy? Is it typically true that parents during the divorce process are so self-absorbed as to use their children as "pawns"? This assumption is certainly behind the proposal that a guardian *ad litem* should be required in *all* divorces, as the legislative assistant proposed to me years ago. After all, the logic flows, pawns are not only sacrificed in games that end up in court, but are equally at risk in negotiated or noncontested cases.

Further, and most importantly, if it is true that a large number of parents can be presumed to tend to sacrifice their children's well-being in this way, does not that mean that there are a lot of unfit parents who are unable to separate out their own needs and act in their children's best interests? Could they *ever* be trusted to do so? Can a parent who views his or her child as "property," or as a "pawn," be expected to change after the divorce decree and custody award? Merely to state these questions is to show how misguided and potentially destructive of the family the assumptions upon which they rest are. But even if the reader does not share that conclusion, it must be clear that this train of thought leads to more and more intrusive interventions by the state. This tendency should be a source of concern for those advocates for children who believe that the interests of children are served by building strong families.

I realize that the response to this critique will be to remind me that divorce is a crisis and parents are not at their "best." My rejoinder to this is two-fold. First, accepting that such may be the case does not resolve the matter entirely because life is filled with stresses and crises (especially for the single parent); there is not likely to be a return to an idyllic state after the divorce. Second is the question of how anyone can even begin to assess a child's best interests if the major sources of information about the child (the parents) are unreliable in regard to their child's interests. Of course, we could assume that the professionals assessing the child's interests can make up for this fact or can see past the unrepresentative behavior, but I am not convinced this is true.

Although I admit that many parents are far from perfect, I have far more faith in the typical parent (even in crisis situations) than in professionals who in most divorce instances have only a superficial appreciation of the family situation. Furthermore, I think those concerned with making policy in this important area should not be satisfied by assertions of wanton self-absorption and blatant sacrifice of children's interests, no matter the degree of professional assurance or force with which they are made.

The net result of the uncritical acceptance of the "child as victim" construction of divorce is state-sponsored substitution of informal nonlegal professional decision making for that of parents *or* that of the courts (Fineman, 1988). The significant *input* into the custody decision-making process is no longer parents, but professionals, inaccurately designated as "neutral" or "disinterested," and legitimized by the notion that they alone are capable of acting in the best interests of children. Furthermore, the *locus* for the decision making is no longer the judge, but these same professionals. I am far from convinced that this is necessary to benefit children and have serious doubts as to whether it is even desirable.

CONSTRUCTION OF THE
CHILD-CLIENT'S BEST INTERESTS

The characterization of the child as a victim of divorce creates a climate in which we easily accept the necessity for legal child advocacy for an independent child-client. The question then is how this client's interests are to be ascertained. When the child is perceived as separate or independent - a client in need of counsel - there must be some way in which to assess the content or goal of the representation. How does the child's legal advocate in the divorce proceeding determine the child's best interests?

This is the second critical element of the current view of the guardian *ad litem* I want to explore. Although this aspect of the problem has been extensively examined, it is usually approached within the context of the inherent role conflict the guardian *ad litem* faces as an advisor or representative. Less attention has been given to the deeper question of the characterization of the child as the victim of divorce in need of representation. The content of such representation is also created by and is dependent upon our acceptance of that characterization. Representation requires the identification of the child's best interests - that which is to be represented or advocated in the divorce proceeding.

There are three potential sources for the determination of a child's best interests. The easiest to dispose of quickly is the child. One way to determine a child's best interests is to ask the child what he or she wants, and then represent that end. This is how an attorney would act in representing a competent adult client. In most instances, this might mean opposing the parents' divorce. It also could result in the attorney doing nothing because the child does not want to be in a position to decide. Yet making choices is what the child's advocate is expected to do. Because many children are unable or unwilling to express a preference between competing potential custodial parents, and because some research indicates that it may even be *harmful* for children to choose between parents at divorce, this approach would leave few official duties for the guardian *ad litem*.

The majority of supporters for legal child advocacy do not adhere to this narrow view. Instead, they urge that the guardian *ad litem* has a duty to make an assessment of the child's best interests that is independent of, though it may consider, the child's wishes. In one study attorneys representing children in divorce cases were found to have many different standards for determining the best interests of the child (Note, 1978). They differed in judging the most important factors: the child's communicated preference, the child's preference perceived by the attorney, the attorney's independent determination, and the data compiled by the social workers.

If the child's choice is not appropriate, the two other contenders for primary determiner of the best interests of a child under the current approach are the guardian *ad litem* and the helping professional. The guardian *ad litem* may act as both investigator and collector of information, and thereafter as an informed expert witness who has examined the evidence and has reached a conclusion as to the best interests of the child. This choice creates the necessity for the guardian *ad litem* to investigate, to collect information from both experts and nonexperts about the child and family, and to make a judgment about appropriate placement.

The role of advocate is one with substantive dimension. Not only has a client been created, but the characteristics of that client necessitate that one necessary and primary function for the guardian *ad litem* is to construct this client's interests in a manner which, to a large extent, is independent of the client's direction. In this instance, where the guardian *ad litem* is making an independent assessment of the quality of evidence accumulated, he or she is no better equipped than a judge to make such an assessment, and would seem, for that reason alone, to be unnecessary to the process.

By contrast, the guardian *ad litem* role may be more limited and the various mental health professionals, who have become increasingly more significant in the divorce context, will serve as the arbiters of the child's best interests. In this process, the guardian *ad litem* often acts as nothing more than the advocate of expert professionals' opinions as to the client's best interests. The guardian *ad litem* then operates to represent the experts' conclusions. In effect, the mental health professional becomes the *substituted* client who speaks for the constructed child-client vehicle through which the child's best interests are realized.

If we choose either the legal or the mental health professionals as the source for the determination of the child's best interests, we encounter important difficulties with the concept of the guardian *ad litem* as a child's independent advocate. It is not clear why one needs a guardian *ad litem* to interpret and assess information and reach a conclusion as to the child's best interests. Is not this what a judge would do? What does a guardian *ad litem* add to this process? In some instances, *perhaps*, some witnesses not called by a parent might be produced, or an expert employed who was not consulted by either parent nor scheduled by court personnel. One wonders how often this positive contribution by the guardian *ad litem* actually occurs, however, and whether the information placed before the judge is typically dispositive, or merely cumulative.

When the guardian *ad litem* represents the mental health professional's opinion as to the child's best interests, the presence of the guardian *ad litem* may, in fact, give added undue weight to professional advice that should be only one factor in fashioning a judge's opinion. The legal advocacy aspect of the role may result in the mental health professional being the ultimate custody decision maker when the guardian *ad litem* uses the professional's recommendations to establish the child's best interests.

One important issue is whether the guardian *ad litem* can be independent of the mental health professional, especially when they agree, for whatever reason (Levy, 1985). The presence of a guardian *ad litem* may be an "easy out" for the judge as another designated neutral actor who is cast as representing only the child's interests and, for that reason, allows the illusion that his or her conclusions can be safely trusted. There is no doubt that the guardians *ad litem* are powerful and can shift the balance of decision making. One study containing interviews of attorneys who represented children in custody cases indicated that they were aware that their recommendations were strictly followed by the judge (Note, 1978). One attorney commented, "[Many judges] view the child's attorney as the judge" (p. 1184). Some also indicated they were annoyed by the sense that some judges shifted the ultimate decision to the child's lawyer.

In fact, the crux of the problem, and what necessitates the development of institutions like guardians *ad litem*, is the substantive standard. The best interests test is so amorphous, undirected, incomprehensible, and indeterminate as to be meaningless without a substantial extra-judicial implementation team. The only response to a degendered, no-fault divorce system, short of scrapping the test, is the creation of alternative decision makers, and the referral of all substantive decisions to them.

THE CHILD ADVOCACY TEAM ROLE
FOR THE GUARDIAN *AD LITEM*

I think that the guardian *ad litem* could perform valuable functions as one type of professional concerned with custody decision making and focusing the system on the interests of children. The first role I envision would be a public function of lobbying for the replacement of the best interests of the child test with a more determinative rule - one more susceptible to the protections of traditional legal decision making. As the substituted rule, I suggest an expanded version of the "primary caretaker" rule as developed by Judge Neely of West Virginia (Neely, 1984). This rule would give custody to the parent who had assumed day-to-day care of the child. One advantage of this rule is that the evidence on which it relies can be gleaned in open court according to our notions of due process and publicly accountable decision making.

The focus of such a rule would not be on the identification of the parent best able to offer the child the best future environment; the rule would, therefore, foreclose speculation in this regard by helping professionals. The only inquiry would be into which parent in the past has accommodated his or her individual life and interests to adapt to the demands of the child.

This type of inquiry is particularly susceptible to legal analysis. For that reason, it has the advantage of being a rule that judges can comfortably apply and lawyers can easily understand. It has an even more important virtue, however. It is a rule that makes the criterion for choice clear to the parents, so that in most instances they can predict the result of litigation of the custody issue. Avoidance of litigation does more than save the system from an overload of family law cases. Custody issues are expensive and time-consuming to litigate. A set of rules that require individualized hearings in order to reveal a plethora of facts or to parade a bevy of experts does not provide "justice" for the majority of divorcing women who cannot afford such expensive procedures.

An additional benefit of the primary caretaker rule is that an appropriate application of it will seldom result in situations where sacrifices can be considered equal. Even when mothers work, their careers (or more likely, "jobs") are usually the ones that must be flexible enough to permit time off initially for the bearing and breast-feeding of infants, and later for school conferences, for the care of ill children, or for mundane day-to-day occurrences as well as family emergencies.

Furthermore, it must be stressed that this proposed test is not a psychological test, which also is an advantage. There should be no speculation as to the quality or extent of emotional bonding between parents and children. The test assumes that these bonds occur on the part of the primary caretaking parent, and they are evidenced by the sacrifice and devotion to the child. As such, these ties will be reciprocated by the child. Criticism can be avoided because the sole custody arrangement that results from primary caretaking does not ignore the different, less sacrificing, actions by the other parent. These can be rewarded by visitation periods with the children.

One possible objection to this test is that it will produce even more awards of custody to the mother than has the best interests of the child test. This may be true but, if it is, then this is the right result. If fathers are "left out," they can change their behavior, begin making sacrifices in their careers and devoting their time during the marriage to the care and nurturing of children. If it is too late in their personal situations for them to change their behavior, or if they choose not to devote their time and attention to the children during the marriage, at divorce they can bargain against the mother's clear entitlement under this test, conceding financial, emotional, or other factors to improve their positions.

This test, which addresses only historic facts, seems the best one of those that have been suggested for insuring a good future for children in our culture. It rewards nurturing and demonstrated concern for children in a concrete way. The messages in the rule that are sent to parents about what is valued by the legal system are clear and unambiguous.

In addition, the guardian *ad litem* as part of a child advocacy team can bring legal values, such as due process and a preference for public decision making, back into a process that has become so informal and nonlegal as to often operate according to the whims of politically unaccountable professionals, or to be driven by professional fads and biases. There have always been voices of doubt raised about the effectiveness of the current system with its reliance on predictions about the future well-being of children based on scanty evidence of questionable validity. Some of these doubts might be eased if it were perceived that the professionals who now seem to make the significant recommendations were in fact subjected to questioning, oversight, and independent evaluation by someone trained in due process and other important legal values.

Under the primary caretaker test or some version of the best interests test that valued past nurturing and sacrifice for children, the guardian *ad litem* could serve the interests of children by viewing himself or herself as an essential and unique part of an advocacy team. The guardian *ad litem* would not be aligned with any other professional, but would remain independent. The mental health professional team members would identify those parents who are *clearly unfit* to care for their children, providing tests and methods that tell us who falls below a legally defined threshold. But, the guardian *ad litem* would be aware that the determinative evidence would be that which addressed historic facts such as which parent nurtured the child.

Professional opinions as to who would be the better parent, or who most resembled some professional ideal, would be viewed as just an opinion. As such, it would be entitled to no more respect than any other opinion. In fact, the guardian *ad litem* might act to insure that it is not overvalued in contrast to information supplied by teachers, neighbors, and others who have more extensive exposure to the individual child. The guardian *ad litem* should act as a check on the informal decision-making process that allows professional biases (such as for shared parenting or other ideological conclusions) by subjecting any conclusion about appropriate placement to vigorous and critical probing.

In this regard, the guardian *ad litem* might initially act by organizing the advocacy team to evaluate a case. Each expert's education and experience would be explored by the guardian *ad litem*. Supervision and a critical assessment of the fact-gathering process of the mental health professional would be essential for the guardian *ad litem* to fulfill his or her responsibility to the child. The goal would be to monitor the process of reaching professional opinions in individual cases.

What has been lost under current practice are legal values such as due process, adherence to clear standards, and the right to cross-examine. These values must be reintroduced into the informal evaluation process by the guardian *ad litem* in order for that process to be viewed as legitimate. This does not mean that all the procedural aspects of a formal hearing have to be followed, but it does mean that openness and fairness are to be goals. The guardian *ad litem* should not feel easier because of a belief that some other professional is taking care of his or her business appropriately.

This relegalization of the child custody decision-making process that I am urging would parallel that which has occurred in the juvenile justice system after *In re Gault* (1967). The development in that area has been to have the child's attorney act as a check on the previously unfettered and unexamined good intentions of mental health professionals. I propose the same role for the guardian *ad litem* in custody determinations at divorce.

REFERENCES

Chambers, D. (1984). Rethinking the substantive rules for custody disputes in divorce. *Michigan Law Review, 83,* 518-567.

Drinan, R. (1962). The right of children in modern American family law. *Journal of Family Law, 2,* 101-109.

Fineman, M. L. (1983). Implementing equality: Ideology, contradiction and social change: A study of rhetoric and results in the regulation of the consequences of divorce. *Wisconsin Law Review, 1983,* 789-886.

Fineman, M. L. (1986). Illusive equality: Review of *The Divorce Revolution, The Unexpected Social and Economic Consequences for Women and Children in America. American Bar Foundation Research Journal, 1986,* 781-790.

Fineman, M. L. (1988). Dominant discourse, professional language and legal change in child custody decision making. *Harvard Law Review, 101,* 727-774.

Fineman, M. L., & Opie, A. (1987). The use of social science data in legal policy making: Child custody at divorce. *Wisconsin Law Review, 1987,* 107-158.

Folberg, J. (Ed.). (1984). *Joint Custody and Shared Parenting.* Washington, DC: Bureau of National Affairs.

Foster, H., & Freed, D. (1972). Bill of rights for children. *Family Law Quarterly, 6,* 343-375.

In re Gault, 387 U.S. 1 (1967).

Goldstein, J., Freud, A., & Solnit, A. (1973). *Beyond the Best Interests of the Child.* New York: The Free Press.

Goldstein, J., Freud, A., & Solnit, A. (1979). *Before the Best Interests of the Child.* New York: The Free Press.

Grossberg, M. (1983). Who gets the child? Custody, guardianship, and the rise of a judicial patriarchy in nineteenth-century America. *Feminist Studies, 9,* 235-260.

Grossberg, M. (1985). *Governing the Hearth.* Chapel Hill, NC: The University of North Carolina Press.

Hansen, R. (1966). The role and rights of children in divorce actions. *Journal of Family Law, 6,* 1-14.

Levy, R. (1985). Custody investigations in divorce cases. *American Bar Foundation Research Journal, 1985,* 713-797.

Litwack, T., Berger, G., & Fenster, C. A. (1979-1980). The proper role of psychology in child custody disputes. *Journal of Family Law, 18,* 269-300.

Mnookin, R. (1975). Child-custody adjudication: Judicial functions in the face of indeterminacy. *Law and Contemporary Problems, 39,* 1-7.

Mnookin, R., & Kornhauser, L. (1979). Bargaining in the shadow of the law: The case of divorce. *Yale Law Journal, 88,* 950-997.

Neely, R. (1984). The primary caretaker rule: Child custody and the dynamics of greed. *Yale Law and Policy Review, 3,* 168-186.

Note. (1978). Lawyering for the child: Principles of representation in custody and visitation disputes arising from divorce. *Yale Law Journal, 87,* 1126-1190.

Okpaku, S. (1976). Psychology: Impediment or aid in child custody cases. *Rutgers Law Review, 29,* 1117-1153.

Stone, O. (1982). *Child's Voice in the Court of Law.* Toronto: Butterworths.

Wallerstein, J., & Kelly, J. (1979). Children and divorce: A review. *Social Work, 24,* 368-375.

Weitzman, L. (1985). *The Divorce Revolution: The Expected Social and Economic Consequences for Women and Children in America.* New York: The Free Press.

Westman, J. C. (1979). *Child Advocacy.* New York: The Free Press.

Westman, J. C., & Lord, G. R. (1980). Model for a child psychiatry custody study. *The Journal of Psychiatry and Law, Fall,* 253-269.

6

THE PROTECTION AND RELIABILITY OF CHILDREN AS WITNESSES

Jack C. Westman

The number of children caught up in the crimes of adults is increasing. They not only are subjected to, and witnesses of, violent and criminal events, but their involvement in those events often makes them important, if not vital, sources of information for the prosecution of suspected offenders.

When children are brought into the legal system, they find that procedural safeguards apply to the accused but not to witnesses and victims. Because children need protection from being harmed by legal procedures even more than do adults, a number of attempts are being made to adapt courts to the special requirements of the young. These adaptations range from excusing the young from testifying to devising means by which they can do so with minimum distress.

This chapter deals with the dilemmas created by the need to obtain accurate information from young witnesses in courtrooms while insuring that they are not harmed by the process.

The juvenile court system was established early in this century because of the recognition that children and youth should not be treated in the same manner as adults in courts. Although the unique questions young people pose are clearly recognized in the principles of law, the widespread abolition of structurally separate juvenile courts has diminished the attention paid in general courts to the procedural implementation of those principles. As a result, instances often occur in which minors are inappropriately treated as adults. This is particularly the case when young persons are called upon as witnesses to adult offenses. For example, in the heat of passions aroused by the polarized designations of offenders and victims, the damaging effect on daughters of being forced to testify against their fathers or grandfathers in the prosecution of sexual abuse often is overlooked.

At the same time children are being exposed to a wider range of individuals and environments under less supervision by responsible parents. Consequently, they are witnesses to and victims of sexual abuse, violence, murder, and other crimes. Accordingly, courts increasingly need children as witnesses without having routine special considerations or protection for them. When a child is the only one who knows the truth, mental health and legal professionals can join together in order to enlist the child's cooperation and protect the child from harm by legal procedures (Goodman, Goldings, & Haith, 1984).

The most common reason for a child to be called as a witness is the allegation of sexual abuse. More than other forms of child abuse, sexual abuse invokes criminal statutes, because it also is sexual assault by definition when the victim is a minor. At the same time, the gravity of the penalty for the perpetrator necessitates the protection of the accused by the Sixth Amendment to the U.S. Constitution, which provides the right to be confronted by one's accuser. Thus, for justice to be served the child must appear in court and face the defendant, regardless of how traumatic that might be for the child. The prosecution of criminal sexual assault of a child also often removes investigative and legal proceedings from the realm of protective services for children to the criminal arena (Yates, 1987). In contrast to the accused, the child witness has no constitutional rights to protection during the investigation or the trial, adding the potential for procedural abuse to the previous abuse of the child.

THE TRAUMATIC LEGAL PROCESS

Repeated interviewing by authorities; the fear of repercussions from alleged perpetrators; the fear of being confronted by the perpetrators in court; the social stigmatization and media publicity; the stress of cross-examination in court; and personal reactions, such as guilt, shame, and bewilderment; all occur in adults who have been criminally assaulted. Children are exposed to the same stressors without the capacity to understand and cope with them. Even the information-gathering process has an impact on children, because they are susceptible to influence both in their reporting of events and by the clinical and legal procedures to which they are exposed (Dziech & Schudson, 1989). It is an expression of prejudice against children that they are expected to be witnesses in court, as are adults, without special considerations, and that the inappropriateness of this expectation is not obvious to all without extensive research documentation.

The intent of child abuse statutes is to help and protect children. However, except when intervention leads to successful treatment of the family or the termination of parental rights, there is real question as to whether the legal process with its investigatory and courtroom procedures is to their benefit. Mental health professionals can help determine whether it is in the interests of a child to be exposed to the courtroom and, if so, how it can be done so as to provide accurate information and minimize the adverse effects of the process on the child. The child's interests may be subordinate to the state's interests in enforcing criminal statutes, but at least the attention of the legal system can be focused on whether or not the statutory intent in a particular case justifies further harming the victim. When children are witnesses to major crimes, such as homicide, their usefulness can be maximized and the deleterious consequences minimized by recognizing that their participation in legal procedures is traumatic for them and by providing mental health professional support (Pynoos & Eth, 1984).

PROTECTION OF THE CHILD WITNESS

Because of these factors, the child advocacy role includes protecting children from harm by determining whether or not their interests will be served by the legal prosecution of offenders. This may mean avoiding prosecution or finding alternatives to the appearance of a child as a witness. However, in certain instances children can benefit from testifying in court with appropriate support by facing a perpetrator and partaking in socially approved retribution against the person who harmed them. Some previously overwhelmed teenagers can be strengthened by the experience (Claman et al., 1986; Terr, 1986). In any event,

the preparation and support of child witnesses is unlikely to interfere with due process and is justified by the legal principle of
serving a child's interests in litigation affecting that child (Bauer,
1983).

INVESTIGATIVE PHASE

The investigative process has been adapted to minimize the
stress for children through joint interviews by multidisciplinary
teams in which police, social workers, attorneys, and other relevant parties interview children together (McPartland, 1984). In
1985 the American Bar Association established guidelines for
multidisciplinary teams in child abuse cases in order to coordinate
prosecutor, police, and social service personnel (American Bar
Association, 1985).

Another adaptation is the use of videotape recordings of
interviews with children for clinical, legal, and investigatory purposes (Bernstein & Claman, 1986). The value of making a
permanent, firsthand record of initial statements is particularly
obvious in a field characterized by the high likelihood of retraction by child victims. The videotape offers the advantages of
avoiding multiple interviews and of corroborating expert testimony in court. On the other hand, prerecorded interviews generally
are not admissible as evidence in courts, and issues of informed
consent and confidentiality are unclear. Furthermore, audio- and
videotapes can be used by defense attorneys to the disadvantage
of the children and might be made available to the media. These
problems have led clinicians who initially advocated the use of
videotapes in court to abandon that usage (MacFarlane & Krebs,
1986).

Another adaptation has been suggested to insure that professionals who carry out investigations are properly qualified to do
so. For example, the proposal has been made that panels of
qualified experts free from financial and political influence be
appointed to validate allegations of sexual abuse (Hechler, 1988).
The court would select panels from a list compiled by a court-
appointed committee. This addresses the court's need for objectivity in validating allegations, but it does not provide for advocacy for a child in a comprehensive sense throughout the legal
process.

The child advocacy team more adequately addresses both the
legal requirements and the needs of the child in the legal, social
service, and mental health spheres. It also can work with all cases

involving children and averts the all-too-frequent fractionation of problems into categories that do not correspond to realistic life situations. We do not need a separate multidisciplinary team for child sexual abuse, for child physical abuse, for child neglect, for child custody, for child murder witnesses, for child civil witnesses, and so on. The child advocacy team can handle any legal matter involving minors.

At a more fundamental level, the option of child-parent privilege should be explored because of the inherent relationship of a child's testimony to self-incrimination and its similarity to husband-wife testimony. The privacy of communication within families is protected when spouses are not required to testify against each other but is violated when children are required to testify against their parents. Because of their psychological identification with their parents, children should not be treated as completely objective witnesses in family sexual and violent crimes. The benefits apparently outweigh the risks when such a privilege exists as an option (Terr, 1986).

COURTROOM PHASE

When a child is required to participate in criminal actions, particularly in instances where that child's interests might be served, the risk of traumatization of the child can be minimized by the judge's use of discretionary power in and outside of the courtroom (Yates, 1987).

A number of innovations have been proposed in an effort to reduce the trauma to children of courtroom testimony and to enhance their credibility (Benedek & Schetky, 1986). One is to broaden the exception-to-hearsay rule, so that children's out-of-court statements can be admitted into evidence. This has been challenged because the child's statements are not made under oath, and there is no opportunity to cross-examine the child. However, there is no assurance that placing a child under an oath or subjecting a child to cross-examination leads to the more accurate determination of facts.

When they are required to provide direct testimony, children's fears of seeing the defendant again and of the courtroom have been handled by having the child sit with a trusted adult, closed courtrooms, and hearings in the judge's chambers.

Increasing numbers of states allow the use of closed-circuit television with children in courtrooms. The techniques vary but essentially allow the child to be physically insulated from the defendant while testifying. In 1988, the U.S. Supreme Court ruled in *Coy v. Iowa* that concealing witnesses behind a screen from the defendant violated "his right to meet face-to-face all those who appear and give evidence at the trial." It left for another day the question of whether any exceptions exist, because there was no individualized finding that the two 13-year-old witnesses in that case needed special protection. In 1990, the U.S. Supreme Court in *Maryland v. Craig* found that the right of the accuser to confront the accused is met when a child deemed to need special protection, because the child will suffer serious emotional distress in the defendant's presence, is able to see selected persons on a television screen, and the child is seen on a screen in the courtroom with two-way auditory communication. These courtroom adaptations are experimental and raise clinical, legal, and logistical issues as courts try to protect children from harmful experiences and simultaneously maintain the constitutional rights of defendants (MacFarlane & Krebs, 1986; Weisberg, 1984). However, closed-circuit television does not protect a child from devious cross-examination, nor does it assure that the child will tell the truth (Terr, 1986). The variations in televised presentations also affect jurors' attention and their perceptions of witness credibility and attractiveness (Melton & Thompson, 1987).

In Israel the use of specially trained interrogators, the admission into evidence of pretrial testimony as an exception to the hearsay rule, the scheduling of special sessions with protracted cases, and the use of a special courtroom have been described as efforts to accommodate to child witnesses (Libia, 1969).

All of these adaptations reflect the need for special procedures that address the fact that children are unique participants in the legal process. However, because the needs of each child differ, there is no simple procedure or policy that can be applied to all children. In the past this was recognized by the separation of the juvenile court system from adult courts. It still is not appropriate to treat minors in the same ways as adults in the legal system. For this reason, courts are struggling with adapting procedures designed for adults to the unique needs of children.

In spite of the validity of all of these adaptations, broad procedural reforms to protect child witnesses are unlikely to pass constitutional scrutiny. A more effective strategy is to identify the special vulnerabilities of each child witness and support that child through the legal procedures (Melton, 1984; Melton & Thompson, 1987). A child advocacy team can do this.

The child advocacy team offers a practical and effective means of managing children in the general legal system while supporting and protecting them and at the same time assisting the court in determining issues of competency and credibility when children must be witnesses. The status of the guardian *ad litem* as a child advocate accommodates the structure of the legal system to the presence of children. The existence of a child advocacy team offers a practical means of providing a specific child with individually tailored support through a particular legal process.

RELIABILITY OF THE CHILD WITNESS

The judgment as to whether a child's testimony is likely to be sufficiently reliable to warrant its admission in court is a legal, not a psychological, decision (Melton, 1988). Still, clinicians can assist the court in determining whether a child is competent, credible, and emotionally equipped to cope with court appearances; whether psychological preparation would enable the child to give more useful evidence; and whether mental health intervention is needed to deal with existing and potential trauma as a consequence of the legal process (Nurcombe, 1986).

Competency refers to a witness's mental capacity to provide reliable testimony and includes the ability to register, recall, and describe events reliably; to distinguish truth from falsehood; and to appreciate one's obligation to tell the truth. The determination of the competency of a witness before a trial is referred to as *voir dire* (Nurcombe, 1986). In contrast, credibility refers to the honesty and accuracy of testimony. One can be competent without being credible, but not the reverse.

COMPETENCY

Because they are evolving areas in law, the rules of evidence, statutes, and relevant case law governing the competency of young witnesses vary from one jurisdiction to another. The majority of states by statute or case law prescribe an age at or above which a child is presumed to be competent to testify in court. That age is 14 in common law, 10 in about half of the states, and 12 in the others. Below the specified age, a court must determine a child's testimonial capacity on a case-by-case basis (Quinn, 1986).

Legal policies regarding the competency of child witnesses generally deal with children's ability to recall and understand the facts about which they will testify and their ability to understand the necessity to tell the truth. The question of legal competency is applied to the child's age at the time of the trial, not at the time of the events at issue. Children are not expected to understand oaths or perjury, but they are expected to understand punishments consequent to the failure to tell the truth. Thus a judge may determine that a child under the statutory age is competent on the basis of the child's ability to carry on a conversation and awareness that telling the truth is desirable. Conversely, a child may be deemed incompetent if unable to communicate well verbally and if very young.

The legal *voir dire* may be sufficient under circumstances in which a child did not experience stress at the time of the event. However, even then the experience of being a witness may be a stressor in itself. Although expert opinions are not required to ascertain a child's competency, clinical evaluations can be useful in assessing a child as a competent source of relevant information (Terr, 1980).

Two kinds of competency are essential in considering children's testimony: the competency to describe events on the witness stand and the competency to accurately recall the events. Related questions include whether the child can comprehend an attorney's questions and the meaning and purpose of the legal proceedings, whether the child's description of events will withstand the stress of testifying, and whether the child can distinguish fact from fantasy (Yates, 1987).

Clinicians can raise additional considerations in order to help attorneys constructively obtain information from children. The first is that the child's age at the time of the events in question must be taken into account in evaluating what is said at the present time. The second is that nonverbal behavioral communications can be helpful both in the form of reports about a child's reactions and the child's behavior during interviews, such as while at play and drawing.

The importance of information obtained from children by other than verbal testimony is illustrated by such examples as the signs of the failure-to-thrive syndrome in infants and the display of sexualized behavior by preverbal children who have been molested in households with promiscuous adults. Furthermore, re-enactment in play may reveal information that cannot be consciously or accurately communicated by a child. Depending on their ages, children may lack an appropriate vocabulary for describing events, especially those involving their bodies. They also may be embarrassed, ashamed, or guilty and consciously hide information as secrets or unconsciously do so by repressing memories.

Children under 9 or 10 years of age have less capacity than older children to recall past events without prompting. They also are more likely to be influenced by suggestive questions. Nevertheless, if prompted, children as young as 3 years of age can recall past events quite well, although children under 9 or 10 have difficulty dating the events or attributing appropriate motivations to other people (Loftus & Davies, 1984; Nurcombe, 1986). The ability of 6- to 8-year-old children to recount events can be as accurate as adults, if free recall and simple, direct questions are used (Flin, Davies, & Stevenson, 1987). Young children have difficulty discriminating what they have done from what they thought they have done, but do not have more difficulty than adults in reporting observations of events that are within their comprehension (Johnson & Foley, 1984).

Although an adult's memory can be facilitated through verbal prompting, a young child is likely to need concrete cues, such as dolls, photographs, or items of clothing (Goodman, 1984).

CREDIBILITY

The common assumption of jurors that children are less credible than adults ignores the fact that adult witnesses commonly are not credible (Goodman et al., 1984). Both adults and children can be influenced by leading questions and have varying degrees of accurate recall. If an event is understandable and interesting to both children and adults, there probably is little difference in their respective suggestibility. Whatever their reasons, children are no less honest than adults who have had more years of experience in deception (Melton, 1981).

In mock investigations of child abuse with 3- and 5-year-old children, Goodman and Aman (1990) found them to be less suggestible than commonly believed when asked about personally significant actions that might be associated with abuse. Still, they found that 10% of 5-year-olds and 18% of 3-year-olds offered misleading responses to questions related to sexual abuse, such as "Did he touch your private parts?" This means that one out of ten 5-year-olds and one out of five 3-year-olds could falsely describe sexual abuse. Caution is warranted in evaluating information from young children about stressful events, particularly when family relationships are strained and parental coaching is possible. If children are inclined somewhat to distort occurrences in comparatively neutral experimental situations, it is more likely that they will do so in affectively charged situations, as do adults.

The evaluation of credibility focuses on detecting misinterpretation, delusion, illusion, confabulation, fabrication, and indoctrination possibilities (Nurcombe, 1986). Mental health professionals have no more inherent ability to detect lying than anyone else. In fact, the ease with which they can be induced to testify in court by one side of a partisan contest conveys an image of their gullibility or availability as "hired guns." Still there are ways in which clinicians can form opinions about the credibility of child witnesses. First of all, a child can be asked to tell the story on different occasions. Although the wording should vary, the facts should remain the same. No variation in wording suggests coaching. Second, verification through dreams and re-enactment in play can be observed. Third, a history of reliability or of pathological lying is helpful. Fourth, although an essential part of the legal investigation, verification of the events by external evidence also should be included in the clinical evaluation.

Depending upon the degree of stress experienced at the time of traumatic events, children may experience perceptual and cognitive distortions. In her study of the Chowchilla kidnapping victims, Terr (1979) found that over half showed cognitive distortions by misidentifying the kidnapper, hallucinating the scene, and confusing the kidnapping with subsequent TV programs or movies.

Loyalty conflicts are the most intense in children who have witnessed, or have been victims of, crimes perpetrated by someone upon whom they are dependent, particularly if they have attachment bonds with them. The situation is even more complex than that between husband and wife, both of whom usually are statutorily exempted from being required to testify against each other.

SUMMARY

Children are being called as witnesses in courts in increasing numbers, usually as alleged victims of sexual abuse. Although participating in legal investigations and courtroom testimony is recognized as stressful for adults, the prevalence of subtle prejudice against children blinds laypersons and professionals alike to the even greater stress experienced by young people.

In an effort to adapt legal investigative and courtroom procedures to children and youth, a number of adaptations are in experimental stages. They represent both restoring the past procedures of juvenile courts and innovations that accommodate protecting young people as witnesses and adults as alleged offenders. During the investigative phase, these adaptations strive to minimize the number of interviews, insure that qualified professionals are involved, and provide ongoing support for the child. During the courtroom phase, the adaptations attempt to minimize stressors for the young witness by physical barriers that limit the visual field of the child, while permitting open communication so that the accused can confront the accuser.

Although the determination of witness reliability is a legal responsibility, mental health professionals can be helpful in assessing competency and credibility. The competence of even young children is greater than most people presume for matters within a particular child's understanding. However, the credibility of children and youth is compromised by the possibilities of misinterpreting affectively charged events, suggestibility, coaching, and loyalty conflicts.

The legal system is searching for institutional ways of accommodating procedures to the unique needs of children, while protecting the constitutional rights of adults. As is true for witnesses and victims in general, there is little regard for the rights of youthful witnesses. Redressing the situation, therefore, depends upon both a greater recognition of the rights of witnesses and victims in general and specific recognition of the unique requirements of children.

The separate juvenile court system fell into disfavor because it was not fulfilling its mission, and because strict adherence to legal principles was not observed. For this reason, it is unlikely that the legal system will make basic structural adaptations to children. A more viable alternative is to accommodate the special requirements of children through the use of child advocacy teams that are assembled on the initiation of legal actions and support the children through the entire process. Mental health professionals have an ethical obligation to add an advocacy component to their diagnostic, treatment, and consultative roles when children are involved in legal actions. Clinicians who limit their roles to expert testimony about information obtained from children ignore their obligation to do no harm to those young persons.

REFERENCES

American Bar Association. (1985). *Guidelines for the Fair Treatment of Child Witnesses in Cases Where Child Abuse Is Alleged.* Washington, DC: American Bar Association, Section on Criminal Justice.

Bauer, H. (1983). Preparation of the sexually abused child for court testimony. *Bulletin of the American Academy of Psychiatry and the Law, 11,* 287-289.

Benedek, E. P., & Schetky, D. H. (1986). The child as a witness. *Hospital and Community Psychiatry, 37,* 1225-1229.

Bernstein, B. E., & Claman, L. (1986). Modern technology and the child witness. *Child Welfare, 65,* 155-163.

Claman, L., Harris, J. C., Bernstein, J. D., & Lovitt, R. (1986). The adolescent as a witness in a case of incest: Assessment and outcome. *Journal of the American Academy of Child Psychiatry, 25,* 457-461.

Coy v. Iowa, 108 S.Ct. 2798 (1988).

Dziech, B. W., & Schudson, C. B. (1989). *On Trial: America's Courts and Their Treatment of Sexually Abused Children.* Boston, MA: Beacon Press.

Flin, R. H., Davies, G. M., & Stevenson, Y. (1987). Children as witnesses: Psychological aspects of the English and Scottish system. *Medicine and Law, 6,* 275-291.

Goodman, G. S. (1984). The child witness: Conclusions and future directions for research and legal practice. *Journal of Social Issues, 40,* 157-175.

Goodman, G. S., & Aman, C. (1990). Children's use of anatomically detailed dolls to recount an event. *Child Development, 61,* 1859-1871.

Goodman, G. S., Goldings, J. M., & Haith, M. M. (1984). Juror's reactions to child witnesses. *Journal of Social Issues, 40,* 139-156.

Hechler, D. (1988). *The Battle and the Backlash.* Lexington, MA: Lexington Books.

Johnson, M. E., & Foley, M. A. (1984). Differentiating fact from fantasy: The reliability of children's memory. *Journal of Social Issues, 40,* 33-50.

Libia, D. (1969). The protection of the child victim of a sexual offense in the criminal justice system. *Wayne State Law Review, 15,* 977-984.

Loftus, E. F., & Davies, G. M. (1984). Distortions in the memory of children. *Journal of Social Issues, 40,* 51-67.

MacFarlane, K., & Krebs, S. (1986). Videotaping of interviews and court testimony. In K. MacFarlane & J. Waterman (Eds.), *Sexual Abuse of Young Children.* New York: Guilford.

Maryland v. Craig, No. 89-478 (U.S. Sup. Ct., June 27, 1990).

McPartland, K. C. (1984). Sexual trauma team. *FBI Law Enforcement Bulletin, 53,* 7-9.

Melton, G. B. (1981). Children's competency to testify. *Law and Human Behavior, 5,* 73-85.

Melton, G. B. (1984). Child witnesses and the First Amendment: A Psycholegal dilemma. *Journal of Social Issues, 40,* 109-123.

Melton, G. B. (1988). Children, ecology, and legal contexts. *Professional Psychology: Research and Practice, 19,* 108-111.

Melton, G. B., & Thompson, R. A. (1987). Detours to less traveled paths in child witness research. In S. J. Ceci, M. P. Toglia, & D. F. Ross (Eds.), *Children's Eyewitness Memory.* New York: Springer-Verlag.

Nurcombe, B. (1986). The child as witness: Competency and credibility. *Journal of the American Academy of Child Psychiatry, 25,* 473-480.

Pynoos, R. S., & Eth, S. (1984). The child as witness to homicide. *Journal of Social Issues, 40,* 87-108.

Quinn, K. M. (1986). Competency to be a witness: A major child forensic issue. *Bulletin of the American Academy of Psychiatry and Law, 14,* 311-321.

Terr, L. C. (1979). Children of Chowchilla: A study of psychic trauma. *The Psychoanalytic Study of the Child, 34,* 552-623.

Terr, L. C. (1980). The child as a witness. In D. H. Schetky & E. P. Benedek (Eds.), *Child Psychiatry and the Law.* New York: Brunner/Mazel.

Terr, L. C. (1986). The child psychiatrist and the child witness: Traveling companions by necessity, if not by design. *Journal of the American Academy of Child Psychiatry, 25,* 462-472.

Weisberg, D. K. (1984). Sexual abuse of children: Recent developments in the law of evidence. *Children's Legal Rights Journal, 54,* 2-7.

Yates, A. (1987). Should young children testify in cases of sexual abuse? *American Journal of Psychiatry, 144,* 476-480.

Part III

THE EDUCATIONAL SYSTEM

INTRODUCTION

A report card on public education is a report card on the nation. Schools can rise no higher than the communities that surround them. It is in the public school that this nation has chosen to pursue enlightened ends for all its people.

Carnegie Foundation for the
Advancement of Teaching, 1985

Since the Northwest Territories were established, the education of children has been seen as a necessary preparation for citizenship in the United States. Yet public education is not a right granted by the U.S. Constitution. It is mandated by state laws, usually state constitutions, as a benefit for, and an obligation of, children and youth.

The educational system powerfully influences the futures of children. It complements the family in preparing young people for adult lives in which there are routines, schedules, obligations, and jobs to be done. However, only when supported by families and other social and economic institutions does the educational system serve society's greater purposes. This is a crucial consideration as educationally oriented institutional care is being extended to children in the early years of life.

For child advocates, it is important to recognize that school systems have their own internal dynamics, and their consumers, the children, are frequently overlooked in their operations. The basic educational problems relate to longstanding issues: teacher-pupil ratios, classroom control, and the practical relevance of curricula. Foremost is the persistent difficulty in providing the individualized education called for in the early decades of this century.

Schools are managed by locally elected school boards, whose budgets are linked to taxation levels and the ideological concerns of the times. The economic pressures confronting schools tend to limit the focus of education to those students who can thrive in competitive group-oriented environments. Furthermore, school administrations are dominated as much by the management of physical plants and personnel as by their educational mission.

Under its constitutional power to provide for the general welfare, the federal government supports about 10% of the national public educational costs, largely for special educational services. The U.S. Constitution's guarantees of equal protection and due process are linked to the expenditure of those funds. Federal initiatives also influence school policies. For example, the release in 1985 of the *President's Report on School Violence and Discipline* signaled a major effort to encourage local school authorities to maintain order in their schools. Supreme Court decisions, such as *TLO v. New Jersey*, which permits school officials to search lockers for suspected drugs, define the authority of school administrators.

Through Public Law 94-142, the Education for All Handicapped Children Act, the federal government has mandated an appropriate education for all children. However, because special education requires additional expenditures, schools often find themselves expected to provide services for which they have no budgeted funds. When they are reimbursed by state and federal governments, local school districts receive funds only for children who meet specific criteria for admission to special educational programs. For this reason, schools have difficulty serving children who do not meet those criteria. These children are left to founder and ultimately drop out of school. To prevent this, parents who can afford to do so turn to the growing industry of tutors and special schools.

Advocacy for children is needed in schools to insure that temperamental, cognitive, physical, and cultural individual differences of children do not become impediments to educational and social progress. Vigilance also is required to insure that the classification of children does not stigmatize and fetter them. Furthermore, efforts to help children with special needs should emphasize that parents are partners in the educational process.

Schools are having a difficult time defining their educational roles amid the priorities of their communities and families. They cannot reorganize society nor provide the love and care that each child requires. Therefore, it is extremely important that there be community agreement on the fundamental purposes of schooling: to produce competent citizens who are literate, creative, articulate, and, above all, who care about working productively.

7

CHILD ADVOCACY
IN DAY CARE

Jack C. Westman

The full-time employment of parents away from home has dramatically altered the lifestyles of many families and has resulted in the placement of infants and toddlers in day-care facilities of various kinds. Although it has been publicly justified as serving the needs of children, in fact the day care of young children is dictated by the interests of employed adults and traditional workplaces, not the children.

Because it seldom enters into discussions of day care, genuine child advocacy at both the individual and class level is needed in order to help parents and public planners recognize the short- and long-term consequences of 8 to 12 hours a day, five days a week, of institutional care of young children, particularly infants and toddlers.

This chapter introduces the perspective of children in their day-care placements. It explicates the nature of parent-child attachment bonds in early life and explains their importance for children, parents, and society. Because erroneous assumptions are being made that full-time employment of most parents away from home is, and will be, a given in American life, and that full-time day care is beneficial for children, there is an urgent need for reasoned consideration of future employment patterns and the interests of the affected children and their parents. This is especially critical because of the commercial and professional interests in promoting day care rather than alternatives that would permit parents to care for their own children.

In the past, America's children generally have come to public attention only when something went wrong in their lives. When they were overworked, we instituted child labor laws. When they created problems on the streets in our growing cities, we instituted public education. When they appeared in hospitals as battered children, we devised programs to combat child abuse and neglect. When they are not as well-educated as foreign children, we devote more attention to their education.

For the first time in our history, we now are concerned not only about what is being done to our children but also about what kind of care is best for them. More specifically, the quality of care young children receive while their parents are employed away from home has become an important social issue.

For young children, there are three kinds of nonparental day care in the United States. The term day care is more accurate than child care, because it is defined and necessitated by the hours of the day during which employed parents are unavailable to their children. The most common form of day care is family or home-based care, which 37% of the children receive in homes other than their own. The second is sitter care in the child's home for 31%. The third is institutional care in school-like centers for 23%.

Because of its especially controversial nature, institutional day care for infants and toddlers is the particular focus of this chapter. The issues posed by very young children differ from those posed by 3- and 4-year-olds. The perspective of the children will be presented by touching on the meaning of children to parents in the United States, the day-care constituencies, the effects of day care on children, the developmental needs of infants and toddlers, day care and public policies, and society's stake in child care.

THE MEANING OF CHILDREN
TO PARENTS IN THE UNITED STATES

The present situation cannot be fully understood without an appreciation of the evolution of parent-child relationships in this country. The styles of parenting in any society vary widely under the influence of cultural and social conventions. In the United States, the contemporary variety of parenting arrangements and apparent dispersion of families has obscured the fact that there has been a gradual evolution of parenting toward more intimate, egalitarian relationships between parents and children.

The significance of parenthood as a socializing agent of society remains as in the past, but as children have become less economic assets and more financial burdens, their value to adults has been stripped to its psychological and affectional core. The motivation of contemporary parents to have and rear children is largely based on love and the potential of lifelong friendships with them. Children are psychological extensions and sources of purpose in life for parents. This is painfully apparent in the bitterness of child-custody disputes resulting from parental divorce. It also is evident when mothers and fathers feel worried and guilty about the available options for placing their children in the care of other people during full-time working hours.

On the other hand, parents are heavily involved in the development of their careers and dependent upon income levels generated by their full-time employment. For many of them, sacrifices are made in their family lives in order to accommodate to their conditions of employment. Unfortunately, these employed parents fail to recognize the power that could be generated from their vast numbers in the workforce and from their critical importance to the functioning of most businesses. They have not fully linked their working conditions and benefits to their responsibilities as parents, in part because they are reluctant to admit that family concerns interfere with their work performance. Fathers especially may hesitate to speak out for family benefits, because doing so does not fit with a competitive, masculine image.

Because of the full-time employment of their parents, many young children are experiencing a completely different world from the one in which their parents were raised. Numerous caregivers in homes and institutions, such as nursery schools and day-care centers, now share child rearing with parents and other relatives (Webb, 1984). Family life is diluted by the busy lives of contemporary parents and their increasing use of full-time day care for young children. Most parents realize that the decision to put their child in someone else's care and the choice as to the kind of arrangement significantly affect their own lives. But few are aware of how full-time day care affects their children.

Moreover, the impact of the extensive use of full-time day care on the nature and direction of our society is not fully appreciated.

Many employed parents would prefer to care for their own babies and toddlers (Ward, 1988). They find that their emotional bonds with their children are overridden and diluted by separation during their hours of employment, often 8 to 12 hours a day, five days a week. The situation is particularly serious for parents who must work to barely sustain a livelihood and who can afford child care of only questionable quality.

There are two categories of women who *have* to work. One consists of women without husbands and the other of women whose husbands earn too little to support a desired standard of living. Forty-five percent of all working women are without husbands, and two-thirds of all single-parent mothers work. For women with husbands, however, the statistical evidence is that wives are almost as likely to work when their husbands earn $35,000 as when they earn less than $25,000 a year (Fallows, 1985). The perception of having to work, therefore, varies considerably and often depends less on straightforward economic pressures than on personal and societal definitions of success, self-fulfillment, family obligations, and material desires.

Many families decide that the financial costs of foregoing one or settling for a part-time income are easier to bear than the emotional costs of trying to earn two incomes. This is suggested by the fact that 34% of mothers of children under the age of 3 are employed only part-time. Thus, nearly two-thirds of the mothers of infants and toddlers do not work away from home or have part-time jobs.

Day-care advocates see day care as essential for women, if they are to fulfill themselves psychologically and if they are to achieve their rightful place in society (Graubard, 1987). They see day care as a positive influence on the social and cognitive development of children and as an antidote to psychiatric problems in family-reared children. These biases obscure examination of day care from the point of view of the affected children and are derivatives of the day-care constituencies.

THE DAY-CARE CONSTITUENCIES

The advocates of institutional day care represent three constituencies: (a) employed parents, (b) day-care child development specialists, and (c) the day-care system itself. Notably absent is a constituency representing the interests of the children.

EMPLOYED PARENTS

The mechanization of housekeeping tasks after World War II, combined with the growing use of birth control, contributed to the availability of women for the workforce. Further encouraged by the advocacy of the civil rights of women following the Civil Rights Act of 1964, the momentum for the employment of women was accelerated by the economic inflation of the 1970s. The resulting decrease in family purchasing power forced many women to find jobs in order to maintain their previous standard of living.

Inherent in the pressure from parents for day care are beliefs and values related to gender. More specifically, attitudes about motherhood and about child rearing reflect the prevailing social values of a particular era. For example, in 1970 popular views about child rearing had changed so completely that social historian Philip Slater (1970) felt compelled to expose what he termed "the magnification of motherhood" among post-World War II middle-class American housewives. He was critical of the views expressed by Anna Freud, Leon Yarrow, and Selma Fraiberg, among many others, that singled out the mother-child relationship as the unique prototype of all later love relationships (Webb, 1984).

In contrast, John Bowlby's writings about attachment (1969, 1973, & 1980) added scientific fuel to the conviction that the mother's role was crucial for the healthy development of the young child. In this view, the attachment to the mother is compromised by competing attachments to other caregivers.

At the same time, Margaret Mead advanced the idea that concepts of gender are principally cultural, not biological (Mead, 1954). Implicit in the new definition of gender was a rejection of the idea that biological destiny, deriving principally from sexual differences, is at work in human affairs. This helped revive feminism as a national movement (Gordon, 1988). Thus, mothers of the 1950s who entered the workforce were made to feel guilty and negligent, but since the 1970s, women who are not employed away from home are made to feel incomplete. Both men and women are imbued with the social value that only remunerative work is worthwhile and personally fulfilling. Domestic work is seen as part of private life and without financial value. The homemaker is treated as a consumer but not as a productive worker. For this reason, the limitation of the term "working parents" to those who are employed away from home contributes to the denigration of the financial worth of the work of parenting (Bose, Feldberg, & Sokoloff, 1987).

In our society, the general view that mothers have the primary responsibility for providing child care has not changed with the return of many mothers to the workforce. One of the most important barriers to thinking clearly about the developmental needs of children is the resentment borne by many women, because they are expected to make greater sacrifices in their lives for their children than are their husbands. The split between family life and employment allows men to ignore the problem of caring for children (Pogrebin, 1983).

The entry of many women into the paid workforce reflects the special obstacles young families must overcome to hold onto the middle-class living standards taken for granted by their parents (Levy, 1988). The social acceptability of divorce also has played a role in increasing the cost of living by creating separate households. More fundamentally, the loss of purchasing power of the still-inflated dollar has forced women to join the paid workforce to maintain family lifestyles. For example, between 1947 and 1973, the average worker's inflation adjusted earnings rose 61%. Since 1973, however, the average earnings have fallen 15%, reflecting a decrease in national purchasing power.

Women are attracted to employment away from home for a variety of reasons beyond financial: professional and intellectual stimulation, escape from perceived tedium and boredom, peer and collegial associations, challenges for greater self-fulfillment and self-development, and a desire for economic independence from their husbands (Physician Survey, 1985). In addition there are several frequently overlooked underlying psychological factors.

The first is the overwhelming challenge for creativity that rearing young children involves. Some parents are attracted to the structure and predictability of work routines as less troublesome than the responsibilities of decision making and leadership inherent in child rearing. They prefer the sense of achievement that comes from self-limited projects with tangible outcomes. For them household tasks do not provide the kind of satisfaction that comes from earning money or accomplishing objectives at the workplace.

A second factor is an aversion to the emotional intensity of interacting with young children. For these parents, the workplace is an attractive haven of relative tranquillity. Many adults wonder if they are cut out to be parents and are attracted by the promotion of day care as desirable for the development of their children. Clinical experience suggests that a major factor behind the delegation of child care by these parents who question their own child-rearing abilities is a lack of modeling of harmonious and competent parenting during their own childhoods. Moreover, many parents have experienced discordant family lives including abuse, sexual molestation, and parental divorce. Their past negative experiences in families and hesitancy in forming intimate relationships affect their relations with other adults, their own spouses, and their children and lead them to avoid the discomfort they experience at home with their children.

The third factor is a desire for adult companionship. The home environment lacks ready access to other adults, and alternative ways of obtaining it for parents and children are more difficult to explore and arrange than is obtaining a job.

In general, the movement of women into the labor force has created a social revolution in its own right. Two out of every three new labor market entrants since 1975 have been women. The employment rate for women with children under 18 years of age has grown from 46% in 1975 to 55% in 1986. For women with children under the age of 3, it has increased from 34% to 51%, including both the part- and full-time employed, over this same time span. This dramatic change in the labor market was completely unpredicted by demographers and forecasters (Briggs, 1987). The resulting need for day care has sorely overtaxed available facilities with resulting stress for parents, children, employers, and society.

Parents of young children currently have less time to spend with their children, more money to spend on them, and higher achievement anxiety in relation to themselves and their offspring. With good intentions, they leave their offspring with different caretakers during the early years of their children's lives (Gallagher & Coche, 1987). The illusion of affluence places them in the position, previously reserved for the wealthy, of hiring others to do what are deemed as the menial chores of child care. Narcissistic parents can use prestigious day care to display their material devotion to their children. Their question is how little time can be spent with infants and toddlers without harming them; not what is best for their children. Behind this question lies the commonly held belief in our society that there are more important things for adults to do than spend time with children. Parenthood often is demeaned. The wealthy hire caretakers for their children, and the status of those who care for them is low.

As a result, the social pressure on parents is to value time spent in remunerative employment more than in parenting. There is little recognition of the pleasures and satisfactions of parenting or of parenthood as a developmental experience.

Still, for most employed parents, their families are the most important source of emotional support (Kamerman, 1980). They seek reassurance that their children are being lovingly cared for while they are working.

DAY-CARE CHILD-DEVELOPMENT SPECIALISTS

Support for day care as a positive influence for children and society is advanced by those child-development professionals who believe that young children in day care benefit from multiple relationships and education.

Beatrice Whiting (1963) pointed out that American culture ranks far above other societies in the importance placed on the mother's presence at home with the children all or most of the time. In 1954, Margaret Mead suggested that cross-cultural studies show that adjustment is most facilitated if a child is cared for by many warm, friendly people. In 1962, Mead further argued that children with multiple caretakers may actually be better off than the child involved in a mother-child pair relationship which, because of its exclusivity, predisposes the child to trauma when this key relationship is disturbed by separation.

In another vein, the points are made to employers that day care is in their interests to protect their investments in the present, as well as the future, workforce and that day care improves parents' performance on the job. Public policy makers also are informed that the future taxpayers of America will pay more taxes if they learn how to work as young children in day care (Gunzenhauser & Caldwell, 1986).

The day care of young children has grown from informally arranged provisions to a commercial industry, a professional field, and a movement with a political constituency of its own. In addition to day-care providers, a bureaucracy has grown in order to administer regulations and monitor programs.

The national state of child-care regulations was surveyed in 1986 (Morgan, 1987). It revealed that 41 states had updated their requirements in the last 5 years, but they fell behind current knowledge. For example, 26 states had no regulations regarding group size for infants and toddlers. In order to improve the day-care field, child-care workers are trying to assume professional status with training requirements, facility standards, training programs, research undertakings, and licensing procedures. Two obvious reasons for this professionalization are to improve the salaries of day-care workers in order to attract and hold competent people and to improve the quality of the care. This means that a growing number of people depend upon day care for their livelihoods. An indication of the boundaries of the day-care "turf" was reflected in Sandra Scarr's expressed concern that physicians and clinical child psychologists are encroaching inappropriately on the field of child care by commenting on day care (Gunzenhauser & Caldwell, 1986).

THE DAY-CARE INDUSTRY

Commercial day-care providers are concerned about marketing their services and are attempting to overcome their image as babysitters by stressing the benefits of their offerings (Gunzenhauser & Caldwell, 1986). The first benefit is quality child care as measured by professional standards and provided by professional caregivers. A second related benefit is that children receive the advantages of child-development research and technologies. A third benefit is that the lack of experience and compromised coping abilities of immature and marginally competent parents can be remedied by the educational and treatment services of day-care facilities.

Because of the institutional nature of their services, day-care providers have their own needs and dynamics that can compete or conflict with a family's. The trend toward viewing day care as a professional activity places caregivers in roles with educational and therapeutic elements. This can create a distance between caregiver and parent as reflected in the statement by Ellen Galinsky: "We should work toward having parent advocates in child care settings . . . to take the parents' perspective" (Gunzenhauser & Caldwell, 1986, p. 68). The intrinsic tension between parents and caregivers is compounded by the fatigue of parents and the low income and status of day-care employees. As an example, stressed parents who believe their children are unhappy at their place of care often blame the particular program and switch centers. Day-care centers, in turn, are sensitive to the financial impact of the withdrawal of children and, therefore, may not report children's distress to their parents.

A day-care center oriented to the developmental needs of children would have a staff-to-child ratio larger than what is

127

commonly recommended or legally required and would be economically infeasible (Blum, 1983). Much less than quality day care costs over $130 a week (Samuelson, 1988).

As is evident, day care involves complexities, ambiguities, and ironies caused by the conflicting needs and goals of each of its constituencies. Tradeoffs to resolve those conflicts are usually at the expense of the other constituencies. Notable by its complete lack of representation is the most important constituency of all - the children.

THE EFFECTS OF DAY CARE ON CHILDREN

The director of Madison, Wisconsin's city day-care center said that she fears we are involved in a social experiment in which we take middle-class children and subject them to the same social problems that only disadvantaged children experienced 10 years ago: overcrowding, lack of planning, lack of stimulation, and lack of adult attention (Coniff, 1988).

Numerous studies of the effects of day care on parents and children report that it both does and does not harm children. In fact, the usual research techniques cannot answer questions that revolve around emotional health, personality development, and family relationships. We do know that early parent-child attachments are important factors in each of these areas, for impairments are found in them with gross disruptions or failures in child-parent attachments. However, the effects of moderate and mild alterations would not be known for years, even until the parent reached the age of infirmity and the son's or daughter's relationship with that parent could be observed.

Research on day care for children also is confronted with almost insurmountable obstacles because of definitional, population selection, site, personnel, control group, duration, and compounding family variables. For example, even how day care is defined varies widely. A child might be in day care from 1 month to 5 years of age and for a duration of a few to 12 hours a day.

Typical of studies demonstrating the benefits of day care is one of a model infant day-care center run by a school of education for children between the ages of 2 months and 22 months for 20 hours a week. It reported the positive influence of day care on child rearing at home (Edwards et al., 1987).

On the other hand, the adverse consequences of interrupting the attachment bonds by separating young children from their parents are well-known to clinicians (Bowlby, 1980). The immediate effect is an insecure parent-child relationship. The widespread use of medications with insecure children and frustrated parents appears to be one result. A pertinent Swedish study of hospitalized children revealed that those who had received day care beginning at 1 year of age showed more anxiety-based behavior at the time of later hospitalization than did those who had not (Elander, Nilsson, & Lindberg, 1986).

Teachers report that contemporary kindergartners look older and seem more mature, self-assured, and assertive than in the past; yet they are less self-disciplined. They show less interest in and respect for other children and teachers. Many exhibit symptoms of stress, low tolerance of frustration, and elevated aggressiveness (Zimiles, 1986). The heightened intensity of their aggressive play (Carlsson-Paige & Leven, 1988) could be a reflection of anger displaced from their parents.

Child psychiatrists also see a vicious circle in which a child's separation anxiety is expressed by excessive seeking of parental attention when at home. This annoys the harried parent and produces growing strain between parent and child. The parent seeks more time away from the child, intensifying the child's provocative behavior. Parents in turn may experience feelings of guilt or loss for having placed their children in day care. In an effort to demonstrate their affection for their children, they may be overly permissive and purchase expensive toys and clothing as atonements.

The effect of interrupting attachment bonds during the first 2 years of life can be a failure to develop a basic trust in constant human relationships and an impaired ability to form committed relationships with other people. One long-term consequence is the alienation of teenagers from adults with resulting alcoholism, drug abuse, and suicide. More subtly, the legendary experience of the wealthy and royalty has been that children raised by surrogates are interested in their parents as sources of wealth and power rather than as persons. Early primary surrogate mothering entails the loss of that relationship for the child and possible alienation from and idealization of the child's biological mother (Hardin, 1985). Gloria Vanderbilt vividly described the adverse affects of such an occurrence in her life (Vanderbilt, 1985).

A review of the literature on infant day care in 1986 concluded that compensated infant-care leaves were preferable to infant day care (Gamble & Zigler, 1986). That review suggested that even children who received quality infant day care are less social-

129

ly responsive, less exploratory, and less attentive than those cared for by their parents.

The rapid expansion of day care, pre-school, and extended kindergarten programs has been accompanied by a widespread tendency to move the elementary school curriculum downward to younger children. In addition, many parents feel obligated to expose their children earlier to educational experiences. The result is what is now referred to as the "hothousing" movement for infants and toddlers devoted to expediting their development (Gallagher & Coche, 1987). This is occurring in spite of the evidence that the long-term outcomes of early didactic, authoritarian approaches with young children relate negatively to intellectual achievement (Sigel, 1986a, 1986b).

Fortunately for us, other societies have tested the limits of adjusting the care of young children to traditional workplaces by institutionalizing infant day care so that parents could work on a full-time basis. The most notable were in nations with communal child rearing objectives, such as Israel, the Soviet Union, Czechoslovakia, and the People's Republic of China. Even in these countries with strong ideological commitments to the full-time employment of parents and the group care of children, each attempt yielded to adjusting the workplace, so that parents could care for their own babies during parenting leaves and return to their jobs with supplementary child care. The experience of the Israeli kibbutzim has been well-documented (Blasi, 1986), as has that of Czechoslovakia (Langmeir & Matejcek, 1975).

Infants and young children generally adjust to whatever is done to them, but there is growing suspicion that short- and long-term harm results from the institutional day care of infants and toddlers, if not in the form of actual emotional or personality damage, at least in the form of weak or ambivalent emotional ties to their parents. In either event, there may be resulting difficulty in finding and sustaining loving, committed relationships in later life and a lack of abiding attachments to their parents.

THE DEVELOPMENTAL NEEDS
OF INFANTS AND TODDLERS

Both children and adults need the basics in life - food, shelter, and love. In the United States, all but a glaring minority have food and shelter, but many are searching for love. The emphasis of the marketplace in our society is on being admired and implicitly on being loved. Often absent is an awareness that the essential ingredient of being loved is the capacity to love others. More critical is the lack of awareness that in order to love as an adult one must have experienced being loved as a child. Even more to the point is that the truly loved child is the recipient of both parental affection and limit setting. For in order to love as an adult, a child needs to learn that respect for the source determines the value of love. Accordingly, parents earn the love of their children by gaining their children's respect. Children who are overindulged with parental attention often do not respect their parents nor return their parents' love.

Most parents intuitively recognize that the formation of attachment bonds with their babies during the early months of life is a time-consuming, intensely personal interaction. Since babies form attachments with whoever cares for them, the development of secure parent-child relationships depends upon babies forming primary attachment bonds with their parents rather than temporary caregivers.

The attachment bonds of infants are their emotional lifelines and the foundation on which self-esteem builds (Brazelton & Cramer, 1990). Since we cannot see these bonds, we infer their existence by observing certain behaviors considered to be hallmarks of attachment. These are proximity-seeking and proximity-maintaining behaviors and protest responses upon separation. Examples are the close following of a mother by a toddling child and the child's despairing cries of outrage when the mother goes away.

It takes 3 to 6 months for infants and parents to establish regular feeding and sleeping patterns. During that time, infants begin forming attachment bonds with familiar adults (Bowlby, 1969, 1973, & 1980). At about 8 months of age the baby demonstrates a clear recognition memory of the face of adults to whom the baby is bonding. In order for the recognition memory of bonding to take place, there must be an indelible tracing of the caregiver's face with its particular characteristics through countless repetitions associated with pleasure and need gratification (Fraiberg, 1977). The attachment process between parent and infant really is falling in love.

Although birth mothers are favored by newborns because of their intrauterine relationship (Hopper & Zigler, 1988), infants form bonds with any available and constant caregivers. The parents of young children employed away from home should be the primary caregivers and make arrangements for their children to be cared for by others with whom they have good relationships

(Goldthorpe, 1987). Many children have more than one figure toward whom they direct attachment behavior; however, these figures are not treated alike. The primary caregivers hold special places in the child's affections, distinct from the attachments to others.

Employed parents often cannot guarantee continuity of caregiving by a few stable individuals who can form attachments with their children. Daily separations are an inevitable occurrence when the parent of a young child is employed away from home. The cognizance of the developmental needs of infants has resulted in a closer examination of the appropriateness of institutional day-care facilities for them. The attachment-bonding process between infant and mother that begins prior to birth provides for the development of the infant's secure relationship with the external world. Separation of a developing attachment relationship, such as by hospitalization, results in protest behavior as part of an anxiety reaction and may affect personality development (Wolkind & Rutter, 1985). Even brief separation can affect young children who lack an appreciation of time and perceive any separation as permanent.

Most parents have difficulty distinguishing significant separation anxiety from transient emotional upsets. Therefore, discerning the effects of day care on children is not easy for them. Because day-care centers generally reward group-oriented compliance, skill learning, and knowledge, a behaviorally mature "false" self may be reinforced, masking underlying loneliness and longing for one's parent (Belsky & Nezworski, 1988). A child regarded as well-adjusted in a day-care center is one who does not demonstrate distressful behavior on parental separation and finds satisfaction in the material distractions available. The fact that crying on leaving and returning to a parent disappears often is interpreted as evidence that a child has adjusted well to day care. In fact, it may be evidence that the child has adapted to stressful situations by entering the stage in which stress is masked, or that the child has adapted by investing less in the parent. The adverse effects of this kind of early life experience may not be evident in more overt ways for years.

The most important question for parents really is not how their child will compete in later educational and vocational activities but what kind of a relationship will that parent and that child have during the rest of their lives. The seeds for a close, supportive, and mutually rewarding lifelong relationship are sewn during the early years of the parent-child relationship. The rancor, alienation, and strain of so many parent-child relationships evident in the past and today can be attributed to the lack of awareness on the part of both mothers and fathers that babies are interacting people who need more than feeding and diapering. Parents who treasured those early years have been rewarded by lifelong, strong family bonds. Those who did not have been disappointed by offspring who have little need for them. The priority parents give to the beginning of life has a bearing on the priority children will give them later.

Child rearing in the past by mothers who stayed at home and fathers who were breadwinners was not ideal in itself. The point is not simply that parents be homemakers; it is that parents be parents in the true sense of the word and both enjoy and bear with the agony and ecstasy of growing up with their children. Simply staying at home is not enough. Children need the full range of spontaneous and intuitive interactions with adults who truly love them enough to sacrifice for them, to absorb their rage when frustrated, and to accept them for what they are. The fact that parenthood is a developmental phase with growth potential for adults often is overlooked. Many parents do not see themselves as growing with their children but simply as caregivers. Parenting is much more than caregiving.

A constituency for representing the developmental needs of children could draw support from parents who want to grow with their children. Then the focus would be not only on a child's need to be with the parent, but also on a parent's need to be with the child. For their own social development, young children do not need full-time day care or nursery school, although 3- and 4-year-olds benefit from part-time group programs with a nursery rather than elementary-school orientation.

DAY-CARE AND PUBLIC POLICIES

Although day care has been available in this country since the 19th century, it always has been with the assumption that parents should arrange and pay for the care of their own children. At certain times of crisis, the federal government has made limited exceptions. During the Great Depression, the Work Projects Administration sponsored day-care services for the children of its workers. During World War II, the Lanham Act provided funds for day-care centers and nursery schools for mothers who were called to work for the war effort. In the 1960s, Operation Head Start programs were begun for disadvantaged children. In 1971, however, the Child Development Act that would have provided more general child-care subsidies for welfare recipients and additional child-care facilities was vetoed by President Nixon.

Because of the magnitude of the social and mental problems in the United States resulting from disrupted or disturbed parent-child relationships, all public policies that affect children must have as the first consideration strengthening rather than undermining parent-child relationships. Self-interest and compromise, which generally determine the allocation of federal funds, do not work well when children and human resources are at stake. None of the lobbyists are asking if institutional day-care programs will serve the developmental needs of children and parents, or if they will nurture and sustain the vital human connections of children.

Conservatives object to publicly funded day care on two grounds. First, they believe that the best child-care provider is a mother at home. To relieve her of this traditional duty is demoralizing to her, to her children, and to society, in this view. Second is the question of fairness. Tax-supported day care is seen as obliging mothers who prefer to care for their own children to pay for the care of children of often more prosperous women, who compete with their own husbands in the labor market (Samuelson, 1988). The only fair way to deal with this situation is to give the mother at home the same kind of child-care allowance received by the mother employed away from home, as is done in Canada and many European countries.

In European countries, the social response to infant care has been adjustment of the workplace to parenting rather than institutional day care; this is because of declining labor forces in addition to the belief that society should share the costs of child rearing. In contrast, in the United States parents have been forced to adjust to their workplaces because of an increasing labor pool that reduces the incentive of employers to accommodate to the needs of employees. Also, the belief exists that parents alone should bear the costs of raising their children. Consequently, with the exception of major corporations, neither private nor public sector workplaces in the United States have accommodated significantly to parenting. The incentive to do so, however, may well increase in the future with a shrinking labor force and the realization that satisfied parents are reliable and productive employees.

Finding the range of alternatives needed to meet the variety of family and employment requirements necessitates rethinking of society's priorities so that men and women are truly equals; solutions are based on the needs of children; and parents fully acknowledge their responsibilities to raise their children. Having a child involves a physical, moral, intellectual, emotional, and financial commitment to take care of that child. Taking care of a child often entails personal and professional tradeoffs, even sacrifices. All of these tradeoffs and sacrifices would be less severe if both parents made them as equal partners (Blum, 1983).

The overlooked essence of child care is that it is purchasing more than a place for physical care, scheduled activities, and supervision. It is purchasing adult guidance and friendships for one's child. That fact introduces a whole range of considerations about the kind of person who is giving the care and about whether love can be purchased. With a vested interest in the child at stake, parental love and attention is given without an automatic association of reward or payment for services rendered. It is not easy, if ever possible, to obtain that kind of devotion from other adults. Quality day care also means play, conversation, and comfort with persons whom the child is fond of and can know over extended periods of time (Rutter, 1981).

The commercial promotion of freestanding infant and toddler day care presents a double-pronged danger. It both attracts parents away from their babies and reduces the pressure to make the needed adjustments of the workplace to permit parents to care for their own children. In those instances when day care is advocated because children are better off there than with their parents, the question is raised as to whether the better course from the child and parent's point of view is treatment of the parent-child unit, foster placement of the child, or termination of parental rights and adoption. The most effective interventions to prevent the maladjustment of young children stress the continuing, active involvement of parents. Parental participation not only benefits the child directly but also increases the parent's own self-concept, autonomy, and sense of competence (Rickel & Allen, 1987).

The assumption that both parents always will be employed full-time in traditional ways and settings is both shortsighted and false. It is popular today to say that the future holds more and more parents employed in traditional jobs, so that we must provide more places for children to be away from home and more professionally trained people to care for them. A new era of nonparental child rearing is forecast as an improvement over the past suburban two-parent home with male breadwinner and female housewife with two children.

The facts are to the contrary. First of all, the nuclear family image is a mythical product of post-World War II consumerism promoted by the builders of housing, manufacturers supplying single-family houses, automobile manufacturers, and a host of other industries that catered to freestanding living quarters. Second, the contemporary image of children living without two parents is contradicted by the fact that 74% do live with two parents now.

Most importantly, the workplace is in a state of flux. The post-agricultural emphasis yielded to industrial manufacturing which is now yielding to service industries. The advent of tele-communication promises even more dramatic changes in work styles offering greater opportunities for parents to combine employment and parenting. Technology is facilitating flexibility in work location, hours, and scheduling that will greatly benefit employed parents. Futurists predict that by the 21st century, computer technology will reverse the urbanization spawned by the Industrial Revolution and create a society of home-based workers (Toffler, 1980). Even in 1987, the number of home-based professionals totaled 9 million and is expected to rise to 13 million by 1990, or 11.4% of the U.S. workforce. Because of their increased productivity, the fastest growing category is of telecommuters - homebound but salaried workers. For example, the Mountain Bell Telephone Company claims that its telecommuters are more productive than other workers (*Time*, October 26, 1987).

For parents who choose to raise their children themselves, there should be rewards, not penalties (Blum, 1983). If one parent chooses to take time off to raise a child, or if parents wish to share in that effort, they should have reassurances about resumption of employment without loss of seniority. There could be mechanisms within our employment and social security systems so that those who do stay home to raise their children are considered employed and are accepted as contributing to the greater good of society. Child-rearing allowances and tax benefits are tangible evidences of a society's commitment to children.

Many corporations have found that child-care benefits for their employees reduce absenteeism and increase productivity in addition to attracting more women to the workforce. Employers can offer more flexibility in terms of hours, work weeks, extended training and promotion ladders, part-time employment, job sharing, and fringe benefits. There can be options for sick-child care, for extended maternity and paternity leaves, and for the care of children during school vacations. A 1984 survey of the Fortune 1500 companies revealed that half of them had unpaid maternity leaves ranging from 1 week to 6 months (Finklestein, 1987). A 1987 survey of 10,345 U.S. companies by the U.S. Department of Labor revealed that 61% had specific policies, such as flextime, to make child care easier, and 11% offered day care or other benefits related to child care (Saltzman & Barry, 1988).

In 1985, the Advisory Committee on Infant Care Leave recommended that infant care leaves should be available for a minimum of 6 months, with partial income replacement included for 3 months and benefit continuation and job protection available for the entire 6-month leave period (Zigler & Frank, 1988). Parenting leaves are preferable to infant day care because they permit parents and infants to form attachment bonds with each other, to establish sleep and feeding patterns, and to recover from the stress of adding another person to the family (Hopper & Zigler, 1988; Zigler & Lang, 1990). Parental leave policies not only support parental child rearing, but they also reduce the cost of public assistance to unemployed parents, reduce the loss of productivity, and reduce the cost to employers of retraining (Spalter-Roth & Hartmann, 1988).

SOCIETY'S STAKE IN CHILD CARE

The contemporary day-care movement raises issues that challenge basic cultural values. The magnitude of the controversy it has stirred up points to a conflict between social and cultural values. Employing the metaphor of a tree, society is represented by the leaves that carry on essential life processes that change with the seasons, and culture is represented by the trunk and roots that provide the enduring underlying structure and nourishment.

Social values are the product of contemporary lifestyles and address the issues of day-to-day living within the organizational structures of society. They are strongly influenced by technology, because they are concerned with the survival of individual members of the species and enhance personal comforts. The societal objectives of child rearing in the United States are producing consumers, who also are competent and productive, and producing educated citizens, who can make informed decisions intelligently.

In contrast to social values which are transient, cultural values are biologically based and endure over generations in order to insure the survival of the species. Cultural values that support harmonious group living and social order are reflected in family structures. Thus, they provide meaning and purpose for life in terms of species survival. The child-rearing objectives of the American culture are producing creative, autonomous, responsible persons capable of committed attachments to others and contributing to the common good.

Society and culture are interdependent. Our society needs adults who are committed to the goals of the commonwealth. This is furthered by our culture's emphasis upon committed attachment to others mediated through cultural institutions of which the family is the centerpiece. Without the support of cultural values, social values cannot endure. When a social and a cultural value conflict, the usual result is short-range dominance of the social value, ensuing controversy, and long-range prevailing of the cultural value.

In recent decades, social values in the United States have stressed materialism and individualism. The importance of committed human relationships and family life has been obscured. Business for profit and the working life have been adulated. However, the social devaluation of parental nurturing of babies and toddlers conflicts with the cultural valuation of the human attachments of children. It is of interest to note that the overriding emphasis on materialism in the United States has not been accompanied by the economic success and quality of life achieved in societies with less conflict between social and cultural values, the most noteworthy being Japan and West Germany.

In many European countries, social and cultural values are less discordant than in the United States. There employment and family life are seen as equally essential and mutually complementary elements of society. The prevailing attitude is that government and private industry must be sensitive to the ever-present needs of employed parents and their children. Many aspects of society in the United States do not support family life (Kagan et al., 1987). There is an impoverishment of the sense of community and of personal intimacy, as materialism and competitiveness are overemphasized. Parenthetically, the rewarding of materialistically oriented activities and achievements in many day-care programs today may propagate this dehumanizing emphasis. Only a strengthening of genuine closeness and connectedness in families and communities can reverse this trend.

The objectives of child rearing are not susceptible to controlled experimentation and the manipulation of variables. Rather they flow from the overall aims of a society and culture. The United States has not clearly articulated its social and cultural goals for its children. The general assumption is that parents will raise their children as they wish, although there are expectations that children will be educated. However, the lack of articulated societal goals for child rearing in the United States does not mean that they do not exist at a deeper level in our culture. As society becomes more involved in child rearing, these goals are being codified in legislation that affects children and draws upon American cultural values. The expectation that children will become competent, committed, and compassionate citizens seems clear, in that order of desirability. We expect adults to be competent in their work and citizenship responsibilities. We expect adults to be reliable and to honor their obligations to others. Especially within families, we expect people to care about each other.

In the United States there is a fundamental emphasis on the autonomy of both adults and children in contrast with other cultures that weight one more than the other. In this context the overall aim of child rearing in the United States is the balanced development of an individual's potential in order to enable competent functioning within our social structure and economic system. The salient qualities needed to achieve this level of competent functioning are social skills, which include the ability to communicate, relate, and be useful to others and the capacity for assuming personal responsibility for self-expression, decision making, and independent living. No society has been able to achieve these expectations without parent-child emotional attachments supported by cultural values. Among other things, the current dilemma over the institutional care of infants and toddlers is a manifestation of a conflict between our society's valuation of paid employment and our culture's commitment to parent-child attachments.

CONCLUSION

There are no easy answers to the problems of child care for parents employed away from home. Those who claim there are deceive both themselves and the public.

On the positive side, day care permits parents to obtain fulfillment in their careers and increased income. Children are

139

exposed to the broader community of adults and peers and enriched in knowledge and skill development. The visibility of groups of young children in communities serves as a tangible reminder that children are a part of society. Employment opportunities for adults, potentially including youths and the elderly, are increased. In general the children are exposed to relatively consistent limit setting and environments, and government is involved in monitoring the quality of care of young children.

On the negative side, parents are enticed away from the mutually rewarding formation of attachment bonds with their young children. Infants and toddlers are exposed to repeated separations from their parents and dilute their personal attachments. Children are programmed in groups managed by adults but dominated by peers. They lack intimate interactions with adults, the freedom to explore, and uninterrupted solitude. They are continually exposed to contagious illnesses. Most importantly, the weight of the evidence is that full-time day care of very young children is contrary to their developmental interests.

In sum, the benefits of day care are clearly in the short-term interests of adults employed away from home and employers. The liabilities are in the long-term interests of parents, their children, and society. The challenge for employers and public planners who are dominated by short-range rather than long-term considerations is to recognize that family life affects productivity and that the children of today are tomorrow's workers. Optimal development in childhood is related to future productivity in the labor market. Unfortunately, this leads to the conclusion in the minds of some that professional child rearing is better than parenting. Consequently, someone must state the obvious: Parenting is the best way of insuring optimal development in early life - children need parents.

In formulating national policies for the care of young children, it is essential that the primacy of the parent-child relationship be supported rather than undermined. For this reason, policies that enable parents to rear their own children are in the long-range interests of the children, their parents, and society. Conversely, policies that favor nonparental care of young children are contrary to these long-range interests. Rather than focusing solely on economic issues, national policies should focus on the quality of parent-child relationships. Short-term research on the benefits of day care for young children is not a reliable basis for policy formulation.

140

At the present time, national policies in the United States do not clearly support the family rearing of children. Even though we have one of the highest rates of women in the labor force, and a rapidly growing number of working mothers with children under the age of 3, the United States stands alone among industrialized nations in having inadequate statutory parental leave policies (Zigler & Muenchow, 1983).

The challenge for parents is to find an optimal balance between the priorities of their families and their jobs. Both cannot be the first at the same time. The priority parents give to their children in early life influences the priority their children will give to them in later life. A shift in social values is needed to help fathers recognize that nurturing relationships with children can be fulfilling for them (Pruett, 1987). In order to further this awareness, boys need opportunities to help care for babies and young children (Brazelton, 1985). The ultimate reward for both mothers and fathers is when children grow into balanced, flourishing individuals who identify with both sides of their parents: the working and the nurturing. Too many parents find that when they finally have time to spend with them, their children have grown up and have little time for them.

In the past, only one breadwinner in a family was needed. Now many parents feel that two incomes are needed to support their families. This reflects both a real diminution in the purchasing power of the dollar and higher material expectations. Many could manage on less income, if they were fully aware of the importance of the early years of their children's lives to both them and their children. The widespread search for meaning and purpose in life is a symptom of the failure of many adults to find fulfillment in their family lives, which often have been dominated by busy activities or spoiled by strained and disrupted relationships.

The challenge for society is to recognize the social value of parenthood and to support rather than undermine family life through workplace accommodations, family benefits, and tax adjustments. Full-time day care, no matter how heavily funded, is not in the interests of young children, their parents, or society, because it is a response to the employment of parents in traditional workplaces by necessity or choice, not to the needs of children nor of their parents. Attention to meeting the developmental needs of children and of parents who want to be with them opens the door to various ways of adapting workplaces to parents and children. The central question is whether the care of infants and toddlers should conform to traditional workplaces or whether workplaces should adapt to permit parents to care for their own young children. The future of our society depends on the welfare of young children during the years in which they are learning to trust, respect, and depend upon adults - the foundation for later citizenship and productivity.

Our evolving society must place a higher priority on child rearing or face losing its leadership in world affairs. There are few limits to what can be done *to* children. The question is what needs to be done *for* them to insure the kind of life we seek for them.

REFERENCES

Belsky, J., & Nezworski, T. (Eds.). (1988). *Clinical Implications of Attachment*. Hillsdale, NJ: Lawrence Erlbaum.
Blasi, J. (1986). *The Communal Experience of the Kibbutz*. New Brunswick, NJ: Transaction Books.
Blum, M. (1983). *The Day Care Dilemma*. Lexington, MA: Lexington Books.
Bose, C., Feldberg, R., & Sokoloff, N. (Eds.). (1987). *Hidden Aspects of Women's Work*. New York: Praeger.
Bowlby, J. (1969). *Attachment and Loss* (Volume I). New York: Basic Books.
Bowlby, J. (1973). *Attachment and Loss* (Volume II). New York: Basic Books.
Bowlby, J. (1980). *Attachment and Loss* (Volume III). New York: Basic Books.
Brazelton, T. B. (1985). *Working and Caring*. Reading, MA: Addison-Wesley.
Brazelton, T. B., & Cramer, B. G. (1990). *The Earliest Relationship*. Reading, MA: Addison-Wesley.
Briggs, V. M., Jr. (1987). The growth and composition of the U.S. labor force. *Science, 238,* 176-180.
Carlsson-Paige, N., & Leven, D. E. (1988). *The War Play Dilemma*. New York: Teachers College Press.
Coniff, D. (1988). Is junior in good hands? *Isthmus*, November 4.
Dreskin, William, & Dreskin, Wendy. (1983). *The Day Care Decision*. New York: Evans & Co.
Edwards, C. P., Logue, M. E., Loehr, S. R., & Roth, S. B. (1987). The effects of day care participation on parent-infant interac-

tion at home. *American Journal of Orthopsychiatry, 57,* 116-119.

Elander, G., Nilsson, A., & Lindberg, T. (1986). Behavior in four-year-olds who have experienced hospitalization and day care. *American Journal of Orthopsychiatry, 56,* 612-616.

Erikson, E. (1963). *Childhood and Society* (2nd ed.). New York: Norton.

Fallows, D. (1985). *A Mother's Work.* Boston, MA: Houghton Mifflin.

Finklestein, A. (1987, September). Parental leave: A policy for the future. *Parents,* pp. 240-242.

Fraiberg, S. (1977). *Every Child's Birthright.* New York: Basic Books.

Gallagher, J. M., & Coche, J. (1987). Hothousing: The clinical and educational concerns over pressuring young children. *Early Childhood Research Quarterly, 2,* 203-210.

Gamble, T. J., & Zigler, E. F. (1986). Effects of infant day care: Another look at the evidence. *American Journal of Orthopsychiatry, 56,* 26-42.

Goldthorpe, J. E. (1987). *Family Life in Western Societies.* Cambridge, England: Cambridge University Press.

Gordon, L. (1988). *Heroes of Their Own Lives.* New York: Viking.

Graubard, S. R. (1987). Preface to learning about women: Gender, politics, and power. *Daedalus, 116,* v-xx.

Gunzenhauser, N., & Caldwell, B. M. (1986). *Group Care for Young Children.* Skillman, NJ: Johnson & Johnson Baby Products.

Hardin, H. T. (1985). On the vicissitudes of early primary surrogate mothering. *Journal of the American Psychoanalytic Association, 33,* 609-629.

Hopper, P., & Zigler, E. F. (1988). The medical and social science basis for a national infant care leave policy. *American Journal of Orthopsychiatry, 58,* 324-338.

Kagan, S. L., Powell, D. R., Weissbourd, B., & Zigler, E. F. (Eds.). (1987). *America's Family Support Programs: Perspectives and Prospects.* New Haven, CT: Yale University Press.

Kamerman, S. B. (1980). *Parenting in an Unresponsive Society.* New York: Free Press.

Langmeir, J., & Matejcek, Z. (1975). *Psychological Deprivation in Childhood.* New York: John Wiley.

Levy, F. (1988). *Dollars and Dreams.* New York: Norton.

Mead, M. (1954). Some theoretical considerations on the problem of mother child separation. *American Journal of Orthopsychiatry, 24,* 477.

Mead, M. (1962). A cultural anthropologist's approach to maternal deprivation. In M. Ainsworth (Ed.), *Deprivation of Maternal Care.* Geneva: WHO.

Morgan, G. (1987). *The National State of Child Care Regulation - 1986.* Watertown, MA: Work/Family Directions, Inc.

Orwell, G. (1961). *1984 - A Novel.* New York: New American Library.

Physician Survey. (1985). The two career family. *Medical Aspects of Human Sexuality, 19,* 43-51.

Pogrebin, L. C. (1983). *Family Politics.* New York: McGraw-Hill.

Pruett, K. D. (1987). *The Nurturing Father.* New York: Warner Books.

Rickel, H., & Allen, L. (1987). *Preventing Maladjustment from Infancy Through Adolescence.* Newberry Park, CA: Sage.

Rutter, M. (1981). Social-emotional consequences of day care for preschool children. *American Journal of Orthopsychiatry, 51,* 4-28.

Rutter, M. (1982). Prevention of children's psychosocial disorders: Myth and substance. *Pediatrics, 70,* 883-894.

Saltzman, A., & Barry, P. (1988, June 20). Child care and fathers. *U.S. News and World Report.*

Samuelson, R. J. (1988, June 27). The debate over day care. *Newsweek.*

Sigel, I. E. (1986a). Early social experience and the development of representational competence. In W. Fowler (Ed.), *Early Experience and the Development of Competence* (pp. 49-65). San Francisco: Jossey-Bass.

Sigel, I. E. (1986b). Reflections on the belief-behavior connection: Lessons learned from a research program on parental belief systems and teaching strategies. In R. D. Ashmore & D. M. Brodzinsky (Eds.), *Thinking about the Family: Views of Parents and Children* (pp. 35-65). Hillsdale, NJ: Erlbaum.

Slater, P. (1970). *The Pursuit of Loneliness.* Boston: Beacon Press.

Spalter-Roth, R. M., & Hartmann, H. I. (1988). *Unnecessary Losses.* Washington, DC: Women's Policy Research Institute.

Toffler, A. (1980). *The Third Wave.* New York: William Morrow & Co.

Vanderbilt, G. (1985). *Once upon a Time.* New York: Alfred A. Knopf.

Ward, A. (1988, September 12). A feminist mystique. *News-week.*

Webb, N. B. (1984). *Preschool Children with Working Parents.* New York: University Press of America.

Werner, E. E. (1989). Protective factors and individual resilience. In S. J. Mosels & M. Schonkoff (Eds.), *Handbook of Early Intervention.* Cambridge, England: Cambridge University Press.

Westman, J. C. (1979). *Child Advocacy.* New York: Free Press.

Whiting, B. (Ed.). (1963). *Six Cultures - Studies of Child Rearing.* New York: John Wiley.

Wolkind, S., & Rutter, M. (1985). Separation, loss and family relationships. In M. Rutter & L. Hersov (Eds.), *Child and Adolescent Psychiatry.* Oxford, England: Blackwell.

Young, K. T., & Zigler, E. F. (1986). Infant and toddler day care: Regulation and policy interpretations. *American Journal of Orthopsychiatry, 56,* 43-55.

Zigler, E. F., & Frank, M. (1988). *The Parental Leave Crisis: Toward a National Policy.* New Haven, CT: Yale University Press.

Zigler, E. F., & Lang, M. E. (1990). *Child Care Choices.* New York: Free Press.

Zigler, E. F., & Muenchow, S. (1983). Infant day care and infant care leaves: A policy vacuum. *American Psychologist, 38,* 91-94.

Zimiles, H. (1986). The social context of early childhood education in an era of expanding preschool education. In B. Spodek (Ed.), *Today's Kindergarten.* New York: Teachers College Press.

8

CHILD ADVOCACY IN SPECIAL EDUCATION

Stanley S. Herr

This chapter outlines the progress made by class and individual child advocacy in the public educational system. Because it is an essential aspect of each child's development, a free, appropriate education has been affirmed as a right for all children. Achieving that status has been the result of the efforts of a number of organizations with advocacy thrusts.

Professor Herr describes the dimensions of class child advocacy. They include legal class actions in which court decisions are sought, regulatory actions to monitor the actual implementation of mandated education, enforcement actions to obtain court supervision of compliance with mandates, and grass-roots political organizing.

At the level of individual child advocacy are such efforts as preparing parents to be informed front-line advocates for their children; lay advocacy through which nonlegal professionals assist parents; and legal advocacy that employs the resources and techniques of the legal system.

The techniques of both class and individual child advocacy include disciplined investigation and fact finding, negotiation, administrative adjudication of complaints and appeals, mediation, and litigation.

Because of the efforts of child advocates, the federal and state governments have mandated an education for all

147

children in the United States. This entitlement must be safeguarded and schools must be assisted in realizing this goal for the many as yet incompletely served children.

*   *   *

Massachusetts admits the right of all her citizens to a share in the blessings of education, and she provides it liberally for all her more favored children. If some be blind or deaf, she still continues to furnish them with special instruction at great cost; and will she longer neglect the poor idiot--the most wretched of all who are born to her--those who are usually abandoned by their fellows--who can never, of themselves, step up upon the platform of humanity--will she leave them to their dreadful fate, to a life of brutishness, without an effort in their behalf?

Dr. Samuel Gridley Howe, 1848[1]

Child advocacy in special education has only recently spawned dramatic positive results. Despite the eloquence of Dr. Howe's plea to the Massachusetts Legislature in 1848, it required another 124 years before that state enacted pioneering legislation to guarantee a right to education for all handicapped children.[2] Not until 1975 did Congress, spurred by the landmark federal district court decisions in *Mills v. Board of Education* and *Pennsylvania Association for Retarded Children (PARC) v. Pennsylvania*, make uniform the "right to free appropriate public education," prescribing that "to the maximum extent appropriate" handicapped children must be educated "with children who are not handicapped."[3]

This chapter examines the "right to education" movement from a child advocate's perspective, and raises several closely

---

[1] S. Howe, *Report Made to the Legislature of Massachusetts Upon Idiocy* 53 (1848).

[2] The Massachusetts Comprehensive Special Education Law, Ch. 766 (1972). Note that Massachusetts was the first state to pass a compulsory attendance law in 1852, but like 49 of the 50 states with such statutes, it exempted many handicapped children from attendance. Children's Defense Fund (CDF), *Children Out of School in America* 55-56 (1978).

[3] 20 U.S.C. §§ 1412(1); 1412(5) (1976). *Mills v. Board of Education*, 348 F. Supp. 866 (D.D.C. 1972); *PARC v. Pennsylvania*, 343 F. Supp. 279 (E.D. Pa. 1972).

related questions. Why were these declarations of rights so long in coming? What types of child advocacy were necessary to create and to enforce those legal mandates? If the right to a free appropriate education in the least restrictive educational environment is to endure and flourish, what techniques of child advocacy are needed? In an era of evident conservatism, can child advocates still redeem the national goal of "providing full educational opportunities to all handicapped children"?[4] Can child advocacy transform the field of special education? Answers to these questions can reveal some of the potentials and pitfalls of child advocacy in general.

TRANSFORMING SPECIAL EDUCATION

Child advocacy can serve as an antidote to society's neglect of the needs of the handicapped child. Before a surge of litigation and critical policy analysis in the early 1970s, the field of special education was a human and legal rights disaster. Nearly 2 million handicapped children were excluded from public schools.[5] An additional 3 to 4 million handicapped children were receiving an inappropriate and inadequate education.[6] According to the staff of the Council for Exceptional Children, only a minority of America's 7 million handicapped children with mental, physical, emotional, or learning handicaps were "receiving the education they need and are entitled to receive."[7] To make matters worse, through culturally biased tests and other means, large numbers of nonhandicapped black and Hispanic children were misclassified and placed in classes for persons with mental retardation.[8]

---

[4] Congress first enunciated this goal for states receiving federal financial assistance in 1974. P.L. 93-380, 88 Stat. 579, 583 (1974).

[5] S. Rep. No. 168, 94th Cong., 1st Sess. 8 (1975), reprinted in 1975 *U.S. Code Cong. & Ad. News* 1425.

[6] *Id.*; H.R. Rep. No. 332, 94th Cong., 1st Sess. 2-7 at n. 12; Weintraub and Abeson, "Appropriate Education for All Handicapped Children: A Growing Issue," 23 *Syracuse L. Rev.* 1037 (1972).

[7] Weintraub and Abeson, *supra* note 6, at 1037.

[8] J. Mercer, *Labeling the Mentally Retarded* (1973); N. Hobbs, *The Futures of Children: Categories, Labels, and Their Consequences* (1975); F. Weintraub, A. Abeson, and D. Braddock, *State Law and the Education of Handicapped Children: Issues and Recommendations* 28 (1971). *Diana v. State Bd. of Education*, C-70-37 RFP (N.D. Cal. 1970); *Larry P. v. Riles*, 343 F. Supp. 1306 (N.D. Cal. 1972); *aff'd*, 502 F.2d 963 (9th Cir. 1974), F. Supp. No. C-71-2270 RFP (N.D. Cal. Oct. 16, 1979) (standardized individual intelligence tests enjoined as basis for placement of black students in classes for the educable mentally retarded); *Covarrubias v. San Diego Unified School District*, No. 70-394-T (S.D. Cal. July 31, 1972).

In too many inner-city schools, inadequate special-education classes were seen as dumping grounds for minority students or holding operations for those found intractable in regular classes.[9] For youngsters in institutions for the mentally ill, mentally retarded or juvenile delinquent, special education was often nonexistent or in short supply.[10] Parents complained of having to go hat in hand begging educational placement for their handicapped children, or of being too intimidated to even protest the denial of their children's schooling.

By altering the power position of handicapped children and their parents, child advocacy in special education changed this inequitable *status quo*. I would define such advocacy along two dimensions: advocacy on behalf of the rights and interests of handicapped young persons, and advocacy by such persons to advance their own rights and interests.[11] Legal reform provided a principle tool of this advocacy campaign. Activists also developed a constituency and a political strategy to articulate children's rights and to implement reform legislation.

That same constituency must now increase the availability and effectiveness of child advocacy to turn symbolic gains and legal entitlements into real improvements in children's lives. One goal of such advocacy is to increase parental participation, efficacy, and knowledge of their children's (and their own) rights. Another goal is to provoke broad-scale, authentic reform through legislation, agency-wide administrative review, regulation, and litigation to correct serious deficiencies in special education.[12]

---

[9] Massachusetts Task Force on Children Out of School, *The Way We Go to School: The Exclusion of Children in Boston* (1970).

[10] *See Wyatt v. Stickney*, 325 F. Supp. 781 (M.D. Ala. 1971), *enforced*, 334 F. Supp. 1341 (M.D. Ala. 1971), *orders entered* 344 F. Supp. 373, 344 F. Supp. 387 (M.D. Ala. 1972), *aff'd in part, rev'd in part sub nom.*, *Wyatt v. Aderholt*, 503 F.2d 1305 (5th Cir. 1974); *N.Y.S.A.R.C. v. Rockefeller*, 357 F. Supp. 752 (E.D.N.Y. 1973) (granting preliminary injunction); *modified* No. 72-C-356/357 (E.D.N.Y. April 30, 1975) (consent decree), *approved sub nom. N.Y.S.A.R.C. v. Carey*, 393 F. Supp. 715 (E.D.N.Y. 1975) *enforced* 409 F. Supp. 606 (E.D.N.Y. 1976) (review panel), *aff'd* 596 F.2d 27 (2d Cir. 1979), *cert. denied*, 444 U.S. 836 (1979), 492 F. Supp. 1099 (E.D.N.Y. 1980), 492 F. Supp. 1110 (E.D.N.Y. 1980), *rev'd*, 631 F.2d 162 (2d Cir. 1980), 544 F. Supp. 330 (E.D.N.Y. 1982), *aff'd in part, rev'd and remanded in part*, 706 F.2d 956 (2d Cir. 1983); *Morgan v. Sprout*, 432 F. Supp. 1130 (S.D. Miss. 1977).

[11] Self-advocacy by older handicapped children and young persons is a neglected dimension of child advocacy. The Education for All Handicapped Children Act does, however, require the child to be a participant, "whenever appropriate," in meetings to develop and revise the Individual Education Program (IEP). 34 C.F.R. § 300.344(a)(4) (1986).

[12] *See* Neal and Kirp, "The Allure of Legalization Reconsidered: The Case of Special Education," *48 L. & Contemp. Prob.* 63, 86 (1985).

In this context, it seems misleading to suggest that child advocacy is a substitute or tonic for insufficient parental advocacy. Even the most conscientious and zealous parents may need the aid and advice of a professional child advocate to claim the services due their child.[13] Although deep-seated conflicts of interests may sometimes exist between handicapped child and parent, most families attempt to pursue the child's right to an appropriate education. But parents often require access to professional advocates to help them understand their rights, to allow them to participate effectively in the Individualized Education Plan (IEP) process, to aid in overcoming the education profession's resistance to parental input, and to marshal evidence and precedents should disputes arise.[14]

Child advocacy in special education seeks to make school bureaucracies more responsive to the law's idealistic norms and the child's individual needs. It is an attempt by persons outside those bureaucracies, with the help of inside allies (e.g., the Council for Exceptional Children), to engineer complex, even monumental social change.[15] That agenda is by now familiar:

1. to ensure the inclusion of all handicapped children in the educational system;
2. to increase fairness in the process of identifying, evaluating, and placing handicapped children;
3. to improve the quality of special-educational services by producing individualized programs of instruction, increasing the resources available for such services, and improving the training of teachers and the teaching technologies at their disposal;
4. to increase parental and child participation in the decision-making process as a check on arbitrary decisions and as a means of arriving at better decisions;
5. to give visibility and legitimacy to the mainstreaming goal; and

---

[13]But see J. Westman, Chapter 1, *supra.*

[14]Clune and Van Pelt, "A Political Method of Evaluating the Education for All Handicapped Children Act of 1975 and the Several Gaps of Gap Analysis," *48 L. & Contemp. Prob.* 7, 33 (1985) ("many educators' studied resistance to any parental input . . . may explain why IEP conferences frequently are highly formal, noninteractive, and replete with educational jargon").

[15]*See,* for example, Council for Exceptional Children, "Basic Commitments and Responsibilities to Exceptional Children: A Position Paper," *38 Exceptional Children* 2 (Oct. 1971).

6. to question assumptions and operating practices that serve administrative convenience at the expense of children's needs.

Although exceptional progress is being made in the first two items of this agenda, advocates still have much cause for concern. Examples of deficient practices abound: dumping mildly handicapped children into ineffective special-education programs; incarcerating truant handicapped teenagers in juvenile correction institutions with inadequate schools;[16] coercing decent parents to relinquish their child's custody to obtain residential schooling; and ignoring the minority of neglectful parents who forfeit their child's right to an education.

Why were the legal rights to challenge these injurious practices so long in coming? The school systems and the public that had long tolerated the *de jure* or *de facto* segregation of blacks from whites were equally insensitive to the injustices inflicted on handicapped children. Indeed, for the states that attempted to justify racial segregation, lawyers argued that such classifications were as right as segregating pupils "on the ground of sex or on the ground of age or on the ground of mental disability."[17] The teaching profession easily accepted and in fact enhanced the rationalizations for the segregation or exclusion of handicapped pupils, by creating categories of the ineducable and untrainable as devices for ridding schools of those children deemed costly to educate. Until the late 1960s, efforts by pioneering child advocates were limited. They made incremental changes, organized the parents' groups that would eventually draw attention to the plight of excluded children, and cautioned that "a slowly developing program may prove to be a stronger one in the long run."[18] Indeed, rather than acting as advocates, many parents' organizations were primarily providing services to the children rejected by the schools. During this period, lawyers acting as child advocates

---

[16] *See* Note, "Enforcing the Right to an 'Appropriate' Education: The Education for All Handicapped Children Act of 1975," 92 *Harv. L. Rev.* 1103, 1121, (1979); Md. Juvenile Services Administration, Consultants' Report (July 1987).

[17] Argument of John W. Davis, Counsel for Appellees in *Brown v. Board of Education*, 347 U.S. 483 (1954), quoted in *Argument* 51 (L. Friedman ed. 1969).

[18] A. Hill, *The Forward Look: The Severely Retarded Child Goes to School* 42 (U.S.D.H.E.W. Bulletin 1952, No. 11); Lazerson, The Origins of Special Education, in *Special Education Policies: Their History, Implementation and Finance* 15, 38-39 (J. Chambers & W. Hartman, eds. 1983).

were virtually unknown, while conspicuously few lawyers had the civil rights experience, initiative, or financial backing to challenge the system of excluding handicapped children. Even if the lawyers had been ready, the courts and the parent organizations seemed reluctant to confront or press that issue. For many individual parents, the stigma of having a disabled child may have been too heavy or the uncertainties of litigation too great to justify the exposure costs. The federal government and the judiciary, embroiled in the massive struggle to end racial exclusion in the schools, hesitated before mounting a protracted and bruising battle to end exclusion based on handicap.[19] These factors, plus barriers of inertia, delayed the coming legal revolution in special education.

CLASS DIMENSIONS
OF CHILD ADVOCACY

LEGAL CLASS ACTIONS

Child advocates used powerful and dramatic forms of intervention to create legal mandates for the free and appropriate education of handicapped children. In the early 1970s, class actions[20] in the federal courts established such rights and decreed procedural and substantive standards to attain them. In *Pennsylvania Association for Retarded Children (PARC) v. Pennsylvania*, the defendants conceded in the face of overwhelming evidence that all retarded children could be educated. By consent decree, school officials agreed to provide "every retarded child access to a free public program of education and training appropriate to his or her learning capacities."[21] On equal protection, due process and statutory grounds, *Mills v. Board of Education* went even further by enjoining any physically or mentally handicapped child from being denied the right to a suitable publicly supported edu-

---

[19]*See Hobsen v. Hansen*, 327 F. Supp. 844 (D.D.C. 1971), No. 82-66, slip. op. (D.D.C. July 23, 1971) (denying handicapped children's motion to intervene in race segregation case to challenge exclusion of black and other handicapped children from DC public schools).

[20]A class action refers to a lawsuit filed in behalf of named plaintiffs and numerous other persons in similar circumstances. In such an action, the court's ruling applies to all class members.

The class action or group dimensions of child advocacy also include other forms of collective advocacy, such as legislation, regulatory advocacy, and political-social organizing.

[21]*PARC, supra* note 3, at 302.

cation. *Mills* mandated detailed procedures. For example, before any child could be removed or suspended from a regular classroom by reason of handicap or disciplinary problem, *Mills* required detailed procedural safeguards including the right to receive a due process hearing and to be represented by an advocate of one's choosing. Perhaps most significantly, the *Mills* opinion placed the interest in educating children who had been excluded above the District's interests in saving money or administrative convenience. As Judge Waddy declared: "If sufficient funds are not available to finance all of the services and programs that are needed and desirable in the system then the available funds must be expended equitably in such a manner that no child is entirely excluded from a publicly supported education consistent with his needs and ability to benefit therefrom."[22]

Mills and *PARC* have had enormous influence on child advocacy and special education. Inspired by these precedents, lawyers filed 36 rights-to-education cases in 27 jurisdictions in the mid-1970s.[23] Shortly after the *Mills* decision, congressional leaders, such as Senator Humphrey and Representative Vanik, proposed nondiscrimination requirements under the Rehabilitation Act, which became known as Section 504. These provisions were intended to ensure equal opportunities for handicapped individuals and to prohibit their exclusion from participation in any program or activity receiving federal financial assistance, such as primary and secondary education.[24] As Senator Humphrey stressed, "the time has come when we can no longer tolerate the invisibility of the handicapped in America . . . children who are excluded from school . . . ."[25] As the United States Supreme Court in *Hendrick Hudson Central School District v. Rowley* made clear in reviewing the legislative history of P.L. 94-142, *Mills* and *PARC* provided the blueprint for that law and inspired its goal of individualized instruction to benefit every handicapped child.[26] With that impetus to a uniform federal standard, Congress rec-

---

[22] *Mills, supra* note 3, at 876.

[23] R. Martin, *Educating Handicapped Children: The Legal Mandate* 15 (1979).

[24] 29 U.S.C. § 794 (1982).

[25] S. 3044 at 118 Cong. Rec. 106-07 (Jan. 20, 1972).

[26] *Hendrick Hudson Central School District v. Rowley*, 458 U.S. 176 (1982).

ognized that "the right to education of handicapped children is a present right, one which is to be implemented immediately," and the federal government's shared responsibility to "assure equal protection of the laws and thus to take action to assure that handicapped children throughout the United States have available to them appropriate educational services."[27]

LEGISLATIVE ACTION

The Education for All Handicapped Children Act (EAHCA, also commonly referred to as Public Law 94-142) emphasized the advocacy process as a means of assessing and obtaining appropriate educational services.[28] In effect, the law made "parents full partners with local school administrators and teachers in making sure that a free appropriate public education is available to each eligible child."[29] In due process hearings, complaints to state departments of education, or adjudications before state or federal courts, the parent as advocate was now empowered to raise disputes over important educational decisions. Those decisions could include the identification of a child's handicap, change of educational placement, and choice of the educational services to be provided. Although only a tiny percentage of special-education decisions are ever formally challenged, the existence of these due process safeguards can deter a school system from noncompliance. The Children's Defense Fund reports that only 0.065% of all children receiving special education challenged any aspect of their program, and only a microscopic 0.007% actually filed a court complaint.[30] As the framers of the EAHCA predicted, parent-school agreement remains the rule, and due process hearings the exception. According to some special educators, this situation prevails "not because we're doing such a good job, but

---

[27]S. Rep. No. 168, 94th Cong. 1st Sess. 17 (1975) *reprinted in* 1975 *U.S. Code Cong. & Ad. News* 1441.

[28]20 U.S.C. § 1400 *et seq.* (1976).

[29]Gerry, "Procedural Safeguards Insuring that Handicapped Children Receive a Free Appropriate Public Education," *News Digest* No. 7 at 1 (1987) (National Information Center for Handicapped Children and Youth).

[30]CDF, Comments of the CDF on the Department of Education's Proposed Regulations Implementing Pub. L. 94-142, at 5 (Dec. 3, 1982) (formal comments), based on data in school year 1979-80, cited in Clune and Van Pelt, *supra* note 14 at 36 n. 172.

because school systems keep parents ignorant of their rights."[31] Nonetheless, the ability of some families to mount well-publicized cases acts as a powerful incentive to reach accords, to correct blatant injustices, and to encourage other activist parents. Individual remedies and private causes of action permitted the parents' enlightened self-interest to be a powerful tool for enforcing the right to a free appropriate public education.

REGULATORY ACTION

To implement federal and state legal mandates, regulatory advocacy was essential. Given the ambiguities of the statutory text and the legislative history,[32] the battle over the regulations implementing P.L. 94-142 was of decisive importance. Were handicapped students entitled to opportunities equivalent to those of nonhandicapped students in terms of tangible and intangible educational inputs? Or were outcomes to be stressed, with the handicapped child provided an equalized educational opportunity through the provision of services to minimize the effects of the handicapping condition, "thereby allowing him to benefit as nearly as possible from the same educational opportunities that are available to his non-handicapped peers"?[33] Did the term *appropriate education* refer to any particular level of services or have operational definitions? Beyond these great debates, there were literally hundreds of new regulatory issues to be resolved. For example, would psychotherapy be required as a related service for seriously emotionally disturbed children? The regulations required that certain counseling and psychological services be provided through qualified social workers, psychologists, guidance counselors, or other qualified personnel.[34] Would psychotherapy provided by a psychiatrist constitute a related service to be provided at no cost to parents if specified in the child's IEP? Administrative rul-

---

[31]Interview with anonymous, special-education teacher, and master's degree candidate in special education, Johns Hopkins University, Aug. 5, 1987.

[32]*See* Wegner, "Variations on a Theme--The Concept of Equal Educational Opportunity and Programming Decisions Under the Education for All Handicapped Children Act of 1975," 48 *L. & Contemp. Prob.* 169, 176-179 (1985).

[33]*Id.* at 176.

[34]34 C.F.R. § 300.13 (b)(2)(8)(v) (1986).

ings on this point were contradictory and avoided a clear answer. (According to those rulings, if the state deems such therapy a medical service, there is no obligation to provide; but if the state deems essentially the same service to be a counseling service, it must be provided to the child at no cost).

Such advocacy issues, as well as efforts to press federal and state bureaucracies to be more interventionist or provide more technical assistance at local school district levels, were not one-time issues. Advocacy groups, such as the Children's Defense Fund, the Parents Federation of Children with Special Needs, and the Disability Rights and Educational Defense Fund, became regular players in the periodic tugs of war to weaken or strengthen the EAHCA regulations. Moreover, given the powerful political lobbies on both sides of those issues, the regulatory arena remains a field for continuing conflict.[35]

ENFORCEMENT ACTIONS

Although all 50 states and the District of Columbia eventually accepted the conditions for P.L. 94-142 funding, advocates were compelled to take enforcement actions to speed compliance. With state education agencies responsible for monitoring local education agencies and for aggregating the necessary special services, advocates could hold the state accountable for failures to discharge its statutory duties to protect handicapped children's rights.[36] In jurisdictions under court order to place handicapped children in appropriate classes, plaintiffs obtained special masters to oversee implementations, sought contempt citations in extreme cases, and otherwise attempted to overcome resistance and obstacles to institutional reform.[37] In jurisdictions without pre-94-142 litigation, class actions were brought against inadequate special-educational systems. For example, *Mattie T. v. Holladay*[38] resulted in a

---

[35] On proposals for more comprehensive federal regulations and substantive guidelines to determine educational benefits and the amount of mainstreaming to be provided based on objective measures, see Comment: "The Education for All Handicapped Children Act Since 1975," 69 *Marquette L. Rev.* 51, 74-75, 77 (1985).

[36] S. Rep. 168, 94th Cong. 1st Sess. (1985); Rosenberg, "Handicapped Kids: America's Stepchildren," 72 *Illinois B.J.* 462, 464 (May 1984).

[37] *See*, for example, *Mills v. Board of Education*, No. 1939-71, (D.D.C. June 18, 1980) 4 MDLR 267 (finding of contempt).

[38] No. DC-75-31-S (N.D. Miss. January 26, 1979) (consent decree); 3 MDLR 98 (1979).

consent decree with specific requirements to overhaul Mississippi's special-education system: least restrictive educational environments for the placement of many institutionalized children into local district day programs, nondiscriminatory testing to reduce the disproportionate number of black children placed in classes for the mentally retarded or excluded from classes for the learning disabled, prohibitions on longer-term suspensions of handicapped children, strong state education department monitoring of local district's compliance with federal law, distribution to parents of a Parents' Rights Booklet, and the provision of compensatory education to children who had been misclassified as mentally retarded in order to enable them to obtain a high school diploma or GED/vocational education program (if beyond the Mississippi school age of 21).

Litigation also contributed to nationwide adoption of the EAHCA standards. After New Mexico opted not to participate in this federal program, a federal court held that the state's failure to provide free appropriate public education to handicapped children might violate Section 504 of the Rehabilitation Act.[39] Faced with that decision and mounting advocacy pressure as the lone holdout among the 50 states, New Mexico agreed to apply for 94-142 funds and to be bound by the Act's requirements.

Class actions can bring recalcitrant school districts into line with the federal time requirements for evaluating and placing handicapped children.[40] Inner-city school districts and districts with large numbers of institutionalized children may be especially vulnerable to such enforcement suits.

GRASS-ROOTS ORGANIZING ACTIONS

As another form of class advocacy, advocates engaged in political-social organizing to consolidate gains and prevent rollbacks of rights. Despite strong efforts by the Reagan Administration, school district lobbies, and other proponents of "deregulation," child advocates defeated proposals to amend P.L. 94-142, Section 504, and their accompanying regulations pertaining to education. They did so by organizing a massive grass-roots response, by flooding regulators and Congress with comments and letters, and

---

[39]*New Mexico Association for Retarded Citizens v. New Mexico*, 495 F. Supp. 391 (D.N.M. 1980), *rev'd and remanded*, 678 F.2d 847 (10th Cir. 1982).

[40]*Robinson v. Pinderhughes*, No. 85-1370 (D.Md. 1986), *remanded*, 810 F.2d 1270 (4th Cir. 1987).

158

by enlisting the aid of influential leaders. For example, the U.S. President's Committee on Mental Retardation courageously urged the retention of those laws in "substantially their present form," and encouraged the President to take "a positive and public stand to halt all efforts to change those laws through regulatory and legislative reform that would adversely affect mentally retarded citizens."[41] The Committee's arguments that implementing such laws were an investment, rather than a burden to society, and that attempts to deny educational and training opportunities to disabled people were antithetical to the concept of equal citizenship, were echoed by scores of disability and advocacy groups. Political organizing also took affirmative rather than defensive forms. Around the country, advocates mobilized parents to lobby for better services and more resources, to assert their rights, and to demand quality education for children with handicaps.[42]

INDIVIDUAL DIMENSIONS
OF CHILD ADVOCACY

Training parents to be informed, front-line advocates for their own children remains a basic objective of child advocacy. Recognizing advocacy functions as a major role of parenting, federal law vests parents with ongoing responsibilities for approving IEPs, authorizing evaluations, and challenging questionable special-education decisions. Furthermore, the parents of severely mentally handicapped children may be obliged to exercise decision-making and advocacy responsibilities of potentially life-long duration. Enhancing parents' advocacy skills and sense of efficacy when the child is young and the parents begin to interact with service providers can therefore decisively affect the child's development. Not only are those first encounters important in themselves, but they can provide the parents with the lessons for successful interventions with other agencies. Unfortunately, paren-

---

[41]Public Law 94-142 and Section 504 Resolution of the President's Committee on Mental Retardation, *reprinted in* U.S. President's Committee on Mental Retardation, *Report to the President: Citizens with Mental Retardation: Equality under the Law* 5-6 (1987).

[42]For examples, D. Biklen, *Let Our Children Go: An Organizing Manual for Advocates and Parents* (1974); Association for Retarded Citizens, Fact Sheet on Public Law 99-457: Amendments to the Education of the Handicapped Act (Oct. 1986); Association for Retarded Citizens, *If You Are the Parent of a Child Who Is Mentally Disabled . . .* (April 1986) (on the importance of advocacy to improve educational services). Technical Assistance to Parents Programs have also been funded on a national basis to provide information clearinghouse services.

tal participation is often limited and ineffective because of historic patterns of parent-professional relations, parental deference to professional educational judgment, and other structural factors undermining the ideal of parents having an equal voice in special-education decisions.[43] Yet parents who have overcome those factors report that by knowing their rights, understanding options for their children, and making demands on the system directly and through legal advocates, they have attained satisfying results. As one parent stated:

> You have to know your rights, know the questions to ask. You can't be intimidated. Parents are the best advocates. You work within the system. You do what you can. You start reasonable and low-key. But you've got to be prepared to go eye-to-eye and toe-to-toe. Consulting with an attorney helps and letting the school know you are consulting an attorney also helps.[44]

What happens to handicapped children who lack parental support? For children under state wardship (i.e., guardianship or custody) or whose parents are unknown or unavailable, *parent surrogates* can be appointed. Although P.L. 94-142 makes this a requirement for state funding, its narrow interpretation by state and local officials has diminished the value of this important tool for child advocacy.[45] Parent surrogates have no authority to make decisions outside the process of special education. Doubt often exists as to the criteria for appointing a surrogate, or the independence of public social workers so appointed.[46] As a result, many eligible children do not receive this service. For

---

[43] *See* Clune and Van Pelt, *supra* note 14, at 32-35, 55, and authorities cited therein.

[44] Interview with Cassaundra Brown, Member of Baltimore City Public Schools Parents' Advisory Council for Exceptional Children, July 13, 1987.

[45] For example, Maryland law defines a ward of the state as "a child for whom a State or county agency or official has been appointed legal guardian, or who has been committed by a court of competent jurisdiction to the legal custody of a State or county agency or official with the express authorization that the State or county agency or official make educational decisions for the child." Md. Educ. Code Ann. § 8-414(a)(9) (1978). A parent is "unknown" when a public agency, after reasonable efforts, cannot identify the child's parents, and "unavailable" when such agency cannot discover the parent's physical whereabouts. *Id.* § 8-414(a)(7)-(8).

[46] By illustration, parents who have been found neglectful of their children often continue to exercise powers to consent to IEPs, even though school principals and teachers may deem these children prime candidates for the surrogate parent program.

example, a recent study of Maryland reports that only 87 children had parent surrogates acting for them out of a special-education enrollment of 75,194 students.[47] In Rhode Island, the Office of the Child Advocate had to obtain a federal court order to insure the appointment of surrogates for all handicapped children committed under abuse, neglect, or dependency laws, and for other eligible children.[48]

LAY ADVOCACY

Lay advocacy (sometimes known as *case advocacy*) is a more common method of representing the interests of handicapped children and their parents in individual special-education determinations. Lay advocates can be specially trained to counsel parents, to assist them at all stages of developing an IEP, and to represent them in administrative hearings. The trained advocate's early involvement in the process of shaping the IEP can produce more favorable and efficient results than trying to change an IEP through taking a due process appeal. Their presence can also give parents an ally in this process and a greater feeling of confidence and empowerment. Lay advocacy is less expensive than legal advocacy. But unlike attorneys' fees, the lay advocates' compensation for assistance at a due process hearing cannot be recouped by the prevailing parent.[49] Although citizen advocates may volunteer their services, organizations must make intensive recruitment and training efforts to muster a significant number of such child advocates.[50]

LEGAL ADVOCACY

Legal advocacy can increase the parents' leverage in negotiating a better IEP or achieving a favorable outcome in a contested

---

[47]Farace, "The Parent Surrogate Program in Maryland: Protecting the Education Rights of Handicapped Children Under Public Law 94-142," 10 *Md. L. Forum* 21, 28 (1987).

[48]*Office of the Child Advocate v. Pontarelli*, No. 82-0091P (D.R.I. 1983) (consent decree).

[49]*Arons v. N.J. State Board of Education*, No. 85-209, 55 U.S.L.W. 2636 (D.N.J. May 12, 1987), *aff'd* 842 F.2d 58 (3d Cir. 1988), *cert. denied* 109 S.Ct. 366 (1988).

[50]Associations for handicapped persons might develop such volunteer advocacy programs in conjunction with service clubs and Protection and Advocacy (P&A) programs.

hearing. With knowledge of administrative law or special education, lawyers who represent many handicapped clients have the advantages of "repeat players." They can influence school officials to adopt a legally required outcome that is favorable to the child and poses the path of least resistance for the officials. They can invest energies in changing the rules, framing test cases, and developing close relationships with school officials and experts. Even if inexperienced in administrative hearings or special education, lawyers can help their clients by interpreting the legal process, collecting information for the hearing, directing the case's presentation, cross-examining witnesses, and keeping their clients calm and poised at the hearing.[51] According to the empirical research, competent representation makes a difference, and a cadre of lawyers and advocates can be recruited that is sophisticated in representing clients at special-education hearings.[52] Lawyers may also be needed to support and train lay advocates. According to Budoff, Orenstein, and Kervick's 1974-1976 Massachusetts study, hearing officers criticized the performance of lay advocates in cases in which complex legal issues were raised, inappropriate arguments were used, or the lay advocates became too emotionally involved to serve as "effective managers of the parents' case."[53] One solution is to link lawyers, paralegals, student-attorneys, and lay advocates in offices or other collaborative arrangements that (a) generate a high volume of cases, and (b) assure case handling by individuals with sufficient expertise, skills, and substantive knowledge to represent effectively a particular client at a particular stage of the process.

TECHNIQUES OF CHILD ADVOCACY: SECURING AN APPROPRIATE, FREE, AND QUALITY SPECIAL EDUCATION

Disciplined investigation and fact finding are essential first steps. Child advocates have often documented systemic failures to implement reform legislation, such as Massachusetts' minimal efforts to provide education to emotionally disturbed children in

---

[51]M. Budoff, A. Orenstein, and C. Kervick, *Due Process in Special Education: On Going to a Hearing* 251 (1982).

[52]*Id.* at 251, 262.

[53]*Id.* at 251.

public schools under Chapter 750 and the disproportionate use of the most restrictive settings,[54] or Maryland's failure to coordinate interagency efforts to serve mentally handicapped children.[55]

Extensive fact finding is also required in child advocacy for the individual. Without careful factual investigation, parents may endorse inappropriate educational goals and objectives, and parent-teacher relationships may suffer from feelings of animosity due to misinformation. By way of illustration, Alan H. was a 6th grader with an IQ of 145. Although his innate abilities were substantial, his school did not appreciate the extent to which his learning disabilities and emotional difficulties had led to his academic failure and social withdrawal in the classroom. His parents sought his placement in a private day school that would both stimulate him intellectually and remediate his serious worsening handicaps. As his counsel, I believed that many factual questions had to be answered in order to persuade a school district that such a placement was appropriate, rather than optimal, under the terms of the law. For example, why was Alan, with his intellectual gifts, failing? Were these failures attributable to any particular handicap or combination of handicaps? What package of services was needed to constitute an appropriate education for this child with his unique abilities and disabilities? In what respects were those services unavailable in the public school system? Would the real costs of the school district be that much greater in a private setting than if the district were to develop its own quality, highly individualized program for Alan? Despite the school district's standard argument that their own program would be less restrictive, would Alan's education in the private school with nonhandicapped peers in fact be less restrictive than the self-contained special-education class that the district was proposing? After the experts' reports, school records, medical records, and parents' written statements were fully mustered, the school district agreed to change Alan's placement to a private day school. Alan's parents now report that he is thriving in his new school, and is eager rather than phobic about attending classes.

---

[54] Task Force on Children Out of School, *Suffer the Children: The Politics of Mental Health in Massachusetts* 38-42 (1972) (less than 1% of eligible children received the special-education services to which they were statutorily entitled).

[55] Leviton and Shuger, "Maryland's Exchangeable Children: A Critique of Maryland's System of Providing Services to Mentally Handicapped Children," 42 *Md. L. Rev.* 823 (1983).

Negotiating an effective IEP program requires particular skills and knowledge. The child's representative must have some understanding of educational evaluation procedures. He or she must know the methods of determining whether a student has been properly evaluated, properly placed, and is making adequate progress in, and deriving sufficient benefit from, the existing program.[56] The advocate must also have a grasp of the detailed federal and state statutes, regulations, policies, and judicial opinions that establish the student's entitlement to a free appropriate public education and the remedies for any violations of the student's statutory and constitutional rights. The advocate must then have the skills and professional judgment to know how to settle disputes informally (e.g., use of experts, demand letters, etc.), how to invoke administrative remedies without creating undue hostility or ill-will, and how to obtain favorable results for the client in the least time-consuming, least expensive, and most satisfying fashion.

When informal methods of negotiation fail, *administrative adjudication* offers a means of challenging school officials' exercise (or lack of exercise) of discretion. For the handicapped child, P.L. 94-142 opens wide avenues for complaint and appeal, with opportunities to present complaints "with respect to any matter relating to the identification, evaluation, or educational placement of the child, or provision of a free appropriate public education to such child."[57] In theory, this makes any special-education decision to serve or not serve a child, to grant or deny a related service such as transportation or counseling, to pay for a private or residential service, subject to potential challenge. But as previously noted, very few parents challenge the school's decisions or invoke these administrative hearings.

Although school officials may wish to be law-abiding and comply with the law for idealistic and professional reasons, they often face counterpressures of budgets, organizational routines, and staff resistance or ineptitude that can undercut P.L. 94-142 mandates. Administrative hearings serve as a means of enforcement when parents are "encouraged or allowed to request or demand compliance from regulated organizations."[58] Sometimes

---

[56]*See* D. Pullin, *Special Education: A Manual for Advocates*, vol. 1, chapters 3-4 (1982).

[57]20 U.S.C. § 1415(b)(1)(E) (1976).

[58]Clune and Van Pelt, *supra* note 14, at 39.

the mere filing of a complaint will spur compliance, while in other school districts even favorable decisions from hearings officers will be ignored or evaded.[59]

Litigation remains a viable mode of redress when other means are exhausted and qualified expert testimony can be presented. Such testimony is especially significant from those with ongoing contact with the child and his or her program.[60] For example, courts have ruled against a district's IEP when the statements of plaintiffs' doctors and teachers recognized the inappropriateness of a public school placement, and the appropriateness of the higher level of therapy available in a special private school.[61] Although courts after *Rowley* often express deference to school decisions and an unwillingness to substitute their own notions of educational policy, they still apply substantive standards and can overturn IEPs that are not supported by a strong factual record.[62] Courts continue to issue significant decisions on such issues as the availability of year-round education for certain children who would otherwise regress during summer breaks;[63] the reimbursement to parents of the costs of individual psychological therapy and group therapy;[64] and the availability of federal civil rights remedies for a district's failure to implement a favorable local hearing officer's decision to place a child in a residential program that could not be found in the public school system.[65] To minimalist arguments by the district that their plans must merely be "of benefit" to handicapped students, courts have insisted that P.L. 94-142 requires a plan of instruction in which educational

---

[59]*See* M. Budoff, *et al, supra* note 51, at 125-127.

[60]*See* Dubow and Geer, "Special Education Law Since Rowley," 17 *Clearinghouse Rev.* 1001 (Jan. 1984).

[61]*See*, for example, *Taylor v. Board of Education of the Copake-Taconic Hills Central School District*, 649 F. Supp. 1253 (N.D.N.Y. 1986).

[62]*See* Zirkel, "Building an Appropriate Education from Board of Education v. Rowley: Razing the Door and Raising the Floor," 42 *Md. L. Rev.* 466, 481 (1983).

[63]*Armstrong v. Kline*, 476 F. Supp. 583 (E.D. Pa. 1979), *aff'd and remanded*, 629 F.2d 269 (3rd Cir. 1980); *Georgia Association for Retarded Citizens v. McDaniel*, 511 F. Supp. 1263 (N.D. Ga. 1981), *aff'd* 716 F.2d 1565 (11th Cir. 1983).

[64]*Doe v. Anrig*, 651 F. Supp. 424 (D. Mass. 1987).

[65]*Robinson v. Pinderhughes*, 810 F.2d 1270 (4th Cir. 1987).

progress is likely, not one that will produce "regression or trivial educational advancement."[66] Workable tests of appropriate education can focus on whether a child is making measurable progress toward the child's IEP goals, or in cases of virtual educational stagnation, whether the child is performing substantially below the norm for "similarly situated handicapped children."[67] In summary, courts continue to subject special-education programs to close scrutiny.

Under certain circumstances, *mediation* offers an attractive alternative method of dispute resolution. Both the 94-142 regulations and researchers have recommended mediation as a less costly and contentious alternative to administrative hearings.[68] Some parents who lack the emotional or financial resources to pursue a formal appeal, even with the support of an advocacy agency, may feel less intimidated by a session with a mediator. If parents at such sessions have bargaining skills, can reach accommodations, and can establish constructive ongoing relationships with school personnel, mediation can offer parents many advantages, while still preserving their appeal rights. In Massachusetts, the state claimed that 90% of parents who initially rejected school IEPs resolved their dispute informally through this pre-hearing mechanism.[69] After one to three sessions with a regionally deployed state education mediator, the parties usually reached an agreement. If unable to clarify and resolve the issues, the mediator would then advise the parents of their hearing rights, the procedures entailed, and the advocacy resources available. Without further research, it is difficult to assess the quality of those settlements, or to gauge whether the parents capitulate to the mediator's opinions or reach reasonable compromises.

---

[66]*Board of Education of East Windsor Regional School District v. Diamond*, 808 F.2d 987, 991 (3d Cir. 1986). *See Crawford v. Pittman*, 708 F.2d 1028 (5th Cir. 1983).

[67]Myers and Jenson, "The Meaning of 'Appropriate' Educational Programming Under the Education for All Handicapped Children Act," 1984 *So. Ill. U. L. J.* 401, 427-440.

[68]Comment to 34 CFR § 300.506 (1986). *See* 20 U.S.C. § 1416(b)(2); M. Budoff *et al., supra* note 51, 305-307, 334-337; R. Martin, *supra* note 23, at 109.

[69]M. Budoff *et al., supra* note 51, at 348.

REDEEMING THE PROMISE OF FULL EDUCATIONAL OPPORTUNITIES FOR CHILDREN AND YOUNG PERSONS WITH HANDICAPS

Child advocates must again formulate an agenda of special-education reform. Contrary to some perceptions, child advocacy in special education is not dead, but merely quiescent. Its task is now to stress issues of quality, in addition to inclusion and appropriateness. Its moral imperative is to define and redeem the promise of full, integrated educational opportunities for all handicapped children and young persons. Its strategy should include a focus on those still most ill-served, especially the homeless, the state-institutionalized, and the impoverished. In an era of shifting federal-state regulations, this advocacy attempts to elevate state standards above minimum federal requirements.[70] Child advocates can also make better use of the family courts to identify the underserved handicapped children who come to those courts' attention and to locate appropriate educational services in the community.[71]

During the Reagan Administration years, defensive efforts consumed much of the available energies. Despite efforts to repeal or dilute P.L. 94-142 and Section 504 or to diminish federal subsidies to local and state special-education programs, those requirements and resources were protected. Federal appropriations for special education which totaled $1.042 billion dollars in 1982 increased to $1.338 billion dollars in fiscal year 1987. In-

---

[70]For states that have set higher standards, see Md. Educ. Code Ann. § 8-401 (a)(2) (handicapped child entitled to special services to achieve educational potential) (1986 Cum. Supp.); Iowa Code Ann. § 281.2 (3) (West Supp. 1987) (special-education students "shall, if reasonably possible, receive a level of education commensurate with the level provided each child who does not require special education"); R.I. Gen. Laws § 16-24-1 (Michie 1981) (schools must provide education which will "best satisfy the needs of the handicapped children"). On federal litigation enforcing higher state standards, see *Bd. of Education of East Windsor Regional School District v. Diamond, supra* note 66 (under New Jersey law, handicapped student entitled to a standard of service exceeding that set by EAHCA, requiring local school district to provide educational services that would afford the student "the best success in learning"); *David D. v. Dartmouth School Comm.*, 615 F. Supp. 639 (D. Mass. 1984), *aff'd*, 775 F.2d 411 (1st Cir. 1985), *cert. den'd*, 106 S.Ct. 1790 (1986) (state law standard that special-education programs "assure the maximum possible development of a child with special needs" incorporated under federal law). *See also Geis v. Bd. of Educ. of Parsippany-Troy Hills*, 774 F.2d 575 (3d Cir. 1985).

[71]For a Chase Manhattan Bank-financed project in the New York City family court system, where an estimated 1/3 to 1/2 of the children before those courts have learning disabilities which contribute to truancy or delinquency, see "Grant to Help Juveniles with Learning Disabilities," *N.Y. Times*, Aug. 9, 1987, at 33, col. 1.

formation services on parental rights in special education were preserved, and improved.[72] A few positive initiatives were launched, such as supported employment and transitional services for school graduates, and a concern with strengthening regular education for some children with exceptional needs.

Although the U.S. Supreme Court has stressed minimum standards, it has left intact the basic statutory promise of individual instruction and related services for the handicapped child. In *Rowley*, the Court adopted a "some benefit" standard in determining whether each child is afforded a meaningful educational opportunity; to wit, whether the child's needs and educational objectives have been properly determined and whether in implementing the IEP the child can reasonably be expected to make some measurable progress toward those objectives.[73]

In *Tatro v. Texas*, the Court held that the related services required as part of that individualized program of instruction could include Clean Intermittent Catheterization by school-based nursing personnel, rejecting contentions that such services were medical and could not be offered in regular public schools.[74] And in *School Committee of the Town of Burlington v. Department of Education of Massachusetts*, the Supreme Court refused to penalize parental activism, by holding that reimbursement for private placement tuition and related expenses incurred pending resolution of a placement dispute was appropriate relief under the Act.[75]

Most recently, the Court decided that the Act's "stay-put" provisions prohibit school districts from indefinitely suspending handicapped children whose disruptive or dangerous conduct arises out of their disabilities. Under those provisions, during the pendency of any administrative hearing, the child must remain in the then-current placement, unless the school and the parent agree to a change in placement.[76] Courts have held that indefinite suspensions constitute a "change of placement," thereby in-

---

[72]On information exchange networks, see M. Gerry, *supra* note 29, and other information from the National Information Center for Handicapped Children and Youth.

[73]*See* Wegner, *supra* note 32, at 192-194.

[74]703 F.2d 823 (5th Cir. 1983), *aff'd in part and rev'd in part*, 468 U.S. 883 (1984).

[75]471 U.S. 359 (1985).

[76]20 U.S.C. § 1415 (e)(3) (1976).

voking the Act's procedural and substantive safeguards, including the right to remain in the *status quo* placement until the contested IEP can be fully reviewed.[77] At stake were two issues: whether the schools may unilaterally suspend a child for over 30 days, thereby creating a vague "disruptive child" exception to the Act's mandate; and whether the state education agency must intervene when a local district defaults in its obligation to provide a publicly supported education for all handicapped children. The Supreme Court has now limited such suspensions to 10 days (unless a parent consents to a change of placement or a court orders it) and affirmed the state agency's duty to be an educator of last resort. To secure the Act's promise of inclusion and a meaningful education for all handicapped children, the judiciary has unequivocally ruled for the pupils and prevented schools from unilaterally transferring students with behavioral disabilities.

Further refinements and extensions of the right-to-education, however, are more likely to come from Congress and state legislatures than the courts. With the Reagan and Bush Administrations' appointments to the U.S. Supreme Court and the lower federal courts, the federal judiciary is less interventionist in disability rights matters, and more likely to emphasize procedural regularity over substantive reforms. Indeed, Congress has twice overturned Supreme Court decisions that weakened the enforcement of handicapped persons' rights. By passing the Handicapped Children's Protection Act of 1986, it reversed the outcome of *Smith v. Robinson* and permitted parents to recover attorneys' fees, including the related costs of expert testimony, when they prevail in administrative proceedings or litigation under the Act.[78] Similarly, Congress responded to *Atascadero State Hospital v. Scanlon* by enacting the Rehabilitation Act Amendments of 1986, thereby lifting a sovereign immunity shield and allowing recipients of handicapped services to sue state agencies on discrimination claims.[79]

---

[77]*Doe v. Maher*, 793 F.2d 1470, 1486 (9th Cir. 1986), *aff'd, as modified Honig v. Doe*, 108 Sup.Ct. 592 (1988); *Eugene B. v. Great Neck Union Free School District*, 635 F. Supp. 753, 758 (E.D.N.Y. 1986).

[78]P.L. 99-372, codified at 20 U.S.C. § 1415 (1986); *Smith v. Robinson*, 486 U.S. 992 (1984).

[79]473 U.S. 234 (1985); 42. U.S.C. § 2000d-7 (Supp. 1988); 1986 U.S. Code Cong. & Admin. News 3554 (as condition of their receipt of federal financial assistance, states subject to suits for violation of federal laws prohibiting discrimination on the basis of handicap, race, age, or sex to the same extent as any other public or private entities).

Congress again proved a champion of disability rights by passing the Education of the Handicapped Act Amendments of 1986, permitting the child's representatives to seek relief concurrently under Section 504 and P.L. 94-142. Even more significantly, those Amendments require the development of "quality early intervention services" for toddlers from birth to age 2, set a 5-year timetable for making those services available to all such handicapped infants, and incorporate now familiar safeguards in these early education programs (child-find systems, procedural safeguards, parent surrogates, written prior notice, timely evaluation, etc.).[80] At state and federal levels, legislators are also addressing the need for transitional services and vocational education for the graduates of special-education programs who often encounter long waiting lists rather than services.[81]

Because of their political powerlessness, handicapped children in institutions may reap better results through litigation than legislation. Through state and federal court actions, advocates for those children have repeatedly challenged the absence of special-educational services, the inferior quality of services offered, and the undue restrictiveness of institutional school settings.[82] Despite longstanding legal requirements of interagency cooperation, litigants turned to courts to resolve impasses between officials of the institution, the local school district, and the state department of education and to assure institutionalized children their rights to education.[83] As a result, judges have appointed special masters to develop remedial plans, ordered institutional schools to conform to state and federal law standards (e.g., requiring new IEPs and the appointment of surrogate parents to assure less restrictive placements), and even issued

---

[80] 20 U.S.C. §§ 1471-1485 (Supp. Pamphlet 1988).

[81] On premature termination of special-education services and the social awarding of a high school diploma without attaining sufficient skills, see *Stock v. Massachusetts Hospital School*, 392 Mass. 205 (1984) (terminating eligibility for special-education services, by awarding diploma, without formal written notice to parents of the graduation decision, and notice of their rights to participate in that decision and seek hearing and administrative review, violates state and federal laws).

[82] *See* cases cited in S. Herr, *Rights and Advocacy for Retarded People* 125-136 (1983). *See generally*, Finn and Coleman, "The Institutional and Educational Abuse of Children in State Care," 19 *Suffolk U.L. Rev.* 227, 246-259 (1985).

[83] *See*, for example, *Mills v. Board of Educ.*, No. 1939-71, 4 MDLR 267 (D.D.C. June 18, 1980); *Jerry M. v. District of Columbia* No. 1519-85, slip op. 24-27 (D.C. Super.Ct. July 10, 1986) (consent decree to remedy violations of educational rights of institutionalized juvenile delinquents).

contempt of court citations.[84] In the controversial field of education for the deaf, eloquent calls to revitalize residential schools for the deaf may signal a different trend. There, a new round of litigation might seek to preserve those schools, validate the legitimacy of sign language, and question narrow interpretations of what constitutes the least restrictive environment.[85] In summary, with approximately 200,000 handicapped school-age children in institutions or other out-of-home placements,[86] advocates must continue to use the courts, along with other strategies, to remedy the all-too-frequent and egregious violations of these children's rights.[87]

Other well-documented gaps in implementing the EAHCA also require thoughtful attention and redress. These include low rates of parental participation, placement in unnecessarily segregated educational environments, and the limited availability of advocacy resources to support individual children. Correcting the first two problems may not be easy. Schools still reinforce patterns of parental inaction, and tout the advantages of more restrictive special education as "special" and therefore better, whereas regular education with ancillary special services has few promoters.[88] Many parents are unwilling or incapable of performing such roles as advocate, educational decision maker, or program evaluator, or lack the training or support to do so effectively.[89]

---

[84]*Mills, supra* note 37; *Rainey v. Tennessee Dep't of Education,* No. A-3100, 1 MDLR 336 (Tenn. Ch.Ct. Davidson Cty. Jan. 28, 1977); *Garrity v. Gallen,* 522 F. Supp. 171 (D.N.H. 1981).

[85]*See* Lane, "Listen to the Needs of Deaf Children," *N.Y. Times,* July 17, 1987, at A35, col. 2.

[86]This estimate includes 59,942 children in institutions and group homes for the mentally retarded, 40,832 children in public and private mental hospitals, 12,455 in facilities for the physically handicapped, and the remainder in juvenile corrections and child welfare facilities and foster homes. Telephone interview with Dr. Ronald Conley, Developmental Disabilities Administration, USDHHS, July 22, 1987.

[87]For a useful discussion of comprehensive strategies and the role of litigation, especially for juveniles in correctional institutions, see S. Bing and D. Richart, *Fairness is a Kid's Game: A Background Paper for Emerging State-Based Child Advocacy Organizations* 58-85 (1987).

[88]Turnbull, Brotherson, Wheat, and Esquith, "The Least Restrictive Education for Handicapped Children: Who Really Wants It?" 16 *Family L. Q.* 161 (1982). For a statement expressing concern on the capabilities of all schools and educators to meet exceptional children's educational needs, see National Education Association, Council for Exceptional Children, and American Association of School Administrators, "The Relationship Between Special Education and General Education" *reprinted in* EHLR SA-156 (Supp. 194, June 5, 1987).

[89]*See* Allen and Hudd, "Are We Professionalizing Parents? Weighing the Benefits and Pitfalls," 25 *Mental Retardation* 133 (1987).

171

Improving the quality and quantity of child advocacy in special education could counter these problems. Advocates could counsel parents to assume more informed, activist roles in their child's education, and could offer a trustworthy analysis of the available options based on research rather than myths. In each state, lawyers and other advocates could prepare and distribute manuals and handbooks on how to secure a quality, free, and appropriate education for the handicapped person from birth to age 21.[90] But even with technical information and support, some parents will need professional advocates to assume roles those parents perform by default rather than by choice. Furthermore, professional advocates can develop alliances with individual teachers and administrators who know how and where violations of students' rights are occurring, but feel powerless to correct those violations without outside support.

Despite beliefs that the "first generation" issues of exclusion from the public schools have been resolved, handicapped children still face serious risks of long-term suspension, expulsion, and outright denial of educational services.[91] To counter those exclusions and pushouts, advocates are most needed for those who can least afford their aid - the homeless, the parentless, the institutionalized, and the poor. Advocates must also focus on the "second generation" of issues, such as educational quality, full integration, and the extension of educational services to pre- and post-schoolers. On the horizon is yet a "third generation" of issues: attempts to reinvigorate regular education as a mode of serving mildly handicapped children and other children whose special needs do not warrant a handicapped label. To realize these ends, a highly sophisticated combination of class and indi-

---

[90]Because state laws and local resources differ, no single handbook can meet this informational need. Even in states with such manuals or handbooks, parents seldom receive particularized information on how to obtain free evaluations of their children's neurological conditions, early education services, post-secondary school education, and access to transitional services as the handicapped person shifts from student to adult roles. For a basic national handbook, see Children's Defense Fund, *94-142 and 504: Numbers that Add Up to Educational Rights for Handicapped Children* (1984).

[91]Jones, "The Education for All Handicapped Children Act: Coverage of Children with Acquired Immune Deficiency Syndrome (AIDS)," 15 *J. of L. & Educ.* 195, 205 (1986) (blanket exclusion of children with AIDS or other diseases is not justifiable under the EAHCA). On risks to homeless children of being handicapped and receiving an inadequate education, see McKinney Homeless Assistance Act of 1987, 42 U.S.C. §§ 11431-11432 (Supp. 1988) (grants for state plans for insuring that homeless children receive an adequate education). Exclusion from school is common: of 104 shelters surveyed, 34% reported denials of access to education to homeless children. National Coalition for the Homeless, *Broken Lives: The Denial of Education to Homeless Children* (Dec. 1987).

vidual advocacy is required to separate realistic objectives from overzealous mistakes.

Organizations such as the Association for Retarded Citizens and other parent groups, the Protection and Advocacy (P&A) agencies,[92] and the Children's Defense Fund must take the lead in shaping that agenda, identifying attainable objectives, and revitalizing advocacy networks to turn the rhetoric of full educational opportunities into realities. P&A agencies, for example, can develop "backup" and support capabilities to aid lay advocates and private attorneys, and to develop special-education units in local legal aid programs.[93]

SUMMARY

Compared to other advocacy efforts for children and disabled persons, child advocacy in special education is a striking, but qualified, success. Class and individual advocacy has produced legal mandates for sweeping change and has given parents new tools for influencing educational decisions in favor of the handicapped child.

Symbolic as well as incremental gain, however, should not blind us to the flaws of a system that differentially rewards handicapped children according to the assertiveness of their parents and the diligence of their advocates. Class bias can result. Children in public institutions frequently suffer. Inequalities between school districts are magnified.

Yet child advocacy can remain a force for transforming special education and renewing our commitments to serve children's interests above narrow professional interests or organizational routines. Broad-based coalitions for *all* disabled children can lobby for more resources and other shared priorities. Free or low-cost advocacy services can give poor children a means to compel respect for their rights. Regulatory and legal advocacy can reduce inequalities in special education based on race, poverty, geography, or institutional residence. These hard tasks are among the child advocate's noblest missions.

---

[92]42 U.S.C. § 6042 (Supp. 1985) (developmental disabilities P&A); 42 U.S.C. § 10801 (Supp. 1988) (P&A for recipients of mental health services).

[93]For example, Massachusetts Disability Law Center, A Project to Help Ensure that Disabled Children Receive the Special Education to Which They Are Entitled: A Proposal Submitted to the Boston Foundation (June 1987).

Part IV

THE SOCIAL SERVICE SYSTEM

INTRODUCTION

The most deadly of all possible sins is the mutilation of a child's spirit; for such a mutilation undercuts the life principle of trust, without which every human act, may it feel ever so good and seem ever so right, is prone to perversion.

Erik Erikson, 1958

Family violence in America was "discovered" as a social problem in the 1870s. It emerged again in the Progressive era of the 1910s and finally surged into public consciousness in the late 1960s (Gordon, 1988). Today, of all developed countries, the United States has the most violent streets and households. Throughout the nation, rape, muggings, and murder are commonplace, and gang wars dominate urban ghettos. Husbands and wives physically abuse each other in 1 out of 6 American homes, so that a person is more likely to be hit or killed at home than anywhere else (Straus & Gelles, 1988). All of this violence is supported by the adulation of sex and violence in the media and the ready availability of pornography and nonrecreational guns (Hutchings, 1988).

Domestic violence is reflected further in the over 2 million cases of child abuse and neglect reported in 1986 - a 12% increase over 1985 and a 223% increase over 1976. The 23% increase in child-abuse-related deaths between 1985 and 1986 is especially significant. In 1986, 1,200 children were reported to have died of abuse; however, the true figure is probably closer to

5,000, because most are reported as accidents or instances of the Sudden Infant Death Syndrome.

On the other hand, in 1985 more than half of the reports of child abuse and neglect were deemed to be unfounded. Furthermore, more than half of the cases involving neglect were latchkey children left unsupervised at home, and fewer than 1% of the total number of reported abuse and neglect cases involved serious injuries. Although confirmed reports of sexual abuse rose to 113,000 in 1985, they still involved a small percentage of the abuse cases. Consequently, there is a risk that public over- and subsequent under-reaction can occur analogous to that surrounding the scare over missing children in the mid-1980s when 1.5 million children were identified as "missing" each year, conjuring up images of widespread abductions by strangers. In fact, the vast majority of the missing children were teenage runaways or children taken by a parent in a custody struggle.

The deluge of child-abuse reports actually endangers truly neglected children, because social workers have such a backlog of complaints that they are unable to respond to them quickly and investigate them thoroughly. For example, in Virginia caseworkers investigated 12,000 more complaints in 1987 than in 1980. Because they had to devote so much time to checking unfounded complaints, they reported 3,000 fewer abused and neglected children than in 1980. In Pennsylvania and Oklahoma one-third of all families in which complaints were deemed unfounded were found later to have been abusive or neglectful. Because child abuse may well be known only to the abuser's victim and family, it is likely that the reported cases of child abuse and neglect fall far short of revealing the full extent of the problem.

Serious neglect and abuse of children is a significant social problem and represents failure of parenting, justifying the intervention of the state on a child's behalf. However, defining the point at which that failure is sufficient to warrant interference with the child-parent relationship depends upon state statutes that deal with physical injury, sexual abuse, and emotional or mental injury (Davis & Schwartz, 1987).

The medical emphasis on physical abuse has obscured the greater damage of parental neglect. The hardships of poverty and the maltreatment of physical abuse pale in comparison to the emotional, mental, and personality damage caused by parental neglect. This is illustrated dramatically by physically abused children who protect their parents, because they fear the greater danger of abandonment by them. A child's need for security may be met by an abusive parent. For this reason, removal of a child from a solely abusive parent usually is not justified; it adds a dimension of externally imposed parental abandonment that can be more harmful to the child than remaining with the parent while family therapy takes place.

In practice, child abuse and neglect often occur together. Parents who are overwhelmed by the responsibilities of child rearing neglect their children and also react violently toward them when frustrated. Moreover, the emotional, mental, and personality damage to children is more difficult to define than physical damage. State statutes usually define emotional and mental damage as overt psychiatric symptoms that can be directly related to a parent's neglect or mental mistreatment of a child, often through denigration and other forms of verbal assaults on the child. Actually the damage often is expressed through delayed or aberrant personality development or, in some cases, failure to thrive in physical development as well. Even the instinctual drives to feed recede in the absence of parental caregiving, and vulnerable infants can die from malnutrition. During later childhood, the development of language and social skills depends upon parental interaction, as illustrated by the extreme case of Genie, who was confined in a room without human interaction from the age of 18 months to 13 years (Lane & Pillard, 1978). When discovered, Genie did not possess the fundamental qualities of a human being. In less extreme examples, children who are deprived of parental contact during hospitalization become withdrawn after initial reactions of protest and despair.

Because society reacts more vehemently to physical and sexual abuse than to parental neglect, focusing attention on the consequences of parental neglect is imperative. Neglected children often become problems for society because of their incapacity to form close relationships with other people. Because their yearnings for parental attachment have been frustrated by repeated experiences of abandonment, they avoid dependency on people and fear the consequent repetition of painful rejection. For this reason, neglected children in foster placement initially fend off intimacy with their foster parents and provoke anger in order to avoid becoming emotionally dependent.

The recognition of parental neglect as an important societal problem has been slow in coming for many reasons. One is that most parents feel varying degrees of guilt for not being sufficiently available to their children. In order to avoid awareness of that guilt, they draw upon the public abhorrence of violence as a standard for defining "bad" parenting. Consequently, "bad" parents are not those who neglect children but those who violently or sexually abuse them. This leads to a societal blind spot for parental neglect. Unfortunately, this emphasis on child abuse and silence about neglect has lulled many parents into believing that if they have enjoyable interludes with their children and provide them with material comforts, they are filling their children's needs. As a result, many children are deprived of secure relationships with their parents.

Even for physical abuse, the high public consciousness contrasts with the low level of help that American society affords victims and perpetrators. The interventions for domestic violence also often punish the victims, as seen in the removal of children from their families in response to an abuse or incest situation supposedly to protect the children. Unfortunately, the level of professional help that abusing and neglectful families need is seldom available. Social workers have overwhelming caseloads, and many are not adequately trained for this demanding, frustrating work.

Because the easiest solution for children in crises is transporting them from one house to another, foster care is becoming a massive industry. Although conceived as a temporary solution for families in distress, for many children, foster care extends for years. More grimly, almost 25% of them move from one foster home to another and become unadoptable (Kadushin, 1979). Furthermore, there is a growing incidence of child abuse by foster parents, because some are unqualified and others are overwhelmed by the behavior of their wards. Thus, removing a child from a family often is the result simply of inadequate child welfare resources and the priority family privacy takes over early intervention. Consequently, providing homemaking support that might prevent a parent from becoming desperate does not occur until child abuse or neglect is reported.

The ambivalent public punishment-treatment attitude toward child abuse and neglect can be understood in the context of the evolution of protective services for children in the United States. The child protection movement began more than 100 years ago with the creation of the New York Society for the Prevention of Cruelty to Children, an offshoot of the American Society for the Prevention of Cruelty to Animals (Carstens, 1921). The prevention of cruelty to animals background firmly focused the early child protection movement on the investigation, prosecution, and punishment of those guilty of abusing children.

After the turn of the century, a new direction advocated by the Massachusetts Society for the Prevention of Cruelty to Children stressed treatment rather than law enforcement. As a result, humane societies and private and public family services emerged with the aim of enhancing the conditions of family life and, thereby, preventing child abuse and neglect (Carstens, 1911-1912). After World War II, the treatment approach was altered radically when pediatricians discovered battered children and extended medical intervention into the child welfare area. This called attention to the inability of social service agencies to cope with the growing problems of troubled families, and the physical abuse of children became a national issue.

The medical influence on child protection has had three important effects: (a) the development of a reporting framework around which most legislative activity on child abuse has focused, (b) bringing physicians through hospital-based identification and treatment programs into child abuse cases, and (c) focusing attention on a disease model of physical abuse by emphasizing the injuries to the child and locating the cause in the personality of the abusing parent. As a consequence of this medical influence, attention was deflected from socio-economic and interactional factors (Kadushin & Martin, 1981). The heritage of decades of social work experience that recognized neglect as the greater problem than abuse, and that called for a broad attack on its underlying social structural causes, became itself a victim of neglect.

Solving the problem of child abuse and neglect requires not simply responding to crises but a fundamental realignment of public priorities. First is the recognition that simply conceiving and giving birth to a child does not insure competence to parent that child. Second is recognition that each child must have minimally competent parenting in order to become a productive citizen. Third is recognition that the early identification of, and interventions to help or, when warranted, replace incompetent parents takes priority over a family's right to privacy and a parent's right to rear a child as that parent sees fit. These are challenging questions that evoke strong feelings and constitutional arguments. Nevertheless, the recognition and legal pursuit of children's rights must be brought to bear on these questions.

The answers lie in more effective efforts first to help troubled families and then with deliberate speed to terminate parental rights and find new homes for children in impossible situations. More important are general preventive efforts to increase parental competence, so that families can form community relationships and help themselves.

REFERENCES

Carstens, C. C. (1911-1912). The prevention of cruelty to children. *Proceedings of the Academy of Political Science, 2,* 616-617.

Carstens, C. C. (1921). The development of social work for child protection. *The Annals of the American Academy of Political and Social Science, 98,* 137-141.

Davis, S. M., & Schwartz, M. D. (1987). *Children's Rights and the Law.* Lexington, MA: Lexington Books.

Gordon, L. (1988). *Heroes of Their Own Lives: The Politics and History of Family Violence, Boston 1880-1960.* New York: Viking Press.

Hutchings, N. (1988). *The Violent Family: Victimization of Women, Children, and Elders.* New York: Human Sciences Press.

Kadushin, A. (1979). Children in foster family care and institutions. In H. Mass (Ed.), *Five Fields of Social Work Practice.* New York: National Association of Social Workers.

Kadushin, A., & Martin, J. A. (1981). *Child Abuse: An Interactional Event.* New York: Columbia University Press.

Lane, H., & Pillard, R. (1978). *The Wild Boy of Burundi: A Study of an Outcast Child.* New York: Random House.

Straus, M. A., & Gelles, R. J. (1988). How violent are American families? Estimates from the National Family Violence Resurvey and other studies. In G. T. Hotaling, D. Finkelhor, J. T. Kirkpatrick, & M. A. Straus (Eds.), *Family Abuse and Its Consequences: New Directions in Research.* Newbury Park, CA: Sage.

9

THE CONTEXT OF
CHILD ABUSE AND
NEGLECT ASSESSMENT

James Garbarino

In recent years reports of child abuse and neglect have been increasing because of greater awareness of the problem and mandatory reporting laws that protect professionals from legal vulnerability in so doing.

In both the reporting and assessing of child abuse and neglect, community standards and the expectations of professionals play key roles. Communities vary in the degree of isolation of families and in attitudes toward violence. Parental behavior tolerated in one community may be grounds for intervention in another. The attitude of professionals toward the validity of statements made by children and youths also varies. Finally, the availability of resources is an obvious determinant of whether or not and how professionals respond to child abuse and neglect complaints.

More than for most professional diagnostic activities, the assessment of child abuse is influenced by social, cultural, and personal biases. For this reason information must be gathered from a number of firsthand sources over a period of time. Although helpful, the usual clinical sources of information in the form of interviews, tests, and questionnaires are not sufficient.

The different perspectives of social service, mental health, health, and legal professionals can be integrated by child advocacy teams in order to understand the needs of children and their families when the questions of abuse and neglect are raised.

The assessment of child abuse and neglect is a context for observing the day-to-day realities of "applied child advocacy." The process of assessment brings into play a host of difficult (sometimes intractable) issues of science, law, and epistemology. The process of assessment is bound up in the process of identification and definition. Even to use the term "child abuse and neglect" is to assert a social judgment, a judgment that parental (or other caregiver) behavior is both inappropriate *and* damaging (Garbarino & Gilliam, 1980; Garbarino, Guttmann, & Seeley, 1986). Assessment thus becomes the task of negotiating a publicly verified and validated interpretation of the child's experience with reference to one or more specific adults who are in parental caregiver roles. The concept of child maltreatment reflects an ongoing process of child advocacy designed to upgrade the minimal standards of child care. This is the context in which to understand assessment.

More specifically, assessment is an attempt to do two things: (a) to clarify, explain, and evaluate the relationships among the processes that characterize the child, the family, and their social environment; and (b) to discover how these processes can be used in intervention aimed at replacing maltreating patterns with healthier ones. Assessment, then, becomes the bridge between defining, identifying, and collecting information about the maltreatment of children, on the one hand, and intervening with the community, family, and child, on the other. It casts the practitioner in the role of "applied researcher."

For the assessment to achieve its goals of explaining processes and orienting intervention, we need to consider several issues: the potentials and limits of information; the role of practitioners in ensuring comprehensive assessment; the relationship between the identified characteristics of a case and its assessment; and "borderline cases," where no clear evidence of maltreatment exists.

THE POTENTIALS AND
LIMITS OF INFORMATION

Information serves as the foundation for intervention by

human service delivery systems. As we think about information as a resource in intervention, we must recognize three themes.

1. *Lay and professional expertise are complementary.* Professional knowledge and expertise are limited and vary across and within practitioner groups. Therefore, we need a variety of assessment approaches, ranging from techniques that require a high level of training and expertise to approaches suitable for use by paraprofessionals and nonprofessionals. In some cases even the most simple assessments, those with "face validity," will do the job. A classic illustration came out of World War II "personnel" screening. In developing an instrument for use in assigning military personnel to arctic bases, complex procedures proved unnecessary. A one-item questionnaire did the job: "Do you enjoy working outside in cold weather?" We have analogous findings from the field of child maltreatment.

Henry Kempe (personal communication, 1985) reports that nurses on maternity wards and in delivery rooms can make excellent assessments of the prognosis for maternal functioning. Byron Egeland (personal communication, 1985) found that the best predictor of subsequent maternal functioning was a 3-point scale rated by hospital nurses: "How interested in her baby does the mother seem?" 0 = not interested; 1 = somewhat interested; 2 = very interested. The point here is not that sophisticated assessment instruments are irrelevant, but that we can sometimes make good assessments just by asking simple questions and searching, perceptively, for the answers. "Simple" clinical insight (such as is commonly found among nurses in direct contact with families) may well do the job, particularly when the larger picture includes "objective testing." Thus, it is important to include assessment instruments that vary in degree of sophistication. A comprehensive evaluation of each case requires that we be open to various sources of information.

2. *Maltreatment is often difficult to predict.* Pencil-and-paper questionnaires designed to identify parents who will eventually maltreat their children have proved ineffective. Such instruments can identify most of the pool of families from which actual maltreatment cases will even-

185

tually come. However, there are many mistakes: Some parents who are maltreaters are not identified as such ("false negatives"), and many parents who are not maltreaters are identified as such ("false positives").

No one source of information gathered "objectively" is likely to succeed in screening. Rarely can such pencil-and-paper questionnaires predict which individuals among a high-risk group will actually maltreat their children. Similarly, it is difficult to determine whether or not a parent will continue to maltreat a child (Starr, 1982).

To deal with the challenge of prediction, we must have as much information as possible, and over as long a time span as possible. Such information must encompass the enduring patterns of parental and child behavior, the ways the parent responds to key situations, and the forces in the parent's enduring environment that reinforce and sustain both the patterns of behavior and the facing of key parenting situations. Even with such comprehensive information, we can make only probabilistic statements rather than definitive predictions. The closer the sources of information to the actual conditions of family life, the better the predictive power. This conclusion has important implications for social policy: Good assessment flows from a preventive orientation that reflects a community relationship with every child, every parent, and every family.

3. *Information about child maltreatment is extremely complex.* It consists of both regular feedback on parent-child relations and general knowledge of appropriate norms, expectations, and techniques concerning child rearing. Adequate information depends on three factors: regular observation and discussion of parent-child relations; informal folk wisdom based on extensive, historically validated firsthand experience; and formal, professional expertise, particularly in the area of solving behavior problems. The need for information is related directly to the situational demands of the parent-child relationship. As these demands increase, so does the need for information. An affluent family with a strong marriage and a healthy "easy" child needs less information than a poor, conflicted family with a sick or disabled child. Formal institutions can also become effective sources of information if they are linked to the family's social network,

either directly through the parent or indirectly through the parent's relationship with some other person. Information is a social phenomenon, and its quality increases when it comes out of real insight into the events and meaning of day-to-day experience.

THE ROLE OF
PRACTITIONERS IN ENSURING
COMPREHENSIVE ASSESSMENT

Ideally, maltreatment is assessed by interdisciplinary or multiprofessional teams. These teams might include child welfare workers, social workers, teachers, psychologists, psychiatrists, attorneys, pediatricians, nurses, and paraprofessional staff, depending on the type of agency with which they are affiliated. The major advantage of conducting an assessment in teams is the potential for variety and comprehensiveness: Practitioners can evaluate a case in the light of their own expertise, and ultimately an integrated assessment can emerge from the dynamic of all the individual, professionally unique evaluations.

More specifically, every practitioner uses the techniques that deal with topics in his or her area of expertise, interprets them, and then integrates the conclusion with the conclusions derived from other instruments administered by other professionals. On the basis of these integrated evaluative conclusions, the team determines the direction of intervention and proceeds to plan for it. In agencies where interdisciplinary teams work with cases of maltreatment, each practitioner's role is professionally unique, and the limits of any one approach are balanced by the strengths of the others.

If one message has emerged from the past two decades of clinical work with child maltreatment cases, it is to avoid professional isolation. If a formal interdisciplinary team is not available, professionals should seek informal collaboration. The wisdom of this statement is borne out ever more strongly as child abuse and neglect matures as a field for professional activity. In isolation, the problem of "burnout" intensifies. (For a more complete discussion of this point, see Helfer & Kempe, 1976; Copans et al., 1979).

The role of the practitioner, then, depends on the situation in which assessment occurs. The goal, however, is always to achieve as much comprehensiveness as possible - whether by using a variety of instruments, administering the same instruments to various family and community members, or combining informal family interviews and observation with the formal assessment. The focus of this discussion is the sociological and psychological issues inherent in the process of assessment. For a review of specific procedures, consult a handbook on assessment (e.g., Knoff, 1986). Identification is a conclusion about whether the family meets our definition of maltreatment. Assessment is an exploration of the dynamics of family life as it exists in a community context. The preferred route of assessment arises from the process of identification. It reflects realistic decisions about the availability of professional resources and expertise. Because assessment is an exploration, the route chosen is always open to modification as preliminary efforts yield new insights about family dynamics or community context.

Often a troubled family is identified, but we do not have clear evidence of maltreatment. Yet the family and the children seem troubled, and we somehow sense that maltreatment is occurring or is likely to emerge. In such cases we can proceed with an assessment of the family, the parents, and the children, according to their identified characteristics, as the basis for intervention. Such an intervention will serve as prevention or will work against the maltreatment too subtle or ambiguous to pinpoint in the initial process of identification This approach gives credence to the reality of practitioner insight. It also recognizes that "unsubstantiated" cases are often "in need of services," and that an exploratory assessment may proceed on a "hunch," a "hypothesis," or a feeling. As long as this exploratory assessment guides intervention, it can proceed. Only where there is a blind mechanistic link between identification and intervention (particularly coercive intervention) is action in borderline or ambiguous cases subject to being ethically compromised. But here, as elsewhere, the operative criterion is the well-being of the child rather than a legalistic commitment for formal process.

When we assess the family's social environment, we seek to analyze the degree of isolation and resourcefulness, in contrast to social connectedness and access to social support. As we do so, we seek to answer the following questions:

What are the community's beliefs about the care of children (recognizing the power of values and norms in turning an otherwise deviant experience into an event that is "normal")?

To what extent and how is the family isolated and lacking social resources? What are the environmental factors that tend to increase the family's isolation, poverty, and resourcefulness (remembering that social impoverishment is both a cause of and a constraint on intervention)?

What are the environmental factors that increase the extent and severity of the maltreatment (remembering that the "stress resistance" of children is very much a social phenomenon)?

What is the community's contribution to the family's environmental situation, as compared with the family's own contribution to it (recognizing that both "directions of effect" exist and have ramifications for intervention)?

What pathways can be found, in the community and in the family, that will help in changing their mutual relationships (remembering that social resources are essential to provide the ongoing structural support necessary to sustain changes in family functioning)? (Garbarino et al., 1986, p. 77)

Such an assessment of the family's environmental context is likely to result in an understanding of various environmental processes: those that maintain and facilitate maltreatment; those that have the potential to reduce maltreatment and promote healthy growth patterns; and those that can be utilized for intervention (e.g., key persons who can serve as "natural neighbors" and members of a supportive social network).

This mandate for exploratory assessment as a form of applied child advocacy focuses attention on the adult as a knower, as a recipient of information. This is our principal concern as we examine the assessment of child abuse and neglect.

Do adults have expectations about child abuse? A recent national survey (National Committee for Prevention of Child Abuse [NCPCA], 1987) revealed that 73% of adults believe that "repeated yelling and swearing at a child" often or very often "leads to long-term emotional problems for the child." In contrast, only 41% of adults believe that "physical punishment of a child often or very often leads to injury to the child."

What are the sources of differences in adult hypotheses about the significance of parent-child interactions? Certainly one source is the adult's personal experience with the behavior in question. There is evidence to suggest that people are less likely to recognize treatment as being abusive if it is similar to that which they themselves experienced as children.

Hertzberger and Tennen (1985) interviewed 139 young adults and asked them to respond to a series of hypothetical "disciplinary interactions between parent and child." Each posed a child misbehavior (previously rated according to adult perceptions of "deservedness for punishment") and a parental disciplinary response (one of eight - four emotionally punishing and four physically punishing, all in the moderate to severe range, rated according to previously established assessments by representative adults). Respondents were grouped according to whether or not they reported having experienced a similar interaction as a child. These 139 respondents then rated the parent-child interactions according to whether or not they classified them as abusive. In general, if respondents had experienced a particular form of punishment, they were much *less* likely to define it as abusive, much *less* likely to predict it would have emotional consequences for the child, and *more* likely to define the situation in which punishment was inflicted as the child's fault.

How then do we interpret the Harris poll reported earlier? Does it mean that few adults had childhood experience with parental yelling and swearing, and that most adults were childhood recipients of physical punishment? Perhaps we can say with some certainty that the latter is true. But the former? Although the extent to which parents used to "yell and swear" at their children is unknown, we know that it is relatively common now (Straus, Gelles, & Steinmetz, 1980). Perhaps the answer lies in the current "processing" of such treatment in the mass media (i.e., the communicating of standards through articles providing advice and other definitions of appropriate conduct for parents).

PROFESSIONAL REPORTING ISSUES

These issues are evident in research on professional reporting of child abuse cases. More than 20 years ago Silver and his colleagues (1967) reported that over 20% of the physicians they surveyed said they would not report cases of suspected physical child abuse that came to their attention. More recently, James and his colleagues (1978) found that 62% of a sample of pediatricians and family physicians said they would decline to report a case of sexual abuse brought to their attention unless the family supported making such a report.

In a study of 18 psychiatrists and 83 psychologists, pediatricians, and family counselors, Attias and Goodwin (1984) found that "more than half the psychiatrists" but "less than a third" of the other clinicians said they would not report a family to child protective services (CPS) in the case of an 11-year-old girl who "describes graphically to her school counselor fellatio and cunnilingus with her natural father, ongoing for more than 2 years," if the child later retracted the allegation. The authors link this in part to widespread misunderstanding of the likelihood that such retractions, rather than the original allegations, are false.

Muehleman and Kimmons (1981) found that 81% of the psychologists they studied said they would report the hypothetical physical child abuse case presented by the investigators. This represented an increase from an earlier study by Swoboda and colleagues (1978), in which 87% said they *would not* report the same hypothetical case. In a much more developed form of the same procedure, Williams, Osborne, and Rappaport (1985) used a 4-point scale (4 = certainly would report; 1 = certainly would not report) and randomly offered four different hypothetical cases to a range of professionals (varying types of abuse - psychological or physical - and "privileged" versus "nonprivileged" communication). Nonprivileged communication regarding physical abuse was most likely to result in reporting (average score 3.68). Among the professional groups studied, school nurses and ministers were most likely to report (average score of 3.35 and 3.32 respectively), and psychologists were least likely to report (with an average score of 2.42). Teachers (2.90), psychiatrists (2.87), and physicians (2.85) stood in between these extremes.

Interestingly, on a separate test of knowledge about reporting statutes, ministers scored highest and nurses lowest, suggesting that knowledge of reporting obligations under the laws was not the decisive factor in differentiating among the professional groups. Whether or not the case involved privileged communication (i.e., legally protected information given in the context of therapy) made a significant difference in likelihood of reporting. As the investigators point out, this is particularly interesting in light of the fact that the child abuse reporting statute in the state in which the study was conducted specifically excludes privilege (excepting attorney-client relationship).

We must note here, as we do in all social problems containing a "moral" dimension, that the distance between the hypothetically and socially desirable "should" and the actual day-to-day "do" can be quite large. Chang and his colleagues (1976) reported that, in a survey of 1,367 physicians, over 90% said they agreed with the statement "physicians in your community *should* report cases." Slightly more than half (61%) said "physicians in their community *usually* report cases." About 30% said they had actually seen cases of abuse in the preceding year (1973), but only about one-third of these cases were "referred to a community agency." This suggests that an even smaller number were actually reported to child protective services.

Using the National Incidence Study as a basis for comparison, it seems safe to say that reporting has improved since the 1960s and 1970s. Nonetheless, a recent study of professionals' reporting of sexual abuse cases tells us the issue is still quite live. Using a self-selected sample of professionals with special interest in and/or responsibility for sexual abuse cases in New England, Finkelhor (1984) found that 64% said they reported such cases to protective services when faced with them. The range across professional groups was from 48% (for mental health professionals) to 76% (for school personnel). Who you are (at least institutionally) seems to affect what you do about assessing the seriousness of a case and then reporting it.

EVALUATION OF PERSONAL EXPERIENCE AND EXPECTATIONS

As adults we must always be careful not to let our own *unexamined* personal experiences inappropriately shape our judgments, *one way or the other.* Research on the intergenerational transmission of child abuse (Kaufman & Zigler, 1987) concludes that one of the most important mediators of intergenerational transmission is the degree to which childhood experiences of maltreatment are unprocessed, unexamined, and left to unconscious forces. Miller has explored these issues in *For Your Own Good* (1983) and *Thou Shalt Not Be Aware* (1984). As a result, the intergenerational transmission rate can vary from 5% to more than 75%.

Unprocessed memories of victimization may be a particular problem in the matter of adults assessing cases of sexual abuse. Survey evidence points to a 20%-25% prevalence of sexual abuse among women and a 10% prevalence among men (Finkelhor, 1984). Thus, the odds are quite high that children will be giving information about sexual victimization to adults who have themselves been victimized and (in light of our historical failure to treat victims) have unprocessed memories that can impede accurate evaluation and response. Denial of such experiences, and their relegation to the unconscious, is common.

When fully processed, however, the experience of victimization might well serve as a powerful motivator to help. On the other hand, "naïve" adults might stand somewhere between "processed" and "unprocessed" former victims. They might be less likely to be biased (one way or the other) because of their lack of exposure to sexual victimization. This issue merits further study. It is clear that "bias" (in the sense of predisposition) is an active element in courtrooms and clinics through the often subtle "tone" set by authoritative figures such as judges and physicians. Research (cf. Blanck, 1985) reveals that a judge's attitude, even though not openly expressed, is evident in the tone set when instructing the jury in criminal cases and appears to be capable of *doubling* the likelihood of a jury returning a guilty verdict, at least in cases where the judge's knowledge of a defendant's prior record of felonies is concerned.

Where children are involved, most of the evidence concerns the power of preconceptions to influence outcome via their impact on motivation and responsiveness. Rosenthal (1977) has reviewed 345 studies consistent with such a model of these effects, a model that emphasizes the role of nonverbal cues as the process linking expectations and altered outcomes. That is, believing or expecting certain things to be true about a child leads an adult to change the way he or she treats the child, and leads ultimately to a different outcome for the child. Nonverbal cues to the child seem to be the principle vehicle for this process. Interestingly, women are, on average, more adept at nonverbal cues (Hall, 1985). This finding has implications for understanding why and how children are better information sources for some adults than for others. It suggests a hypothesis to explain why women *generally* are more successful at building rapport with children in clinical interview situations.

How relevant are adult expectations in understanding adult responses to children as sources of information in child abuse allegations? Research by Boat and Everson (1986) testifies to the possibly dramatic importance of such expectations. In their study they surveyed Child Protective Service workers in all 100 counties in North Carolina. The survey focused on rates of substantiation in sexual abuse allegations and on expectations concerning the incidence of false statements about sexual abuse by children and adolescents (i.e., both fictitious accounts and false retractions).

Boat and Everson (1986) reported that of 124 cases involving children under the age of 3, 48% were substantiated (52% were unsubstantiated) and 1.6% were "false reports" among the unsubstantiated (with no retractions). Among the 301 cases involving 3- to 6-year-olds, 60% were substantiated, there was a "false report" incidence of 1.7%, and a false retraction rate of 2.7%. Among the 6- to 12-year-olds, there were 414 cases, with a 55% substantiation rate, 4.3% "false reports," and 5.8% false retractions. Among the 410 adolescent cases there was a substantiation rate of 57%, with an 8.0% lying incidence, and a 5.0% false retraction rate. Note, of course, that the determination that a child's account was a "false report" reflects the protective service investigation.

These age-related differences in the incidence of false reports (some of which may have been "lies") are particularly interesting given three findings about developmental trends in honesty. The first is that "the data for specific tests of overt moral conduct . . . provide little evidence of a continuing development of honesty with age" (Burton, 1976, p. 178). The second is that "the evidence has confirmed the expectation of age-related increases in the complexity of moral thought" (Burton, 1976, p. 179). The third is that researchers have observed a trend toward growing consistency with age: Older children become more consistently honest *or* more consistently dishonest, than younger children (Burton, 1976). To what do we attribute the higher rate of false reports among adolescents?

Among the protective service workers reporting in Boat and Everson's study, some reported a rate of fictitious accounts of 15% or more. This led to a separate study of 24 (of the original 34) workers who had described at least one fictitious report of sexual abuse in their experience. These 24 were randomly matched with 24 of the original respondents who did *not* report detecting a false report in the original survey.

Boat and Everson asked these workers to report on their *expectations* about the frequency of lying by children and adolescents in allegations about sexual abuse. They asked: "Suppose you saw 100 children . . . who said they had been sexually abused. On average, how many of those children do you think would be lying or not telling the truth about the abuse?" They asked this question for each of the following categories: "below age 3," "3 to 6," "6 to 12," and "12 to 18 years old."

Within the group of 46 workers, the average expectation of lying across all age groups was 8.7%. It averaged 4.3% for under

3-year-olds, 2.7% for 3- to 6-year-olds, 6.6% for 6- to 12-year-olds, and 15.8% for 12- to 18-year-olds (with the most significant comparison being between adolescents and all other ages). This gives some baseline for professional expectations about children as sources of information in the important matter of child sexual abuse allegations. This is not the whole story, however.

The workers who had actually reported lying *expected higher rates* of lying by children than those who did not report having had an experience of a child lying. Overall, they expected 12.2% of children alleging sexual abuse to be lying, versus 5.2% from those who did not report having had a child lie. This difference was particularly evident for expectations about adolescents (19.6% vs. 11.9%, respectively). The most interesting finding in Boat and Everson's analysis is that those who reported having had a child lie had an overall substantiation rate of 47.8% in the previous year, as opposed to a rate of 69.4% for those who did not report a case of a child lying. The differences between the two groups (i.e., those who reported fictitious accounts and those who did not) did not seem to derive from years of service as a protective service worker, number of cases of sexual abuse dealt with, or perceived comfort in dealing with such cases.

Boat and Everson offer the following conclusion based upon their study: "We believe that these findings suggest that many CPS workers may have difficulty believing that children tell the truth when they report sexual abuse. Rather than beginning an investigation with the attitude that the child is to be believed unless there is convincing evidence to the contrary, these workers seem to view the child, and especially the adolescent, with a great deal of suspicion. A retraction is then accepted, not as a predictable phase of the disclosure process, but as evidence that the child is lying, confirming the worker's worst suspicions" (p. 6). Some adults begin with the working hypothesis that "children often lie about sexual abuse," and others start with the hypothesis that "children rarely lie about sexual abuse." *Both* of these are more valid than "children always lie about sexual abuse" or "children never lie about sexual abuse." But the truth of the matter is probably closer to the belief that "children rarely lie about sexual abuse." In the Boat and Everson study it is not possible to be sure about the direction of effects. Did one group expect more lies because they encountered more liars? Or did they believe they encountered more liars because they expected more lies? Once "burned" by a false report, a worker may be much more skeptical in the future. Once having dismissed a true account, a worker may bend over backwards to avoid the same mistake in the future.

This report from the field leads us to consider the results of laboratory studies conducted by Mahoney (1986) dealing with the processes adults use in confirming and discarding hypotheses. Mahoney's research has dealt with factors that influence the strength of convictions about hypotheses, and its relevance to our concerns should become apparent in light of Boat and Everson's study.

Mahoney (1986) has conducted and reviewed research on the tendency to select and reinforce evidence that conforms to our hypotheses about the world. In laboratory studies, subjects remained certain that their hypothesis was correct after 20 trials, even though only 50% of their predictions were confirmed by the evidence. Mahoney notes that, "Even more interesting was the finding that *subjects tended to consider positive results as valid and negative results as invalid.* They rated 94% of their successes as valid tests, while they rated only 25% of the disconfirming results as being valid" (p. 5). Two-thirds of the participants rated all their successful outcomes as valid, an example of what Mahoney calls "confirmatory bias."

That "confirmatory bias" operates in the assessment of child and abuse seems extremely likely. How? DePaulo and Pfeifer (1986) report that one such area is the selective success of professional interrogators in discerning lies. DePaulo and Pfeifer had college students and police investigators listen to audiotapes of 16 people's statements, each of which contained two lies and two truths. The two groups were equally unable to discriminate between truths and lies in this situation, but the police were more confident of their judgments. The more experienced police officers became more confident of their judgments as the test progressed. These results parallel Starr's findings (1982) in studying the inability of professionals (and students) to identify abusive parents on the basis of a brief observation.

Interestingly, Starr (1982) reported that psychiatrists achieved a success rate lower than chance (and lower than that attained by college students and nurses). Perhaps the professional confidence of the police and the psychiatrists stems from similar origins (e.g., peer support in the absence of empirical validation) and thrives when information is fragmentary and selective perception of results is possible. We must bear in mind that confirmatory bias can imply both that some adults will invariably reject accounts given by children, and that others invariably *accept* accounts given by children. Both are threats to the integrity of the assessment process. There are two points to be made here, however. The first is that it is extremely difficult to make valid assessments on the basis of tiny samples of behavior (or in only one modality, as in the case of the audiotapes). The second is that any of us, including professionals, may overestimate our ability, be inappropriately confident of our ability, and overvalue our own "hypotheses" about what we see and hear. These "hypotheses" may do a disservice to the needs of children and the pursuit of truth. This is certainly consistent with recent evidence disputing the validity of the customary interview of the child by a trial judge to determine the child's competence to testify. The *voir dire* appears to be of very limited validity (Melton, 1986).

Adult hypotheses about children as sources of information are embedded in institutional policy, in community ideology, and in individual psychology. Some examples will serve to illustrate this contention, at least with respect to the veracity of children.

Institutional Policy. Until recently, children (unlike adults) were presumed incompetent to testify in court unless proven otherwise. The guiding "hypothesis" was that children are unreliable witnesses in general, and that the good child witness is a rare exception. As several historical reviews make clear (e.g., Bross & Michaels, 1987; Melton, 1986), there has been a strong confirmatory bias at work. In Michigan, for example, police routinely ordered polygraph (lie detector) tests for child witnesses. Over 147 were administered with only one child failing the test before the practice was abandoned (Melton, 1981). How well would adults have fared under such a policy?

Community Ideology. Fueled by an overextension of Freud's psychoanalytic model of child seduction fantasies (or even misled by Freud's own work - cf. Masson, 1984), many professionals have assumed that the preponderance of sexual abuse allegations made by children (particularly girls) are fictitious, and result from seduction fantasies. The tenacity with which this "hypothesis" is held seems all the more interesting in light of studies demonstrating the empirical rarity of *child-initiated* fictitious allegations. The most commonly cited recent study is Jones and McGraw's (1987) analysis of 309 allegations, only 45 of which were found to be fictitious (when evaluated by staff predisposed to believe them or at least without a strong bias against them). The fictitious allegations were of two types: 36 were *adult-initiated* false allegations (typically involving custody disputes, many by adults who had themselves been sexually abused), and 9 were false allegations by adolescents who had been sexually assaulted on some earlier occasion. False allegations that are taken seriously are apparently rare.

In contrast, Benedek and Schetky (1985) report that only 8 of the 18 cases in their study of *adult-initiated* allegations of sexual abuse in the context of a custody dispute could be confirmed. Many child protective service units now shy away from such cases because of this problem. One result, of course, may be to leave some children at heightened risk for victimization because adults have retreated from a commitment to investigate all allegations.

Are children likely to lie and fantasize about sexual abuse *on their own*? One view says no: "The fantasy of young children is so inextricably interwoven with actual experience, so reflective of wishful thinking and pleasure principle material, so likely to have mastery as a theme, and so easily differentiated from reality, that sexual abuse is not likely to be a theme of the fantasy in the first place, and therefore, will not be the stuff of lies" (deYoung, 1986, p. 557). The classical Freudian view asserts "seduction fantasy" as a plausible, common source of false allegations about sexual *abuse*.

How do we reconcile these positions? Perhaps the bridge between these two contradictory viewpoints is the finding that *real* traumatic stress can produce negative fantasies - a "post-traumatic stress syndrome" - that *can* generate false allegations subsequent to actual assault (and thus explain Jones and Mc-Graw's findings of adolescent victims falsely asserting new victimization). Severe trauma can and does produce negative fantasy, even in young children (Terr, 1983). This view is actually consistent with one rendering of Freud's view, namely that his female patients had been sexually assaulted, and that "seduction fantasies" were the *result* of these real traumatic experiences.

Individual Psychology. One important source of adult confirmatory bias is unconscious cognitive processing as evidenced by denial and repression. Denial and repression play important roles in adult psychology, particularly in sexual matters, and can thus influence the process of assessment. Recent developments in neuroscience have begun to document not only the existence of unconscious filtering of information, but the processes involved as well (Goleman, 1986). Although they have questioned the exact sequence of mechanisms proposed by Freud for this censoring process, contemporary students of cognitive science have validated the existence of unconscious and preconscious censorial processes.

Zajonc (1984) has demonstrated that even when a person is not aware of having perceived something (such as a geometric shape flashed on the screen), the unconscious reception and storage of that information can influence later behavior (e.g., which shape is chosen from among a group containing the original "unseen" one). This perceptual filtering of affectively neutral information is not the whole story, of course.

In a process that takes only tenths of a second, unconscious processors can screen out (from conscious awareness) upsetting or troubling information. In the words of one popular review: "Our capacity to deceive ourselves seems to depend upon our ability to deflect attention away from whatever might be too troubling to face" (Goleman, 1987, p. 28). That child sexual abuse is a prime candidate should come as no surprise, for few things are more threatening. One veteran (Summit, 1986) of dealing with child sexual abuse puts it this way:

> What makes the issues so difficult is not their power but their paradox. Most of us are survivors of childhood. We are intimidated and embarrassed by the shadows of our past. It was good to become enlightened, imperative to become strong and sure, vital to replace fearful feelings with comforting beliefs. It is normal to be an adult. It is healthy to take charge. It is necessary to *know*. Who can dare slip back to experience the feelings and vulnerabilities of a dependent child? (pp. xii-xiii)

Besides all those basic growth and power issues, each of us is challenged in our personal beliefs and loyalties. If we are loyal and respectful to the memorial image of our own parents, and if we are protective of appropriate hierarchies of enlightenment and power, can those securities stand the test of believing that a pediatrician has molested a patient or that a father has sodomized his own 3-year-old? If mothers are vital to our experience of caring and being cared for, can we contemplate that a woman could enjoy forcing feces into the mouth of her infant? And could such a woman be at the same time the trusted organizer of a parent cooperative pre-school? Most of us insist that she would be found, if at all, only in Bedlam.

Even beyond the challenge to positive anchors of security, sexual abuse of young children assaults our psychological defenses. Anyone betrayed and molested by loving caretakers in childhood will try to establish a protective mythology: "They were right and good; I was bad and provoked my own suffering (and if I could only learn to be good they would love me)." By learning to be hyperalert and intuitively sensitive to clues of displeasure, abused children can learn to protect adults and to scapegoat themselves, making reasonable order out of intolerable chaos. An adult survivor of such a childhood may be very good at helping others in distress even while despising the child who elicits that distress. Many practitioners in the helping professions are themselves victims, hidden even from themselves. Some will be incapable of empathy with abused children. Others, further along in their partial recovery from abuse, can feel only for the children and against the offenders. Child sexual abuse gives new meaning to the old adage "Physician, heal thyself."

The use of denial in dealing with information from children is not homogeneous or universal, of course. Although every consciousness is shielded by a censoring unconsciousness to some degree, some are more shielded than others. Beyond issues of technique in assessing child abuse we must address our own censoring processes. We owe that openness to abused and neglected children if we are to advocate for them from a position of knowledge and unambiguous confidence. This demands that we restructure the protective service systems to include a preventive orientation. Such an orientation would legalize and normalize the flow of information to and from families. If the community demonstrates its relationship with children early and often, then the assessment process can occur early, naturally, and in a context of support rather than investigation of allegations. Protective services should be child advocacy rather than law enforcement.

REFERENCES

Attias, R., & Goodwin, J. (1984, September). *Knowledge and Management Strategies in Incest Cases: A Survey of Physicians, Psychologists, and Family Counselors.* Paper presented to the Fifth International Congress on Child Abuse and Neglect, Montreal, Canada.

Benedek, E. P., & Schetky, D. H. (1985). Allegations of sexual abuse in child custody and visitation disputes. In D. H. Schetky & K. P. Benedek (Eds.), *Emerging Issues in Child*

Psychiatry and the Law (pp. 160-175). New York: Brunner Mazel.

Blanck, P. (1985, November). The appearance of justice: Judges' verbal and nonverbal behavior in criminal jury trials. *The Stanford Law Review, 38,* 89-164.

Boat, B. W., & Everson, M. D. (1986). *Using Anatomical Dolls: Guidelines for Interviewing Young Children in Sexual Abuse Investigations.* Chapel Hill, NC: University of North Carolina.

Bross, D., & Michaels, L. (1987). *Foundations of Child Advocacy.* Longmont, CA: Bookmakers Guild.

Burton, R. (1976). Honesty and dishonesty. In T. Lickona (Ed.), *Moral Development and Behavior: Theory, Research, and Social Issues* (pp. 173-197). New York: Holt, Rinehart & Winston.

Chang, A., Oglesby, A., Wallace, H., Goldstein, H., & Hexter, A. (1976). Child abuse and neglect: Physicians knowledge, attitudes and experiences. *American Journal of Public Health, 66,* 1199-1201.

Copans, S., Krell, H., Grundy, J., Rogen, J., & Field, F. (1979). The stress of treating child abuse. *Children Today, 8,* 22-27.

DePaulo, B., & Pfeifer, R. (1986). On-the-job experience and skill at detecting deception. *Journal of Applied Social Psychology, 16,* 249-267.

deYoung, M. (1986). A conceptual model for judging the truthfulness of a young child's allegation of sexual abuse. *American Journal of Orthopsychiatry, 56,* 550-559.

Finkelhor, D. (1984). *Child Sexual Abuse.* New York: Free Press.

Garbarino, J., & Gilliam, G. (1980). *Understanding Abusive Families.* Lexington, MA: Lexington Books.

Garbarino, J., Guttmann, E., & Seeley, J. (1986). *The Psychologically Battered Child.* San Francisco: Jossey-Bass.

Goleman, D. (1986). *Vital Lies, Simple Truths: The Psychology of Self-Deception.* New York: Simon & Schuster.

Goleman, D. (1987, March). Who are you kidding? *Psychology Today,* 24-30.

Hall, J. (1985). *Nonverbal Sex Differences.* Baltimore: Johns Hopkins Press.

Helfer, R., & Kempe, C. H. (1976). *Child Abuse and Neglect: The Family and the Community.* Cambridge, MA: Ballinger.

Hertzberger, S. D., & Tennen, H. (1985). The effect of self-relevance on judgements of moderate and severe disciplinary encounters. *Journal of the American Medical Association, 240,* 1145-1146.

James, J., Womack, W. M., & Strauss, F. (1978). Physicians' reporting of sexual abuse of children. *Journal of the American Medical Association, 240,* 1145-1146.

Jones, D. P. H., & McGraw, J. M. (1987). Reliable and fictitious accounts of sexual abuse in children. *Journal of Interpersonal Violence, 2,* 27-45.

Kaufman, J., & Zigler, E. (1987). Do abused children become abusive parents? *American Journal of Orthopsychiatry, 57,* 186-192.

Knoff, H. (Ed.). (1986). *The Psychological Assessment of Child and Adolescent Personality.* New York: Guilford.

Mahoney, M. (1986, May 28). *Self-Deception in Science.* Paper presented at the annual meeting of the American Association for the Advancement of Science, Philadelphia, PA.

Masson, J. M. (1984). *The Assault on Truth: Freud's Suppression of the Seduction Theory.* New York: Farrar, Straus & Giroux.

Melton, G. (1981). Children's competency to testify. *Law and Human Behavior, 5,* 73-85.

Melton, G. (1986). Litigation in the interest of children: Does anybody win? *Law and Human Behavior, 10,* 337-353.

Miller, A. (1983). *For Your Own Good: Hidden Cruelty in Children and the Roots of Violence.* New York: Farrar, Straus & Giroux.

Miller, A. (1984). *Thou Shalt Not Be Aware.* New York: Farrar, Straus, and Giroux.

Muehleman, T., & Kimmons, C. (1981). Psychologists' views on child abuse reporting, confidentiality, life, and the law: An exploratory study. *Professional Psychology, 12,* 631-638.

National Committee for Prevention of Child Abuse. (1987). *Public Attitudes and Actions Regarding Child Abuse and Its Prevention.* The Results of a Louis Harris Public Opinion Poll, Chicago, IL.

Pennebaker, J. (1982). *The Psychology of Physical Symptoms.* New York: Springer-Verlag.

Rosenthal, R. (1977). Biasing effects of experiments. *Etc., 34,* 253-264.

Silver, L., Barton, W., & Dublin, C. (1967). Child abuse laws: Are they enough? *Journal of the American Medical Association, 199,* 65-68.

Starr, R. H. (Ed.). (1982). *Child Abuse Prediction: Policy Implications.* Cambridge, MA: Ballinger.

Straus, M., Gelles, R., & Steinmetz, S. (1980). *Behind Closed Doors*. Garden City, NY: Doubleday.

Summit, R. in McFarlane, K. (1986). Foreword. *Sexual Abuse of Young Children: Evaluation & Treatment* (pp. i-xv). New York: Guilford.

Swoboda, J., Elwork, A., Sales, B., & Levine, D. (1978). Knowledge of and compliance with privileged communication and child abuse reporting laws. *Professional Psychology, 9,* 448-457.

Terr, L. (1983). Life attitudes, dreams, and psychic trauma in a group of "normal" children. *Journal of the American Academy of Child Psychiatry, 22,* 221-230.

Williams, H., Osborne, Y., & Rappaport, N. (1985). *Child Abuse Reporting Laws: Professionals' Knowledge and Compliance*. Unpublished manuscript, Louisiana State University, Baton Rouge, LA.

Zajonc, R. (1984). On the primacy of affect. *American Psychologist, 39,* 117-123.

203

10

INTERVENTIONS IN
CHILD ABUSE AND NEGLECT

Patricia A. Schene

*Protective services for children exist in every state to re-
ceive reports of child abuse and neglect from professionals,
friends, relatives, and neighbors. Patricia Schene points
out, however, that we have placed social service agencies,
families, and children in a no-win situation. We mandate
the acceptance of reports and the provision of services.
However, as increasing numbers of reports pour in, we fail
to provide a proportional increase in services. We then
criticize the agencies for the high number of unsubstantiated reports and for the failure to provide quality services.*

*Because efforts have been focused on case finding
rather than on diagnostic and treatment services, the advocacy steps of identifying the needs of the affected children
and families and then meeting them often are not effectively carried out. We have created a system for monitoring
parental failure rather than for helping families succeed.*

INTRODUCTION

Over 2.1 million children were reported to child protection
agencies nationwide in 1986 (American Association for Protecting Children, 1988; see Figure 1, page 206), and many more were
abused and neglected but not reported. More than 98% of
Americans now view child abuse as a serious social problem, but

205

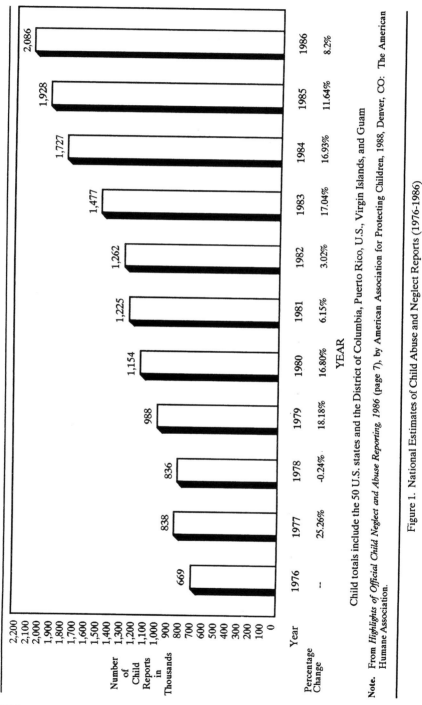

Year	1976	1977	1978	1979	1980	1981	1982	1983	1984	1985	1986
Number of Child Reports in Thousands	669	838	836	988	1,154	1,225	1,262	1,477	1,727	1,928	2,086
Percentage Change	--	25.26%	-0.24%	18.18%	16.80%	6.15%	3.02%	17.04%	16.93%	11.64%	8.2%

YEAR

Child totals include the 50 U.S. states and the District of Columbia, Puerto Rico, U.S., Virgin Islands, and Guam

Figure 1. National Estimates of Child Abuse and Neglect Reports (1976-1986)

Note. From *Highlights of Official Child Neglect and Abuse Reporting, 1986* (page 7), by American Association for Protecting Children, 1988, Denver, CO: The American Humane Association.

we have not yet seen an effective advocacy effort resulting in resources to protect children from abuse and neglect and strengthen family functioning.

It is clear our reporting systems do not capture all the cases. The 1980 and 1986 National Incidence Studies (Westat Associates, 1987) found that for every one case substantiated by public child protective services (CPS), there are almost two others known to professionals in their communities but not identified to CPS. These two cases are of equal or greater severity than the one reported.

A study undertaken in 1986 by Murray Straus of the University of New Hampshire and Richard Gelles of the University of Rhode island through a Louis Harris telephone survey estimated that, based on parental admission, 1.5 million children over 3 years old from two-parent families were subjected to very severe violence in 1985 (Gelles & Straus, 1987). This appears to be a conservative estimate in that data from single-parent households were not included, the parents had to identify their own behavior, and the survey did not address other forms of child maltreatment, such as sexual abuse and physical neglect. At the same time, this very conservative estimate of 1.5 million children severely physically abused is 700% greater than the sum total of cases of physical injury - mild as well as severe - documented by CPS agencies nationwide in 1984.

The dimensions of the problem are truly staggering. What do we have in place to respond? The "intervention system" can be broadly conceptualized to include all official and nonofficial ways we respond to children who are abused and neglected. The more formal part of that system involves at least child protective services (a public agency function existing in every county's department of social services), law enforcement, the court system (both juvenile and criminal), district attorneys, lawyers representing parents and children, the medical community, hospital emergency rooms, mental health and other local community agencies providing treatment services, schools, and the foster care system. This is quite an impressive apparatus, yet in most communities the "intervention system" is not truly adequate to the challenge of protecting children.

Resources are, of course, an issue, but it is not simply a resource issue. We have not yet made the political decisions about the nature and extent of our commitment. Nor have we truly sorted out some boundary issues. Problems not adequately addressed include: the relationship between chronic neglect and severe poverty; when the rights of truly inadequate parents need to be sacrificed to the rights of children to be protected from maltreatment; and how to find and fund supportive alternative homes for children when their parents cannot provide the care. These are just a few examples of our unfinished mandate and the tentativeness of our commitment.

THE INTERVENTION SYSTEM -
CHILD PROTECTIVE SERVICES

In every state there are agencies responsible by law to receive reports of child abuse and neglect from concerned professionals, friends, relatives, and neighbors. These agencies investigate the reports and, if warranted, plan for services to the children and families reported. The focus of child protective services' initial intervention is not primarily on the investigation, but on what is needed by the child and family. The questions to be answered are not only "Did it happen," but "What can be done to make this situation safe for this child?" Law enforcement officials often will be involved in their own investigation, particularly in cases of severe physical abuse or sexual abuse. The focus of their work is quite different - it is to determine if charges should be brought against the alleged perpetrator. There may also be a simultaneous medical evaluation both to ascertain the nature of the injury and to provide treatment.

If child protective services are warranted, the next step is usually to have the caseworker develop a service plan outlining the goals of intervention and the service resources to be accessed within the department of social services as well as the community at large. Service resources vary tremendously: Some communities have the capacity to immediately assign a parent aide to the family; others can offer only a 6-month waiting list for even basic mental health evaluation services to children who have been sexually abused.

A common situation currently is the growing inability to provide casework services beyond the initial investigation unless the court has ordered protective supervision. Even then, the lack of resources often results in "monitoring" families rather than providing services. *We often are monitoring parental failure rather than helping families succeed.* In many places there are no appropriate services available for some children and families involved in abuse and neglect. In one major state it is the *goal* of the CPS program to serve 43% of the substantiated cases. The other 57% cannot be served. This situation is not unique, only uniquely admitted and thus made visible. The inadequacy of resources is apparent in most communities, resulting in what some refer to as "agency supervised neglect." The case is substantiated, remains open, but no treatment resources are applied.

The intervention system just described has assumed that the child remains in his or her home. More than 70% of the children on substantiated cases do remain at home. These children, at least initially, are not placed outside their homes even on an emergency basis. An even smaller percentage of abused and neglected children go into foster care. Services to prevent placement are the preferred way of strengthening families and protecting children. Yet the majority of the children in foster homes in the United States are placed because of abuse or neglect.

HOW DID THE
PRESENT SYSTEM DEVELOP?

The maltreatment of children is not a phenomenon of the 20th century. Early history records children as victims of abandonment, maiming, torture, and infanticide. The value placed on a child was equated with rights of "chattel" or "property," and, as such, children were within the exclusive control of their parents in many cultures.

It was not until the 19th century, characterized by social reform, that for the first time it was recognized that parents' rights in relation to their children were not limitless. In the 19th century, concerns about the welfare of children were not well articulated. What intervention existed was largely private - family, friends, and neighbors. Toward the end of the century, local societies developed to protect children from cruelty.

THE "MARY ELLEN CASE"

The Mary Ellen Case in New York in 1874 resulted in the first case law granting children a right to be free from unreasonable physical discipline.

Mrs. Wheeler was called by a woman dying of tuberculosis. Through this woman she heard the story of a child being beaten by her relatives and of her crying in the next room. Mrs. Wheeler first turned to the police, who said there was no proof of a crime. She then went to the New York Department of Charities, which refused aid on the grounds that the agency did not have legal custody of the child. She then went to Henry Bergh, founder and president of the Society for the Prevention of Cruelty to Animals. Bergh responded that Mary Ellen should have "the same rights as the stray cur in the street." Bergh acquired a lawyer by the name of Elbridge T. Gerry (1837-1927), and the case went to court in April, 1874.

Jacob Riis, a young police reporter, wrote in his report, "I saw a child brought in, carried in a horse blanket, at the sight of which men wept aloud, and I heard the story of little Mary Ellen told again, that stirred the soul of a city and roused the conscience of a world that had forgotten; and as I looked, I knew I was where the first chapter of the children's rights was being written."

Mary Ellen's testimony gives some insights into the dynamics of isolation and lack of knowledge operating in child neglect and abuse. She stated, "I don't know how old I am . . . I have never been allowed to go out of the room . . . I have never been allowed to play with children . . . Mama has been in the habit of whipping and beating me almost every day . . . I never know for what I was whipped. Mama never said anything . . . ."

AGENCIES FOR PROTECTING CHILDREN

As a result of the Mary Ellen case, the Society for Prevention of Cruelty to Children was founded in 1875 in New York City. A number of local agencies were started in other cities, and by 1877 they met to form The American Humane Association, which became the leading agency for setting standards for the protection of both animals and children since that time.

The orientation of these early interventions was toward "rescuing" children from their families. Children were taken off the streets of New York City and Chicago, for example, and brought to farms in the midwest.

Local private societies for the protection of children developed in many communities, particularly in the northeast and midwest in the early 20th century. The depression of the 1930s forced the closure of many of them; law enforcement and public welfare agencies endeavored to protect children when voluntary agencies were unavailable. The first county to establish a public responsibility for the protection of neglected and abused children was Hennepin County, Minnesota, in 1944. It was not until the 1960s, under the Social Security Act, that federal funds became available to states that established child protective services.

As we progressed into the 20th century, child protection became more family oriented. *Rather than rescuing the child from the family, the hope was to rescue the family for the child.* As we moved from the private to the governmental sector as the leading source of intervention, the words of Vincent de Francis, the Director Emeritus of the American Humane Association, that child protective services should be "child-centered and family-focused," made their way into the laws passed by many states in the 1950s and 1960s mandating the reporting of child abuse and neglect. This remains the value basis for our work; it is hard to be for children without also supporting families.

REPORTING LAWS

Another milestone in protective services practice occurred almost simultaneously in the 1960s. Improved radiology had enabled radiologists and orthopedists to refine diagnostic skills. As a result, children were increasingly being seen at hospitals with injuries of a suspicious nature, incompatible with the history offered by the parent. In addition, injured children were being shunted from hospital to hospital by parents to prevent a diagnosis of a pattern of repeated abuse. The medical profession and the few remaining private child protective service professionals were consequently alarmed by the lack of protection for these neglected and abused children. Lobbying fostered the passage of reporting laws, mandating medical professionals to report suspicion of "nonaccidental" injuries, which in turn would activate the child protective service inquiry.

Over the years reporting laws have increased the classes of individuals who are required to report and have expanded to include reports of all forms of suspected maltreatment. Today all 50 states have mandatory reporting laws.

As public awareness of child abuse and neglect grew, reporting increased considerably. Between 1976 and 1986 reports of child abuse increased 212% nationally. A great deal of attention has been drawn to the problem, and yet, in the past few years, intervention in child maltreatment has become increasingly controversial.

WHY HAS INTERVENTION
IN CHILD ABUSE AND NEGLECT
BECOME SO CONTROVERSIAL?

A generation ago the direction to be taken to protect children from abuse and neglect seemed clear. Laws had to be written defining and proscribing child maltreatment. A process to report neglect and abuse needed to be established. A system of services needed to be developed and expanded to intervene to protect children and work with families. It was clear that without a process of reporting, and in the absence of expanded specialized services to respond to the cases identified, children would remain unprotected. With clear direction from a concerned public, the "system" of laws, central registries, and child protective services was put in place. Once again, as a country, we saw a need and responded.

We now seem to be in a more "mature" stage of development. Decision making about the future requires careful judgments as we pick a course through what sometimes seem to be conflicting currents. On the one hand, we learn of ever-increasing numbers of children being reported, the burden on existing CPS systems that are largely underfunded and understaffed, and the uncovering of "new" areas of child maltreatment in institutions, day care centers, and so on. On the other hand, some are alarmed at the level of "unwarranted" intervention into private family affairs under the banner of protecting children.

Some of the crucial areas of current controversy facing the field are (a) the proportion of unsubstantiated reports, (b) the potential conflict in parental rights versus children's rights, (c) the futility of trying to reduce abuse and neglect, (d) the inadequacy of our current intervention system, and (e) the costs of truly protecting our children. In presenting some considerations related to each of these issues, a framework for advocacy emerges.

UNSUBSTANTIATED REPORTS

There is a tremendous concern that the high levels of "unsubstantiated" reports suggest inappropriate interference in family life or, at minimum, a clear waste of social service resources in conducting fruitless investigations. The national reporting data analyzed at The American Humane Association reveal that each year slightly more than half of the reports are not able to be substantiated. It is not always possible to counter parental denial with clear evidence. There is often no "evidence" in cases of sexual abuse; and even in cases of physical abuse, injuries cannot always be clearly attributed to abuse. Additionally, when there is no reason to open a case, either because the parents are truly willing to change, or if needed services are simply not available, the report in some places is not substantiated. Sometimes it is difficult to locate the family, or there are not enough staff persons to do a thorough investigation. In these cases also the report could not be substantiated. For all these reasons, an unsubstantiated report cannot be considered synonymous with a false report.

It is extremely misleading to use substantiation statistics as a measure of the "true" amount of reported child abuse and neglect. Issues *other* than "did it happen?" affect the rate of substantiated cases. Studies indicate that factors such as the volume of cases reported to child protective service agencies, time spent on the investigation, who reported the case, resources available in the community, and variations in policy and practice are among those which may affect whether a report is confirmed.

Although the national rate of substantiated reports hovers at 40% of total reporting, there is a disturbing range of rates between states, and even among the counties of any one state. For example, the county substantiation rate within one relatively homogeneous state varied from 20% to 80%. This variation suggests factors extrinsic to the cases themselves that affect the substantiation decision.

To focus our public concern only on the rate of substantiation is short-sighted. We then fail to address (a) those unsubstantiated reports which are indeed at risk and do not receive services, (b) those substantiated cases which receive no services or inadequate services, and (c) those identified cases of maltreatment which are never reported to the local CPS agency.

We have placed our local agencies, families, and children in a no-win situation. We mandate both acceptance of reports and the provision of services; when reports pour in, we fail to provide a proportional increase in services or clear decision-making criteria for which cases will remain unserved. We then criticize the agencies for the high number of unsubstantiated reports and the failure to provide "quality" services. We become disenchanted, and families and children needing protection are the losers.

Since the substantiation decision is the principal mechanism for intervention into the lives of families, it is indeed relevant to be concerned about the quality of that decision. The concern, however, should not be restricted to the cases where intervention occurs, but also where it does not. Moreover, the concern about the "unsubstantiated" cases needs to go beyond a simplistic assumption of "false reporting" to a fuller recognition of the need for consistency in standards, decision rules, and the wider need for resources to adequately respond to abused and neglected children and their families.

PARENTS' RIGHTS VERSUS CHILDREN'S RIGHTS

To some extent the issue of parents' rights versus children's rights goes back to the beginning of time or at least to the initiation of a public response to child maltreatment. Yet it possesses increased currency in today's political climate.

In our society we believe parents have the right to raise their children according to their own values and beliefs. This right connotes a responsibility and cannot be considered a license to harm. There are minimal standards of care for children that are basic to their protection and development.

To be advocates for children, we must be advocates for families. Children require functioning families to grow adequately. The good news is that most parents do want to provide adequate care; and with supportive services, most of those involved with abuse and neglect can learn to be the best source of protection for their children.

It is in all of our interests, across the political spectrum, to have well-functioning families; the controversy around this subject today is really not so much one of parents' rights as it is one of confidence with the decision-making capacities of our systems of intervention.

CAN WE REALLY HELP CHILDREN AND
FAMILIES INVOLVED IN ABUSE AND NEGLECT?

There are numerous empirical studies documenting the value of intervention. Many formerly abusive parents are now functioning well due to the intervention of child protective services. Of course, the content of the intervention makes a great difference, but it is an incontrovertible fact that we *can* protect children and strengthen families. The clients themselves have testified to the value of intervention in improving their ability to parent effectively. The area of prevention is also very promising. As we establish more prevention programs through trust funds and local community organizing we see evidence of progress.

ADEQUACY OF OUR CURRENT
SYSTEM OF INTERVENTION

It is clear that many children suffering from abuse and neglect are not reported; many of those who are identified do not receive the quality response necessary to turn their situations around. Looking only at cases both reported and substantiated, the volume has vastly outstripped the available resources. The United States House of Representatives Select Committee on Children, Youth and Families noted a 55% increase in reporting between 1980 and 1985, but only a 2% increase in resources at federal, state, and local levels combined (U.S. House of Representatives Select Committee, 1987). We have been uncovering a problem that is much more widespread than many believed. The Gelles-Straus survey (1987), which revealed a level of severe physical violence against children 700% greater than substantiated by CPS systems, also found that this level represented a significant drop over the decade. We can simultaneously be making real progress in reducing child maltreatment and increasing reporting rates because so many cases are being identified which would have remained hidden a decade earlier. What this means is that the value of our current intervention efforts may not be felt until a future time when the fruits of primary and secondary prevention efforts are manifested. At that point, increased reporting would clearly be identifying an increased incidence of child maltreatment, rather than simply initial identification. Obviously, much depends on the resources we commit to the families and children involved in abuse or neglect.

What we currently do for the cases identified is a serious concern. Too often our limited resources support the investigation of the report and the placement of the child, but do little for those children who remain at home. The most successful intervention programs are based on a serious commitment of both time and resources to serving children and families. Research has shown this usually requires at least 6 months of effort by a combination of CPS and other community services, well-targeted to the particular needs of each family. This is a luxury for most communities.

CAN WE AFFORD WHAT IS NEEDED?

So much of the current "controversy" regarding child protection intervention is informed by real doubts as to whether we are willing to tax ourselves sufficiently to truly protect children from abuse and neglect. This certainly is a legitimate issue to address, considering public policies over the recent past. There are some hopeful signs; public opinion polls recently found Americans becoming "more compassionate" regarding social problems and less sustained by pursuing higher levels of personal material well-being. This may be one of those "windows of opportunity" for child advocates to clearly demonstrate the value and efficacy of intervention.

We need to not only clearly define a national consensus on what intervention in child protection must include, but also contribute to a public climate of sustained commitment. There are no "quick fixes." We Americans tend to believe we have a large social agenda demanding our limited resources and would, therefore, like to feel justified in diverting these resources to other social problems as we "solve" child abuse. Moving from one "quick fix" to another has characterized much of our public policy approaches in the area of human services and, in my opinion, has contributed to the enormous weight of frustration and helplessness we feel when the problems do not "go away."

Another way of responding to the "cost" issue is to ask, "Can we afford not to intervene?" Dr. Deborah Daro of the National Committee for the Prevention of Child Abuse has summarized some of the immediate and long-term costs surrounding child maltreatment, which should give policy makers pause (Daro, 1988). Some examples include: $640 million in foster care, $14.8 million in juvenile court and detention costs, a minimum of $685 million in loss of future earnings, and so on. Besides the dollar costs, we of course have the human costs of lives diminished or even ended.

DIRECTIONS FOR CHANGE

As indicated earlier, our intervention system goes far beyond child protective services to reach into a variety of community agencies and even to individuals who respond to the needs of abused and neglected children. The challenge for intervention is to mobilize and integrate this system to truly work to protect children. Dr. Richard Krugman, director of the Kempe National

Center on Child Abuse Prevention and Treatment, spoke of his first child abuse fatality during his medical residency. A total of 27 separate agencies had seen the little 2-year-old boy in his short life, but none knew of the others' involvements or concerns. We surely have the imagination to coordinate our response more effectively.

In the 1980s, a remarkable new public policy was formed in the Child Welfare and Adoption Assistance Act (P.L. 96-272). This law requires that demonstrable, albeit reasonable, efforts be made to prevent the placement of children and to reunify families, as well as to secure permanent homes when necessary. The "family preservation" ethic and the "placement prevention" obligation can be used to build response systems that are better able to protect children. People all across the country are doing this; we need to share the results of these efforts in our design or redesign of intervention systems.

The Children's Defense Fund reports that a growing number of organizations that provide a range of services designed to help children are pursuing strategies that involve parents, empowering them to help their children, and thus strengthening the whole family. In widely varying formats and under many different labels, child-care providers, teachers, and child-welfare professionals have been experimenting in recent years with ways to help children by providing new resources to families. In many cases, their successes are attracting political support for increased public investment in this kind of program.

The National Association of Public Child Welfare Administrators have outlined needed public child protective services and provided both guidelines and a framework for consensus on intervention. Through joint efforts of the American Bar Association's National Legal Resource Center, the American Public Welfare Association, and the American Enterprise Institute, a national forum on the focus of intervention was convened. As a result, the volume *Child Abuse and Neglect Reporting and Investigation: Policy Guidelines for Decisionmaking* was published (Besharov, 1988).

The American Humane Association's meetings from 1986 to 1988 indicated a clear and growing consensus on broad policies. The Child Welfare League of America has revised its child protective service standards with the help of a national group of organizations and individuals to contribute to the generation of consensus on standards.

The sum total of these efforts is truly remarkable and reflects a clear direction toward focused commitment to intervention.

IMPLICATIONS FOR ADVOCACY - WHAT WE DO WITH WHAT WE KNOW

We have learned what works: research and experience shows what intervention needs to be. It includes:

1. Support services to families to improve parenting, organize home life, access medical and mental health services, provide respite care, and offer concrete help with housing and employment.
2. The relatively long-term presence of stable, caring help for families in the form of a professional, a volunteer, or another parent.
3. The availability of crisis intervention resources in every community.
4. A system of intervention and decision making that is clearly focused, coordinated, and accountable - in CPS, in law enforcement, and in the courts.
5. Treatment services for children to heal some of the trauma.
6. Stable homes available when placement is necessary.

A process has been defined in P.L. 96-272 and in several states' laws. It is relatively straightforward:

1. All legitimate reports of abuse and neglect need to be investigated and assessed.
2. All children needing protection from abuse and neglect where the parent or guardian is unwilling or unable to provide protection should receive services.
3. Adequate services must be provided to strengthen families and to prevent future maltreatment; these services should be provided while children remain at home whenever their safety permits.
4. When services do not prevent placement, a safe, stable foster home needs to be identified along with a plan for family reunification and a process of parental visitation. Within a reasonable time frame, family reunification should be attempted and evaluated.
5. When it is not possible for children to be safe in their homes, a permanent plan should be developed for long-

218

term foster care, adoption, or other stable, out-of-home placement supported by the courts

These procedures are straightforward and noncontroversial but are beyond the resources of most communities. They are breaking down at every stage due to the absence of:

1. Adequate numbers of people - social workers, paraprofessionals, juvenile officers, judges, health professionals, volunteers, and so on.
2. Adequate training for all of the above.
3. Development, coordination, and access to available resources.
4. Accountability around a clear focus for social intervention.
5. Development of new service resources.

What happens to our children ought to concern each of us as private individuals and as members of society. This concern is manifested publicly and privately every day in homes and communities across the country. We need to become more able to mobilize public and private resources in response to abused and neglected children. Child maltreatment violates our conscience and our values as well as our laws. We may argue among ourselves about how to respond, who should finance the response, and even about what constitutes child maltreatment. What we cannot argue about is whether to respond.

Child abuse and neglect reports are overwhelming social service systems nationwide. We all know that, but we cannot stop there. Standards exist to measure capacity to respond to reports - not only to investigate but to serve. Beyond that point of capacity, if cases increase, either resources have to increase, or another response capacity needs to develop. We cannot pretend to be doing the job, nor can we leave the job undone.

Our concern for abused and neglected children generated the present laws. Resources must be made available to meet that obligation. As citizens and professionals we need to insure that an adequate system of response exists in every community. It can be a mix of public and private services, it can be donated or paid resources; it can be in the form of both volunteers and professionals.

Our children depend on us and learn from us how to care for those unable to care for themselves. We must define a standard of resource capacity needed to respond to abused and neglected children. This calculation should be done for every county in the

United States so that communities are held accountable for providing the level of services needed.

REFERENCES

Adoption Assistance and Child Welfare Act of 1980 (P.L. 96-272). (1980). Washington, DC: U.S. Department of Health and Human Services.

American Association for Protecting Children. (1988). *Highlights of Official Child Neglect and Abuse Reporting 1986.* Denver, CO: The American Humane Association.

Besharov, D. J. (1988). *Child Abuse and Neglect Reporting Investigation: Policy Guidelines for Decisionmaking.* Washington, DC: American Bar Association.

Daro, D. (1988). *Confronting Child Abuse: Research for Effective Program Design.* New York: The Free Press.

Gelles, R. J., & Straus, M. A. (1987). Is violence toward children increasing?: A comparison of 1975 and 1985 National Survey results. *Journal of Interpersonal Violence, 2,* 212-222.

Mitchel, L. (1987). *Child Abuse and Neglect Fatalities: A Review of the Problem and Strategies for Reform* (Working Paper #838). Chicago, IL: National Committee for the Prevention of Child Abuse.

U.S. House of Representatives Select Committee on Children, Youth and Families. (1987). *Victims of Official Neglect.* Washington, DC: U.S. Congress.

Westat Associates. (1987). *Study of the National Incidence and Prevalence of Child Abuse and Neglect.* Washington, DC: U.S. Department of Health and Human Services.

11

CHILD ADVOCACY IN THE MANAGEMENT OF SEXUAL MOLESTATION AND INCEST

Jack C. Westman

The public reaction to incest and the sexual molestation of children focuses attention on the punishment of the perpetrator and ignores the welfare of the affected children. For this reason, all professionals who deal with children need to become informed about the management of child sexual abuse, so that children are not further traumatized by legal and clinical procedures.

This chapter discusses definitional issues, the prevalence, the consequences, public reactions, the distinctions between child molestation and incest, professional responses, and the treatment of perpetrators, children, and families.

The management of sexual molestation and incest requires sensitivity to the needs and welfare of affected children and their families and the cooperation of all relevant disciplines.

Sexual child abuse differs from other forms of child abuse in the motivations of the perpetrators, the dynamics of the situations, and the combined emotional and physical impacts on the children (Jason et al., 1980). Its two forms are sexual molestation by nonfamily members and incest.

Our knowledge about the actual prevalence of child sexual abuse today is limited by its secretive nature, by under- and over-reporting, and by definitional problems. Although the peak age for child sexual abuse reporting usually has been between 8 and 13 years of age, in Los Angeles County in 1986 it was 4 years of age. When this is coupled with the fact that, for older children, the abuse may have been going on for several years before its disclosure, the vulnerability of young children to sexual abuse becomes apparent (Waterman & Lusk, 1986).

Few topics elicit the intense emotional responses, ranging from vehement denial to hysterical accusations, seen in child sexual-abuse matters (Ganzarain & Buchele, 1988; Hechler, 1988). At one extreme is a tendency by professionals to ignore sexual abuse, such as when physicians attribute venereal diseases in young children to nonsexual causes. At the other extreme are false accusations and the presumption that sexual abuse has occurred whenever it is alleged (Schuman, 1986).

DEFINITIONS

Distinguishing between sexual molestation and incest is an important first step in defining child sexual abuse. Even then, the definition of sexual molestation varies widely and includes interactions without physical contact and with persons close in age. Accordingly, Finkelhor urged establishing more precise criteria to insure that the definition is limited to children and to much older persons in order to exclude developmental sexual experimentation (Finkelhor & Hotaling, 1984). For example, he suggested 5 or more years' difference between children under 12 and 10 or more years' difference for teenagers. He also proposed that sexual molestation should be characterized by exploitation through force, threat, deceit, or authority by a nonfamily member.

Incest also is defined both narrowly as sexual intercourse and broadly as sexually arousing behavior between family members (Nadelson & Rosenfeld, 1980). The definition of incest must take into account the commonplace genital contact that takes place between young children and parents. For example, over 30% of a sample of parents answered other than "never" when asked if their daughters touched their father's genitals, and 45% when asked if their sons touched their mother's breasts or genitals (Rosenfeld et al., 1986). In a study of New England college students, 15% of the females and 10% of the males reported some type of sexual experience with a sibling (Finkelhor, 1979). Reactions were divided evenly between those who considered it positively or negatively.

Studies of child sexual abuse offenders variously reveal that from 10% to 43% are family members with father figures identified as 2% to 8%, that from 11% to 51% are strangers, and that from 33% to 49% are extrafamily acquaintances (Bagley & King, 1990).

Because of the ambiguous nature of erotic behavior between family members, the term "sexual misuse" defined as "exposure of a child to sexual stimulation inappropriate for a child's age and role in the family" has been proposed as more appropriate than "sexual abuse" for incest (Brant & Tisa, 1977). This merits consideration because the charge of sexual abuse often automatically invokes criminal prosecution under a variety of different laws that apply to child molestation, sexual assault, rape, indecent exposure, and corrupting the morals of minors.

The definitional problem in child sexual abuse was illustrated by the sexual assault charge against a 38-year-old female high school teacher resulting from a teenage boy's testimony that he had sexual intercourse with her. Her lawyer successfully argued that the state's sexual assault law defined sexual intercourse as requiring penetration by the defendant, thereby exempting her.

The key to sexual abuse is sexual activity that causes harm (Bagley & King, 1990).

PREVALENCE

In the 1880s, social agencies knew that incest was common. However, with the subsequent decline in the influence of the women's rights movement, concern about domestic abuse in general subsided, so that by the 1940s textbooks tended to deny that incest occurred (Gordon, 1988). Instead of focusing on the abusive actions of men, it became fashionable to focus on the provocation of abuse by women. This viewpoint obscured the significance of the report in 1956 by Landis that one-third of the college students surveyed reported sexual experiences as children with adults. These figures were confirmed for women by Gagnon in 1965.

More recent estimates of the prevalence of childhood sexual abuse, including both molestation and incest, vary from 8% in Great Britain (Baker & Duncan, 1985) and Texas (Kercher & McShane, 1984) to 62% in Los Angeles County (Wyatt, 1985). These studies reveal the importance of cultural, social, and methodological factors in surveys of this nature. The carefully conducted Badgley survey in Canada (1984) found that of the female respondents, 15% had been molested under the age of 15, and 22% under the age of 18. Of the males, 6% had been molested under the age of 15, and 9% under the age of 18. Sixty percent of the molestations were construed to have been under physical coercion or threat by the offender. In the United States a 1985 national survey conducted by the *Los Angeles Times* suggested that 16% of the population had been sexually abused as children.

Until recently, it has been widely assumed that child sexual abusers are exclusively male. In recent years, however, descriptions of incestuous mothers and female molesters are beginning to appear (Marvasti, 1986; E. L. Rowan, J. B. Rowan, & Langelier, 1990). Because of their greater intimacy with children, female caregivers have opportunities to sexually stimulate children in unnoticed ways. In its 1988 study, the American Humane Association revealed that 14% of the sexual abusers of boys and 6% of girls were females. Because of their larger numbers, more girls were abused by females than boys.

Substantiated cases of child sexual abuse in the United States increased almost twenty-fold between 1976 and 1985, rising from 6,000 to 113,000 (American Humane Association, 1988). The number of reported cases of incest, which constitute 20% to 40% of the reported cases, probably represents only the tip of the iceberg (Baker & Duncan, 1985; Conte & Berliner, 1981; Finkelhor, 1983; Mrazek & Kempe, 1981; Thornton & Carter, 1986). From the available data, it is clear that the reporting of child sexual abuse has increased dramatically, but it is not clear that the actual prevalence has increased over the years.

CONSEQUENCES

The current perspective on child sexual abuse is influenced by the perception that childhood sexual experiences inevitably leave lasting negative effects. Clinical studies of patients who have been sexually abused as children point to the high incidence of general signs of psychopathology, such as mistrust of others, poor self-image, depression, hysterical symptoms and character traits, social withdrawal and impaired peer relations, poor school performance, post-traumatic stress disorder, multiple personality disorder, borderline personality disorder, and disturbances in sexual behavior and gender roles (Bryer et al., 1987; Schetky & Green, 1988). Furthermore, 57% of adult child molesters have histories of being sexually abused as children (Seghorn, Prentky,

& Boucher, 1987). Aggressive, depressive, and withdrawal symptoms also have been reported in 3- to 12-year-old sexually abused children (Friedrich, Urquiza, & Beilke, 1986). In these clinical populations, however, there often are compounding factors, such as parental neglect, mental illness, and antisocial behavior.

The widely held assumption that sexual abuse inevitably has an adverse impact on psychosexual development has not been confirmed by some investigators (Gelinas, 1983; Tsai, Feldman-Summers, & Edgar, 1979; Vesterdal, 1983). They point out that the effects of sexual abuse must be understood in terms of the personality strengths of the individual and the general functioning of the family. For example, sexual molestation by a nonfamily member of a child with adequate coping mechanisms and a supportive family may have few lasting adverse effects (Gelles, 1982).

The reports of adults who experienced sexual abuse as children do not support a uniformly negative outcome and generally lack empirical bases (Finkelhor & Browne, 1988; Tong, Oates, & McDowell, 1987). One half of a sample of adult women from both an outpatient clinic and community sample with histories of incest reported recovering well from their childhood incestuous experiences (Herman, Russell, & Trocki, 1986). The other half had suffered forceful, prolonged, or highly intrusive incest and reported long-lasting negative effects. A survey in Great Britain found that 49% of the adult women did not feel they were harmed by childhood sexual abuse (Baker & Duncan, 1985). Still, these self-reports may be defensive and conceal subtle adverse effects. Moreover, the public sentiment condemns incest, as seen in the case of a Santa Ana, California, woman who was awarded financial damages against her stepfather for sexually molesting her 15 years before.

The biographies of adolescent and adult sexual molesters suggest that the traumata of humiliation and punishment for normal sexual rehearsal play and of experiences with partners of widely disparate ages predispose individuals to paraphilic sexual behavior (Money, 1988).

PUBLIC REACTIONS

In recent years revelations about the sexual abuse of children have evoked strong public reactions, so that we have shifted from under-reporting to over-reporting the problem. On the positive side, these reactions focus attention on children and families who need help. On the negative side, the reactions embroil children in society's ambivalence about crime and punishment and many adults' needs for scapegoats to assuage guilt about their own sexuality and neglect and misuse of children (Gardner, 1990).

An example of the public reaction is seen in an organization, Mothers Against Raping Children, that helps hide abused children and their mothers from abusive fathers. Most of the organization's members are mothers who have accused the fathers of their children of sexual abuse but who cannot find relief in the courts. Rather than acceding to court orders allowing the father's custody or visitation rights or fighting such orders and going to jail, an increasing number of mothers are "going underground" and in the process breaking the law. In contrast, divorced fathers have banded together to protect their rights in the national organization, Victims of Child Abuse Laws.

With the dramatic increase in reported cases of child sexual abuse, there has been a corresponding increase in unsubstantiated cases, especially when parents are involved in custody battles or visitation disputes (Green, 1986; MacFarlane & Waterman, 1986). For this reason, when a child's mother suspects sexual abuse because of the child's unusual behavior or statements, she may be regarded as having an ulterior motive for accusing or discrediting the father. It is easier to regard a mother as hysterical than to recognize an otherwise seemingly rational and caring father as capable of sexual abuse (MacFarlane & Waterman, 1986). The majority of truly unsubstantiated allegations appear to have been made in good faith but are based upon misinterpretation of the interaction between child and adult or misreading of physical or psychological symptoms of the child.

On the spectrum of cases of child sexual abuse ranging from substantiated to patently false, the majority probably fall in between. A study of 439 child sexual abuse reports in Denver found that 8% were plainly fictitious and another 22% were unsupported by evidence (Spiegel, 1986). Three-fourths of the false accusations came from adults, not children. Sexual abuse charges occur in about 30% of Michigan's contested custody case, up from 5% in 1980. Some ex-wives use false accusations as a weapon of last resort in custody and visitation disputes.

False allegations seem to occur under the following circumstances: (a) when a child is used by a vindictive parent attempting to punish the other parent; (b) when a delusional mother projects her own unconscious sexual fantasies on the father; (c) when the allegations are based on a child's sexual fantasies; and (d) when a child seeks revenge (Schetky & Green, 1988).

The systems designed to protect children at times malfunction by failing to screen out false accusations (Spiegel, 1986). Children can come to believe and testify to events that have not happened, and they can accommodate to the wishes of parents or custodians who, for various reasons, want to believe that sexual abuse has occurred. Thus, the belief that children never lie, combined with an emphasis on protecting them, may lead to events in which the guilt of the accused adult is inaccurately presumed. The following examples illustrate the timelessness of this point:

Principal Loses Job

Nearly 3 years after accusations of sexual misconduct threw the life of an elementary school principal into turmoil, the 12-year-old girl who accused him of fondling her recanted her story (*Wisconsin State Journal*, December 4, 1987). In early 1985 after he helped the girl off a piece of playground equipment, she alleged that he had illicitly touched her. Two other children subsequently complained that they also were touched by him. Although investigations found no basis for legal action and concluded that the children could have been influenced by a lecture on child abuse just before the accusations were leveled, the principal resigned under pressure and was unable to find employment in his field after that time.

Teachers Falsely Accused

Dr. William C. Niederland (1988) recalled an anecdote from his childhood in the 1920s in Germany. When his classmates learned about sexual intercourse, a group of boys asserted that they had seen two of their teachers having intercourse in their classroom on the floor directly in front of the blackboard. According to their lurid and convincing details, they had seen the whole intimacy through the keyhole. The "event" turned out to be totally invented, when an adult committee found that one could not observe anything that was close to the blackboard through the keyhole.

Behind public over-reactions against child sexual abuse is the unspoken social fact of incest (Crewdson, 1988). The fear of sadistic molesters is understandable, but it also can be a displacement of anxiety about hidden sexual abuse in the home. Only about one-third of incarcerated child molesters are pedophiliacs (Finkelhor, 1979) and a smaller percentage have dangerous antisocial or psychopathic personalities (B. Justice & R. Justice, 1979). We would rather think children are being violently kidnapped than that they are being skillfully seduced.

In order for sexual abuse to take place, the perpetrator must have the opportunity. An absent, conspiratorial, or depressed parent or an alienated child may offer a perpetrator that opportunity (Salter, 1988). Incest can happen when a father under job stress turns to his daughter for reassurance, or when a father prepares his daughter from infancy to expect and enjoy his touch. Feeling disappointment with their spouses, mothers also can turn their sons into lovers. Pre-adolescents and teenagers can experiment sexually with younger children. Even pedophiles, like any wise suitor, may try to build sexual intimacy on friendships with lonely children.

The popular response to the sexual abuse of children is to warn them against the minor threat of sexual molestation by strangers and to leave them open to the greater risk of being seduced by familiar adults (Crewdson, 1988). In fact, the adults who sexually abuse children are likely to be fathers, sitters, teachers, and next-door neighbors. The abused children can be Cub Scouts in a Midwestern town or wealthy children at a prestigious nursery school. At home they may have incestuous relationships with their parents, or away from home they may be raped or sodomized. In either instance they may agree to keep it secret.

CHILD MOLESTATION

It is of unappreciated significance that, although most sexual molesters are males, the victims are both males and females. Child molesters can be differentiated on the basis of whether their pedophilic behavior is based upon a fixation or a regression in their sexual lifestyle (Groth, 1978).

Three types of male child molesters have been identified: (a) a pedophile-fixated type who has never been able to maintain mature relations with his peers and consistently selects an underage person for compulsive sexual activity; (b) a pedophile-aggressive type who mainly selects boys for sexually sadistic acts; and (c) a pedophile-regressed type who has mature peer relationships but regresses after confrontation by a threat to his masculine image and displaces his sexual impulses to children. The fixated and aggressive types share an insensitivity to the needs and feelings of others, little insight into their own behavior, a lack of genuine remorse or shame, and denial or minimization of their behavior.

Fixated and aggressive pedophiles usually have a history of sexual abuse and neglect in their own childhoods (Seghorn et al., 1987). They experience their sexual behavior as a compulsion and may be obsessed with sexual thoughts that interfere with leading productive lives. Because they often are severely maladapted psychosocially, they usually need institutional treatment and typically do not respond unless confronted with incarceration (Barnard et al., 1988). The direct physiological assessment of sexual arousal has been useful in the diagnosis and monitoring of their treatment responses (Travin et al., 1986).

Regressed pedophiles usually have sexual relationships with adults but regress under circumstances in which they perceive a loss of power or sexual adequacy. They act impulsively when depressed and are unconcerned about the consequences. They later experience shame, guilt, and disgust with themselves and are candidates for outpatient treatment.

Approximately 20% of all rapes and 30% of all child sexual abuse are perpetrated by adolescents (Becker & Kavoussi, 1989).

Adolescent child molesters who are not of the fixated type appear to have motivations in addition to sexual gratification. They may be expressing displaced hostility, exerting power over a helpless victim, attempting to master past victimization of themselves, or validating heterosexuality (James & Nasjleti, 1983). Their prognoses are favorable when these other issues are resolved.

Child pornography and prostitution are prevalent forms of sexual molestation with a profit motive. They are fostered by family problems and the failure of society to deal with the exposure of children to exploitation by the media and organized crime (Schetky & Green, 1988).

INCEST

An avoidance of human inbreeding results from the interaction of genetic predispositions and environmental conditions (van den Berghe, 1983). Incest avoidance probably is widespread among the vertebrates and innately propels individuals into new relationships and social territories (Parker, 1976). However, the evolution of sexual behavior in humans has resulted in hypersexuality, which allows sex for its own sake. Therefore, for many humans, sexual activity and reproduction are distinct functions. As a consequence, incest has little to do with reproduction. The fact that incest occurs in humans most likely is cultural and psychological in origin, rather than an expression of human nature (Arens, 1986). The incest taboo has not kept incest from occurring as much as it has kept people from reporting it, becoming informed about it, and taking steps to prevent and treat it (B. Justice & R. Justice, 1979).

A factor contributing to incest in Western culture is that men have difficulty developing intimate interpersonal relationships that do not have a sexual component (Finkelhor & Browne, 1988). Boys are socialized in ways that deprive them of opportunities to meet their needs for tender touching and intimacy. They satisfy those needs only later in sexual relationships. In contrast, girls are socialized to understand a distinction between the touching and closeness of tenderness and that of sexuality. As a consequence, in our society males need more opportunities to express tenderness and to have close relationships without sexual components.

Although the law considers a child involved in incest as an innocent victim of an adult perpetrator, other family members usually play roles in an incestuous situation. When this is the case, the incest serves as a tension-reducing mechanism for the father and mother so that the family can remain intact (Nadelson & Rosenfeld, 1980). The children may feel guilty and confused, because they enjoy the attention they receive while involved in incest, and some find the sexual activity itself pleasurable. The children often are silent because of intimidation, bribes, or affection for family members. In some instances, the incestuous parent is perceived by the child as, and may actually be, the better parent. The incestuous acts may be revealed because of medical problems, such as venereal disease or genital trauma, or they may be suspected because of a child's behavioral, emotional, and psychophysiological symptoms.

The gradual societal recognition of incest as a harmful experience for children is illustrated by the writings 200 years ago of Jeremy Bentham: "There were inconveniences of incest, which would include rivalry between house members and relaxation of domestic discipline." He also added that incest could be dangerous to the health of the young, as the result of "premature indulgence" and the absence of a prohibition against incest would deprive a girl "of marriage and its advantages" (cited in Arens, 1986, p. 29).

Contrary to popular assumptions, many incestuous fathers appear to be otherwise well-adjusted, as are other members of the family (Arens, 1986). These families do not demonstrate undue role confusion, but they insulate themselves from prevailing moral standards and influences. They show an uncommon exercise of paternal authority with the father as the sole arbiter of morality and a corresponding withdrawal of the mother from a position of influence. The mother, daughter, and other members of the household become passive bystanders and victims of an overbearing male, who maintains rigid standards of proper social behavior in other areas, while contravening sexual standards. For the father, incest implies a sad and futile attempt to reconstruct a personal universe, which decays with the father's own physical decline and the maturity of its female members, who in the normal course of events would establish their own marital arrangements. The incestuous father constructs his family on the model of a kingdom, in which his own authority, rather than society's, reigns supreme. This has led some to suggest that incest in some form is an inevitable feature of feminine social experience in a patriarchal culture (Arens, 1986).

Other incestuous families have obvious dysfunctional characteristics with confusion of boundaries and roles, poor impulse control of a parent weakened by drugs and alcohol, and social isolation of the family (Thornton & Carter, 1986). There also is suggestive evidence that the risk of incest between stepfathers and stepdaughters is 1 in 6, compared to 1 in 50 for biological fathers and daughters (Russell, 1986).

When their sexuality is violated at a young age, children may be uncomfortable but not complain, because they do not know there is anything to complain about. The harm of adults having sexual relationships with children results from the powerlessness of children who are no match for adult authority (Miller, 1984). For example, in most cases of father-daughter incest, the authority of the father is enough to quell the little girl's doubts. The harm of his exploitation of her is less being repelled by his touch and more by being put in a situation that denies her working through normal development experiences. The incestuous father robs his daughter of a relationship to him as a parent. The forbidden fantasies of the Electra complex are brought to life and interfere with the normal processes of repression, the formation of the conscience, and the maturation of a differentiated self. Like any moral cruelty, it can be a humiliation so great that the victim eventually trusts neither herself nor anyone else and enters adulthood lacking self-esteem.

The tolerance of children for their parents knows no bounds. Their dependency on their parents insures that conscious or unconscious acts of mental and physical cruelty against them go undetected. Their naïveté makes it difficult for them to recognize traumatizations which often remain hidden behind the idealization of their parents.

Alice Miller found that a child is more likely to opt for a terrible inner isolation and splitting off of one's feelings than to "tattle" to outsiders about one's father or mother (Miller, 1984). The plight of an abused child could have more serious consequences than the plight of an adult in a concentration camp. The latter would not need to convince oneself that the abuse experienced was for one's own good and would find others with feelings of outrage, hatred, and despair. The abused child has none of those options. In the privacy of their homes children are almost totally at the mercy of their parents.

The great cruelty inflicted on children by incest is the repression of their anger and suffering because of the risk of losing their parents' love and affection. These children often do not encounter problems until they reach puberty, when they are taken by surprise by the intensity of their true feelings, after having succeeded in keeping them at a distance during earlier life. One result is substance abuse. As adults, they try to rid themselves as quickly as possible of the helpless, dependent child within them in order to become independent adults deserving respect. The resulting repression of their anger and helpless rage can lead to its transformation into more or less conscious hatred directed against themselves or substitute persons. When they have not dealt with the cruelty they endured as children because it was experienced early, beyond the reach of memory, they must demonstrate cruelty to themselves and others.

It is so natural to feel outrage at the adult and pity for the abused child that one is tempted to only condemn the adult. However, the most common reason why parents mistreat their children is that they were mistreated themselves as children. They often were humiliated and demeaned victims, on the one hand, and commanded to respect and love those who victimized them, on the other hand. Under no circumstances, however, were they able to give expression to their own suffering. One study found that adults who had experienced incest as children were comparatively insensitive to hypothetical situations similar to the type of abuse they experienced themselves (Ginsburg et al., 1989).

PROFESSIONAL RESPONSES
TO CHILD SEXUAL ABUSE

The first priority on behalf of the children should be early entry into a therapeutic environment for the child, abuser, and family. Although the state has an interest in punishing those who violate the laws against child abuse, due process simultaneously guarantees the accused a presumption of innocence and a fair trial. When criminal action is involved, it should not be permitted to interfere with, but be used to insure, treatment of the child and family. Professionals from all disciplines must collaborate to balance these often conflicting interests (Landwirth, 1987).

The existence of state statutes that require professionals to report reasonable suspicions of child abuse offer them protection from allegations of negligent or false reporting. At the same time, professionals are open to legal action if they do not report reasonable suspicions. A literal interpretation of the statutes may well restrict the exercise of professional judgment in reporting, since that may be regarded legally as decision making outside of the role of one charged with only reporting cases. On the other hand, investigations frequently neither prove nor disprove the allegations. For this reason, the most important step from the child's point of view is not prosecution of an offender but treatment of the family.

The traumatic effect of sexual abuse on children is not only related to the nature of the sexual acts or the bond between the child and the perpetrator. Just as important is the way in which professional systems handle the situation. When systems react with anger and disgust and focus on punishing the offender, the resulting drastic responses allow society and professionals to feel vindicated but often traumatize the victims further.

From the perspective of the child, the disclosure of sexual abuse by a parent can lead to the appearance of police officers, interrogation by a succession of strangers, physical examinations, lie detector tests, placement in foster care, alienation from the child's parents, and breakup of the family. For these reasons, it is important to recognize that acknowledging that a child or adolescent has been sexually molested or misused by a family member is an upsetting event for the family. In instances of incest, the family must face the question of loyalty to the offender versus loyalty to the affected child.

Therefore, when any form of incest reporting is being considered or being done, informing the parents is important for both ethical and therapeutic reasons. Informing parents allows for more collaboration with protective services, because the reporting professional can actively participate in designing the least intrusive and most therapeutic response (Racusin & Felsman, 1986).

To accurately evaluate an allegation of sexual abuse in a young child a clinician must understand the cognitive, emotional, familial, and social factors that surround the allegations (American Academy of Child and Adolescent Psychiatry, 1988). In addition, evaluators must be sensitive to their verbal and nonverbal communications with the child and approach the evaluation in an objective and unbiased manner (Benedek & Schetky, 1986). They also should be aware of their ethical obligation to cause no harm to the child. Treatment of the child actually begins at the first point of contact through arranging constructive handling of the case and assisting the child and family to confront and deal realistically with the situation, ideally through the work of a child advocacy team.

The medical examination is the most over-rated and inadequately applied component of evaluating sexual abuse (Durfee, Heger, & Woodling, 1986). It should be conducted only as a protective and supportive intervention to help the child deal with the situation, to gather medico-legal evidence, and to detect associated medical problems (Finkel, 1988). An immediate examination is indicated where there has been genital penetration within 72 hours, and when there is the possibility of pregnancy.

Special training in the protocol of conducting the medical examination of children is necessary. It should begin with an interview during which rapport is established by playing and talking with the child. Because the examination directly involves the child's body, it is simultaneously both potentially revealing and traumatic. On the other hand, because it is in the context of a general physical examination, it can be carried out easily if the child is with a supportive adult and feels in control of the situation. The history, physical examination, and laboratory studies may reveal evidence of bodily injuries, genital manipulation and penetration, and sexually transmitted diseases. Color photographs should be taken of significant physical signs.

For validating sexual abuse, the verbal report of the child remains the most significant piece of evidence. Physical signs are reliable but rarely present. Certain other symptoms, such as inappropriate sexual behavior, somatic complaints with sexual content, paternal jealousy, and running away from home are all specific enough to be suggestive of sexual abuse. Other frequently cited symptoms, such as depression, poor school performance, aggressive behavior, and regressive behavior are too unspecific to be useful (Salter, 1988).

The psychiatric evaluation of sexually abused children requires a period of time for establishing rapport (Green, 1986). In sexual abuse matters collateral information is even more important than in other clinical evaluations. In situations of alleged incest, the child should be seen with both parents separately and together even though this may be resisted by the alleging parent. The joint interview can resolve important discrepancies for the evaluator. An examination of each parent also should be carried out. In nonstranger sexual molestation situations, the alleged offender should be interviewed, when possible, in order to obtain that person's perspective.

Common sources of difficulty facing the evaluator are the lack of consensus regarding behavioral indicators of child sexual abuse and of standardized validation procedures, problems regarding competency and reliability of very young children as discussed in Chapter 6, and the strong bias and polarization of parents and family members. Incest offenders usually deny their actions and are not easily identified by psychological profiles or psychiatric diagnoses.

Since normal developmentally-determined sexual behaviors in children may generate anxiety and might be misinterpreted as evidence of sexual molestation, it is imperative that mental health professionals be acquainted with them. The universality of sexual arousal in parents in the context of early child rearing has been described by Reitman and Robson (1987). Erotic parental responses toward their offspring are a component of being in love with one's child. Conversely children show curiosity about sexual anatomy and functions. Touching of a young child's genitals and anus by parents or caregivers occurs during bathing, diapering, and toileting and usually is not invested with sexual significance. However, many cases of sexual misuse begin with touching and physical contact that escalates into genital manipulation.

Even when an evaluation is conducted for therapeutic purposes, the information divulged by the child may necessitate reporting suspected child abuse and could result in legal action. In such instances, the way in which the interview was conducted may be subject to legal scrutiny. It may call into question the validity of the interviewer's opinion or the child's words. Accordingly, verbatim notes should be kept of the child's statements.

In interviewing children it is important to establish a common terminology for naming people and things and for describing body parts and sexual acts. In the context of play with dollhouses, dolls, puppets, and toys the child's fears can be elicited, particularly of people. Inquiry should be made about secrets and about what they have been told will happen to them if they divulge secrets. It is important to convey to the child that this is the time to tell the truth, so that the interviewer can understand what really happened. The interviewer should also bear in mind the responsibility to honor the trust of the child. Too often children have revealed their personal experiences only to find that their revelations aid professionals' reports but not their life situations. When denial is suspected, children can be asked what they think an experience would have been like, if it had happened to them or if it happened sometimes. Children's thoughts and memories often are fragmented, so that they need help in piecing them together.

Because sexually abused children frequently blame themselves for past events, questions should be phrased so as to avoid the appearance of blaming the child. Questions should begin by being as open-ended as possible and slowly narrow down, giving the child a range of alternative answers in order to avoid suggesting an answer. They also should provide a choice of answers rather than inviting a "Yes" or "No." One should not assume that the sexual experience was all bad or painful for the child or that anger is felt toward the abuser. In incest, the child's anger toward the mother for the lack of protection may be closer to the surface than anger toward the father. When a child is seductive, it is helpful to remember that seductive behavior is learned by the child and often reinforced by the abuser (Schetky & Green, 1988).

Children who have been traumatized by sexual abuse may suffer from post-traumatic stress disorders and show denial in fantasy and inhibition of spontaneous thought that can seriously compromise their testimonial capacity (Pynoos & Eth, 1985). Furthermore, children may produce ambiguous reports that are magnified and projected back onto the child by other adults in a positive feedback loop which increases the ultimate distortions (Schuman, 1986). The accuracy of sexual abuse reports by children also should be assessed with awareness that incest frequently is reported only after the offender has moved out of the home, because children fear retaliation if they report it earlier (Salter, 1988). When sexual misuse has occurred, children benefit from having their perceptions validated. However, questioning their allegations can play into their fears that they will not be believed. For this reason, it can be done in the third person. "What would you say if someone asked you whether or not you made this up?"

True and false allegations of incest tend to have the following distinguishing characteristics (Green, 1986). True cases involve delayed, conflicted disclosures, often with retractions and accompanied by painful affects; the child uses age-appropriate terminology; the child initially is reticent to discuss the sexual behavior with the mother or others; the child does not confront the father, even with the mother present; the child is fearful in the father's presence; the mothers often are depressed; and the child demonstrates emotional and behavioral symptoms. One study disclosed that sexually abused children showed more sexual content in doll play than did controls (Jampole & Weber, 1987). However, from 6% to 20% of nonabused young children show explicit sexual doll play in structured anatomical doll interviews (Everson & Boat, 1990).

By contrast, in false cases the disclosure is more likely to be easy and apparently spontaneous in the absence of painful affect; the child uses adult terminology; the child discusses the abuse when prompted by the mother and checks with her; the child confronts the father in the mother's presence; the mother has paranoid or hysterical psychopathology; and the child might be sexually preoccupied but does not show emotional and behavioral symptoms related to the abuse.

When young children erroneously accuse a parent of sexual misuse, they may believe their own stories. Young children can be induced to allege sexual abuse on the suggestion of a parent, by their own sexualized perceptions emanating from the Oedipal or Electra complexes, and by secondary involvement of the child in the projective identification of one parent with the other (Yates & Musty, 1988). In the last instance, the accusing parent projects sexual and aggressive impulses onto the other parent in an attempt to devalue and control that parent. The attack is engendered by the unconscious wish to cling parasitically to the other person. In spite of the fury of the attack, the attacker often wishes to be reunited with the accused. In custody disputes, this becomes intensely frustrating and confusing for all concerned, and cases tend to drag on without clear resolution.

A technique has been developed for therapeutically interviewing children who have recently witnessed extreme acts of violence (Pynoos & Eth, 1986). The easily learned, three-stage approach can be adapted to sexual abuse situations by establishing rapport, exploration, support, and closure within a 90-minute interview. The format proceeds from projective drawing and storytelling to discussion of the actual traumatic situation and its impact, to issues centered on the aftermath, and to the situation's consequences for the child. The Draw-A-Person, Draw-A-Family, spontaneous drawings, and anatomical dolls are valuable sources of information as well (White et al., 1986). However, because of the suggestibility of young children, the exposure to anatomical dolls in itself may influence a child's later perceptions and memory, especially when children are induced to make associations between the dolls and people (Terr, 1988). One controlled study disclosed only 53% accuracy in distinguishing sexually abused and nonabused children on the basis of anatomical doll interviews alone (Realmuto, Jensen, & Wescoe, 1990). For these reasons, courts are beginning to place restrictions on the admissibility of evidence obtained from doll interviews, as they have for hypnosis and lie-detector examinations. The current confusion concerning legally acceptable and admissible aspects of doll interviews, in addition to the ease of discrediting such testimony in court, makes it necessary for investigators to meticulously document their methods of gathering data. The least contested usage in court is to demonstrate the doll play and avoid the issues of hearsay, validity, and reliability of the technique (Quinn, 1986).

Therapeutic interviewing of young children who have been sexually molested can be facilitated by written aids, such as *The Secret* (McCoy, 1986).

TREATMENT

The most important aspect of designing a treatment program is the assumption that child molestation and incest are either the result of deviant arousal patterns or the inappropriate conversion of nonsexual problems into sexual behavior (Salter, 1988). The goals of therapy for the perpetrators are to learn to control their deviant arousal patterns and to solve displaced problems in non-sexual ways in order to minimize the risk of recurrence. The perpetrators must take responsibility for their behavior, and dysfunctional family patterns that provide the opportunity for, or result from, the sexual abuse must be addressed. The children must be helped to recover from the sexual abuse, to develop ways of resisting further abuse, and to pursue age-appropriate sexual development.

In general, the focus of treatment of sexual molesters is on control rather than cure. New skills can be taught to overcome stressors, self-esteem can be strengthened, and social supports can be increased. Antiandrogen medications can be helpful when closely monitored. Because of the high incidence of recidivism incarceration without treatment usually is ineffective (Bagley & King, 1990).

As with physical abuse and neglect, incest is more appropriately handled through children's codes and family law than through the criminal system (Terr, 1986). Statutes have established sexual assaults as crimes to life and bodily security and are aimed at sexual actions upon an individual without the consent of that person. The degree of sexual assault usually ranges from a felony for acts of sexual intercourse to a misdemeanor for sexual contact. The actions usually are regarded as sexual assault when the victim is under age 16, whether or not there was consent. These statutes have come to be applied to cases of incest and juvenile sexual experimentation. When cases are reported to the police or prosecutors, the chances of criminal action are twice as high as when reported to social service departments. Even then, however, one study revealed that only 1 in 5 ultimately was prosecuted (Finkelhor, 1983).

In 1985, the American Bar Association established guidelines for a multidisciplinary team in child abuse cases involving the prosecutor, the police, and social service personnel (American Bar Association, 1985). A specific example is the Norfolk Family Sexual Trauma Team, which involves the Norfolk Police Department and the Division of Social Services (McPartland, 1984). The team is composed of a youth division investigator and a child protective services worker who work closely with the prosecutor, psychiatric treatment team, courts, and the probation department. The team's goal is to reduce the trauma to the child by eliminating successive and repetitive questioning, provide rehabilitation for the offender as a mandatory condition of probation, stabilize the family through therapeutic intervention, and prevent recurrence by long-term follow-up.

In every jurisdiction there is a statutory child protective services agency that has the authority and responsibility for receiving reports of all types of child maltreatment, investigating cases, and validating complaints. By defining sexual misuse by familiar adults within general child abuse rather than criminal statutes, further traumatization of the child by legal and clinical procedures can be minimized. When an incestuous parent is criminally charged and incarcerated, the child may feel enormous guilt over the breakup of the family in addition to the incest itself. Overlooked is the powerful bond between parent and child that usually is the key to successful treatment of the child and the parent. Furthermore, the entire family system is disrupted, and economic repercussions can be severe. At the same time, the possibility of criminal prosecution can be used as a motivating tool in obtaining the cooperation of family members in treatment.

An effective child sexual-abuse treatment program involves, simultaneously, the treatment of perpetrators, victims, spouses, and siblings (D. S. Everstine & L. Everstine, 1989; Friedrich, 1990; Horton et al., 1989; Salter, 1988). Extrafamilial offenders can be treated without involvement of their victims (Maletzky, 1990). An authoritative legal incentive is essential for the perpetrators of child molestation and incest (Sgroi, 1982). The perpetrators must acknowledge that they have committed the acts without projecting responsibility onto other factors. They must be held accountable for their actions and make some form of restitution related to the harm caused. The result of treatment should be the development of more appropriate alternative modes of self-expression, need gratification, and impulse management (Groth, 1978).

The treatment of choice for incest is reconstructive family therapy for available members of the family. Peer group self-help also is a useful adjunct. The authority of the court usually is necessary in order to initiate and maintain treatment over the extended period of time necessary for changes in attitudes and behavior to occur. The power of a court can be used to prevent recurrence of the sexual misuse while these changes are occurring (James & Nasjleti, 1983). Even when sexual abuse is not substantiated, the allegation, in itself, usually is an indication for treatment of the family.

In order to reverse this situation, child rearing must be directed toward the welfare of children, not toward satisfying their parent's need for affection, power, or revenge. At the same time, abusive parents need help in mourning their own childhood mistreatment. In psychotherapy, the expression of resentment toward one's parents can provide access to one's true self, reactivate repressed feelings, give expression to mourning, and possibly lead to reconciliation.

The format of reconstructive family treatment varies between sessions with individuals, dyads, triads, and the entire family and may involve a single or multiple therapists (Giarretto, 1982; Sgroi, 1982).

The phases of the family treatment of incest can be conceptualized as the disclosure-panic phase lasting from several weeks to 3 months; the assessment-awareness phase, lasting from 6 to 18 months; and the restructuring phase, lasting from 18 to 24 months (James & Nasjleti, 1983). During the disclosure-panic phase, it is important to firmly insist that incestuous behavior is unacceptable and at the same time to handle the family's anger, denial, projection, intellectualizing, and diversionary efforts. During the assessment-awareness phase, the misuse is no longer denied, and the possibility of a new lifestyle leads to dependency on the therapist and a degree of excitement about the newly discovered potential for personal growth. There still is a need to work through blaming the victim, alcohol, or other extenuating circumstances. This is a vulnerable time for backsliding and interruption of therapy. During the restructuring phase, parents usually separate emotionally from their families of origin and strengthen the parent-child boundaries in their present family. Parents in incestuous families are sensitive to rejection and abandonment, so termination usually is a gradual process.

"Victim therapy" is a form of brief psychotherapy that focuses on encouraging the victim to experience the feelings and thoughts about the sexual activity that were initially avoided and not discussed with anyone. The meaning of the experience to the child is critical. If the feelings experienced in incest were pleasurable or within the child's control, the child may not feel abused (Newberger & Devos, 1988). Psychotherapy then can be directed at altering beliefs about the self and others that have been distorted by the experience. Children can be helped to "talk out" instead of "acting out" their memories and fantasies (Weil, 1989). After successful resolution of the traumatic experiences, victims feel increased self-esteem, gain more control of their lives, and resume less conflicted life patterns.

SUMMARY

Child sexual molestation and incest can be distinguished from physical abuse, because they usually represent different populations and have different legal, social, and clinical consequences. Sexual molestation is more likely to involve pedophiles, incest is more likely to involve collusion in an outwardly stable family, and both are more likely to result in criminal action against the perpetrators than physical abuse itself.

Definitions of child sexual abuse need to be more precise in order to separate developmental from exploitative sexual behavior and to distinguish child molestation from incest. The failure to make these distinctions has led to inappropriate allegations and criminal prosecutions, because it is unclear as to whether the perpetrator constitutes a danger to society. The evidence suggests that nearly 1 in 5 girls and 1 in 11 boys experience child sexual abuse with about half of them reporting few lasting adverse effects.

Incest avoidance appears to be innate in vertebrates and human beings, so that the occurrence of incest is a cultural and personal over-riding of that taboo. It appears to be related to patriarchal cultural factors and the lack of socialization of boys in nonsexualized expressions of affection and nurturance.

The early incest literature assigned the responsibility for child sexual abuse to the victim. The fashion turned from holding victims responsible to regarding mothers and other nonparticipating family members as colluding. More recently the perpetrator is seen as being ultimately responsible (Salter, 1988). The strong current tendency is to assign responsibility to perpetrators of any socially unacceptable action, whether that person be a teenage delinquent, an incestuous father, or a disruptive kindergartner. Missing is an awareness of the transactional nature of human relationships in which the genesis of a given behavior is in the interplay of multiple factors. Still the person wielding the ultimate behavior bears the responsibility for the consequences of his or her own actions.

We have passed from an era of under-reporting to an era of over-reporting of childhood sexual abuse, largely in the context of group exaggerations and in the aftermath of divorce. The challenge is to identify dangerous child molesters in order to protect society and to identify incestuous families for treatment interventions that do not further harm the affected children.

242

Unfortunately, child sexual abuse has become a war with battles, backlashes, and community-wide scandals. The criminal prosecution of alleged perpetrators actually further victimizes the children through the publicity and inevitable legal procedures that concentrate on whether or not sexual abuse occurred. As efforts are made to protect them from adults who sexually exploit them, the children's welfare often is overlooked, because interventions are focused on the offender, not the victim. Consequently, children fall prey to the general orientation of the legal system, which ignores the rights and needs of victims while protecting the rights of the accused.

Incest is a problem growing out of parents' ineffective meeting of their needs for intimacy and sexual stimulation and ineffective dealing with stressors. Protective service and legal interventions should be used to help incestuous families, not to remove children from their homes, send a parent to prison, or break up a family.

The responsibility of mental health professionals, as child advocates, is to manage sexually abused children in such a way as to protect the children from further harm by insensitive systems and to insure treatment of their families in addition to themselves, even when the perpetrator is not a family member. The most important issue is not determining whether or not sexual abuse occurred; it is recognizing even an allegation of sexual abuse as a cry for help, and it is responding to a troubled child and family without further harming them.

REFERENCES

American Academy of Child and Adolescent Psychiatry. (1988). Guidelines for the clinical evaluation of child and adolescent sexual abuse. *American Academy of Child and Adolescent Psychiatry Newsletter, Fall,* 9-11.

American Bar Association. (1985). *Guidelines for the Fair Treatment of Child Witnesses in Cases Where Child Abuse Is Alleged.* Washington, DC: American Bar Association, Section on Criminal Justice.

American Humane Association. (1988). *National Study on Child Neglect and Abuse Reporting.* Denver, CO: American Humane Association.

Arens, W. (1986). *The Original Sin: Incest and Its Meaning.* New York: Oxford University Press.

Badgley, R. (1984). *Sexual Offenses Against Children: Report of the Committee on Sexual Offenses Against Children and Youths.* Ottawa, Canada: Government of Canada.

Bagley, C., & King, K. (1990). *Child Sexual Abuse: The Search for Healing.* London: Tavistock/Routledge.

Baker, A. W., & Duncan, S. P. (1985). Child sexual abuse: A study of prevalence in Great Britain. *Child Abuse and Neglect, 9,* 457-467.

Barnard, G. W., Fuller, A. K., Robbins, L., & Shaw, T. (1988). *The Child Molester: An Integrated Approach to Evaluation and Treatment.* New York: Brunner/Mazel.

Becker, J. V., & Kavoussi, R. J. (1989). Diagnosis and treatment of juvenile sex offenders. In R. Rosner & H. J. Schwartz (Eds.), *Juvenile Psychiatry and the Law* (pp. 133-143). New York: Plenum.

Benedek, E. P., & Schetky, D. H. (1986). The child as a witness. *Hospital and Community Psychiatry, 37,* 1225-1229.

Brant, R., & Tisa, V. (1977). The sexually misused child. *American Journal of Orthopsychiatry, 47,* 80-90.

Bryer, J. B., Nelson, B. A., Miller, J. B., & Kral, P. A. (1987). Childhood sexual and physical abuse as factors in adult psychiatric illness. *American Journal of Psychiatry, 144,* 1426-1430.

Conte, J. R., & Berliner, L. (1981). Sexual abuse of children: Implications for practice. *Social Casework, 62,* 601-606.

Crewdson, J. (1988). *By Silence Betrayed: Sexual Abuse of Children in America.* Boston, MA: Little, Brown & Company.

Durfee, M., Heger, A. H., & Woodling, B. (1986). Medical evaluation. In K. MacFarlane & J. Waterman (Eds.), *Sexual Abuse of Young Children: Evaluation and Treatment.* New York: Guilford.

Everson, M. D., & Boat, B. W. (1990). Sexualized doll play among young children. *American Journal of Child and Adolescent Psychiatry, 29,* 736-742.

Everstine, D. S., & Everstine, L. (1989). *Sexual Trauma in Children and Adolescents: Dynamics and Treatment.* New York: Brunner/Mazel.

Finkel, M. A. (1988). The medical evaluation of child sexual abuse. In D. H. Schetky & A. H. Green (Eds.), *Child Sexual Abuse.* New York: Brunner/Mazel.

Finkelhor, D. (1979). *Sexually Victimized Children.* New York: Free Press.

Finkelhor, D. (1980). Sex among siblings & a survey of prevalence, variety, and effects. *Archives of Sexual Behavior, 9,* 171-194.

Finkelhor, D. (1983). Removing the child - prosecuting the offender in cases of sexual abuse: Evidence from the national reporting system for child abuse and neglect. *Child Abuse and Neglect, 7,* 195-205.

Finkelhor, D., & Browne, A. (1988). Assessing the long-term impact of child sexual abuse: A review and conceptualization. In G. T. Hotaling, D. Finkelhor, J. T. Kirkpatrick, & M. A. Straus (Eds.), *Family Abuse and Its Consequences: New Directions in Research.* Newbury Park, CA: Sage.

Finkelhor, D., & Hotaling, G. T. (1984). Sexual abuse in the national incidence study of child abuse and neglect: An appraisal. *Child Abuse and Neglect, 8,* 23- 32.

Friedrich, W. N. (1990). *Psychotherapy of Sexually Abused Children and Their Families.* New York: W. W. Norton.

Friedrich, W. N., Urquiza, A. J., & Beilke, R. C. (1986). Behavior problems in sexually abused young children. *Journal of Pediatric Psychology, 11,* 47-57.

Gagnon, J. (1965). Female child victims of sex offenses. *Social Problems, 13,* 176-192.

Ganzarain, R. C., & Buchele, B. J. (1988). *Fugitives of Incest: Perspective from Psychoanalysis and Groups.* New York: International Universities Press.

Gardner, R. A. (1990). *Sex Abuse Hysteria: Salem Witch Trials Revisited.* Cresskill, NJ: Creative Therapeutics.

Gelinas, D. J. (1983). The persisting negative effects of incest. *Psychiatry, 46,* 312-332.

Gelles, R. J. (1982). Child abuse and family violence: Implications for medical professionals. In E. H. Newberger (Ed.), *Child Abuse.* Boston, MA: Little, Brown & Company.

Giarretto, H. (1982). *Integrated Treatment of Child Sexual Abuse: A Treatment and Training Manual.* Palo Alto, CA: Science and Behavior Books.

Ginsburg, H., Wright, L. S., Harrell, P. M., & Hill, D. W. (1989). Childhood victimization: Desensitization effects in the later lifespan. *Child Psychiatry and Human Development, 20,* 59-71.

Gordon, L. (1988). *Heroes of Their Own Lives: The Politics and History of Family Violence. Boston, 1880-1960.* New York: Viking Press.

Green, A. H. (1986). True and false allegations of sexual abuse in child custody disputes. *Journal of the American Academy of Child Psychiatry, 25,* 449-456.

Groth, A. N. (1978). Patterns of sexual assault against children and adolescents. In A. W. Burgess, A. N. Groth, L. T. Hemstrom, & S. M. Sgroi, *Sexual Assault of Children and Adolescents.* Lexington, MA: Lexington Books.

Hechler, D. (1988). *The Battle and the Backlash: The Child Sexual Abuse War.* Lexington, MA: Lexington Books.

Herman, J., Russell, D., & Trocki, K. (1986). Long-term effects of incestuous abuse in childhood. *American Journal of Psychiatry, 143,* 1293-1296.

Horton, A. L., Johnson, B. L., Roundy, L. M., & Williams, D. (Eds.). (1989). *The Incest Perpetrator: A Family Member No One Wants to Treat.* Newbury Park, CA: Sage.

James, B., & Nasjleti, M. (1983). *Treating Sexually Abused Children and Their Families.* Palo Alto, CA: Consulting Psychologist Press.

Jampole, L., & Weber, M. K. (1987). An assessment of the behavior of sexually abused and unisexually abused children with anatomically correct dolls. *Child Abuse and Neglect, 11,* 187-192.

Jason, J., Williams, S. L., Burton, A., & Rochat, R. (1980). Epidemiological differences between sexual and physical child abuse. *Journal of the American Medical Association, 247,* 3344-3348.

Justice, B., & Justice, R. (1979). *The Broken Taboo.* New York: Human Science Press.

Kercher, G. A., & McShane, M. (1984). The prevalence of child sexual abuse victimization in an adult sample of Texas residents. *Child Abuse and Neglect, 8,* 495-501.

Landis, J. (1956). Experiences of 500 children with adult sexual deviation. *Psychiatric Quarterly Supplement, 91,* 91-109.

Landwirth, J. (1987). Children as witnesses in child sexual abuse trials. *Pediatrics, 80,* 585-589.

MacFarlane, K., & Waterman, J. (1986). *Sexual Abuse of Young Children: Evaluation and Treatment.* New York: Guilford.

Maletzky, B. M. (1990). *Treating the Sexual Offender.* Newbury Park, CA: Sage.

Marvasti, K. (1986). Incestuous mothers. *American Journal of Forensic Psychiatry, 7,* 63-68.

McCoy, D. L. (1986). *The Secret: A Child's Story of Sex Abuse for Children Ages 4 Through 6.* Knoxville, TN: Magic Lantern Publications.

McPartland, K. C. (1984). Sexual trauma team. *FBI Law Enforcement Bulletin, 532,* 7-9.

Miller, A. (1984). *For Your Own Good: Hidden Cruelty in Child Rearing and the Roots of Violence.* New York: Farrar, Straus, Giroux.

Money, J. (1988). *Gay, Straight, and In-Between.* New York: Oxford University Press.

Mrazek, P. B., & Kempe, C. H. (1981). *Sexually Abused Children and Their Families.* Oxford, England: Pergamon.

Nadelson, C. C., & Rosenfeld, A. A. (1980). Sexual misuse of children. In D. H. Schetky & E. P. Benedek (Eds.), *Child Psychiatry and the Law.* New York: Brunner/Mazel.

Newberger, C. M., & Devos, E. (1988). Abuse and victimization. *American Journal of Orthopsychiatry, 58,* 505-511.

Niederland, W. C. (1988, June 16). Letter to the editor. *Psychiatric News.*

Parker, S. (1976). The precultural basis of the incest taboo: Toward a biosocial theory. *American Anthropologist, 78,* 285-305.

Pynoos, R. S., & Eth, S. (1985). Children traumatized by witnessing acts of personal violence: Homicide, rape, or suicide behavior. In S. Eth & R. S. Pynoos (Eds.), *Post-Traumatic Stress Disorder in Children.* Washington, DC: American Psychiatric Association Press.

Pynoos, R. S., & Eth, S. (1986). Witness to violence: The child interview. *Journal of the American Academy of Child Psychiatry, 25,* 306-319.

Quinn, K. M. (1986). Competency to be a witness: A major child forensic issue. *Bulletin of the American Academy of Psychiatry and Law, 14,* 311-321.

Racusin, R. J., & Felsman, J. K. (1986). Reporting child abuse: The ethical obligation to inform parents. *Journal of the American Academy of Child Psychiatry, 25,* 485-489.

Realmuto, G. M., Jensen, J. B., & Wescoe, S. (1990). Specificity and sensitivity of sexually anatomically correct dolls in substantiating abuse. *Journal of the American Academy of Child and Adolescent Psychiatry, 29,* 743-746.

Reitman, M., & Robson, K. (1987, October 23). *Erotic Aspects of Normal Parenting.* Presented at the 34th Annual Meeting of the American Academy of Child and Adolescent Psychiatry, Washington, DC.

Rosenfeld, A., Bailey, R., Siegel, B., & Bailey, G. (1986). Determining incestuous contact between parent and child: Frequency of children touching parent's genitals in a nonclinical population. *Journal of the American Academy of Child Psychiatry, 25,* 481-484.

Rowan, E. L., Rowan, J. B., & Langelier, P. (1990). Women who molest children. *Bulletin of the American Academy of Psychiatry and Law, 18,* 79-83.

Russell, D. E. H. (1986). *The Secret Trauma: Incest in the Lives of Girls and Women.* New York: Basic Books.

Salter, A. C. (1988). *Treating Child Sex Offenders and Victims.* Newbury Park, CA: Sage.

Schetky, D. H., & Green, A. H. (1988). *Child Sexual Abuse: A Handbook for Health Care and Legal Professionals.* New York: Brunner/Mazel.

Schuman, D. C. (1986). False accusations of physical and sexual abuse. *Bulletin of the American Academy of Psychiatry and Law, 14,* 5-21.

Seghorn, T. K., Prentky, R. A., & Boucher, R. J. (1987). Childhood sexual abuse in the lives of sexually aggressive offenders. *Journal of the American Academy of Child and Adolescent Psychiatry, 26,* 262-267.

Sgroi, S. M. (1982). *A Handbook of Clinical Intervention in Child Sexual Abuse.* Lexington, MA: Lexington Books.

Spiegel, L. (1986). *A Question of Innocence.* Morris Plains, NJ: Unicorn Publishing Co.

Terr, L. C. (1986). The child psychiatrist and the child witness: Traveling companions by necessity, if not by design. *Journal of the American Academy of Child Psychiatry, 25,* 462-472.

Terr, L. (1988). Anatomically correct dolls: Should they be used as the basis for expert testimony? *Journal of the American Academy of Child and Adolescent Psychiatry, 27,* 387-388.

Thornton, C. I., & Carter, J. H. (1986). Treatment considerations with black incestuous families. *Journal of the National Medical Association, 78,* 49-53.

Tong, L., Oates, K., & McDowell, M. (1987). Personality development following sexual abuse. *Child Abuse and Neglect, 11,* 371-383.

Travin S., Bluestone, H., Coleman, E., Cullen, K., & Melella, J. (1986). Pedophile types and treatment perspectives. *Journal of Forensic Science, 31,* 614- 620.

Tsai, M., Feldman-Summers, S., & Edgar, M. (1979). Childhood molestation: Differential impacts on psychosexual functioning. *Journal of Abnormal Psychology, 88,* 407-417.

van den Berghe, P. L. (1983). Human inbreeding avoidance: Culture in nature. *The Behavioral and Brain Sciences, 6,* 91-123.

Vesterdal, J. (1983). Etiological factors and long-term consequences of child abuse. *International Journal of Offender Therapy and Comprehensive Criminology, 27,* 21-54.

Waterman, J., & Lusk, R. (1986). Scope of the problem. In K. MacFarlane & J. Waterman (Eds.), *Sexual Abuse of Young Children: Evaluation and Treatment.* New York: Guilford.

Weil, J. L. (1989). *Instinctual Stimulation of Children, Volume 1: Clinical Findings.* Madison, CT: International Universities Press.

White, S., Strone, G., Santelli, F., & Halpin, B. (1986). Interviewing young sexual abuse victims with anatomically correct dolls. *Child Abuse and Neglect, 10,* 519-529.

Wyatt, G. E. (1985). The sexual abuse of Afro-American and white-American women in childhood. *Child Abuse and Neglect, 9,* 507-519.

Yates, A., & Musty, T. (1988). Preschool children's erroneous allegations of sexual molestation. *American Journal of Psychiatry, 145,* 989-992.

12

THE TERMINATION OF PARENTAL RIGHTS AS A THERAPEUTIC OPTION

David L. Kaye and Jack C. Westman

Subsequent to abuse and neglect by their biological parents, "children of the state" grow up in a series of foster homes and institutions under the guardianships of agencies. This ill-fated course can be prevented by the initial rehabilitation of the child's biological family or, if that is not possible, the expeditious termination of parental rights and adoption of the child.

This chapter identifies the numerous factors that interfere with compliance with termination of parental rights statutes. The lack of continuity and fragmentation of services combine with the ineffective use of the legal system to produce lengthy delays and later disruptions in legal proceedings. As a result, most of the affected children pass through multiple foster homes and institutions.

The benefits to parents of involuntary termination of their parental rights often are overlooked. They are spared the responsibilities of child rearing so that they can pursue their own self-development. Decision making by the court also assuages their guilt and assists them in facing reality.

In most jurisdictions, statutory grounds for the termination of parental rights exist when parents persistently fail to meet the basic needs of their children and are not amenable to treatment. This chapter outlines criteria for assessing how a parent meets the basic needs of a child, evidence of damage to that child, and amenability of the parent to treatment.

Jack Henry Abbott, a convicted murderer, received literary acclaim when he was released from a federal prison in June of 1981. Six weeks later he impulsively killed a restaurant waiter. In his book, *In the Belly of the Beast* (1981), Abbott revealed a chilling attitude toward murder:

> The enemy is smiling and chattering away about something. You see his eyes: green-blue liquid. He thinks you are his fool; he trusts you. You see the spot . . . you have sunk the knife to its hilt into the middle of his chest . . . As he sinks you have to kill him fast or get caught . . . You can feel his life trembling through the knife in your hand. It almost overcomes you, the gentleness of the feeling at the center of a coarse act of murder . . . It is like cutting hot butter, no resistance at all. They always whisper at the end: "Please."

In an increasingly violent world, one asks how human beings develop the frame of mind evidenced by Abbott. Explanations range from genetic defects to the effects of the penal system itself. Many factors undoubtedly are involved; however, one pattern repeatedly emerges from the histories of violent persons and is captured by what Abbott called "children of the state." Subsequent to abuse and neglect by their biological parents, these children grow up in a series of foster homes and institutions under the guardianship of agencies.

Abbott's life dramatically illustrates the outcome for many "children of the state." He was in and out of foster homes from the time of his birth. At the age of 9, he began serving long stints in juvenile detention quarters. At the age of 12, he was sent to the Utah State Industrial School for boys. When he reached 18, he was released as an adult, but 6 months later, further offenses resulted in sentencing to the Utah State Penitentiary. There, he killed one inmate and wounded another. Between the ages of 12 and 37, Abbott had been outside of an institution for less than a year and had been in solitary confinement for 14 years.

All children who experience gross parenting failures, lack of continuity in parenting, and multiple foster homes do not become murderers like Jack Abbott. In fact, most children who receive only foster care do not become problems for society (Fanshel & Shinn, 1978). However, for many vulnerable children, multiple foster placement and institutionalization are the factors that permanently tip the balance toward an antisocial life (Westman, 1979). We know that the vast majority of violent offenders have been seriously abused as children (Lewis, 1985; Lewis et al., 1979, 1983; Tanay, 1969), and that the annual incidence of reported abuse and neglect has doubled to a level of over 2 million since 1980 (American Humane Association, 1989). Because large numbers of abused and neglected children experience multiple foster placements punctuated by return to their biological parents, this problem represents a major public health concern (Winnicott, 1984).

In 1980 Congress passed the Adoption Assistance and Child Welfare Act, P.L. 96-272, that called for a combined effort on the part of the judicial, executive, and legislative branches to preserve families and, if necessary, to form new ones. It requires that judges determine whether reasonable efforts have been made to enable children to remain safely at home before they are placed in foster care and to reunite foster children with their biological parents. The Act directs professionals both to expeditiously rehabilitate foundering families and to provide new families for children when that is not possible.

With this public awareness of the plight of abused and neglected children, there is an increasing desire to assist and rehabilitate their families. On the other hand, there is pressure to provide these children with safe, supportive environments. In many situations the desires to treat families and protect children reflect either-or biases without regard for the specifics of a given child and family.

In our view, rehabilitation of the original family is the optimal solution for a child, family, and society. However, in some instances this cannot be accomplished for a specific family with available sources within the time frame of a child's developmental needs. The treatment of abusing and neglectful parents is a difficult task. In a review of the literature on treatment outcome for abusing families, Jones (1987) noted that 20% to 87% with a mean of 53% of abusing families were judged to be unchanged or worse at the end of treatment. Moreover, the recidivism rate was between 16% and 60% with a mean of 38%. Obviously treatment resources vary widely and even with the best available, almost 30% of the parents do not have lasting positive responses to therapeutic interventions. For this reason, the presumption that all parents will make necessary changes is not justified. Therefore, close monitoring of treatment within specified time limits is warranted. We agree with Wald's (1982) recommendation that for children under 3, the period of trial treatment be a maximum of 12 months and for children over 3, 18 months. The longer the delay, the less likely is subsequent adoption to be successful.

Although the termination of parental rights often is seen as a punitive action, our experience confirms that of others (Reinhart, 1985; Schetky et al., 1979) that for many abusive and neglectful families, it can be therapeutically useful for both parents and children. At the least, the prospect of the termination of a parent's rights can help motivate a parent to improve. In some instances, parents come to recognize the value of voluntarily terminating their parental rights. In untreatable situations, it does not serve the interests of the children or their parents to continue to make rehabilitative efforts that are rejected or that are too unproductive to benefit the children. When carried out through legal action, the involuntary termination of parental rights makes a decision for parents that they are unable to make for themselves because of guilt, shame, extended family pressures, or monetary incentives. They may experience relief after the action has taken place or in subsequent years when they come to appreciate the opportunities that adoption or permanent foster care offered their children.

For all of these reasons, we favor methodically providing treatment for abusive and neglectful parents and moving expeditiously toward the termination of their parental rights when circumstances warrant it. The remainder of this chapter will provide a clinical framework for the evaluation of these cases by mental health professionals and end with a case example. The first section highlights some of the system issues that influence the conduct and legal application of the evaluation and treatment of families. The second section outlines an evaluation procedure.

SYSTEM ISSUES

Typically, abusive and neglectful parents already have been involved with the social service, legal, and health care systems prior to their referrals to mental health professionals. Usually a petition initiated by the social service system is made to the legal system to determine if a child is in need of protective services and to outline a dispositional plan.

Later, after a child has been adjudicated to be in need of protective services and a treatment plan implemented, the mental health professional may be asked to give an opinion as to whether a child in foster care is ready for return to the original home or whether an extension of foster care is indicated. In other instances, a social worker or foster parents initiate a request for treatment because of a child's behavior.

In all of these situations, the possibility of the termination of parental rights usually is not raised as an issue unless done so by the mental health professional. Hence, as in many other clinical situations, raising questions about the parents' ability to respond to treatment and their progress is important. This shifts the emphasis to evaluating the overall status of the child and family rather than focusing on a single question about the child. In so doing a variety of system level factors may surface in which the mental health professional can play a useful bridging and integrating role (Faller, 1981):

1. *Courts deal with facts and due process.* Based on their past experiences, child protective services workers may believe that a particular judge would never terminate parental rights. This often has been the result of the incomplete presentation of evidence in court. Frequently the opinions and information presented to the court are disjointed, unclear, and speculative. The language used by professional disciplines differs and obscures areas of agreement. Consequently, the court's practical questions are not addressed. When critical information is brought into focus and due process procedures are followed, judges do terminate parental rights as statutes require.

2. *Mandated family preservation policies.* Departments of social services usually have the mandate to preserve the family unit. For this reason, a tendency to inordinately delay involuntary termination of parental rights may permeate a department's practice. Awareness of the adverse effects on specific children can alter this trend.

3. *"Battle fatigue" of child protective services workers.* Social workers in these agencies often are young, inexperienced, and carry high caseloads of severely disturbed families. This leads to high staff turnover rates which result in the lack of continuity in case management. The mental health professional's support and empathy can be helpful for social workers.

4. *Orientation of the prosecuting attorney.* The prosecuting attorney must be convinced of the merits of a case if it is to come to court and be pursued vigorously. The prosecuting attorney plays a key role in organizing and presenting testimony to meet the requirements of the law as well as the policies of a particular judge.

5. *Informing the parents' attorney.* Because the parents' attorneys can pursue legal actions and appeals to a child's detriment, mental health professionals can insure that the parents' attorneys are aware of all the facts regarding parental behavior with children. A defense attorney may be helped to recognize that zealous defense of a parent's wishes may be contrary to the parent's long-term interests.

6. *Collaboration with the guardian* ad litem. In the adversarial format, children need legal representation of their interests. In a number of states this is provided by a guardian *ad litem* or counsel for the child. The optimal role of the mental health professional is as an expert appointed by the judge as a member of a child advocacy team initiated by the guardian *ad litem.*

THE EVALUATION OF PARENTING

The task of assessing a parent's ability to meet a particular child's needs is guided by the statutory requirements of each state. Generally the expectation is that parental rights will not be terminated if parents meet minimal, not optimal, child-rearing standards. The critical issue is the fit between what a specific child needs and what a particular parent can provide.

A parenting evaluation includes a complete history of the child's development and of the parent-child relationship as well as a current assessment of the child in the context of the family (Schetky et al., 1979; Schetky & Slader, 1980; Schoettle, 1984; Steinhauer, 1981). For this, access to social workers, lawyers, foster parents, professional and school records, and the nuclear and extended families is necessary. Usually multiple interviews, observations of family interactions, and home visits are necessary. Psychological and neuropsychological testing also can be useful. All of this can be most effectively accomplished by a child advocacy team as described in Chapters 1 and 4.

In order to establish grounds for the termination of parental rights in most jurisdictions, the following must be demonstrated: (a) a repeated or continuous pattern of failure to meet the basic needs of a child; (b) evidence that this pattern has been damaging to the child; and (c) indications that the parent-child interaction is not amenable to treatment nor likely to change in the natural course of events soon enough to benefit the child. Although usually not specified in statutes, an additional consideration is the primary attachment to a person other than the biological parent.

THE BASIC NEEDS OF THE CHILD

The following criteria can be employed in determining whether an adult fails to possess minimally sufficient capacities to parent a specific child:

1. *Clothing*
   a. Lack of variety commensurate with family income
   b. Insufficient to protect from weather
2. *Hygiene and Cleanliness*
   a. Evidence of repeated rashes or infections as a result of inadequate bathing
   b. Attention-attracting body odor
3. *Health Care and Supervision*
   a. Inadequate immunizations and routine health and dental care
   b. Failure to attend to medical emergencies
   c. Failure to attend to medical and mental health appointments, the administration of medications, and other prescribed treatments
4. *Nutrition*
   a. Inadequate physical growth due to insufficient nutrition
   b. Infections as a result of contaminated food
   c. Nutritional deficiency diseases
5. *Shelter*
   a. Insufficient heating or insulation of house
   b. Insufficient bedding and blankets
   c. Lack of provision for undisturbed sleep
   d. Food or excrement on floor or furniture
6. *Safety*
   a. Accidental overdoses or ingestions of chemicals

    b. Exposure to injury or property destruction by dangerous people
    c. Dangerous electrical connections
    d. Accidents related to inadequate supervision or repeated exposure to situations in which accidents are likely to occur
    e. Inadequate supervision when parent not present

7. *Attachment to Parent*
    a. Lack of affectionate holding, touching, and talking to child by parent
    b. Parent insensitive to child's initiatives and reactions
    c. Parent erratic, inconsistent, abrupt, or rough with child
    d. Lack of comfortable reaching out to parent by child
    e. Lack of child's affectionate gaze, vocalization, touching, or smiling at parent
    f. Negative, fearful, or indifferent attitudes toward parent by child
    g. Fearful, disruptive behavior before, during, or after visits with parent

8. *Acceptance by Parent as a Developing Person*
    a. Parent views child as object rather than person
    b. Parent misperceives innocent behavior of child as willful or hostile
    c. Parent omits care as a result of misperception, preoccupation, or lack of motivation
    d. Parent is sadistic or excessively critical of child
    e. Parent fails to appreciate child's cognitive and physical level of development
    f. Parent fails to understand a child's need for autonomy by infantilizing or restraining the independent activity and exploration of the child
    g. Parent fails to appreciate child's need for limit setting by overindulgent or excessively permissive behavior
    h. Parent's daily routine incompatible with child's schedule and needs

9. *Socialization*
    a. Parent models irresponsible behavior, such as failure to manage finances and carry out day-to-day tasks
    b. Parent models violent or antisocial behavior
    c. Severe conflict between parents in their expectations of a child
    d. Flagrant exposure of child to adult sexual behavior

10. *Continuity of Relationships*
    a. Instability of home location
    b. Instability of household composition

When evaluating whether parents have met the basic needs of the child, we look for a pattern of repeated and longstanding failure. Exceptions are cases of heinous failures by the parents (e.g., premeditated or sadistic abuse, Münchausen syndrome by proxy, murder of a sibling). In most cases in which the termination of parental rights is being considered, the failure to meet the basic needs of a child is evident by most, and sometimes all, of the criteria.

In the assessment of the fit between the basic needs of a given child and the parenting capacities of a particular parent, one must consider the ameliorating effects of other available persons interested in parenting the children, such as older siblings, grandparents, aunts, uncles, and others living with the family.

EVIDENCE OF DAMAGE TO A CHILD

Determining whether a child has been damaged involves a medical, developmental, and psychiatric assessment of the child as well as data about a child's adjustment away from the home environment, such as in a foster home or residential center. The developmental and psychiatric findings are usually more important than physical findings because of the more devastating effect of neglect on a child's personality and coping abilities than of physical abuse to the body.

Although the presence of a developmental delay does not in itself prove inadequate parenting, significant developmental delays in a child of normal intelligence, particularly if associated with other signs of a disturbed parent-child relationship, are highly suggestive of inadequate parenting. The presence of longstanding symptomatic behavior reflecting anxiety or depression and of a conduct disorder also may be indicators of damage. Care should be taken to relate the manifestations of psychiatric disorders to parenting patterns and environmental events.

Rapid progress in developmental level or symptomatic improvement in a substitute family environment are indications of previously inadequate or damaging parenting (Steinhauer, 1981). Assessment of progress made away from the original home can be made from data gathered from teachers, foster parents, social workers, and the children themselves.

AMENABILITY OF A
PARENT TO TREATMENT

The last area of evaluation is the likelihood that a parent will develop minimal parenting skills soon enough to be of value in a specific child's developmental course. Three questions are helpful in this assessment.

The first question concerns the highest level of overall functioning that a parent has achieved and whether there has been a pattern of deterioration. A psychiatric diagnosis is necessary but not sufficient for this part of the evaluation. Although some workers (Green, 1981; R. Kempe & C. H. Kempe, 1978) have identified diagnostic groups likely to be untreatable (e.g., sociopaths, psychotics whose delusions include the child, alcoholics, drug abusers, and the mentally retarded), we must assess the impact of these disorders on parenting. This is done by investigating the actual past functioning of a parent in terms of psychiatric symptoms, employment, arrests, relationships, past medical history, and daily routines. The parents' personal history of parenting during childhood also is relevant. If there is an established history of chronically poor functioning, any rehabilitation plan will require motivation of the parent and optimal community resources for a chance of success.

Neuropsychological testing of the parent is a valuable part of the evaluation. Areas of deficit are specified in a concrete way that can be persuasive in court. Psychological findings of defective judgment may be more amenable to education and psychotherapy than a memory deficit which appears to be more fixed. For example, a child may have a medical condition for which accurate and appropriate administration of medication is necessary. If a parent fails to administer the medication appropriately, this may be attributed to poor judgment which may be amenable to intervention, or to a memory deficit which may be more difficult to remedy.

The second question concerns the parent's response to past treatment efforts. In this regard one can consider all professional attempts to assist the parent, such as by homemakers, caseworkers, parent trainers, nurses, teachers, physicians, lay therapists, guardians, and psychotherapists. For each treatment effort one should inquire about the reasons for referral, the frequency and nature of the intervention, the parent's cooperation and attitude, and the circumstances of termination. By reviewing past treatment efforts, the often stated plea for "one more chance" by parents can be seen in the larger context in which they have previously received many "one more chances." A careful review of each treatment effort reveals one of four patterns:

1. The parents have repeatedly and consistently refused treatment and denied problems.
2. The parents have acknowledged difficulties, have attended regularly, but have had mixed results from their efforts.
3. The parents have acknowledged difficulties, have attended regularly or irregularly, have improved their material parenting but not their psychosocial parenting.
4. The parents have acknowledged difficulties, participated regularly, and have consistently made significant improvement in their physical and psychosocial parenting.

Our experience and that of others (Jones, 1987) indicates that the first pattern has an extremely grave prognosis. The second pattern requires a closer look at the circumstances and nature of the treatment efforts. Did the parents make improvements with certain professionals and not with others or with certain treatment components or formats and not with others, or with agencies near their homes but not those far away? The third pattern represents the most difficult to evaluate. In these cases, the mental health professional needs to weigh the severity of the current abuse or neglect, how much damage has been done to the child, and how much progress has occurred. The fourth pattern represents the optimal outcome.

The third question has to do with the parent's view toward future intervention. Often parents deny problems and state that they "don't need treatment." If this response has been observed consistently by different professionals, we feel secure in making an immediate determination of untreatability. Commonly parents admit vague deficiencies as a means of appeasing the professional while omitting substantial specifics. They often attribute their difficulties to the mismanagement of their case by other professionals. A review of past treatment efforts reveals a pattern of begrudging motivation, sporadic attendance, and limited progress. They also may insist that they will change when their children are returned to them, claiming that their problems are the result of the placement of their children.

The following case illustrates the steps that can be taken to constructively terminate parental rights. In this example the methodical pursuit of an involuntary termination procedure led to a voluntary termination.

CASE EXAMPLE

One-year-old Kathy was brought to an emergency room after being dropped on her head by her 23-year-old mother's live-in boyfriend, Mr. G. She had 4- and 5-year-old sisters. Each child was fathered by a different man, none of whom were married to the mother. Shortly after this incident, a neighbor reported Mr. G to the police, alleging sexual behavior toward the three girls. He was subsequently arrested and convicted. At that time, all three children were removed from the home and placed in foster care.

Investigation by the Department of Social Services (DSS) revealed grossly inadequate food, clothing, shelter, and supervision. Kathy's 5-year-old sister provided supervision and guidance for the two younger children and was called "mom" by her 4-year-old sister. When examined by a physician, Kathy was noted to be filthy, anemic, malnourished, and with feces in her vagina.

The mother denied that there were any problems and wished to have her children returned home. The DSS recommended psychological evaluation, homemaker services, counseling, and parent training with indefinite foster placement of the children. Over the next 1-1/2 years, numerous specialized services were offered to the mother. After a few meetings, she typically dismissed them, saying that she "knew everything already." Despite her claims, however, observation of her functioning as a parent revealed little if any improvements, so that the DSS filed for the termination of her parental rights. The case became bogged down, however, because the attorney for the mother viewed her as an unfortunate person being unfairly punished by society.

At this point, the authors were contacted by the guardian *ad litem* to become involved as experts for the court. Our first step was to meet with the district attorney, guardian *ad litem*, and DSS workers to clarify the history and to organize a child advocacy team. In this meeting their desperation over the gravity as well as the seeming futility of pursuing the case vigorously became apparent. Our plan was to shift the emphasis away from punishing the mother by involving the mother's attorney so as to increase his appreciation of the DSS workers' observations of her realistic capacities, and by supporting the mother's efforts to forge a relationship with her new husband, Mr. F. Concurrently, our aim was to shift the mother's basis for self-esteem from possession of the children to pride in herself and her personal gains. To carry this out we met with her, her husband, and the children in various combinations nine times over the next 6 months. In addition, the foster parents were interviewed, the children were observed on visits in the mother's home twice, and her attorney was informed of our activities and impressions. Many telephone calls to and from the DSS workers occurred. Neuropsychological testing also was performed on the mother.

With the children in foster care and the possibility of an involuntary termination of her parental rights facing her over a 6-month period, the mother stopped drinking, solidified her relationship with her husband, and began to look for employment. Still, her parenting skills remained grossly inadequate. During a home visit she smiled and verbally greeted the children but had no physical contact with them. Mr. F watched cartoons on television and did not acknowledge the children's presence nor interact with them throughout the visit. The children appeared wary of him and stayed away from him. The mother's only words were instructions to the children such as, "Eat your vegetables." When the children left, there were no good-byes and no expressions of parting from the mother. Mr. F continued watching television. After a subsequent unsupervised visit, the 4-year-old had an unexplained burn on her hand.

Because of the mother's lack of improvement in parenting skills in spite of vigorous treatment efforts, the child advocacy team decided to pursue involuntary termination of her parental rights. A number of dramatic last-minute occurrences followed, including the mother's failure to retain legal counsel until a few days before the scheduled hearing. Her first attorney resigned from the case soon after the team was formed. Because of her tardiness in pursuing new legal aid, she was refused representation by the Public Defender. Her initial attorney agreed to take up the case again but re-entered the case with a broader perspective of his client's interests. With his support and encouragement, she proceeded to voluntarily terminate her rights to all three children. She apparently recognized that the responsibilities of raising three young children would jeopardize the progress she had made in improving her personal life adjustment.

SUMMARY

Contemporary conceptions of minimally adequate parenting have been evolving out of public dialog between legislators, professionals, and the media. This ongoing refinement of what constitute the basic psychological and developmental needs of abused and neglected children is at the heart of the question of terminating parental rights. Although we hope that the future will bring more effective prevention and treatment in this realm, the unfortunate fact is that a sizable number of children and parents benefit from a permanent change in parenting and homes.

Some argue that professionals have no business "playing God" in these complex situations. This viewpoint overlooks the body of knowledge of child development and the clinical assessment techniques that permit valid judgments regarding the fit of parenting capacities and a child's needs. More importantly, this argument overlooks the fact that making no recommendations under these circumstances and tacitly or overtly agreeing to return a child to a questionable parent is no less "playing God."

Although cases in which the termination of parental rights is considered are challenging, there are rewards. The voluntary termination of parental rights can provide relief for overtaxed parents who make this painful decision in their children's interests. The involuntary termination of parental rights can relieve parental guilt, because an external authority has made the decision. For the child, the benefits are early adoption and the avoidance of an uncertain future resulting from multiple foster placements. The careful and methodical assessment of parenting capacities provides a structure for formulating treatment goals and monitoring progress. This saves anguish, prolonged indecisiveness, and futile efforts. Last, for society, facilitating the adoption of abused and neglected children reduces the ultimate burden on everyone imposed by "children of the state."

REFERENCES

Abbott, J. H. (1981). *In the Belly of the Beast.* New York: Random House.

American Humane Association. (1989). *Highlights of Official Aggregate Child Neglect and Abuse Reporting.* Denver, CO: Author.

Faller, K. C. (Ed). (1981). *Social Work with Abused and Neglected Children.* New York: Free Press.

Fanshel, D., & Shinn, E. (1978). *Children in Foster Care.* New York: Columbia University Press.

Green, A. H. (1981). Factors associated with successful and unsuccessful intervention with child abusing families. *Child Abuse and Neglect, 5,* 45-52.

Jones, D. (1987). The untreatable family. *Child Abuse and Neglect, 11,* 409-420.

Kempe, R., & Kempe, C. H. (1978). *Child Abuse.* Cambridge, MA: Harvard University Press.

Lewis, D. O. (1985). Biopsychosocial characteristics of children who later murder: A prospective study. *American Journal of Psychiatry, 142,* 1161-1167.

Lewis, D. O., Shanok, S. S., Grant, M., & Ritvo, E. (1983). Homicidally aggressive young children, neuropsychiatric and experiential correlates. *American Journal of Psychiatry, 140,* 148-153.

Lewis, D. O., Shanok, S. S., Pincus, J. H., & Glaser, G. D. (1979). Violent juvenile delinquents. *Journal of Child Psychiatry, 18,* 307-319.

Mitchell, L. (1987). *Child Abuse and Neglect Fatalities: Review of the Problem and Strategies for Reform.* Denver, CO: National Committee for Prevention of Child Abuse.

Newby, R. (1981). *Review of Outcome Research on Family Oriented Interventions for Physical Child Abuse.* Unpublished manuscript.

Polansky, N. A., Chalmers, M. A., Buttenwieser, E., & Williams, D. P. (1981). *Damaged Parents: An Anatomy of Neglect.* Chicago, IL: University of Chicago Press.

Reinhart, J. B. (1985). Termination of parental rights. *Journal of Child Psychiatry, 24,* 238-239.

Schetky, D. H., Angell, R., Morrison, C. V., & Sack, W. H. (1979). Parents who fail: A study of 51 cases of termination of parental rights. *Journal of Child Psychiatry, 18,* 366-383.

Schetky, D. H., & Slader, D. (1980). Termination of parental rights. In D. H. Schetky & E. P. Benedek (Eds.), *Child Psychiatry and the Law* (pp. 107-118). New York: Brunner/Mazel.

Schoettle, V. C. (1984). Termination of parental rights - ethical issues and role conflicts. *Journal of Child Psychiatry, 23,* 629-632.

Steinhauer, P. (1981, May 7). *Assessing for Parenting Capacity.* Paper presented at Ontario Family Court Clinic Conference, Ontario, Canada.

Tanay, E. (1969). Psychiatric study of homicide. *American Journal of Psychiatry, 125,* 1252-1258.

Wald, M. S. (1982). State intervention on behalf of endangered children. *Child Abuse and Neglect, 9,* 3-45.

Westman, J. C. (1979). *Child Advocacy.* New York: Free Press.

Winnicott, D. W. (1984). *Deprivation and Delinquency.* London: Tavistock Publications.

Part V

THE POLITICAL SYSTEM

INTRODUCTION

The quality of a civilization may be measured by how it cares for its elderly. Just as surely, the future of a society may be forecast by how it cares for its young.

Daniel Patrick Moynihan, 1986

We live in a world that permits 40,000 children to die each day from malnutrition and disease while nations, led by the United States, have spent $2.7 billion a day on military weapons (Edelman, 1987). We live in a nation that, for every dollar spent on Aid to the Families of Dependent Children, spends $11 on veterans' benefits and military retirement programs for a smaller number of people. In this context, the need for class child advocacy is clear.

Still, recognizing that each generation views its successors with alarm, the federal and state governments are seeking an objective perspective from which to gauge the seriousness of contemporary problems of children and youth (U.S. Department of Education, 1988). The media tend to stress that teenagers are dropping out of school, getting pregnant out of wedlock, taking drugs, running away from home, and otherwise getting into trouble at increasing rates. But the reality is more complex, and in some ways, encouraging. For example, more teenagers are finishing high school than ever before, the rate of births to teenagers has not increased over the last 10 years, and teenage drug use has eased somewhat in the last 5 years. On the other hand, the overall indicators reflect a totally unacceptable rate of troubled children and youth for a modern civilized society and a deterioration in the status of many.

As examples of the deterioration in the welfare of children in the United States, between 1970 and 1985 the percentage of children living in poverty rose by one-third. The year 1985 was the first year since 1960 that the overall neonatal mortality rate failed to decline in the United States, which placed 19th in the world. Nearly 25% of all infants were born to mothers who received late or no pre-natal care. Medicaid and Supplemental Food for Women, Infants, and Children failed to reach half of all the eligible women and children in poverty (Hughes et al., 1988). One-sixth of white children, but two-fifths of black and Hispanic children, live in poverty. Almost half of white youths continue their education beyond high school, but only one-third of blacks and one-quarter of Hispanics do so. Blacks and Hispanics are catching up in reading and mathematics proficiency, but they still lag far behind their white classmates. When it comes to unemployment among youths, the races are far apart. For youths who drop out of school, fewer than half find jobs, and those who do not often commit crimes. Moreover, juvenile justice has been plagued by the extremes of over-reaction and undereffectiveness (Sandhu & Heaseley, 1981). It has overcriminalized, overprocessed, overincarcerated, and undermonitored the problems of children and youth brought to the courts. But one statistic cuts across all of the others. Among young people, suicide has become the second-leading cause of death, out-distanced only by motor-vehicle accidents.

More specifically, the federal government has consistently discriminated against families. For example, special interest groups influence tax legislation from which the most important part of our economic system - mothers, fathers, and children - are left out. The standard federal income tax deduction for a dependent would have been $5,600 in 1988, if it had kept abreast with inflation.

The United States now is experiencing a simultaneous increase in wealth and poverty (Moynihan, 1986). There are three different kinds of poor families: the single-parent family, the working poor, and the ghetto poor. About a quarter of the nation's children live in single-parent families, most of them poor, but only 1 single mother in 3 receives any child support, and the average annual payment is only $2,300. Two-parent working poor families receive so few government benefits that they generally end up even poorer than families who depend entirely on the welfare system. This situation creates intense bitterness, discourages the work ethic, and encourages long-term dependency on government benefits. The ghetto poor need most the things no welfare system can provide: (a) fair-wage jobs for adults, unless aged, disabled, or rearing young children; (b) fluency and literacy in English; (c) work skills; and (c) prosocial values (Mead, 1986).

In addition to the plight of the disadvantaged, another important reason for class child advocacy is the influx of mothers with children into the labor force. Many married women return to work on either a part-time or full-time basis when their children grow up, or earlier as economic necessity or personal choice dictates (Statistical Bulletin, 1987). In 1986, over 30 million wives - 55% of all married women - were either employed or seeking work. At ages under 25, over three-fifths were in the labor force. Between the ages of 25 and 44, the years when most women formerly remained home to care for their children, the percentage of part- and full-time employed was two-thirds. As the workplace increasingly dominates family life, advocacy for affected children is needed.

At the present time, there is evidence of progress in class child advocacy, as exemplified by the Association of Child Advocates, a national association of local and state groups. States also have varying levels of class advocacy for children and their families. For example, the New York State Council on Children and Families produced the *State of the Child in New York State* in 1988.

All programs intended to deal with children and youth require specific attention to mental health, including the prevention and treatment of developmental disabilities, emotional disturbance, and mental illness. An estimated 5 million young people in the United States have disorders requiring psychiatric care; another 5 million also need help but less urgently. Psychiatric services are available for only 5% of these children, in contrast with 75% for the physically handicapped. As an example of addressing this need, the Wisconsin Advocacy Coalition has developed the principles that mental health services for children should be: (a) based on comprehensive assessment; (b) individualized; (c) available on a voluntary basis at the early stages of a problem; (d) designed to maintain a child in the community; and (e) coordinated through case management systems (Greenley & Ungrodt, 1987).

The steps in the class advocacy process (Children's Defense Fund, 1978) typically are to: (a) ascertain how many children are in need, how existing systems work, and what ombudsman mechanisms for case advocacy exist; (b) identify sources of authority and examine budgets, licensing regulations, administrative procedures, laws, and statistical and program reports; (c) decide what corrective action is necessary in the interdependent parts of the child-care system and formulate realistic short- and long-term remedies; (d) mobilize support for the desired change by encouraging civic and church groups to become familiar with the identified problems and to understand why corrective action is needed; (e) identify the impact of federal funding on state budgets, the competitors for funds, and the timetables for the preparation of local and state budgets; (f) use as many strategies as necessary to effect change beginning with persuasion and, if that fails, publicity, litigation, and coalition building between agencies and organizations affecting children; (g) monitor the changes effected to be sure that they are carried out; (h) keep records of all stages of the advocacy process and obtain administrative decisions and timetables for changes in writing; and (i) be patient but persistent.

A cloud hangs over the various forms of class child advocacy, because it often is unclear whether the interests of adults or of children are being promoted. The reformers of the Progressive Era early in this century fought for the creation of juvenile courts, protective child labor laws, and compulsory education laws because their agendas for children also met adult needs (Mnookin, 1985). Now, as then, lobbying efforts or organizations controlled by parents, teachers, mental health professionals, probation officers, and other professionals often serve their own interests rather than those of children. This was illustrated vividly by school desegregation, which imposed substantial burdens on many children, some of whom suffered greatly. The lives of children rather than adults were altered to promote social change with short-range disadvantage for them in order to achieve potential long-range social gains. This was favored rather than addressing the underlying socio-economic causes of segregation.

Because of the likelihood of bias against children, courts are confronted with three dilemmas in class action suits: (a) deciding which policies best serve the interests of children; (b) defining the appropriate role for courts in democratic policy making on behalf of children; and (c) the paradox of needing advocates to speak for children's interests without a mechanism to hold those advocates accountable to those children (Mnookin, 1985).

Broad public support for class advocacy for children and families cannot be expected until there is awareness that crime and social dependency are directly linked to poverty, child abuse, and child neglect (Wilson & Herrnstein, 1986) and then that crime and dependency directly threaten public safety and increase taxes. The public needs to know that early intervention now is possible by identifying both child and parent populations at risk for later crime and dependency. Examples include teenage pregnancy; high-school dropouts; juveniles in custody; abused and neglected children; children who have experienced loss of a parent by death, desertion, divorce, or serious illness; and children with developmental handicaps and learning disabilities (National Governors' Association, 1987).

An over-riding consideration in class advocacy for children is recognizing the need of each child for competent parenting. Most public debate focuses on the economic well-being, health, and education of children, because the resources of government can be directed at those factors. However, these elements are not sufficient to prepare children for citizenship and productivity. Competent parents are needed to foster the development of the motivation, values, and social skills needed for participation in our society. When children have had competent parenting, poverty and social disadvantage have not prevented their self-fulfillment and success in later life. Without competent parenting, even wealth and social advantage have not been enough to insure later success.

The pivotal question for our society is: Should we expect children to continue to be the victims of adult failures and inadequacies or should the fact that children are affected stimulate adults to more competently resolve their problems?

REFERENCES

Association of Child Advocates, P.O. Box 5873, 3615 Superior Avenue, Cleveland, OH 44101-0873.

Children's Defense Fund. (1978). *Children Without Homes.* Washington, DC: Children's Defense Fund.

Edelman, M. W. (1987). *Families in Peril.* Cambridge, MA: Harvard University Press.

Greenley, D., & Ungrodt, J. (1987). *Kids in Crisis: A Plan for Action.* Madison, WI: Wisconsin Coalition for Advocacy.

Hughes, D., Johnson, K., Rosenbaum, S., Butler, E., & Simons, J. (1988). *The Health of American's Children: Maternal and*

Child Health Data Book. Washington, DC: Children's Defense Fund.

Mead, L. M. (1986). *Beyond Entitlement: The Social Obligations of Citizenship.* New York: The Free Press.

Mnookin, R. H. (Ed.). (1985). *In the Interest of Children: Advocacy Law Reform and Public Policy.* New York: W. H. Freeman.

Moynihan, D. P. (1986). *Family and Nation.* New York: Harcourt, Brace, Jovanovich.

National Governors' Association. (1987). *The First Sixty Months: The Next Steps.* Washington, DC: The Council of State Governments.

New York State Council on Children and Families. (1988). *State of the Child in New York State.* Albany, NY: New York State Council on Children and Families.

Sandhu, H. S., & Heaseley C. W. (1981). *Improving Juvenile Justice.* New York: Human Sciences Press.

Statistical Bulletin. (1987). Profile of the American Wife, *68,* 18-21.

U.S. Department of Education. (1989). *Youth Indicators 1988.* Washington, DC: U.S. Government Printing Office.

Wilson, J. Q., & Herrnstein, R. J. (1986). *Criminals Born and Bred: Crime and Human Nature.* New York: Simon & Schuster.

13

SELLING ADULTS ON CHILDREN'S ISSUES: PROBLEMS OF CLASS CHILD ADVOCACY

Gary B. Melton

The aim of this chapter is to orient practitioners to the evolving concept of class child advocacy. It highlights the key issues and the difficulties in defining general advocacy goals.

Professor Melton warns that the "interests of children" are used for a variety of political agendas. The emotional appeal of protecting our children is used to justify massive military spending at one extreme and both pro- and antia-bortion positions at the other. As a result, obtaining consensus for effective class child advocacy depends upon clearly defining limited, specific objectives for particular classes of children.

Adults generally assume that they know what is best for children without having an accurate data base. This stems from the fact that children are not freestanding individuals. By definition they are parts of child-parent units; when they no longer are so, they are adults. Still the inclusion of children in decision making and events that affect them enhances the validity of adult actions on their behalf and need not give them inappropriate responsibility and power for self-determination. The model of healthy family life in which the opinions and needs of children are included in family decision making is more appropriate than a political model in which children represent themselves in legislative

*bodies. Thus the empowerment of children means includ-
ing their viewpoints and needs in establishing advocacy
agendas.*

*The inclusion of a child's views and interests inheres
more readily in individual than class advocacy because the
child participates in the clinical process. Because young
people ordinarily are not included in class advocacy, a
deliberate and planned effort to do so can help to insure
that advocacy agendas truly reflect their concrete interests
rather than abstractions about what is best for children.
Because they are aware of the problems encountered by
children through their work with individuals, practitioners
are in a strategic position to initiate and support effective
class advocacy.*

*The most important antidote to ageism and the exploi-
tation of children is respect for children and youth as people.*

For the most part, child advocacy is a social movement that is
directed neither by nor toward children themselves. Although I
do not believe that fact to be fully intrinsic to the enterprise, I do
believe it to be basic to the two major problems of child advocacy:
(a) establishment of an agenda and (b) selection of strategies.
Although both of these problems also arise in case advocacy, they
are more acute when advocates purport to represent the interests
of children as a class.

ESTABLISHMENT OF AN AGENDA

IDEOLOGIES OF ADVOCACY

The major problem in establishing the goals of child advocacy
is that neither advocates nor children themselves share a common
understanding about the values and social facts underlying child
advocacy. Definitions of the interests of children involve symbolic statements of fundamental beliefs about proper social order-
ing: how children, parents, and the state *ought* to relate to each
other (Melton, 1987e). Debates about children's policy typically
rest on broad assumptions about the nature of childhood, family
life, and the human condition. Views about the nature of childhood and children's issues are entwined with world views that
organize one's understanding of the social world. At such a basic
level of social cognition, empirical observation and normative be-

lief are conflated. Assumptions about child development and family life are so basic as to be largely intuitive, a priori (and, therefore, largely inarguable), and deeply and emotionally held. Child advocacy is especially difficult, therefore, because the nature of the arguments that will be persuasive (if indeed any can be) often is elusive. Apparent questions of fact may turn out instead to be problems of ethics and politics that are not answerable by amassing empirical evidence.

The significance of this observation is illustrated by examining child advocacy itself. The notion that there is a single movement for children is both philosophically and politically naïve. There are at least three conflicting perspectives found among child advocates. One school of thought emphasizes recognition of children's liberty and privacy interests. Such "kiddie libbers" typically believe children and youth to be more like, than different from, adults. They regard those differences that do exist to be morally insignificant; children's personhood is not doubted.

By contrast, "child savers" typically perceive children as incompetent, vulnerable, and irresponsible. They generally favor stringent limits on the self-determination of children and youth, at least when choice is exercised in the direction of refusing what's "good for them." In recognition of children's dependent status, child savers emphasize entitlements to solicitude and protection. Although they are convinced of children's innocence, they tend to doubt parents' competence, motivation, or resources to provide such nurturance. As a result, they favor expansive state involvement in protection of child welfare.

The third group (e.g., J. Goldstein, Freud, & Solnit, 1973, 1979; J. Goldstein et al., 1986) perceives children's interests in a manner similar to the child savers, but believes that children's primary psychosocial need is for authoritative parents. Thus, although they share a belief that children and youth are not autonomous members of the community, they advocate parents' rights and, for the most part, state neutrality, in the name of children's rights.

Note the ambiguous foundation of assumptions in all three perspectives. Both of the latter groups view children as properly dependent. It is unclear when such an assumption reflects an assessment of the realities of children's abilities and needs, and when it instead indicates an ethical/political theory about what the status of children in society should be.

Regardless, it is clear that the child advocacy movement, when viewed as a single movement, lacks a consensus even about the nature of its purported constituency (even whether they are persons) and whether, as a general matter, children's interests are better served when authority for their lives is vested primarily in the state, parents, or children themselves. Indeed, the only assumption that child advocates are apt to share is that children are important. Although the resulting injunction to "be nice to kids" is a warm sentiment, it is hardly a ringing slogan for a political movement or a guiding principle for social reform and legal decision making.

AVOIDING QUESTIONS

Because child advocates themselves hold such widely divergent views about their agenda, the tendency is to gloss over or, alternatively, to dwell on basic disagreements about the nature and status of children and youth. Questions of child mental health policy are illustrative. For example, Nebraska's unicameral legislature recently enacted a Family Policy Act (1987), the language of which is so broad as to be either all-encompassing or meaningless, because it purports to amend the entire state code![1] Potentially the most far-reaching provision is encompassed in the following sentence:

> When children and families require assistance from a department, agency, institution, committee, or commission of state government, every reasonable effort shall be made to provide such assistance in the least intrusive and least restrictive method and to deliver such assistance as close to the home community of the child or family requiring assistance as possible. (sec. 1, para. 2)

In a small planning group charged with developing precise goals and objectives to implement the Act, I began to point out some of the ambiguities about legislative intent. For example, the subsection quoted requires a particular style of action "[w]hen children and families require assistance." By use of that phrase, did the legislature intend to create an entitlement to services for

---

[1]The Family Policy Act (1987, sec. 1, para. 2[a]) is to "be interpreted in conjunction with all relevant laws, rules, and regulations of the state" and to be applied "to all children and families who have need of service or who, by their circumstances or actions, have violated the laws, rules, or regulations of the state and are found to be in need of treatment or rehabilitation."

needy children and families? Alternatively, did the legislature intend instead to express an over-riding libertarian policy minimizing state involvement in the lives of children and families even when assistance is requested? And for whom did the legislature intend to minimize intrusiveness and restrictiveness - children or parents?[2]

As I raised such questions, it became clear that they had never been considered by the legislature or the advocates who were lobbying for passage of the Act. Indeed, there was no formal legislative history at all; no legislators had a doubt that they wanted to be on record in favor of families, and there was no floor debate. It also became clear as the planning group discussed the Act that the individuals in the room - some of whom had been involved in drafting the legislation - had markedly divergent views about the nature of the policy that had been enacted.

Ultimately, though, if the Family Policy Act is to be more than mere dicta, the child advocates in Nebraska will have to resolve hard questions about the goals of policy for children and families. As long as such questions are sloughed off, I doubt whether significant development and re-structuring of children's services - the general goals that the advocates share - will be possible. Failure to confront broad policy dilemmas may result in avoidance of concrete plans for change.

On the other hand, advances in child mental health policy are sometimes forestalled when *only* the overarching questions - indeed, sometimes the *wrong* questions - are addressed, because of the desire for symbolic assertion of various principles. An excellent example is the debate about psychiatric hospitalization of minors. That debate has focused on the question of who the primary decision maker should be in admission of children to mental hospitals. Unsurprisingly, the issue has aroused great verbiage about the nature of children and families. For example, *Parham*

---

[2]Although services that are minimally restrictive for seriously disordered children also tend to be minimally intrusive on family privacy (intensive home-based services being a good example), it must be recognized that minimization of restrictions on children's liberty and intrusions on their liberty also may directly intrude on parental liberty and privacy interests (e.g., when children are permitted to consent to treatment independently). Conversely, unfettered parental freedom to make decisions regarding the family obviously may result in significant restrictions and intrusions on children. For example, parents' decisions to commit their children to psychiatric facilities result in outright deprivation of freedom of movement and association and substantial intrusion on privacy of mind and personal space.

v. J. R. (1979), the landmark decision on the topic, was the long-
est opinion that the U.S. Supreme Court issued in its 1978 term -
an opinion that was long on myths, short on facts, and uncertain
in influence (Perry & Melton, 1984).

Although I do not minimize the symbolic significance of full
recognition of the personhood of youth (to belie my own position
in the debate), it is clear to me that the question of who decides is
not the critical problem. Whether correct or not, a given in child
policy is that children and youth have to be somewhere; even the
most dogmatic kiddie libbers generally are prepared to concede
that minors should not be left on their own. The unfortunate
realities are (a) that many of the youth in psychiatric hospitals
were rejected by or removed from their families long before the
hospitalization, and (b) that few less restrictive (and, I would
argue, more appropriate) settings for difficult youth exist in most
communities. In this instance, concentration on the largely symbolic question of allocation of decision-making authority among
child, family, and state has obscured the more pressing policy
questions: What can we do to protect the integrity of families in
crisis, and how can we insure the availability of humane settings
that are relatively unrestrictive and unintrusive for troubled and
troubling adolescents who have no place to go (see Melton &
Spaulding, 1991)?

Regardless of whether assumptions about the nature of
childhood are ignored or obsessed over, social reality is obscured,
and attention to practical dilemmas of social policy is diverted.
Any sense of shared mission is apt to be lost or transformed. As
several accounts of the development of child and family policy
have illustrated (see, e.g., Melton, 1983a; Mnookin, 1985b; Steiner, 1976), a common result of class advocacy is that child advocates themselves are left in disarray and political strife, as their
underlying differences ultimately predominate.

I believe that we currently are on a collision course in which
each of the major schools of child advocacy has obtained some
success in limited contexts but without reconciliation or even ac-
knowledgement of advocates' fundamental differences in their
approach to problems of child policy. As I have summarized
elsewhere:

> We currently are confronted with unprecedented child
> self-determination, family privacy, state intervention to
> protect children (especially in regard to their health), and
> state intervention to disrupt families and constrain child

autonomy! Each of the major schools of thought about children's rights seems to have identified issues in which it can pursue its agenda with little controversy. On the other hand, the ultimate incompatibility of such perspectives cannot be avoided. If, for example, a school district relies on the new paternalism to provide the ideological foundation for establishment of school health clinics, it eventually will be confronted with the question of who may give (and refuse) consent to the clinics' services. It also eventually will have to decide whether to seek state authority to coerce receipt of services, to require parental involvement, or to enforce confidentiality against parents. (Melton, 1987c, p. 86)

THE USE OF CHILDREN

The potential political conflict is intensified by the fact that child advocates' agendas rarely are derived directly or exclusively from an analysis of the interests of children and youth. To use an example of an issue that has been the focus of much of my own work in recent years,[3] consider the debate about policy on adolescent abortion.[4] In political arguments and legal struggles over the limits to be put on minors' access to abortion, I doubt that either side would approach the issue substantially differently if it did not involve minors. When the American Civil Liberties Union or Planned Parenthood lobbies or litigates for recognition of privacy rights, and right-to-life groups argue for parental notification requirements, they do so ostensibly in the name of the protection of minors' interests. Although such a declaration can be part of a cynical political strategy, I suspect that in this instance both sides really believe that they have adolescents' interests at heart. Nonetheless, it is clear that the "children's rights" issue emanates from other political and ethical concerns and that the danger is real of *using* children and youth to serve the interests of particular adult constituencies.

---

[3]See *Hartigan v. Zbaraz* (1987), brief of amicus curiae American Psychological Association (APA); *Hodgson v. Minnesota* (1989), brief of amicus curiae APA; Interdivisional Committee on Adolescent Abortion (1987); Melton (1983c, 1986, 1987d); Melton & Russo (1987).

[4]An excellent account of the divisions among child advocates on the abortion issue is presented in Mnookin's (1985a) journalistic discussion of *Bellotti v. Baird* (1979).

The images of childhood that have underlain public policy differ (Melton, 1990). One such image is that of "little warriors for social change." Whether the direction of change is toward the left or the right, the tendency is to rely on children to implement it. Just as liberals have focused their efforts to remedy inequality on the schoolhouse, so conservatives have centered their attempts to achieve their moral agenda in the schoolhouse and the home. Similarly, the Reagan Administration (Working Group on the Family, 1986) curiously rejected social programs intended to support children's healthy development - for example, day care, government-sponsored health care, school health programs - on the rationale that such programs ultimately increase the tax bite, force mothers into the workplace, and reduce the birthrate. "Pro-family" has become a buzzword for (a) opposition to public support for programs intended to enhance child development and family life and (b) advocacy of individual responsibility coupled with a *laissez-faire* approach to social and economic policy.

KNOWING WHAT CHILDREN REALLY THINK

Distortion of the agenda of child advocacy to serve adult political and social interests is not limited to those whose primary agenda is not child-centered. Even specialists in services to children often unwittingly fall prey to imposition of their perspective on children. In his provocative book on the political lives of children, Coles (1986) pointed out the central place of the adverb "really" in the vocabulary of child mental health professionals. A good rule of thumb is that a reference to what children *really* think, feel, or intend is likely to mask a falsification, even if inadvertent, of children's experience and behavior.

The unfortunate reality is that attributions about children's concerns often are mistaken, even when made by professionals expert on child development (see, for review, Melton, 1987b). For example, children's own rankings of stressors depart markedly from the rankings that mental health professionals typically believe that children *should* give. Moreover, child and youth issues, as reported by children and adolescents themselves, turn out not to be too dissimilar from the sorts of social, economic, and political problems that preoccupy adults, although perceived in terms of children's own interests. Elementary-school-age children are modally concerned about crime, because children, especially those from economically impoverished backgrounds, often find that they have no safe place to play. Rather than ostensible

282

"youth issues" like preservation of the environment, adolescents tend to identify economic issues - being able to get a job - as their primary concern.

I mention these discrepancies between the subjective realities of children and youth and the attributions by child advocates and helping professionals for three reasons. First, child advocates must acknowledge the fact that they act ostensibly on behalf of children, but they do not *represent* them. Because of the risk of using children to promote one's own political agenda (even if one's intention is beneficent), special and difficult ethical problems arise in child advocacy.[5] When acting as a child advocate, one must take care to insure as far as possible that one is promoting children's interests rather than exploiting them. Beyond the ethical dilemma, if one is attempting to advocate children's interests, then a practical first step as a practical matter is to insure that those interests are accurately perceived. The problem in that context is that, unlike advocates for most other groups, child advocates are unlikely to hear the views of their constituents, absent some form of affirmative effort to learn children's own concerns.

Second, if fully pursued, child advocacy will take one well beyond the arena of issues that commonly are identified as children's issues. This fact has important strategic implications. Even if a united front can be maintained in regard to a basic ideology of children's rights, coalitions may break apart over broader political issues (e.g., the role of the federal government in promoting economic well-being of single-parent families). Alternatively, as discussed earlier, the coalition may be maintained, but the emphasis on children's rights may be lost in the service of other economic and political goals.[6] Regardless, with children's issues covering the gamut of social concerns, child advocates will find that the targets of their work necessarily will be quite diffuse. For example, legislative advocacy cannot focus just on a key committee or two. As a result, the proper investment of re-

---

[5]I discussed these ethical issues at length in my presidential address to the Division of Child, Youth, and Family Services of the American Psychological Association (Melton, 1987b).

[6]An example of such a loss of perspective may be the report of the Carnegie Council on Children (Keniston, 1977). Claiming that its goals were achievable within a decade, the Council's top priorities were for full employment and control of inflation. Although the significance of general economic well-being for child welfare is undeniable, such broad recommendations were politically naïve and probably diluted the credibility of the report.

sources for lobbying and public relations campaigns becomes a difficult but critical strategic issue.

Third, the fact that the concerns of children and youth are so closely tied to the general sociopolitical environment in which they live heightens the difficulty of advocacy for children as a class. I do believe that it is possible to identify issues that affect most children, particularly in regard to protection of their privacy and promotion of respect for their dignity and self-determination. Even when children share the values of their parents (as most do), I also believe that children have a unique perspective, because of their particular situations, that should be heard, as matters of both ethics and rational policy making.

Nonetheless, the point should not be lost that, for most critical issues, it may be impossible to advocate the interests of *the* child. Class advocacy by its nature demands joinder of presumably similar interests.[7] However, just as the targets of child advocacy are diverse, so is the constituency. Indeed, unless one limits the scope of the class for whom advocacy is intended (e.g., institutionalized children), child advocacy often is no more meaningful than adult advocacy. This point was dramatized for me in my study of children's concepts of their rights (Melton, 1980, 1983a). Older children and adolescents from affluent backgrounds tended to identify with the adult authorities in the vignettes that I presented, not the children who might have asserted a right (cf. Coles, 1977). To a large extent, their perceived interests were closer to those of adults who would limit children's access to resources than those of children in need of them.

CAN THE PUZZLE BE SOLVED?

The problems that I have raised are not fully tractable. However, I do believe that they can be alleviated by a relatively simple maneuver: Involve children themselves in advocacy on their behalf (see Melton, 1987b, for a more thorough discussion of this idea). When children and youth themselves participate in setting the agenda for advocacy, less danger lurks of either inadvertent exploitation of children for other political purposes or neglect of the central concerns that children actually have.

---

[7]*See* Federal Rule of Civil Procedure 23(a).

I recognize, of course, that such a solution is only partial. Young children will be unable to contribute much to identification of key factors in their lives. Although older children and adolescents may be astute in recognizing the situations most in need of change, they (like most adult advocates) are apt to lack savvy about ways of effecting that change or at least to lack the economic resources, political clout, and legal standing to obtain access to the policy-making arena.

These gaps can be partially addressed by establishing a requirement for preparation of a children's impact statement before official actions are taken (see Melton, 1987b). Such statements would *not* be fora for advocacy. Rather, they would be intended as a catalog of potential positive and negative effects of proposed policies on various groups of children. Compilation of such statements would be intended to stimulate advocates to come clean about values and uncertainty and to set the tone for a thoughtful approach to children's policy, with due attention to social reality (apart from political mythology).

Looking ahead to potential criticisms of involvement of children in decision making about child advocacy, let me just mention a few counterpoints, which I have discussed in more detail elsewhere (see, e.g., Melton, 1983b, 1987b; Tapp & Melton, 1983). Some might argue that children should be "protected" (i.e., excluded) from involvement in advocacy. However, a substantial body of research shows that, unsurprisingly, perceived control is correlated with numerous aspects of general adjustment (see generally Perlmuter & Monty, 1979). Involvement in self-advocacy also would be expected to facilitate legal and political socialization.

Even without such effects, though, the concern about protecting children from the political process is misplaced. The view that children are apolitical is itself mythical (see Melton, 1987b, for review). Although most children and youth, like most adults, are not political activists, it is nonetheless true that the cumulative proportion of the population involved in some form of political activity peaks by junior-high age. Even elementary-school-age children often are remarkably attuned to power relations and concerned about political and social issues. Thus the goal is not so much to sensitize children to something that they would not otherwise experience, as it is to systematize that involvement and develop it in such a way that child advocacy is richer and more attuned to the issues that are relevant to children's everyday lives.

There are many ways in which such participation can occur. A good model is *Children's Express (CE)*, a children's journalism project that includes syndicated newspaper columns and a former PBS prime time series. CE uses an interview format in which elementary-school-age children serve as reporters, teenagers act as editors, and adults act as advisors and trainers. CE has the advantage of giving children and youth some supervised responsibility and personal and peer-group control, while at the same time providing an opportunity for expression by both the CE staff and those whom they interview.

I do not mean to suggest that empowerment of children is easy.[8] Many children's experiences in home, school, and community tell them that children's opinions are unvalued and that ostensible freedom of expression is not real. Elicitation of frank views from children and youth, especially from underprivileged backgrounds, often may require explicit approval of such expression, modeling, and reward (cf. Belter & Grisso, 1984; Lewis, 1983; Melton, 1980). Nonetheless, both the ethical and the practical rewards justify the effort.

SELECTION OF ADVOCACY STRATEGIES

As a general matter, advocacy for children as a class is not an easy task. Just reaching the starting line - defining the agenda - is a significant intellectual and moral accomplishment. Actually reaching the goal may seem to require the wisdom of Solomon, the moral force of Martin Luther King, and the political acumen of Mayor Daley.

The obstacles to establishing a coherent agenda for child advocacy are omens of the roadblocks along the way to adoption of a comprehensive child policy. At a macro level, child advocates find themselves attempting to influence broad political, econom-

---

[8]"Empowerment" does not necessarily imply outright control. Rather, my point is that children and especially adolescents should be given a chance to have a say and that the views that they voice should be taken seriously. At least in some circumstances, those views will not be dispositive, just as similar expressions of viewpoint by adults need not be translated into action.

I also am suggesting that children themselves have a place in advocacy. As has been the case with other groups subject, sometimes with good reason, to paternalistic responses (e.g., mentally retarded, physically disabled, and mentally disordered people), the ultimate test of child advocates' recognition of their constituents' personhood may be whether they are willing to share the stage with them. As suggested in the accompanying text, there are many instances in which at least older children and adolescents can be participants in class advocacy.

ic, and social decision making. The strategic questions are no smaller in scale than those faced by far more powerful, far richer, and usually far more politically sophisticated interest groups. The questions are even more complicated than those encountered by organized labor, for example, because of the uncertainty about the agenda and the diffuseness of targets as well as the paucity of loot and clout (cf. Ryan, 1971).

At an individual level, adults may perceive child advocacy as a threat to their personal freedom, especially if advocacy either entails or promotes increased self-determination by children. Particularly given the centrality of beliefs about children and families in our social system, child advocacy may elicit intense reactance motivation (cf. Brehm, 1966). Moreover, given the evidence that espousal of civil liberties is related to individuals' confidence in their own ability to generate novel ideas (Zalkind, Gaugler, & Schwartz, 1975; Zellman & Sears, 1971), individuals who are generally inclined toward rigidity and who lack such intellectual self-confidence are apt to be especially threatened by expression of ideas by someone perceived as dependent and small: "The implication is that success in increasing sensitivity to the rights and needs of children is likely to be related to the degree to which the threat to authoritarian adults can be minimized" (Melton, 1983a, p. 15) and their concepts of childhood reformed.

This task may not be quite as difficult as it sounds. Recent public opinion polls suggest that most adults may be more prepared to take the needs and rights of children seriously than their leaders think that they are. A Louis Harris poll conducted in 1986 (Taylor, 1987) found, for example, that 70% of Americans want teenagers to have access to birth control services, and 70% want the government to provide health care coverage for children without it. Large majorities say that they would even pay higher taxes if the funds were spent on public schools (76%) or day care (83%). The Harris pollsters concluded:

> If you look at all of these data, you can only reach one conclusion. The American people have come to a new consciousness about children, the problems of children and the need to address them. It is plain that the American people would welcome leadership that will call upon them for some sacrifice to make it possible for government and the private sector to take action at last on behalf of children. Our survey indicates a massive public concern about these issues and a willingness to support

real leadership on them if such leadership emerges. (Taylor, 1987, p. 13)

Nonetheless, the point remains that child advocacy, to be more than mere exhortation, requires careful and thoughtful attention to selection of both goals and strategies. Moral cheerleading has some value in motivating and guiding the converted, but it does little to persuade the skeptics, and it does nothing to effectuate policy. Child advocacy does require commitment, but it also demands rationality and a large dose of technical skill in social planning and political action.

CONCLUSION

In the end, the answer to the potential conflict of interest between advocates and children must be the consciousness and conscience of individual child advocates. Advocates should not be paralyzed by uncertainty, but neither should they ignore or deny it. They must be careful to scrutinize their own motives and behaviors in order to identify when their advocacy on behalf of children is no longer *for* them - when it has been clouded by personal interests and ideology. Above all, they must listen to children and use their voices as guides to an agenda for advocacy.

At the same time, it should be emphasized that the ethical and pragmatic imperatives to involve children in advocacy does not mean that adults' responsibility can be shirked or diffused. Neither does it reduce advocates' need for expertise in the technology of advocacy, the means of inducing change on behalf of children (see, e.g., Melton, 1983a, 1987a). Children should be involved in advocacy, but that principle does not imply that child advocacy can or should be *all* self-advocacy. Power rests with adults. If child advocacy is to be more than mere paternalism or gratuitous platitudes, adults must become partners with children and youth in advocacy for their interests. Perhaps at root, my point is that adult advocates for children must show them respect. That sort of modeling ultimately may be the most potent source of change in the status of children and youth.

REFERENCES

Bellotti v. Baird, 443 U.S. 622 (1979).

Belter, R. W., & Grisso, T. (1984). Children's recognition of rights violations in counseling. *Professional Psychology: Research and Counseling, 15,* 899-910.

Brehm, J. W. (1966). *A Theory of Psychological Reactance.* New York: Academic Press.

Coles, R. (1977). *Children in Crisis: Privileged Ones: The Well-Off and the Rich in America* (Vol. 5). Boston: Little, Brown & Co.

Coles, R. (1986). *The Political Life of Children.* Boston: Atlantic Monthly Press.

Family Policy Act of 1987, Neb. Rev. Stat. §§ 43-532 to 43-534 (Supp. 1987).

Goldstein, J., Freud, A., & Solnit, A. J. (1973). *Beyond the Best Interests of the Child.* New York: Free Press.

Goldstein, J., Freud, A., & Solnit, A. J. (1979). *Before the Best Interests of the Child.* New York: Free Press.

Goldstein, J., Freud, A., Solnit, A. J., & Goldstein, S. (1986). *In the Best Interests of the Child: Professional Boundaries.* New York: Free Press.

Hartigan v. Zbaraz, 108 S.Ct. 479 (1987), *reh'g denied,* 108 S.Ct. 1064 (1988).

Hodgson v. Minnesota, 853 F.2d 1452 (8th Cir. 1988), *cert. granted,* 109 S.Ct. 3240 (1989).

Interdivisional Committee on Adolescent Abortion. (1987). Adolescent abortion: Psychological and legal issues. *American Psychologist, 42,* 73-78.

Keniston, K. (1977). *All Our Children: The American Family Under Pressure.* New York: Harcourt Brace Jovanovich.

Lewis, C. E. (1983). Decision making related to health: When could/should children act responsibly? In G. B. Melton, G. P. Koocher, & M. J. Saks (Eds.), *Children's Competence to Consent* (pp. 75-91). New York: Plenum.

Melton, G. B. (1980). Children's concepts of their rights. *Journal of Clinical Child Psychology, 9,* 186-190.

Melton, G. B. (1983a). *Child Advocacy: Psychological Issues and Interventions.* New York: Plenum.

Melton, G. B. (1983b). Decision making by children: Psychological risks and benefits. In G. B. Melton, B. P. Koocher, & M. J. Saks (Eds.), *Children's Competence to Consent* (pp. 21-40). New York: Plenum.

Melton, G. B. (1983c). Minors and privacy: Are legal and psychological concepts compatible? *Nebraska Law Review, 62,* 455-493.

Melton, G. B. (Ed.). (1986). *Adolescent Abortion: Psychological and Legal Issues*. Lincoln, NE: University of Nebraska Press.

Melton, G. B. (1987a). Bringing psychology to the legal system: Opportunities, obstacles, and efficacy. *American Psychologist, 42*, 345-354.

Melton, G. B. (1987b). Children, politics, and morality: The ethics of child advocacy. *Journal of Clinical Child Psychology, 16*, 357-367.

Melton, G. B. (1987c). Law and random events: The state of child mental health policy. *International Journal of Law and Psychiatry, 10*, 81-90.

Melton, G. B. (1987d). Legal regulation of adolescent abortion: Unintended effects. *American Psychologist, 42*, 79-83.

Melton, G. B. (1987e). The clashing of symbols: Prelude to child and family policy. *American Psychologist, 42*, 345-354.

Melton, G. B. (1990). *Images of Childhood: Children, the Law, and Social Policy*. Lexington, MA: Lexington Books.

Melton, G. B., & Russo, N. F. (1987). Adolescent abortion: Psychological perspectives on public policy. *American Psychologist, 42*, 69-72.

Melton, G. B., & Spaulding, W. J. (1991). *No Place to Go: Civil Commitment of Minors*. Lincoln, NE: University of Nebraska Press.

Mnookin, R. H. (1985a). *Bellotti v. Baird*: A hard case. In R. H. Mnookin (Ed.), *In the Interest of Children: Advocacy, Law Reform, and Public Policy* (pp. 149-264). New York: W. H. Freeman.

Mnookin, R. H. (Ed.). (1985b). *In the Interest of Children: Advocacy, Law Reform, and Public Policy*. New York: W. H. Freeman.

Parham v. J. R., 442 U.S. 584 (1979).

Perlmuter, L. C., & Monty, R. A. (1979). *Choice and Perceived Control*. Hillsdale, NJ: Erlbaum.

Perry, G. S., & Melton, G. B. (1984). Precedential value of judicial notice of social facts: *Parham* as an example. *Journal of Family Law, 22*, 633-676.

Ryan, W. (1971). *Blaming the Victim*. New York: Vintage.

Steiner, G. Y. (1976). *The Children's Cause*. Washington, DC: Brookings Institution.

Tapp, J. L., & Melton, G. B. (1983). Preparing children for decision making: Implications of legal socialization research. In G. B. Melton, G. P. Koocher, & M. J. Saks (Eds.), *Children's Competence to Consent* (pp. 215-234). New York: Plenum.

Taylor, H. (1987). Opening remarks. In A. Sheffield & S. Keenan (Eds.), *The Media and Children's Issues* (pp. 12-13). New York: Children's Express.

Working Group on the Family. (1986, December). *The Family: Preserving America's Future.* Washington, DC: White House Domestic Policy Council.

Zalkind, S. S., Gaugler, E. A., & Schwartz, R. M. (1975). Civil liberties and personality measures: Some exploratory research. *Journal of Social Issues, 31*(2), 31-54.

Zellman, G. L., & Sears, D. O. (1971). Childhood origins of tolerance for dissent. *Journal of Social Issues, 27*(2), 109-136.

WORKPLACE DILEMMAS FOR MOTHERS AND THEIR CHILDREN: DOMESTIC IDEOLOGY AND PUBLIC INDIFFERENCE

Valerie Polakow

The aim of this chapter is to familiarize practitioners with the issues involved in class advocacy for children whose mothers are employed away from home. This is a controversial area that needs the enlightenment of objective analysis.

Professor Polakow points out that antifamily policies often are obscured by euphemistic rhetoric. She clearly describes the past and present exploitation of women and children and demonstrates that this is occurring now in ways such as the widespread commercial promotion of institutional day care.

This chapter is a comprehensive and well-documented statement of the past and contemporary status of mothers employed away from home. Reacting to the removal of women from the cash economy that occurred in the transition from family farms to industrialized urban life at the turn of the century, "material feminists" argued that the redesign of feminine households and neighborhoods was a more important factor than winning the right to vote. However, in the 1930s the fashion was single-family homes on their own lots with the father as breadwinner and the mother as an unpaid domestic housewife. This was reinforced after World War II by the expansion of suburban living. The resulting invisible domesticated wife and the visible family-wage-earning husband effectively sealed the divisions between private and public life, the domestic and political economies, and unremunerated and remunerated labor. Thereafter, domestic labor was not regarded as work, and the rearing of children was reinforced as a private responsibility.

Most contemporary feminist organizations have represented the interest of professional women rather than mothers and children, thereby perpetuating the dichotomy between domestic and public life that the earlier feminists struggled against. Because mothers who work away from home and their children generally have not been recognized as having special needs, a de facto *antifamily orientation has existed in our society, particularly in the workplace. This climate, together with the tension between the right of mothers to work and the entitlement of children to bond to their own parents, creates an untenable situation for many mothers and their children. Although fathers now play more significant roles in child rearing, the fact is that mothers remain burdened with most of the responsibilities.*

In contrast with all other industrialized democracies, the United States stands alone in the absence of pro-family policies, such as free pre- and post-natal care, statutory parental leaves, job protection, sick days for sick children, and flexible work schedules.

*   *   *

"We have so arranged life, that a man may have a home and family, love, companionship, domesticity, and fatherhood, yet remain an active citizen of age and country. We have so arranged life, on the other hand, that a woman must 'choose'; must either live alone, unloved, unaccompanied, uncared for, homeless, childless, with her work in the world for sole consolation; or give up all world-service for the joys of love, motherhood and domestic service." (Perkins Gilman, 1906, p. 496)

"As for me, I get up in the morning, I get dressed; I fix everybody's breakfast; I clean up the kitchen; I get the children ready for school and the baby ready to go to his babysitter; I take him to the babysitter. Then I first go to work, I work all day; I pick up the baby; I come home. The two older kids come home from my neighbor who takes care of them after school. Everybody wants me for something but I can't pay them any mind because I first have to fix dinner." (Rubin, 1976, p. 101)

"Women like me go to work because we 'have' to; there's no alternative but living poorer lives. None of my friends want to go to that factory . . . I worry about my own children, while I take care of other people's children. That's the way it has to be, I know. I need the money. They have the money!" (R. Coles & J. H. Coles, 1978, pp. 235-236)

"Upon first entry into the newly opened KinderCare Learning Center in Ann Arbor, Michigan, one of over 1,000 for-profit KinderCare chain centers, we were alarmed by the large numbers of children herded into the barest minimal space facilities as permitted by the state licensing requirements. This center is licensed for 135 children. Children from six weeks to six years spend 11-12 hours a day, mostly restricted to small age-segregated areas. In the infant room, eight babies and eight cribs were crowded into a small rectangular room -- leaving little space or materials for active exploration. The locally hired teachers received minimum wage pay ($3.40-$3.70 an hour) and most had little or no training.

While KinderCare's glossy brochure and marketing techniques taking advantage of working parents' vulnerability, offer 'the finest of indoor and outdoor equipment' and 'our program helps your child explore,' we wondered about the rigid overall building design, age-segregated areas with a few flashy looking toys, sparse materials, no soundproofing, no soft cozy corners, no places to run or tumble inside. And above all, lethargic children, all doing the same 'busy' work, coloring the pre-cut shapes, sitting in silence to an expressionless story, marshalled from inside to outside, from work-station to work-station. The enchantment of discovery was leveled here and could not surface in this children's compound -- attended by minimum wage employees, trained in KinderCare jargon to enforce rules of conformity and obedience -- cramming as many children into minimum square footage as permitted.

The child as commodity was nowhere more in evidence here." (Polakow, 1987)

Unfortunately these narratives of daily life are *not* windows into a world of ever-widening possibilities for women and children, from the turn of the century to our contemporary milieu. On the contrary, they are grim reminders of the strident antifamily policy in this country, which creates hardship, suffering, confusion, and worlds of pain for millions of children and their working mothers, whose hardships increase in inverse proportion to their socio-economic status.

Before we even begin to address the issues of parenting and the workplace, and the place of children, I wish to make my own position clear by reformulating the topic as workplace dilemmas for mothers and their children. The term *parenting*, rather than *working mother*, often serves to obscure further the *gender-specific* hardships and struggle that working mothers[1] rather than working fathers have experienced, and continue to do so. A legacy of discrimination and patriarchal control does not unravel rapidly. The language of parenting creates images of democratized families; unfortunately that is not yet the case. Most single parents continue to be women, and most married women continue to take major responsibility for their young children. Hence, by and large, the family continues to be role segregated and hierarchical. Parenting and the workplace can be meaningfully addressed only when the specific problems and conflicts that beset *working mothers* are addressed by education and public policy. To fail to critically address working women and *their* workplace democracy is to locate the problem outside of economic injustice and a discriminatory antifamily policy, in which mothers and their children are the primary casualties.

The everyday metaphors we live by in regard to families, children, and work are in urgent need of reformulation. We need to critically examine the ideology behind the policies that wreak havoc with the lives of working women and their children and frequently destroy those who are poor and exist on the margins of public indifference. The Reagan Administration did untold harm to children - particularly poor children - but public policy indif-

---

[1]In this chapter I use the term working mothers to denote mothers in the labor force. I do not wish to imply that mothers who are homemakers do not work. They, too, are compromised by public policy indifference.

ference has its roots in successive administrations of antiwoman and antichild legislation since the beginning of the Industrial Era.

It is important, in this context, to question the prevailing concept of the family as a static entity, and the current image of domestic reality as a natural law. Family forms are enormously diverse and have been so throughout history. Our current images of the family are fixed, unidimensional, and rooted in a patriarchal Victorian paradigm.

THE MEANING OF FAMILY -
A BRIEF HISTORICAL FRAMEWORK

In exploring the meaning of family, it quickly becomes apparent that historians have not only ignored central issues of domestic space, reproduction, and the raising of children from a woman's point of view, but also the socio-cultural conditions in which children have experienced daily life. As the social historian, Peter Laslett, has remarked, "Crowds and crowds of little children are strangely absent from the written record" (1965, pp. 104-105).

If we trace the change from a society based primarily on a familial domestic economy, in which women shared economic power, to an industrial one, in which the family unit no longer determined the organization of labor and production, it becomes apparent how patterns of authority have changed, as well as the position of women in relation to work. This had profound consequences for their young children. As the division between the private household and public workplace grew, so, too, did the invisibility of a woman's labor and her dependence on her husband's earnings.

The social form of the family during industrialization underwent a transformation in response to economic and political factors, with corresponding changes in the images of daily life. Similarly, the social forms of the family in our time have undergone dramatic shifts, and a similar change in consciousness and practice is required. To understand familial groups only in terms of kinship, reproduction, and biology is to ignore the dialectic of meaning which evolved as part of our social-historical experience. Such a limited view illustrates the preconceptions many sociologists, psychologists, and historians of the family still hold, imprisoned in specific social constructs which foster a denial of the unstable, changing patterns and social forms in which the family has moved historically.

It was not until the 18th century that the German term *Familie* came into general use and was linked to the French *Famille*. Both derived from the Latin *Familia*, a term that referred to the household, meaning the total number of people, related and unrelated, living together. The term *"paterfamilias"* (father of the household) was a collective term applied to the composite household. (This was also true of *famille* in the Romance languages.) During the 18th century these terms came to connote a more nuclear unit, corresponding to the change in social structure resulting from industrialization (Mitterauer & Sieder, 1982, pp. 1-24). As the separation of the workplace from the dwelling was institutionalized, a sentimental, rather than functional, image was ascribed to the family. This was based on blood ties and reflected the strengthening of the exclusivity of the parent-child bonds in the Age of Enlightenment.

However, when unquestioned assumptions about the durability of emotional bonding in "traditional" families and the historical necessity of the mother-child couplet are propounded as natural laws, we should begin to question the accuracy of our own history of meanings. As Peter Laslett points out in Mitterauer and Sieder (1982, p. ix), family membership was always "evanescent, familial relationships brief, intermittent and presumably unstable." In fact, the family has assumed so many diverse social forms over the course of our human history that it is grossly inaccurate to portray it as a static entity, or a "natural unit of human communal life, remaining the same over time" (Mitterauer & Sieder, 1982, p. 2). The family, then as now, has been a constantly shifting class- and gender-based lived reality. What perhaps has remained unchanged in recent times is an *image* of family, fixated in a particular moment of our early industrial history in North America and Western and Central Europe.

This patriarchal image of the family in father's shadow fits well with Victorian morality and Freudian constructions of the historical necessity of the mother's central presence in the psychosexual development of her child. Infant-mother bonding, separation anxiety, and attachment theory (as argued by Spitz, 1945; Bowlby, 1951; and Ainsworth et al., 1978) all find roots in the stable fixed image of a patriarchal family with mother as nurturer. This persists despite the fact that, very often in our human history, neither the babies of the rich, nor the bourgeoisie, nor the poor were nursed by their own mothers. Frequently it was the poor women who gave sustenance and nurturance to the babies of the rich and bourgeoisie, while their own babies often died for lack of nutrition (Ariés, 1962; de Mause, 1982).

In this country our image of family is not a social one, but a highly individualized reality, taking place behind closed doors and fenced patios in private domestic space. This has not only created the invisibility of the suburban female laborer, but also the invisibility of conflicts, struggles, and parent-child relationships which take place behind the shutters. Shadowed by the imperatives of individual attention, this scene casts father as central breadwinner and mother (if she works outside the home) as secondary breadwinner and primary caretaker of the family. This public image persists, despite the fact that more than one in five children lived in female headed families in 1988, and of these 53.2% were living in poverty, without entitlement to health and home and child care (*CDF Reports*, 1989, p. 4). If Mommy goes to work, she literally goes to work double, arranging the domestic as well as the public spheres. If poor, she is also desperately negotiating how to plug the cracks of the vast antifamily edifice, which daily confronts her as a fact of life in this society.

Guilty employed mothers, married and single, worry about their babies in the haphazard hodge-podge of child-care alternatives. As spring brings chicken pox, and winter brings strep throats, sick-day leaves for sick children are distant and illegitimate dreams, as are job-protected maternity leaves for most women. Working out of choice and necessity, they become the wage slaves of crippling corporate indifference, while federal policy perpetuates a system that Jacob Riis (1912, p. 2) a century ago described as "the evil offspring of public neglect and private greed."

Viviana Zelizer (1985) argues that our public attitudes toward children have undergone a radical change since children were expelled from the cash nexus of the economy at the turn of the century; their economic value has been replaced by a sentimentalized "sacralization" of children's lives. Now the child has very little market value, as in the 19th century, but rather has become an emotional, affective asset. This sentimental view of children was given prominence by reformers during the late 19th century as they fought to remove children from very exploitative and brutalizing work conditions. Yet, in the 1990s, behind the prevalent sacralized images of children living happily in their nuclear suburban families (although less than 10% currently live in a two-parent traditional nuclear unit, with wage earner father and stay-at-home mother) lies the shadow of what Michael

Rothenberg (1980, pp. 15-24) has called the "national conspiracy against children." Alice Miller (1984) argues that we have developed a poisonous pedagogy - a revengeful child-rearing which springs from the poisoning of our own childhoods. This is an argument shared in part by psychohistorian Lloyd de Mause (1982) and other family historians who are appalled by our public and private treatment of children.

The history of childhood in Central and Western Europe, as well as in North America, reveals widespread abuse, both physical and emotional. Neither our historical child, nor our contemporary child, can claim any existential respect in standing before the adult world with entitlement to care and concern. Rather, across class and gender, children have been, and continue to be, objects of our sexual desires and commodities for our narcissistic dreams. Historical, cultural, and class forms have shaped the constructions of reality with which we carpet our daily lives with children. Both our public images of childhood and our notions of family are in need of demystification. Today, the "commoditization" of childhood, with its corresponding array of experts "developing" children's lives, has reached a peak. This process is embedded in a materialistic individual ethic which corresponds to a cost-benefit analysis of parenting and pedagogy. Hence to begin to talk about the family - and the place of parents and children - is to render the romantic images of the past and the complacent images of the present obsolete. However, the call for a reformulation of the notion of family should not be read as a demeaning of the significance of family bonds between parents and their children. For most, the family as a "unit" - in all its diverse realities - is often a life-long sought-after dream despite the reality of pain, suffering, and hostile relationships that many children experience growing up. Although Alice Miller (1984) has argued that families are hell, reminiscent of Sartre's "hell is other people," we recognize that both families and people are our existential fate.

But in order to transform historical and contemporary structures of indifference, in which women and children find themselves suspended in flimsy, unraveling, public-support webs, we need to radically re-examine the antifamily policy in this country that masquerades as "pro-family." Behind the publicspeak lie blaming-the-victim bureaucracies. Behind closed doors lie children's lives, inextricably intertwined with their mothers' legacy of domestic and economic domination. It is in the shameful *placelessness* of working mothers and their children in public life, and the invisibility of their preoccupations and conflicts, that a shifting of metaphors needs to develop. Understanding the geography of this experience can point to new directions for child advocacy and critically reformulate the workplace dilemmas of our time.

THE PLACELESSNESS OF WORKING MOTHER-AND-CHILD IN PUBLIC LIFE

Dolores Hayden in *The Grand Domestic Revolution* (1981) gives a fascinating account of the lost tradition of material feminism during the latter part of the 19th and early 20th centuries in this country. These material feminists, including Melusina Fay Peirce, Charlotte Perkins Gilman, and others challenged the split between domestic and public life as experienced by women during the period of industrial capitalism. Although cooking, caring for the young, and cleaning the household have always been thought of as women's work, performed without pay in domestic environments, these duties have always been central to the world's necessary labor. This has created a sexual division of labor leading to ever-widening circles of economic exploitation of women by men, originating in the domestic environment. The material feminists challenged the whole notion of "women's" sphere and "women's" work, specifically in regard to the physical separation of the household from the workplace, as well as the creation of two parallel economies - the domestic and the political (Hayden, 1981, pp. 3-5).

The material feminists, in redefining the housework and housing needs of women, argued for the redesign of feminist households and neighborhoods as central to the question of equality - and far more important than winning the right to vote. Clearly, having the right to vote for men as the sole occupiers of public office gave women no guarantees of economic justice or opportunities for workplace and career advancement! Many urban planners and architects adopted the visions of the material feminists and designed collective urban residential space in several cities. Their commitment to "kitchenless houses," socialized domestic work, and collectivized child care were incorporated within the apartment blocks designed for the middle classes and the model tenements for the poor. Many of these kitchenless house designs were influenced by the famous Fourierist Socialist experiment in Guise, France, known as the Familistère (Social Palace). Melusina Fay Peirce, Marie Howland, and others influenced many architects and designers to incorporate these ideals into cooperative family "hotels" in Connecticut and Boston (Hotel Kempton).

Other diverse communities, feminist and nonfeminist, such as Amana, Iowa, the Oneida Community in New York, the Shakers in Massachusetts, and the Women's Commonwealth in Texas also attempted to redesign domestic space to incorporate egalitarian alternative forms of collective living, which socialized household labor (Hayden, 1981).

The key argument of the materialist feminists was that a reorganization of human work and physical environment would end the exploitation of domestic labor and free women to enter the market economy on an equal basis with men. Spatial analysis became the key to the transformation of the domestic sphere, which the material feminists claimed should be placed under women's control, thereby linking their campaigns for social equality, economic justice, and urban reform. The bourgeois Victorian home represented in spatial form the patriarchal hierarchies of public man-at-work and private woman-at-home-with-her-babies taking care of the nurturant underlife that propelled her man to face the world outside. "Space is where discourses about power and knowledge are transformed into actual relations of power . . . both designs and ordinary buildings, offer privileged instances for understanding how power operates" (Wright & Rabinow, 1982, p. 14).

Interestingly, it was in the pre-industrial era that women, as working members of the household, were often substantial contributors to the family economy and thus did not suffer the far-reaching consequences of the split between private and public life. Their labor on the household, farm, or estate was very visible, as was their children's, and their presence marked the value of an integrated domestic economy in which men, women, and children all participated. However, the growth of manufacturing industries took poor women and children into factories as wage laborers under brutalizing conditions or kept women at home as consumers of manufactured goods. By 1890 only 5% of married women worked outside the home. "The private home was the spatial boundary of women's sphere, and the unpaid domestic labor undertaken in that space by the isolated housewife was the economic boundary of women's sphere. 'A woman's place is in the home' and 'a woman's work is never done' were the usual basic definitions of woman's sphere. Above all the woman's sphere was to be removed from the cash economy" (Hayden,

1981, p. 13). Hence, although class conditions determined the fabric of women's comfort *or* their desperate struggle for survival under industrial capitalism, it was gender that united women under a common umbrella of exploitation by the patriarchal structures of industrial life.

The material feminists battled for almost 60 years to push their program of women's control over reproduction and domestic transformation, amid swift attacks by corporations, trade unions (who were campaigning for men to receive a "family" wage, thereby excluding women), and public red-baiting. Their program for the redesign of urban households and neighborhoods suffered a severe setback during and after the depression. Hoover's National Conference on Home Building and Home Ownership in 1931 supported home ownership for men of "sound character and industrious habits," encouraging men as homeowners and women as domestic managers. Banks, architects, and builders all promoted the single-family suburban home on its *own* lot - with father as breadwinner and mother as invisible full-time unpaid domestic housewife. (The term housewife is in itself evocative of the assumed union between woman and house - effectively accentuating her removal from the public sphere.)

This trend of domestic isolationism continued after the Second World War, when in the 2-month period following the war, women who had held essential wartime jobs were laid off at a rate of 175 per 1,000 workers. Layoffs were particularly resisted in the heavy industrial sector because women desperately wanted to retain their well-paid jobs. During the war years 4.7 million new women workers had entered the labor force, with approximately 3.5 million of those taking jobs they might otherwise not have taken (Kessler-Harris, 1982).

Federal support for child care, part of a recruiting campaign for women workers during the war years, together with the promise of "mansized wages," had by 1942 resulted in $4,000,000 being devoted to local building of child-care centers. By 1945, 100,000 children were enrolled in federally supported facilities which went hand in hand with the recognition that, as three-fourths of the new wartime female workforce were married women, some mandatory assistance had to be given to the care of their children (Hewlett, 1986).

However, after the war, jobs were needed by the returning veterans, and the strategy of evicting women from the workplace was accompanied by the coercive shutting down of federal child-care facilities. "Public child care was terminated as part of a national movement to return children to their mothers and working mothers to their homes. 'The women, so lately the darlings of the nation's factories were sent home to stay'" (Hewlett, 1986, p. 242).

The G.I. Bill followed, providing extremely low cost mortgages (30 year loans at 3% to 4% interest), free college tuition, and subsistence allowances for self and dependents - what greater incentive for a nice home in suburbia with a commuting, breadwinning husband and stay-at-home wife? The Highway Act of 1944 completed the suburban isolationism with road networks around and between the cities. Hence the invisible domesticated wife, ringed by young children in isolated nuclear suburban communities, and the family-wage-earning husband in public life, effectively sealed the divisions between private and public life, domestic and political economy, and invisible and visible labor.

The Norman Rockwell vision of middle America sentimentally extolled female domesticity as the ideal of family life, a vision that meshed with economic strategies to keep women out of the workplace, buttressed by psychoanalytic and developmental arguments, which placed pathology in the laps of insufficiently bonded, and insufficiently domesticated, mothers. Helene Deutsch (1944), one of the prominent women psychoanalysts, argued for satisfactory feminine sublimation through husband and children in the 1940s, and the research of Spitz (1945) and Bowlby (1951) on attachment, separation, and loss, all contributed to the hysterical and peculiarly ahistorical assumption about the natural necessity of the mother-child couplet as central to the healthy development of the infant. At no other time in the history of this country had hearth and home, encapsulated in the nuclear image of the family, been so effectively entrenched as a vital mainstay of civilization!

As Grubb and Lazerson have pointed out, blaming Chicanos and blacks for the instability of the so-called deprived minority family finds its parallel in blaming the working mother for the deterioration of family life. "Working mothers have been accused of ignoring their children's 'birthright' to full-time mothering, and single mothers have been castigated for denying children the care and influence of fathers" (Grubb & Lazerson, 1982, p. 333). This blaming-the-victim syndrome locates the source of the problem within the individual or the dyad of mother-and-child. Rarely are the sources of economic injustice, poverty, discrimination, and the ideological and practical eviction of women from public life, seen as contributing to a growing social pathology evidenced by indifference and neglect on the part of the federal and state governments.

The continuing tendency to blame women for family crises has failed to locate responsibility in the social-public realm, and has relegated families to individual problem solutions. This has hampered the development of public policies which take responsibility for maternal employment, childbearing, expansion of child care, part-time work, flexible hours, and job protection. Women have often been forced into the dilemma of making the choices outlined by Charlotte Perkins Gilman at the beginning of this chapter - staying at home, earning a low income, working under conditions of hardship and stress, or disengaging from marriage and children.

As late as 1964 the U.S. Women's Bureau publicly announced that its policy was *not* "to encourage married women and mothers of young children to seek employment outside the home. Home and children are considered married women's most important responsibilities" (Carl Degler quoted in Grubb & Lazerson, 1982, p. 34).

In 1980, the White House Conference on Families was another occasion for the reassertion of so-called traditional family values and antiworking-women sentiment. These traditional values, when situated in historical context, form part of an image of family that is tied to a prevailing patriarchal hegemony of ideas and practice in this society. The notion of traditional mother-at-home, which was in reality a bourgeois Victorian image of the upper middle class European woman, represents no more than a brief moment of our social history; yet somehow we are fixated in the social temporal constructions of that milieu. The hegemony of domestic ideology that masquerades as "pro-family" has effectively impeded the development of social policies aimed at protecting and enriching the lives of children who are the victims of a strident antifamily policy in the United States.

This argument concerning the centrality of a social structure and public policy that supports the entitlement of children and their mothers to economic justice and promotes their well-being should not be misconstrued as a mechanistic versus organismic model of human development. Personal development cannot be seen solely as the result of forces external to the child. On the other hand, without insuring the social conditions that promote the possibilities for existential development, it becomes a largely academic, developmentalistic debate abstracted from the daily reality of the "worlds of pain" (Rubin, 1976) to which the growing majority of our children are subjected. This indifference to the lives of working women and their young children is unparalleled in all other industrialized Western democracies.[2]

WINDOWS ONTO THE LANDSCAPE OF THE WORKING MOTHER: MARGINALIZATION AND NEGLECT IN THE MILIEU OF THE MODERN WAGE SLAVE

In most other Western industrialized societies, mothers who work take for granted social support structures which assist, rather than impede, their abilities to be competent workers and mothers; such as free pre- and post-natal care, a statutory right to childbirth and maternity leaves, job protection, sick days for sick children, and flexible hours. These concrete pro-family policies are still distant legislative dreams in the United States, which stands out as the most *underdeveloped* society as regards family justice and child care. Compare these stories of working women on opposite sides of the ocean, described and cited in Sylvia Hewlett (Hewlett, 1986, pp. 95-96):

Gail (who lives in the U.S.) is a writer employed by a T.V. network. At 35, pregnant with her first child she negotiated that she would work right up to labor and take 2-1/2 weeks off for her delivery. One and one-half of this time was her paid vacation time, and the other week was defined as leave at half-pay. Gail had a difficult cesarean birth but was forced to return to work for fear of losing her job and $1,800 of her medical expenses that were not covered by insurance. "I don't know how I lived through those first weeks back at work. I was exhausted and in pain from the surgery. The worst thing was the lack of sleep. Annie woke to be fed at least three times a night, and by midday I was ready to kill for sleep. But somehow I had to work - and to smile and pretend to my boss that I didn't have a family care in the world."

---

[2] This indifference is also unparalleled in socialist societies and in Third World nations. Cuba, Guinea - Bissau, Zimbabwe, Czechoslovakia, the Soviet Union, and China, all have far more progressive social policies for working mothers and their children and have devoted large amounts of time, education, and national budget to their development.

Susan, on the other hand, works as a secretary in Stockholm and has three children, eight, three, and two. When each of her children was born, she was entitled to a nine month paid leave at 90% of her salary plus a six-month job-protected additional unpaid leave. Since her two youngest children were born within a year of each other, she merged her maternity leaves into a consecutive 2-1/2 year period. In addition, her husband was entitled to share parental leave with her and took a four month leave at the birth of their first child.

These stories are not unusual and point to the vast differences that exist in social support structures between women of the United States and Europe. Gail's story is not unique; rather it resonates with stories of other women in this country, similarly struggling to lead double lives. Consider Marian, poor and single, pregnant at 15, who went back to school when her daughter was 3, struggling to get off welfare. Her babysitting arrangements kept breaking down - first her sister, then an irresponsible lady on the block; there was no subsidized day care in her neighborhood, and she could not afford private day care (Polakow, 1986). What to do? Again the constant struggle and desperate will to survive on the part of these women comes through. Could Marian dream of Sweden, or France, or Italy, where she would be guaranteed subsidized all-day child care for her daughter?

If we examine current demographic data from the Bureau of Labor Statistics, we see that one-half of pre-school age children today have mothers employed outside the home. By the year 2000 it is expected that figure will rise to almost 7 in 10 (Children's Defense Fund, 1990). In the decade between the mid-1970s and 1980s, labor force participation for married women with babies under 1 year increased by an astonishing 70% (Kamerman, 1986, p. 54). See Table 1 on page 308.

Given that almost one-half of the labor force is now female and that women with young children comprise the majority of new labor force participants, we realize how unrealistic and distorted our images of *family life* are. Most children today have working parents. Fewer than 10% of American households follow the vision of wage-earner husband, stay-at-home wife, and two children nestled in suburbia. Single, nuclear, reconstituted, or extended, families are now as diverse as they ever have been in our social history. Yet domestic ideology has a tenacious hold on

TABLE 1: U.S. WOMEN WHO GAVE BIRTH IN THE LAST YEAR
AND PERCENTAGE WHO WERE IN THE LABOR FORCE,
1976, 1980, 1983, 1984 (Number in Thousands)*

Age of Women and Survey Year	Number of Women	Percentage in Labor Force
Ages 18 to 44		
1984	3,311	46.7
1983	3,625	43.1
1980	3,247	38.0
1976	2,797	30.9
Ages 18 to 29		
1984	2,375	44.5
1983	2,682	42.4
1980	2,476	38.2
1976	2,220	31.8
Ages 30 to 44		
1984	936	52.2
1983	942	45.1
1980	770	37.3
1976	577	27.6

*Note. From U.S. Bureau of the Census, Current Population Reports (Economic Policy Council of the UNA - USA-Family and Work, 1986). Cited by Kamerman, 1986, page 54.

public consciousness with dire consequences for the private lives of families.

The denial of family-form diversity and the persistent tendency both to blame adolescent violence, drug-alcohol abuse, and poor school performance on the "broken" family, and to hold up the "intact" family as a model of social health shift the consequences of public indifference and social neglect, economic injustice, and a legacy of discriminatory practices against women to the most vulnerable members of our population - young children. This situation and that of their mothers in 1990 is not that far removed from the industrial wage slaves of the 19th century. Let us consider the plight in which women and children find themselves by virtue of gender and age.

In 1984, 70% of mothers with children 6 to 13, 60% with children 3 to 5, and 50% with children under 3 were in the labor force. In addition, according to the U.S. Department of Labor, 50% of current marriages will end in divorce in the 1990s, and 50% of all American children will spend part of their childhood in a single-parent household (Bureau of Labor Statistics, 1985).

Despite these realities, institutional structures serving women and children display a historical lag. We experience life in the present but make policy according to our myths of a past era.

In addition, as a group children are the most disadvantaged, comprising 40% of the poverty population. Between 1979 and 1988, the proportion of American children living in poverty grew by 23%. One in five children lives in poverty and one in four young children under the age of 3 is poor. The Children's Defense Fund also estimates that in 1988 more than one in five children lived in female headed families and of those, 53.2% were poor. If we break that statistic down further, we note that among female headed families living in poverty, 45.1% are White children, 65.2% are black children, and 68.6% are Hispanic children (*CDF Reports*, 1989, pp. 1-8).

During the 1980s over 33 million Americans were completely without health insurance, and Medicaid reached only 40% of the eligible poverty population (Family Policy Panel of the EPC of UNA/USA, 1985). An appalling consequence is that more than 12 million children and more than 14 million women of childbearing age are currently without health insurance (Children's Defense Fund, 1990).

The United States also is unique among over 100 countries (including Western industrialized nations as well as so-called developing nations) in having no national legislation for pregnant women and their babies. Pregnant women have no rights to (a) a specified period of leave from work; (b) job protection while on leave; and (c) a cash benefit equal to or a partial portion of her wage (Kamerman, 1986, p. 60). When we compare the antiworking-women policies of the United States to European countries, the differences are striking:

France

Employed mothers are guaranteed 16 weeks of job-protected leaves for childbirth, including up to 6 weeks

309

before and 10 weeks after birth, seniority, and pension rights included. They are entitled to an additional 2 weeks with full wage replacement if there is a complicated or multiple delivery. An additional job-protected unpaid leave is available to either parent for up to 2 years in companies with 100 or more employees. Low-income parents can also qualify for cash benefits during this time. (Family Policy Panel of the EPC of the UNA-USA, 1985)

Great Britain

Employed mothers are entitled to an 18-week maternity leave with job protection and seniority and pension rights. They receive 90% of their wage for a maximum of 6 weeks. If they have worked 2 years for the same employer, they are entitled to an additional unpaid leave up to a maximum of 40 weeks.

Sweden

Parents are entitled to 1 year, and the mother can use a pre-natal 60-day leave. Ninety percent of their salary is guaranteed for 9 months, with an additional 3-month flat rate benefit. Job protection, seniority, and pension rights are guaranteed and either parent has the right to unpaid leave until the child is 18 months old. Additional benefits include the right to work a 6-hour day until the child is 8 years old, as well as up to 60 days per year for each employed parent to care for sick children under 12 at home. (Family Policy Panel of the EPC of the UNA-USA, 1985)

In the United States, the only form of maternity benefits are those mandated by states for temporary disability insurance, collective bargaining agreements, or voluntarily-provided employee benefits. The only federal legislation that exists is the 1978 Pregnancy Disability Act (see Kamerman, 1986), which requires that firms treat pregnant employees the same as employees with any other temporary disability. But not all employers provide temporary disability insurance or even paid sick leave. Only five states - California, Hawaii, New Jersey, New York, Rhode Island - and the railroad industry have temporary disability insurance laws.

When we look at corporations, the national data of employer/employee provisions for working mothers are significantly more limited than for health insurance or pensions. Kamerman and colleagues (Kamerman, Kahn, & Kingston, 1983) conducted a 1981 survey of 1,000 companies and found coverage to be much lower than popularly believed. As the survey tended to cover large- and medium-sized firms, and because the "generosity" of benefit coverage was proportionately better in bigger firms in states that have temporary disability insurance, Kamerman concluded that coverage probably extends to less than 40% of women who could claim income protection during pregnancy and childbirth. At least one-third of all working women have no right to even an unpaid but job-protected leave that covers their "temporary disability."

Catalyst, a private nonprofit organization, surveyed the policies of leading industrial and financial service companies (Catalyst, 1986). It is disturbing, even in these "progressive" companies, to note how limited the health care provisions are, and how low American mothers' expectations are as regards their labor rights. Apparently the vast majority of women who take maternity-related leave stay away for extremely brief periods - less than 3 months - and yet, compared to other major industrial societies, these employer-sponsored initiatives for women workers are substandard. Unfortunately, it also is apparent that in this abysmal overview of scarce social-support structures for working women, the post-childbirth reality has hardly been discovered. When the child is born and mother goes back to work, who takes care of the baby born into a world that places the infant's needs for care and nurturance in direct contradiction to the mother's need to work?

FALLING THROUGH THE
CRACKED LANDSCAPE OF CHILD CARE

In Pennsylvania I was taken to the KinderCare facility, which was one of several in the state. It was housed adjacent to a large shopping mall, with "Sale of the Century" signs plastered in nearby windows. The infant room was very small, with no natural lighting and filled with the din of crying babies in cribs, propped up in feeding seats, and the remainder sucking thumbs in play-pens. The toddler room was even more disturbing -- eight toddlers lying on their tummies -- having their "art" activity and using one crayon to color an outline. In all of these rooms, only one harried aide appeared to be in charge. The three-year-old room smelled, and I observed cockroaches crawling under the snack table. One little boy was screaming, having been forced to go to the bathroom when he didn't want to. The rigid schedule on the wall testified to the management of these children's bodies as well as their minds, organizing their eating-time, sleeping-time, potty-time, creative play-time, "free" time in calculated 15 minute intervals. The teachers, frequently shouting at the children, were hostile managers of limited space resources and functioned as police; yet here it was babies and young children who were under surveillance. (Polakow, 1983)

In the midwest, a visit to a smaller local for-profit child-care chain exhibited strikingly similar problems.

As I entered, Teacher Nellie appeared self-conscious and suspicious of me at our first meeting. She told me that the "kids are unusually wild today." They were fighting each other, using assorted makeshift weapons -- a baseball bat, a wooden pole, wooden blocks, plastic trays were all being thrown at the other children. Teacher Nellie continually shouted, "Stop it," but no one took any notice. She dragged two children out of the room, pushed one into a corner, and ran back to switch off the lights as the room turned to near chaos. One boy hit another on the head with a baseball bat. The environment was dangerous. I was hit twice by flying tennis balls and ducked to avoid a baseball bat. I noticed one boy beating up other children, hitting one on the head with a truck, and pummeling and punching another. When he noticed me, he came up and asked me, "Would you stay all day?" and "Will you come back another day?" I told him I would, and he spoke to me for a few minutes. When the children were told to line up for the TV room, he seemed to randomly attack two other children who began to cry. He was sent to the back of the line. As the children walked out, four were screaming, and one little girl was holding her head. (Polakow Suransky, 1982, pp. 120-121)

These two narratives sadly are typical of the hundreds of visits I have made to child-care chains and for-profit corporations across the country. In my view, the for-profit corporate chains, of which KinderCare with over 1,000 units is the largest and most successful, repeatedly provide the worst possible kind of care for young children. Because child care is a labor-intensive enterprise, the quality of programs is severely compromised when cost-benefit management objectives and company profits become the dominant factor in designing, planning, and running them. KinderCare proudly states that each child of a given age in their centers across the country gets the identical curriculum on any given day. These packaged programs give minimal attention to the children's needs and maximum benefit to the corporate managers, who employ minimum-wage workers at maximum adult-child ratios in order to keep costs down. Most high-quality centers struggle to make ends meet, trying to attract caring professionals into an underpaid low-status profession. Yet KinderCare makes huge profits from parent fees. In 1985, its net income was $123.7 million - more than 12% profit from every parent dollar!

What is life like for these young children in such early childhood institutions? Unfortunately, they are not atypical of our child-care landscape. This is the question I posed in 1982 (Polakow Suransky, 1982), 10 years after Mary Keyserling conducted her comprehensive study *Windows on Daycare* and characterized the situation as a "national daycare crisis" (Keyserling, 1972). Fifteen years later, we still have a national day-care crisis - inaccessible, unaffordable, and often poor-quality care frequently provided by profit-run corporations, rushing to fill the gaps created by the increasing number of mothers in the labor force and the decreasing amount of federal support since 1980. For example, Title XX funds which provided child-care subsidies to poor families have been drastically cut since 1980, and Title XX is now funded at levels less than half of 1977, adjusted for inflation (Children's Defense Fund, 1990). The others are a disarray of alternatives ranging from the large commercial profit-chains, such as Mary Moppets, Children's World, Gerber, and KinderCare (whose snapshots of "child-care-less" environments have already been depicted), to private nonprofit community-based centers. Many young children and infants are cared for in informal family day-care homes which are unregulated. Although all states except two have minimal regulations, they are rarely enforced.

During the 1980s, estimates indicated that there were only 1 million day-care slots available, half of which were Title XX funded. Due to the 1980 Reagan budget cuts, despite the increased need for child-care services, 32 states served fewer children in 1983 than 1981. More than 6 million children were estimated to be in informal family day-care arrangements. Only

1,850 of the 6 million employers in this country provided any form of child care (Kamerman, 1983). Currently, Head Start serves fewer than one in six eligible children, while the child poverty rate has risen, and the need for safe, accessible, affordable, high-quality child care has increased dramatically.

The various forms of employer-supported child care include on-site care and contracts with family day-care homes. One of the unfortunate trends in employer-sponsored care is the tendency to contract with existing child-care centers, frequently for-profit commercial chains, to provide on-site child care. Corporations tend to favor day-care corporation chains, praising their efficient management policies in turning child care into a subsidiary industry with their employees which often results in poor quality child care. The notable exceptions to this trend are several progressive corporations such as Merck & Company, Steelcase, and American Can Company, each of which provides a variety of flexible benefits, maternity leave, job protection, and child-care support services for their employees.

It is not surprising that day care should present a national crisis for this country; it is a natural consequence of a consistently indifferent set of policies for employed mothers and their children. There was a brief optimistic period in 1971 when Congress passed the Comprehensive Child Development Bill, but it was promptly vetoed by Nixon, who succeeded in re-establishing day care as an un-American activity, as he talked about the importance of the veto in order to "cement the family in its rightful position as the keystone of our civilization" (Hewlett, 1986, p. 280). In 1975, a diminished version of the Bill was introduced by Mondale and Brademas, but neither the House nor the Senate took action.

Continued efforts have been underway for several years to obtain comprehensive child-care legislation sponsored by broad based coalitions such as the Alliance for Better Childcare. The Act for Better Childcare (ABC Bill) has received bipartisan support and was designed to provide a $2.5 billion federal investment in child care with financial assistance provided to low and moderate income families with full cost to the poorest families. Minimum state and national standards to insure the health safety and educational experiences of children were proposed, as were measures to increase the supply of child-care services. But as of 1990, the first session of the 101st Congress failed to give final passage to the ABC Bill, thereby also failing to provide child

314

care for the poorest 500,000 of the 10.5 million young children with mothers in the labor force (Children's Defense Fund, 1990).

When we turn to other countries, we note how their governments not only promote and maintain progressive social legislation for working mothers, but also dedicate a great deal of public resources to providing child care for their babies and young children.

Sweden has the best record for providing high-quality subsidized care in the form of public day-care centers to all children of employed parents as well as after-school care and parental-leave sick days for young children. In addition, there are licensed municipal day-care mothers who care for three to four children in their homes. They also are reimbursed by their municipalities.

In France, out-of-home care is assumed to be a normal part of the fabric of daily life. Since the 1950s the *école maternelles* (free public pre-schools) enroll nearly all 3- to 6-year-olds. *Crèches* are set up for children 6 months to 3 years of age, and they too are partially subsidized with parents paying on an income-adjusted basis.

Similarly Denmark, Italy, Israel, and Great Britain all have made considerable progress in creating a support network of publicly funded child care, with the expressed aim of easing the lot of working mothers.

Yet, once again, in this country, child care is perceived to be the individual responsibility of the family, rather than a social responsibility. It also is disturbing that employed mothers and child care have, until recently, been a low priority on the agenda of the mainstream feminist organizations such as N.O.W. The E.R.A. and abortion have been top priorities. Frequently maternity leave has not even been part of the feminist agenda, because a comprehensive maternity policy means that women who work and who are mothers need special treatment (as do their children); this recognition conflicts with the spirit of the E.R.A. The paradox between the American feminists' fight for equal *individual* rights and opportunities contrasts sharply with the social feminists of Europe, who demand that special recognition be accorded to employed women and their children. Sylvia Hewlett cites an interview with Dana Friedman, a child advocate and lobbyist who spent many years in Washington lobbying for child-care legislation and researching work and family issues: "The feminist groups never took the lead on childcare issues. It's not that in the end they didn't sign off on childcare initiatives, but they never put any real effort into this area" (Hewlett, 1986, pp. 190-191).

When we analyze the complex web of inter-relationships that characterize the employed mother's presence in domestic and public life, we realize how in this country, with the notable exception of the materialist feminist movement, these dilemmas are couched within an individualistic ethic which has framed most of the struggles for equal rights. Most often, the mainstream feminist organizations have represented the class interests of professional women, frequently excluding mothers, their children, and the poor, thereby perpetuating the same dichotomy between domestic and public life that the materialist feminists struggled so valiantly against.

The question of working mothers' rights and their children's rights cannot be answered simply by meeting the demand for universal day care or workplace child care. Once these basic institutional provisions are met, the vital question "What kind of care?" must be posed. The creation of a *laissez-faire* system in which commercial for-profit day-care chains are promoted is not the answer; nor is the early institutionalization of young babies and toddlers in large impersonal centers. The early lives of children are in the balance here - as is the healthy maintenance of family structures. Creating the grounds for diverse child-care options is a necessary starting point. There must be a commitment that does not permit the use of children as commodities in a profit market but rather safeguards their entitlement to care, nurturance, and creativity in child-centered landscapes.

How to create child-centered institutions that are small enough and personal enough to make each child special, catering to class and ethnic diversity and soliciting parent participation, is a challenge. Not the least part of the challenge is the necessary change in public consciousness about "women's work" and the correlative low status accorded child-care employees and early-childhood teachers. As Modigliani (1986) points out, carpet and drywall installers, parking lot attendants, and animal caretakers all earn higher wages than child-care workers! In her interviews with child-care professionals, she reports that there is a bitter tension between their own appreciation for what they do and society's lack of appreciation. Modigliani convincingly argues that the devaluation of young children goes hand in hand with the devalued labor of child-care professionals. She questions whether our devotion to materialism and production is stronger than our devotion to our children, for "children in such a value system don't have much worth" (Modigliani, 1986, p. 53).

Perhaps the turmoil between domestic and public life, so starkly mirrored by the plight of working mothers and their children today, is an indicator of the narcissistic individualism that corrupts our experience of community. The profit ethic dominates private and public life, from corporations to families, to schools, to day-care centers, and to hospitals. A technical rationality pervades our institutional decision making and takes a short-term rather than a long-term view of public commitment and social responsibility. As long as we frame our social problems in terms of individual pathologies and dilemmas, the greater the possibility for powerlessness and inaction. Families in poverty are increasing, single mothers and their children are falling into destitution and homelessness, and this appalling reality reveals a corrupt and indifferent social and public ethic in need of transformation. The road to transformation also involves the recognition that women and their children are here to stay as visible participants in public and domestic life.

CONCLUSION

> For most people the issue is not whether the family has a future, but what that future will look like . . . It is there -- in those families -- that the stresses and strains of everyday life are played out -- that children are born and brought to adulthood; that women and men love and hate; that major interpersonal and intrapersonal conflicts are generated and stilled; and that men, women, and children struggle with the demands from the changing world outside their doors. (Rubin, 1976, p. 5)

Child advocacy must be seen as a changing praxis embedded in the context of diverse and shifting family forms. It also is centrally located in the complex and conflict-ridden ideological milieu of women's right to work and children's entitlement to care. It is as if the dilemmas posed by Charlotte Perkins Gilman (1898) in *Women and Economics* in the late 19th century are being replayed once more. Gilman argued that the evolution of the human race would be hastened by removing the burdens of housework and child care from the home, thereby allowing women to experience motherhood and paid employment on an equal basis with men through socialized domestic work and collective living.

However, in 1990 the same tensions and contradictions remain, couched within the pursuit of individual rights at the cost of social concern and responsibility. When individualism as a *Weltanschauug* is promoted within a class- and gender-stratified society, the resulting scenario does not differ much from past patriarchal frames of historical inequities.

One of the painful paradoxes in this country is that an individualistic rather than a social feminism has dominated the political agendas of the leading women's organizations, so that the struggle by mothers in the domestic and public spheres has created another set of contradictions - my rights versus my child's! In this country the employed woman has been pitted against her child in a series of unremitting contradictions fostered by economic injustice and lack of child-mother support policies.

Hence child advocacy also is working-mother advocacy. I argue primarily that a new relationship between working mother and child needs to be nurtured, not because the presence and role of fathers is secondary, but because the reality of families today is that most mothers still bear the significant responsibility for their children.

My specific recommendations at the public policy level closely follow and extend those of the Economic Policy Council's *Report on Work and Family in the United States: A Policy Initiative* of December 1985 and include:

- Pay equity for women and the reduction of occupational segregation.
- Free and universally available maternal and child health services including pre- and post-natal care which can only be realized within a universal health care system.
- A guaranteed 16-24 week job-protected maternity leave with income replacement for all women workers.
- A further job-protected unpaid leave for all working mothers and fathers until the child is a year old.
- Subsidized, regulated, sliding-scale, high-quality child care organized by federal/state/communities, private nonprofit organizations, and family day-care homes, the latter particularly for infants and toddlers.
- Parent participation in child-care centers and family day-care homes and "special leave" days for parents as part of flex-time policies.

- Respect and dignity for early-childhood teachers, reflected in equitable and professional level salaries.
- Before- and after-school programs in the elementary schools as well as consideration for an optional all-day kindergarten and alternative care provided for teacher preparation days.
- Flexible hours at the workplace as well as leave for sick children for mothers and fathers with children under 12.
- A vast expansion of early intervention programs for poor children and those considered "at risk." This expansion should involve Head Start as well as other innovative early childhood programs, and be modeled on the ABC Bill proposals.

If these recommendations seem rather impractical in the 1990s, we should remember that it was not so long ago that paid vacation leave, health insurance, and pension plans for workers were, too, a distant dream, as was suffrage for women.

Above all, we need to support families with children, recognizing the special vulnerabilities that temporarily attend single mothers and young children, the hardships encountered by working mothers who are poor, and the institutional assistance needed by all working mothers who, by virtue of their dual position in domestic and public life, need recognition and aggressive social-support networks.

Mothers and their children, once the invisible majority curtained behind the domestic hearth, are fast becoming the visible victims of a far-reaching antifamily policy, whose burgeoning contradictions affect our society. As child advocates, we need to promote critical and controversial discourse about these issues. It is not only the pragmatics of policy that need to change, but also our own consciousness about the meaning of family and the landscape of childhood.

REFERENCES

Ainsworth, M., et al. (1978). *Patterns of Attachment*. Hillsdale, NJ: Erlbaum.

Ariés, P. (1962). *Centuries of Childhood: A Social History of Family Life*. New York: Knopf.

Bowlby, J. (1951). *Maternal Care and Mental Health*. Geneva: World Health Organization Monograph Series.

Bureau of Labor Statistics. (1985, September 19). Washington, DC: U.S. Department of Labor.

Catalyst. (1986). *Report on a National Study of Parental Leaves.* New York: Catalyst's Career and Family Center.

CDF Reports, 11(5), December, 1989.

Children's Defense Fund (CDF). (1990). *Children 1990. A Report Card, Briefing Book and Action Primer.* Washington, DC: Author.

Coles, R., & Coles, J. H. (1978). *Women of Crisis: Lives of Struggle and Hope.* New York: Delta/Seymor L. Lawrence.

de Mause, L. (1982). *Foundations of Psychohistory.* New York: Psychohistory Press.

Deutsch, H. (1944). *The Psychology of Women: A Psychoanalytic Interpretation.* New York: Grune and Stratton.

Family Policy Panel of the Economic Policy Council (EPC) of UNA-USA. (1985). *Work and Family in the United States: A Policy Initiative.* New York: United Nations Association.

Grubb, N., & Lazerson, M. (1982). *Broken Promises: How Americans Fail Their Children.* New York: Basic Books.

Hayden, D. (1981). *The Grand Domestic Revolution: A History of Feminist Designs for American Homes, Neighborhoods and Cities.* Cambridge, MA: MIT Press.

Hewlett, S. A. (1986). *A Lesser Life.* New York: William Morrow & Co.

Kamerman, S. B. (1986). Maternity, paternity and parenting policies. In S. A. Hewlett, A. S. Ilchman, & J. J. Sweeney (Eds.), *Family and Work: Bridging the Gap* (pp. 53-65). Cambridge, MA: Ballinger.

Kamerman, S. B., Kahn, A. J., & Kingston, P. W. (1983). *Maternity Policies and Working Women.* New York: Columbia University Press.

Kessler-Harris, A. (1982). *Out to Work: A History of Wage-Earning Women in the United States.* New York: Oxford University Press.

Keyserling, M. D. (1972). *Windows on Daycare.* New York: National Council of Jewish Women.

Laslett, P. (1965). *The World We Have Lost.* New York: Scribner.

Laslett, P. (1982). Foreword. In M. Mitterauer & R. Sieder (Eds.), *The European Family* (pp. vii-xii). Chicago: University of Chicago Press.

Miller, A. (1984). *For Your Own Good: Hidden Cruelty in Childrearing and the Roots of Violence*. New York: Farrar, Straus & Giroux.

Mitterauer, M., & Sieder, R. (1982). *The European Family*. Chicago: University of Chicago Press.

Modigliani, K. (1986). But who will take care of the children? Childcare, women and devalued labor. *Journal of Education, 168*, 46-49.

Perkins Gilman, C. P. (1906, June). The passing of matrimony. *Harper's Bazar, 40*, 496.

Perkins Gilman, C. P. (1966). *Women and Economics: A Study of the Economic Relations between Men and Women as a Factor in Social Evolution*. New York: Harper Torchbooks. (Original work published in 1898)

Polakow, V. (1983). Excerpts from field observations conducted at a KinderCare Center.

Polakow, V. (1986). An excerpt of interviews with mothers of young children in Washtenaw County, Michigan.

Polakow, V. (1987). Excerpts from field observations conducted at a KinderCare Center.

Polakow Suransky, V. (1982). *The Erosion of Childhood*. Chicago: University of Chicago Press.

Riis, J. A. (1912). *How the Other Half Lives: Studies among the Tenements of New York*. New York: Scribner.

Rothenberg, M. (1980). Is there an unconscious national conspiracy against children in the United States? *Clinical Pediatrics, 19*, 15-24.

Rubin, L. B. (1976). *World of Pain/Life in the Working-Class Family*. New York: Basic Books.

Ryan, W. (1971). *Blaming the Victim*. New York: Pantheon Books.

Spitz, R. A. (1945). Hospitalism. *Psychoanalytic Study of the Child, 1*, 53-74.

Wright, G., & Rabinow, P. (1982, March), Spatialization of power. *Skyline*, pp. 14-20.

Zelizer, V. A. (1985). *Pricing the Priceless Child: The Changing Social Value of Children*. New York: Basic Books.

15

PUBLIC POLICIES FOR DISADVANTAGED CHILDREN AND THEIR FAMILIES

Judith H. Weitz

The Children's Defense Fund has become the most articulate and effective voice for disadvantaged children in the United States. This chapter outlines the ways in which current public policies do not adequately address the needs of disadvantaged children and their parents. In fact, the situation is deteriorating rather than improving with the passage of time.

Judith Weitz calls attention to six fundamental needs of children: to grow up in families with adequate incomes; to be born and to stay healthy; to grow up in caring, protective, and secure environments; to have shelter; to have a sound education; and to develop the self-esteem, knowledge, and skills required for productive work.

In order to meet these fundamental needs, the Children's Defense Fund advocates investing in a preventive and early intervention agenda that helps children before they drop out of school, become pregnant, or lose hope; supporting the young in their efforts to acquire basic skills and job experience needed for the workplace; assisting parents to mobilize the support they need for their children while they are employed away from home; and assuring families of a viable income.

In America, parents bear the primary responsibility for meeting the needs of their own children. Rich or poor, most parents make every effort to give their children not only food, clothing, shelter, and health care, but the intangibles of self-esteem, motivation, and hope.

But American society is complex, and no family shoulders this burden alone. From the day they are born, our nation invests in all children:

- Most children are born either in public hospitals that are directly supported by a state or local government, or in private, nonprofit hospitals built mainly with loans and grants from the federal government and tax-deductible private gifts.
- Most children are educated in public schools that are funded by the taxes of parents and nonparents alike.
- Most American children who pursue higher education receive public support, either by enrolling in public institutions or by receiving government-subsidized grants or loans.
- Millions of families receive federal or state housing subsidies through programs such as the Federal Housing Administration or Veterans Administration insurance and tax-exempt revenue bonds. Millions receive federal tax relief when they pay property taxes and mortgage interest payments.
- Most families pay many of their medical bills with the help of employer-paid insurance, which the government subsidizes by not treating it as taxable income.
- Most Americans live in neighborhoods that provide parks, libraries, playgrounds, and other enriching services underwritten by the government.

In these and many other ways, local, state, and federal governments invest in children and help support families. We do this to enhance, not to detract from, the role of the family. The relationship between family, community, and government is synergistic, strengthening both the family and the society in the complex undertaking of caring for children and building the future for them.

We extend this help to children not solely because of our moral obligations, but because we have faith in the future of our society, its progress, its values, and its traditions, and we want our children to have every opportunity to participate in the society and contribute to it.

In addition to our societal investment in children is an inter-generational compact that protects our future security. Children need help during the 18 years it takes them to reach adulthood. But today's adults will later turn to these children. Today's children are tomorrow's workers and taxpayers: our future leaders, artists, teachers, and scientists. Today's children will shoulder the trillion dollar national debt, finance our Social Security system, and lead this country into the 21st century. All Americans have a stake in our younger generation.

This partnership between family and government has its roots far back in American history, before the War on Poverty, before the New Deal, before the first federal funding for maternal and child health programs in 1921, and before the Civil War era, back to the period before the adoption of the Constitution, when the Congress of the Confederation granted federal lands to help maintain public schools.

We have made national progress on behalf of children. In 60 years, the number of 16- and 17-year-olds enrolled in school rose from less than 50% to almost 90%. More than 4 million handi-capped children are attending public school thanks to the passage and implementation of the Education for All Handicapped Chil-dren Act. Currently, 95% of our children are fully immunized by the time they enter first grade. It is within our reach to eradicate polio, diphtheria, measles, rubella, and whooping cough. From 1965 to 1979, technological advances in the field of medicine and increased access to health care helped reduce infant mortality rates 40%, from 25 deaths per 1,000 live births to 13.

However, any national report card on our current perform-ance for children would include many warnings of slowed prog-ress and some failing grades. A Louis Harris and Associates na-tional survey of public attitudes toward the problems of children found that nearly three out of four Americans think problems affecting children have gotten worse since they were growing up. Less than half of the public believe that most American children are basically happy, get a good education, or live in safe neigh-borhoods. A majority of those sampled believe that as a society we spend too little effort on our children and too little public money on programs for them.

A recent Harris survey of 3,000 families nationwide found that although the majority of families reported satisfaction with family relationships, many are stressed, pressured, and worried about the impact of external perils that beset children, including: drugs, alcohol, teen pregnancy, and dropping out of school. Over 90% worry about how their children are treated as individuals, whether they have inspirational teachers and mentors, whether they are learning how to concentrate and to think for themselves, and whether they are making close friends. The survey also found that one in four of all families shows signs of despair. "The singular mark of these families on the thin edge is that, by and large, their troubles are economic. Though money will not solve many family tensions, it is striking that the lack of money seems to go hand in hand with a dismal family life."

And, indeed, the data give cause for concern. Of 4- and 5-year-olds in today's America:

- One in four is poor;
- One in five is at risk of becoming a teen parent;
- One in six has no health insurance;
- One in six lives in a family where neither parent has a job;
- One in two has a mother working outside the home, but only a minority receive quality child care; and
- One in seven is at risk of dropping out of school.

The nurturing unit - the family - is imperiled by extraordinary change and economic instability. Of every 100 children born today:

- Twenty will be born out of wedlock;
- Twelve will be born to parents who divorce before the children reach 18;
- Six will be born to parents who separate before the children reach 18;
- Four will be born to families in which one parent will die before the children reach 18; and
- Forty will live in a female-headed household before adulthood.

Poverty and related ills also affect millions of families. Of every 100 children born today:

- Thirteen will be born to a teenage mother;
- Fifteen will be born into a household where no parent is employed;

- Fifteen will be born into a household with a working parent earning a below-poverty wage; and
- Twenty-five will be on welfare at some point prior to adulthood.

WHAT CHILDREN NEED

What is it that our children need that our national public policies are not providing for them?

CHILDREN NEED TO GROW UP IN FAMILIES WITH INCOMES ADEQUATE TO MEET BASIC NEEDS

Childhood should be a time of exploration, growth, and joy, with the security of knowing that, however financially pressed they are, parents can put food on the table and a roof over their heads. Yet we are failing to provide this most basic security to many of America's children.

In 1985, 12 million children lived in families with incomes below or at the poverty level (the "bare-bones" level the federal government estimates is necessary to meet a family's minimal subsistence needs), which in 1985, was set at $8,573 for a family of three. Even more startling is the fact that over 40% of these 12 million children lived in families whose incomes were less than $4,280.

Minority children suffer a far higher poverty rate. In 1985, over 43% of black children and 40% of Hispanic children were poor, as contrasted with 16% of white children.

Younger children too suffer a far higher poverty rate. They are disproportionately likely to be poor, and have grown increasingly so since 1979. Twenty-three percent, or nearly one in four, American children under 6 are poor, compared to 20% of children 6 to 17.

Children in female-headed single-parent families also are more likely to be poor. Over half of the children living in female-headed families are poor, a rate over four times the rate for children in other families. In 1985, 72% of Hispanic, 67% of black, and 45% of white children in female-headed households were poor.

It also is significant that almost as many poor children live in two-parent families as in single-parent homes. In 1985, 5.5 million poor children were living in two-parent families.

Overall, children in America have become far poorer than other age groups. Over 3 million children fell into poverty from 1979 to 1982, and only 210,000 children were lifted out of poverty in 1983 and 1984. At that rate of improvement, and assuming no more recessions, it would take 30 years - almost two generations - to get the number of poor children back even to the 1979 levels (when nearly one out of every nine children, two out of every five black children, and more than one of every four Hispanic children were poor).

Poverty increased most significantly among white (37%) and Hispanic (43%) families between 1979 and 1985; the corresponding increase for black families was 6%. Poverty among children in two-parent families also increased significantly during that period - and represented a 38% increase in the poverty rate.

Why are so many of our children poor? There is certainly no single factor or sole cause of this growing disadvantage among our nation's young. But at least four major factors can be identified that are pushing more and more children and families into poverty.

Children are poor because of persistently high joblessness among parents. Today, unemployment continues at historically high levels for a period that is more than 3 years into an "economic recovery." Roughly 8 million Americans are still unemployed. Another 5.6 million Americans (up from 3.9 million in 1979) work part-time because they cannot find full-time jobs. An additional 1.1 million are not counted as unemployed - they are the so-called "discouraged workers," those who have stopped actually looking for work, because they believe job prospects are too bleak.

Children are poor because their working parents cannot earn high enough wages to escape poverty. Research by Danziger and Gottschalk at the Institute for Research on Poverty at the University of Wisconsin found that roughly two-thirds of heads of poor households (who are not disabled, elderly, or taking care of young children) worked either full- or part-time during all or part of 1984.

For a growing number of Americans, a paycheck is not enough to escape poverty. Some of the most dramatic increases in poverty since 1979 have occurred among the working poor. The number of working-age persons who work but still remain poor was 9.1 million in 1985 - and has increased by 40% since

328

1979. More than 2 million Americans work full-time year-round but still remain in poverty. The ranks of the working poor have grown in significant part as a result of the declining real value of the minimum wage, which has dropped by more than 25% since 1981. As recently as 1979, earnings from a full-time minimum wage job were sufficient to lift a family of three out of poverty. Now a minimum wage job brings earnings equal to only 75% of the poverty line for a family of three. The larger numbers of hourly workers having low-wage jobs that do not produce enough income to lift their families out of poverty have also added to the ranks of the working poor. In 1979, 2.8 million of the Americans who were paid hourly wages earned less than $2.90 an hour, leaving them unable to lift a spouse and one child family above poverty through full-time, year-round work. By 1985, because of inflation, a worker would have needed $4.30 per hour to equal 1979's $2.90. The government does not keep data on workers earning less than $4.30, but it does tell us that more than 10.6 million hourly workers earned less than $4 per hour in 1985.

Children are poor because of changing family demographics, including growth in the number of children living in female-headed households. Over the past two decades the nation has experienced a significant movement away from the formation of two-parent families. Between 1970 and 1984, although the birth rate among women dropped, the proportion of births that were out of wedlock increased significantly, especially among white women. The divorce rate also increased. As a result of these trends, one in every five American children now lives in a female-headed household. Children living in female-headed families in 1985 were over four times more likely to be poor than those living in other families.

Although about half of all poor, able-bodied mothers with school-age children work at some point during the year, their earning power is still dramatically lower than men's and makes their families even more likely to remain in poverty. Danziger and Gottschalk found that the weekly earnings in 1984 of 45% of able-bodied female heads of households with children over 6 were so low that they did not meet the poverty level for a family of four; only 21% of comparably situated men earned this little.

Divorce or failure to form a two-parent family also often spells economic disaster for the custodial parent. Too frequently child support is a failed promise. In 1983, only 58% of the 8.7 million mothers raising a child whose father was absent from the home had been awarded child support. And of those, only half received the full amount; a quarter received partial payment, and a quarter received nothing. Even when paid in full, child support alone usually can do little to lift a child from poverty. The mean amount of child support paid under court order in 1983 was $1,330 per year, or 58% of what was due. In 1983 alone, absent parents failed to pay $3 billion in child support they owed their children.

Children are poor because the federal safety net has been shredded. Cutbacks in national survival programs for poor children and families have had a lasting impact. The effects of the $10 billion cut in 1981 are still felt - in spite of some partial restorations since that time. The gap between need and service has been growing.

These cuts have exacerbated the problem of poverty among families with children. An analysis by the Center on Budget and Policy Priorities of data from recent Census reports covering the period 1979 to 1985 shows that 30% of the increase in poverty among families with children since 1979 (and half of the increase since 1981) is due to the declining help government programs give in removing families from poverty. In 1979 nearly one out of every five families with children who otherwise would have been poor was lifted out of poverty by cash benefits such as Social Security, unemployment insurance, or public assistance. The comparable figure for 1985 was only one out of every nine families. The Center's research shows that the decline in the antipoverty impact of government benefits programs is even greater if the value of certain noncash benefits is included.

CHILDREN NEED TO BE BORN HEALTHY AND TO STAY HEALTHY

For a child to be born healthy, his or her mother needs early and continuous prenatal care and nutrition. Yet, in 1984, there was no change in the percentage of American women who received no prenatal care or only late care (during the last 3 months of pregnancy). This follows 3 years of movement in the wrong direction, with more and more pregnant women not receiving adequate prenatal care.

For 3 consecutive years, the improvements in our national infant mortality rates, already placing us 19th among industrialized nations, have slowed. In 1984, for the first time in over 30

330

years, there was virtually no improvement at all. Our black infant mortality rate is almost twice the white rate.

Although the majority of the nation's children are in better health than ever before, 40% of pre-school children are still not immunized against measles, rubella, or polio. Between 1983 and 1984, there was a 69% increase in the cases of measles reported. Nearly one-third of all children under age 17 have never visited a dentist.

Sexually active teens have the highest overall rates of sexually transmitted diseases among Americans. A reported 1 million teenage girls a year contract chlamydia, the fastest growing sexually transmitted disease and a leading cause of infertility and infant pneumonia. Each year over 1 million teenagers become pregnant: one in every eleven between the ages of 15 and 19 and one of every four sexually active girls.

Children and teenagers do not receive the health care they need for many reasons. One critical factor, however, is that many families cannot afford to pay for health care except in emergencies; many have no health insurance coverage. Experts estimate that anywhere from 4.8 million to 10.8 million U.S. children under the age of 18 are without health insurance today.

CHILDREN NEED TO GROW UP IN CARING, PROTECTIVE, AND SECURE ENVIRONMENTS

For a growing number of children with working parents, this need includes access to decent out-of-home child care. Over half of women with children younger than 3 work, as do an even higher percentage of women with pre-school and school-age children; most work full-time. In the next decade, the number of children younger than 6 needing child care will grow by more than 50%. If current trends continue, by 1995 more than three-quarters of all school-age children and two-thirds of pre-school children will have mothers in the labor force.

For low-income families, whether headed by a single parent or by two parents, child care is a critical rung in the ladder to economic security and stability for the whole family. However, poor and near-poor families cannot bear child-care costs without help. The typical cost of full-time child care is about $3,000 a year for one child, or one-third of a poverty-level income for a family of three.

The federal government thus far has avoided a leadership role in meeting the nation's child-care needs. The majority of direct federal assistance for child care comes through the Title XX Social Services Block Grant. In 1981, the President and Congress reduced federal funds for Title XX for 1982 by 20%. Despite subsequent minor boosts, Title XX funding is now one-half (in real terms) of what it was a decade ago. In response to the federal cuts, 23 states today offer Title XX child care to fewer youngsters than in 1981, though there are more poor children with working parents needing services.

Children also need to grow up in a home environment free of threatened or actual maltreatment. Yet, in 1985 1.9 million children and adolescents were reported abused or neglected, an increase of over 10% since 1984 and a 58% increase since 1981.

Between 1974 and 1980, the federal government stepped up its efforts to help these vulnerable children. The Child Abuse Prevention and Treatment Act, enacted in 1974, authorizes grants to states to assist them in developing and strengthening programs designed to prevent child abuse and neglect and to provide treatment for its victims. The Adoption Assistance and Child Welfare Act, enacted in 1980, is aimed at providing alternatives to prevent unnecessary out-of-home placements, encouraging permanency planning for children who are in care, and insuring quality care for children in placement.

Despite important strides in recent years, the federal commitment to meeting the special needs of troubled children and families still is inadequate. State and local systems set up to provide help are underfunded and are being swamped by rapid increases in demand for their services.

The National Committee for Prevention of Child Abuse recently reported that the number of child deaths due to maltreatment increased dramatically in 1986. In the 24 states for which survey data were available, the number of confirmed or suspected child deaths due to maltreatment increased 27% over 1985, whereas overall deaths in those same states had declined by 2% between 1984 and 1985.

CHILDREN NEED SHELTER
AND HEAT IN THE WINTER

The number of low-income households paying more than one-half of their incomes for rent and utilities rose from 3.7 million to 6.3 million (or nearly one-half of all low-income households) between 1975 and 1983. Between 1970 and 1980 the median rent rose 120%, but renters' median incomes rose only

66%. More than 8 million low-income renters were in the market for the 4.2 million units renting at affordable prices in 1985. This gap - 4 million units - is 120% larger than it was in 1980.

Low-income families have been hard hit by a 60% drop since 1981 in federally assisted housing funds targeted to help the poor and near-poor. In September of 1985 only 4 million of the 35 million potentially eligible households received any federal housing assistance.

A 1986 U.S. Conference of Mayors survey found that 92% of the cities surveyed reported an increase in the number of homeless families with children seeking shelter. Members of families with children now represent an estimated 28% of the homeless population nationwide, and much more in some areas.

At a recent hearing on homeless families and children held by the House Select Committee for Children, Youth, and Families, research was reported indicating that one out of every six homeless children suffers from cardiac diseases, anemia, or other chronic health conditions, a far higher rate than that for children in general.

Equally troubling is the December, 1985 report of the Governor's Task Force on Homeless Youth in Illinois, which indicated that in that state there were over 7,000 pregnant teenagers and teenage mothers without permanent living situations, 3,900 of them younger than 18. The odds for poor birth outcomes for these young mothers are overwhelming.

CHILDREN NEED A SOUND EDUCATION TO GROW INTO SELF-SUFFICIENT ADULTS

Every year, some 10 million children are held back a grade in school. The segment of the school population that had repeated at least one grade grew by 25% between 1977 and 1983. About 14% of white students, 24% of black students, and an estimated 40% of Hispanic students do not complete high school. University of California at Los Angeles Assistant Professor of Education, James S. Catterall, estimated that in 1985 the total lifetime earning loss for the dropouts in the high school class of 1981 alone will be $228 billion.

The future for a young person without strong basic skills is seriously limited. According to data from the National Longitudinal Survey of Young Americans analyzed by Andrew Sum of the Center on Labor Market Studies at Northeastern University, youths by age 18 with the weakest reading and math skills, when compared to those with above-average basic skills, are:

- eight times more likely to bear children out of wedlock;
- seven times more likely to drop out of school before graduation;
- four times more likely to be both out of work and out of school; and
- four times more likely to be forced to turn to public assistance for basic income support.

Recently, the federal government's crucial role in enhancing educational opportunity has diminished, due to funding cutbacks in most programs and the exacerbating erosion caused by inflation.

The Chapter I Compensatory Education Program (P.L. 97-35), which provides basic instructional services to disadvantaged elementary and secondary students, has significantly improved participants' test scores. Yet, it served only 54 students for every 100 poor school-age children in 1985; in 1980 this ratio was 75 per 100. Federal support for college education for disadvantaged students has failed to keep pace with skyrocketing tuition costs. Partially as a result, enrollment rates among youths with annual family incomes less than $10,000 dropped by 17% from 1979 to 1982, and those of youths with family incomes of less than $20,000 fell 9%. Enrollment increased among students from families with higher incomes during the same period. In 1977, 51% of white and 50% of black high school graduates went on to college. Since then the racial disparity has grown substantially.

CHILDREN NEED TO DEVELOP
SELF-ESTEEM, KNOWLEDGE, AND
SKILLS REQUIRED FOR PRODUCTIVE WORK

As children mature, they need a broad range of experiences, exposures, and relationships with their parents and other adults that will build their own self-esteem, extend their vision beyond neighborhood boundaries, continue their education, and expand their knowledge of the challenges of the skills required in the world of work.

Work is the bedrock of America's society and economy. For a young person, entry into the world of work is a key milestone in the transition to adulthood and sets the stage for future roles as parent, provider, and contributor to community and nation. Parental modeling of competence is an essential foundation.

Youths, in turn, need help from society to prepare for and make this transition. Each teenager needs a firm foundation of basic academic skills and a chance to explore vocational interests, develop good work habits, learn about employer expectations, and receive advice on finding suitable employment. Young people leaving high school or college need an opportunity to work and earn a wage that will support them and their families.

Yet, the overall teenage unemployment rate in January, 1986 was 18%, compared to 16% at a comparable point in time after the last big recession ended. The rate among black youths was almost 42%. Hispanic youths also faced a higher rate of 27% in November, 1985.

HOW WE CAN RESPOND

There are no foolproof ways in which to provide vulnerable families with the supports they need to raise healthy, happy, and productive children and teenagers. However, based on our national experience of what works and our understanding of what children need to prosper, we can begin to fill in the essential gaps.

*CHILDREN NEED PREVENTIVE
AND EARLY INTERVENTION HELP*

We need to invest in a preventive agenda that helps children before they get sick, drop out of school, get pregnant, or lose hope.

Before birth and during the early years, a child is growing and developing at an extraordinarily rapid pace. This is the time during which a youngster is most responsive to his or her environment and during which the foundation for a child's capacities in later years is built.

By providing prenatal care, for instance, to enough pregnant mothers to achieve the Surgeon General's 1990 goals of reducing infant mortality from its current rate of 10.8 to 9 deaths per 1,000 live births, the lives of more than 68,000 American babies can be saved by the year 2000.

By stepping up efforts to provide prenatal care so as to reach the Surgeon General's 1990 goal of reducing the incidence of low-birthweight births from its present rate of 6.7 to 5, we can reduce the total number of low-birthweight babies born by more than half a million and assure these babies a healthy start in life. Low-birthweight babies are 20 times more likely than others to die in the first year of life and are at significantly greater risk of developing such permanent handicapping conditions as developmental retardation, cerebral palsy, and autism. Yet, Medicaid, our national public health insurance program for low-income families, reaches fewer than half of all low-income pregnant women and newborn babies who need its services, and programs that provide care in medically underserved areas are underfunded. Twenty million Americans live in federally underserved communities.

Major new research funded by the United States Department of Agriculture and issued in January, 1986 tells us that there is a direct link between the provision of nutritional supplements to pregnant women, infants, and children and: (a) a reduction in fetal deaths; (b) a decrease in the rate of premature births; (c) an increase in the proportion of poor pregnant women seeking prenatal care; (d) increased head circumference of infants born to women receiving supplements during pregnancy; and (e) improved diets for women, infants, and children. The research also indicated a possible link between food supplements and improved cognitive development in children. If we provided The Supplemental Food Program for Women, Infants, and Children to women and children in the 100 counties that now have no program and to the over 3 million women and children now eligible but not receiving the services, we could make a difference.

In early childhood, children need stimulation and patient teaching to attain a beginning grasp of basic skills. Recognizing the importance of making this early investment, more and more Americans are enrolling their children in early childhood development programs. Sheila Kamerman and Alfred Kahn at the Columbia School of Social Work analyzed primary school data provided by the U.S. Department of Education's Center for Statistics and found that 67% of 4-year-olds (and 54% of 3-year-olds) whose families have incomes of $35,000 a year or more attend pre-school programs. In 1985, fewer than 33% of 4-year-olds and 17% of 3-year-olds whose families had incomes of less than $10,000 a year were enrolled in pre-school programs. Poor children are not getting an equal opportunity to participate in early child development programs.

The Head Start Program provides children pre-school education, parent involvement, and comprehensive service delivery.

This comprehensive approach mirrors Head Start's broad objectives: improving and expanding children's ability to think, reason, and speak clearly; working to improve children's health; aiding their emotional and social development; and helping children and their families gain greater confidence, self-respect, and dignity.

Head Start makes a difference for children. Head Start children are more likely to be able to meet the basic requirements of school and less likely to be held back a grade or assigned to a special education class. Children in Head Start receive more adequate levels of health care, have fewer absences from school, and perform better on physical tests. It also makes a difference for parents. Four out of five of the parents of Head Start children are providing volunteer services in the program. The program encourages parents to seek jobs in Head Start and elsewhere. Thirty-one percent of the program's paid staff are parents of current or former Head Start children. Yet despite its proven effectiveness, the program now reaches only 16% of the 2.5 million children who could benefit from its services. Increased investments in Head Start, and other similar comprehensive child development programs, would constitute a substantial building block for healthy children and families.

YOUNG PEOPLE NEED SUPPORT FOR VOCATIONAL PREPAREDNESS

We need to support young people in their efforts to acquire the basic skills and job experience they need to find a place in the workforce.

An effective education is necessary for the personal development of young people and for the development of the knowledge and skills they need to be productive and thoughtful members of our society. The vast majority (87%) of American children from all income groups are educated in our public school system. Many schools are doing very well. Schools located in middle-income or more affluent communities are most likely to have the resources and teaching staff to offer children a full range of opportunities to learn. But, the public school system is failing to educate many children, especially those from economically disadvantaged backgrounds. There are several symptoms of this failure including a high dropout rate, and persistent achievement gaps between well-off and poor children, and between blacks, Hispanics, and whites.

337

Although often helpful to most students, the state education reform movement, now in its fourth year, has not focused on disadvantaged students. In addition, the education reform movement has meant that many states have required students to meet higher standards without providing sufficient resources to enable those who need help to meet them.

Schools can make a difference for poor children. For too long many people have thought otherwise. But recent research on effective schools is showing that there are many things that schools can do to insure that all students learn. Five general characteristics distinguish effective from ineffective schools. They are: strong leadership from the principal in setting the tone of the school, in deciding on instructional strategies, and in managing school resources; high expectations for students both academically and in life in general; an orderly, pleasant school environment; heavy emphasis on the acquisition of basic academic skills; and program evaluation based on measured student outcomes.

Bilingual education, Magnet School Assistance, handicapped education, Chapter I assistance for disadvantaged elementary and secondary school children, and Pell grants to provide assistance to low-income students for college and university expenses are all important pieces of education assistance. In addition, special investments targeting dropout prevention, incentives for putting in place effective schools, and creation of community learning centers that complement school activities in out-of-school settings should be explored. Such "second chance" programs are essential if we are to reach any of the one in six youths who currently drop out of school.

In addition to a renewed commitment to education, we need to develop a system of vocational training and employment assistance for noncollege-bound youths. Expanding current successful federal investments in employment training and school-to-work transition programs for teenagers holds promise. The Summer Youth Employment Program, Job Corps, and Job Training Partnership programs all serve important functions in providing disadvantaged youths the work experience and job training they need. But we also need to be investing in Youth Opportunity Accounts which would allow at-risk children to earn credits toward future education, training, or subsidized work experience by reaching educational goals or performing community service. Creating school-to-work transition programs that give counseling and assistance to young people using the successful model of the Jobs for America's Graduates Program also makes sense.

PARENTS NEED SUPPORT

We need to assist parents to mobilize the supports they need for their children while they go to work and to insure that families receive income which at least meets basic needs.

All working parents, as well as parents in school or training programs, need access to affordable, quality child care to insure their children a safe and nurturing environment while they participate in the workforce. But the supply of child care lags behind need. The Children's Defense Fund, in collaboration with over 70 national organizations, has launched a major campaign to foster a new national child-care policy. The goal of this collaboration, the Alliance for Better Child Care, is to pass a major national child-care initiative which would make new federal funds available to help low- and moderate-income families meet the cost of child care while, at the same time, providing states with direct funds and financial incentives to improve the quality and expand the supply of child care for all families.

The bill addresses a wide range of gaps and problems in our current child-care system. It would help to eliminate a growing 2-tier system of child care by insuring that states pay an adequate amount for each child to provide incentives for child-care providers to serve children receiving federal and state child-care funds. A better child-care system for all families would result, with funds targeted to help states develop resource and referral systems to help families find appropriate child care; support programs to fund organizations to provide services to strengthen family day care programs; develop training programs to reach all child-care providers; expand the supply of child care; and strengthen both child-care standards as well as the enforcement of those standards.

There are many who believe that the key to a family's well-being is a job. It is true that a job gives young people and adults an important sense of self-worth and independence as well as an income. However, having a paycheck does not always mean that a family is free of the disabling effects of poverty.

Employment growth during the 1980s has been dominated by low-paying jobs. Since 1979, over half of all jobs added to the economy paid less than $7,000 per year (in 1984 dollars), according to a recent study by economists Barry Bluestone and Bennett

Harrison. A portion of this growth in low-paying jobs can be traced to increases in part-time or intermittent employment. Yet even among full-time, year-round workers, more than one in five new jobs created between 1979 and 1984 paid less than $7,000 a year.

In addition, our "safety nets" for the unemployed have many holes. Since the 1930s, Americans have counted on the unemployment insurance system to cushion the financial impact of job loss. However, in recent years the system has been weakened so that only one-fourth of all unemployed workers receive any benefits, compared with between only one-half and two-thirds in a typical month a decade ago.

Many jobless Americans do not qualify because they have not worked long or steadily enough at their previous place of employment. Others are not covered because they have been unemployed for longer than the benefit lasts. The unemployment insurance system is particularly ineffective for young parents, women, and minorities. Because eligibility is based on work experience and wage levels during the previous year, these groups are less likely than older, male, or white counterparts to collect benefits.

Our other national income safety-net program, Aid to Families with Dependent Children (AFDC), also is inadequate. First, many needy families cannot qualify for AFDC. To be eligible, families must not only meet certain income and resource tests but also certain "categorical" eligibility requirements. In 24 states, children in two-parent families, however poor they are, do not receive AFDC. Since 1981, pregnant women with no other children have been barred from receiving federally matched AFDC benefits for the first 5 months of pregnancy. A 1986 Children's Defense Fund survey found that 27 states begin AFDC coverage in the 6th month; 5 begin in the 7th month; and 2 begin in the 9th month. Only nine of these states also use state funds with no federal match to provide cash assistance at the AFDC rate prior to the 6th month. Seventeen states provide no AFDC help to first-time pregnant women.

Second, both benefit levels and eligibility levels are very low. As of July, 1986, the standard of need, which represents the state's assessment of the amount a family requires to support a minimum standard of living in a state, was below the poverty line for a family of three in every state. Actual AFDC benefits are often far lower than the need standard. In July, 1986, the maximum benefit for a family of three was less than half the federal poverty level in 32 states. The national average monthly AFDC payment per individual was $118.86 compared with the average federal public assistance for poor and disabled persons which was $336 per month per person. One child's pro-rata share of an AFDC grant for four in July, 1986 was only $36.75 in Alabama and $36 in Mississippi.

In addition, because few states have adjusted benefits to keep up with inflation, the real AFDC monthly benefit fell by 33% between July, 1979 and January, 1985. In 41 states, even the combined AFDC and food stamps benefits are less than 75% of the poverty level, nearly double the number in 1981.

Third, current restrictions on AFDC eligibility mean that many recipients have little financial incentive to seek low-wage employment. Since 1981, any earnings reduce a recipient's AFDC benefit virtually dollar for dollar.

Finally, the AFDC program falls short in enabling families to overcome barriers to employment. The obstacles most AFDC recipients face in the job market are well-documented. Three-fifths of all adults on AFDC have not graduated from high school, and at least one in four has no prior work experience. Those parents who do have the skills and work experience to compete for jobs frequently are unable to shoulder the costs of child care. Nearly 90% of all AFDC households are headed by single women. In 1983, 60% of all AFDC parents had children younger than 6 and 38% had children younger than 3. Even if a parent does find work, earnings may not meet subsistence needs or carry such job-related benefits as health insurance coverage. Loss of Medicaid deters some families from moving into the workforce.

A long-term agenda to help poor families must address the root causes of the poverty cycle: being born in poverty, insufficient opportunities to work or to work full-time, wage levels that are inadequate to support even small families, and a welfare system that rarely meets the most basic subsistence needs of poor families or provides parents with the basic skills and supports to become self-sufficient. However, we can also make a difference by making some immediate changes. For instance, we can:

- raise the minimum wage so that a full-time minimum wage earner can support his or her family at a level above the poverty line;
- enforce federal and state child-support laws and establish paternity for children born out of wedlock (even when

paid in full, however, child support alone usually cannot lift families out of poverty); and
- turn the AFDC program into more of a real "safety net" for poor families by establishing a national minimum benefit level and requiring states to provide AFDC to poor two-parent as well as single-parent families.

REFERENCES

[For up-to-date information on children's needs and the programs and policies in place to address them, the following sources are suggested.]

Carnegie Council on Adolescent Development. (1989). *Turning Points: Preparing American Youth for the 21st Century.* Washington, DC: Author.

Center for National Policy. (1989). *Giving Children a Chance.* Washington, DC: Center for National Policy Press.

Children's Defense Fund. (1990). *S.O.S. America: A Children's Defense Budget.* Washington, DC: Author.

Committee for Economic Development. (1987). *Children in Need: Investment Strategies for the Educationally Disadvantaged.* New York: Author.

Edelman, M. W. (1987). *Families in Peril: An Agenda for Social Change.* Cambridge, MA: Harvard University Press. (Available from the Children's Defense Fund, Washington, DC)

National Center for Children in Poverty. (1990). *Five Million Children.* New York: Columbia University, School of Public Health.

National Commission on Children. (1990). *Opening Doors for America's Children.* Washington, DC: Author.

U.S. House Select Committee on Children, Youth and Families. (1989). *U.S. Children and Their Families: Current Conditions and Recent Trends, 1989.* Washington, DC: Government Printing Office.

CONCLUSION

*A society in which more and more people become less and
less involved in nurturing their own children will inevitably
be less human, less understanding, and less compassionate.*

Margaret Mead pointed out long ago that public efforts to
protect children often harm them, because the responses are to
symptoms rather than to underlying causes (Mead, 1976). She
cited a still frequently repeated pattern in which troubled children are removed from their homes, from their school classes,
from their foster homes, from child-caring institutions, and ultimately to penal institutions. Furthermore, she called attention to
the time bomb of disadvantaged children in urban ghettos and
correctly predicted the large-scale explosion of gang wars. She
called for mechanisms for continuously confronting society with
thinking about the futures of our children.

In the United States we have removed children from factories, abusive homes, ghettos, and, most recently, from the daily
care of their parents with the rationalization that we are helping
them. In fact, these actions usually are motivated by adult needs
rather than the children's welfare. Children actually were
removed from factories because labor unions and the National
Consumer's League sought jobs and better working conditions
for adults (Teplitz, 1979). They are removed from abusive homes
because of society's need to point a finger at blameworthy par-

343

ents; from ghettos to summer camps as the gestures of charities of the wealthy; and from routine parental care, because parents are employed away from home.

Even though dramatic crises involving children regularly recur, society's responses typically follow the "issue-attention" or "crisis-recoil" cycle (Downs, 1972; Rhodes, 1972). In this cycle, an event is urgently catapulted to public attention, which then diminishes rapidly as people are distressed by facing the underlying causes, become bored with the issue, and shift their attention to the next dramatic event. As a result, the basic causes of these crises and their remedies rarely are addressed.

The intent of child advocacy, however, is not to rebuke society or adults for willfully harming or exploiting children, but to highlight children's unique needs that underlie crises and that can be addressed effectively. Child advocacy is a means of incorporating knowledgeable awareness of children into child-caring systems, professional practice, and public policies (Westman, 1979). It is assuming responsibility in varying degrees and ways for meeting the developmental needs of individual and classes of children. At the core of child advocacy is the recognition that children are parts of child-parent units and, by definition, are not freestanding individuals. When they are so, they become adults. Therefore, child advocacy is founded upon the child-parent relationship.

Individual child advocacy is a function of competent parenting; it is also a professional role and an ethical obligation of those who work with children. The professional tradition of relying upon the voluntary initiative and cooperation of individuals to be helped generally is a viable approach with adults, who are free to prosper or fail. However, because children are unable to fend for themselves, society accepts the responsibility to promote and protect their interests. Accordingly, professionals are expected, and in matters of abuse and neglect required, to take the initiative in helping children. When clinicians restrict themselves to diagnostic and treatment roles, they overlook the fact that children are unable to assume full responsibility for seeking appropriate help and following through on treatment procedures for themselves. Ignoring this inherent need of children for advocacy can be harmful to them, and clinicians have an ethical responsibility not to harm their clients or patients.

Because many professionals are unaware of their ethical advocacy responsibilities, there is a compelling need for education in advocacy knowledge and skills. Most professionals lack confidence in advocacy roles. They feel helpless in the face of the

344

painful and vexing dilemmas posed by children and erect defenses against the resulting anxiety. For example, health workers can become absorbed in the treatment of disease, lawyers in courtroom procedures, social workers in administrative policies, educators in the mechanics of teaching, psychiatrists in administering medications, and child-development specialists in short-term studies of day care. These defenses relieve personal anxiety and enhance the homeostasis of professional systems, but they are antithetical to the interests of children.

These barriers to empathic involvement in children's lives can be overcome by the mastery-enhancing techniques of child advocacy. Through increased child-development knowledge, skills for communicating with children, interdisciplinary teamwork, awareness of the rights of children, and coordination of resources for children, the helplessness and anxiety generated by the seemingly overwhelming life situations of vulnerable children can be minimized. Universities bear a special responsibility for providing training in child advocacy at all professional educational levels.

In the broader picture, professionals who are advocates for individual children are in unique positions to identify issues for, and participate knowledgeably in, class advocacy. In so doing, a background of awareness of the status of children in contemporary society is helpful. The value of children has changed as our society has evolved from stable rural to mobile, urban-based families. The newborn child in 19th century rural America was welcomed as a future laborer and as security for the parents later in life. Now children are economically unproductive and only sentimentally valued. In strict economic terms, they are financial burdens for their parents; the cost of raising a child in 1980 was between $100,000 and $140,000 (Zelizer, 1985). Consequently, the costs of raising children cause parents and society to regard child rearing as an economic liability in competition with other priorities rather than as a fundamental investment in future family relationships and in society's productivity.

Furthermore, there has been a downgrading of the satisfactions of parenthood, because it does involve financial, vocational, emotional, social, and physical sacrifices. Many adults are diverted from family life by preoccupation with their personal problems or with their vocational lives. Consequently, more people are openly questioning whether or not to become parents. They need to become more aware of the rewards of family life to counteract misconceptions about the onerous burdens of child rearing. In both tangible and intangible ways, children enrich the lives of adults. They provide emotional support, meaning, and purpose in life for their parents. Moreover, people who avoid having or working with children miss the stimulating effect of the young on their own personal growth.

Children really do not need specialized expertise from parents. Although professional aid may be required in managing certain children, the day-to-day needs of children, whether they are troubled or not, can be met by dependable, competent, and compassionate persons. To be a parent and raise a child requires common sense more than technical knowledge. And with guidance, children can be useful contributors to the economic welfare of their families by assuming household responsibilities, especially for parents employed away from home (Zelizer, 1985).

Because a child's most basic need is for a committed, competent parent, the welfare of families is the most important thrust of class child advocacy. Because the family is the source of socialization, the health of society depends upon vigorous families. However, since the late 1970s a shift has taken place in the distribution of wealth in the United States, more sharply defining class distinctions that discriminate against women and children (Thurow, 1987). The top 20% of all families received 44% of the national income in 1985, whereas the bottom 60% received only 32%. One result is the feminization of poverty: 77% of those living in poverty are women and children. Since 1979 the poverty rate of children has increased from 16% to 20% (Smeeding & Torrey, 1988).

If present trends continue without corrective actions, the American economy will have a severe workforce crisis in the 1990s (Committee for Economic Development, 1987). The impact of new technologies is expected to increase the total demand for employment to 157 million jobs, nearly twice the 1978 level. The nation's manufacturing sector will rely less and less on unskilled, manual labor, and the growing service and knowledge industries will require more literate, skilled workers. If these estimates hold, there will be a shortage of over 30 million Americans willing and able to work. This scarcity of qualified workers will seriously damage this country's position in an increasingly competitive global marketplace. Our nation's need for a qualified workforce to compete in the fast-changing global economy makes it intolerable that each year nearly 1 million marginally literate and virtually unemployable youths drop out of high school.

346

The most destructive political-economic process for families in the United States has been the longstanding development of a military economy, which means increasing stocks of ever more dangerous armaments and the dependency of industry on military expenditures. This has alienated young people's trust in adults and has deflected public funds away from using our society's brainpower to address the deteriorating lives of disadvantaged children. Furthermore, because some 3 million jobs in the United States depend upon spending on military armaments, the economic adjustment of communities, industries, and workers to required reductions in military spending is important (Melman, 1988). An economic alternative to the production of military weapons is urgently required.

More fundamentally, public policies are needed to enhance, rather than undermine, family life (Haveman, 1988). For example, the federal income tax deduction for a dependent would be $5,600 now, if it simply had kept up with inflation over the years. Family planning and family life education also are essential, because frequently an unwanted or an additional child sets off family disintegration and becomes its principal victim. Children's mental health services that have been eclipsed by community mental health services for adults should be restored with a family focus. The conflicts between family life and employment also must be addressed.

The Committee for Economic Development (CED), an independent research and educational organization of business executives and educators, has proposed policies to bring about steady economic growth in the United States with high employment, stable prices, increased productivity, improved living standards, and greater opportunities for every citizen (Committee for Economic Development, 1987). The CED calls for new partnerships among families, schools, businesses, and community organizations devoted to bolstering the health, education, and well-being of children beginning with their formative years. The CED points out that improving the prospects for disadvantaged children is an essential investment that can be postponed only at great cost to society.

The CED urges policy makers to adopt a three-part strategy for improving the prospects for disadvantaged children. First is prevention through early intervention in the form of programs that focus on children from birth to age 5 and on teenagers who are at risk of pregnancy. Second is restructuring the foundations of education by changing the organization, staffing, management, and financing of schools. Third are retention and re-entry-targeted programs that combine educational, employment, health, athletic, and social opportunities for students still in school and for dropouts.

We need a national vision that recognizes that human productivity depends upon competent child rearing. A short-sighted focus on immediate financial gain ignores long-range considerations, such as the fate of the earth and the productivity of future citizens. On the other hand, a society that understands research and development concepts can appreciate the importance of nurturing family life as an essential foundation for present and future economic productivity. The heart of the solution to our national economic and social problems is the rearing of competent children by competent parents. This is the aim of both individual and class advocacy.

Yet, parents are handicapped in the United States by the assumption of the media and government that they have the sole responsibility for their children and will protect their children from adverse influences in life. For example, the responsibility for protecting young people from drugs, pornography, and alcohol is seen as lying with parents, not society and communities, although general laws exist regulating these items. Thus, adults ignore the fact that children and youth are watching and are influenced by the public conduct of their affairs. Societal, community, and media standards would be quite different if all adults were aware, as should be parents, that they are modeling values and behavior for the young. Because parents are limited in their abilities to shield young people from destructive peer and adult influences that can be irresistible for some, society and communities have a responsibility to recognize the existence of, and to protect, their largest permanent minority - children and youth.

At the state and federal levels, the interpretation of laws and regulations that affect the media and raise First Amendment constitutional issues should take into account the fact that the public consists of both adults and minors. Accordingly, public standards should be appropriate for children and youth. In the private sector business and professional organizations should establish and refine ethical codes that incorporate the principles of class child advocacy.

At the community level individual and class advocacy can be brought together through child, youth, and family advocacy that relies on the direct participation of youths in formulating community goals and processes in collaboration with adults. It involves a series of stages beginning with needs assessment and prioritizing, continuing with identifying existing and projected resources for meeting those needs, developing those resources, and then establishing a mechanism for maintaining the advocacy process. The essential point is that significant sectors of a community demonstrate an interest in adapting their adult orientation to the population of children and youth. The inclusion of the adjective "family" along with child and youth advocacy at this level is important to convey to the uninitiated that the basic unit to be addressed is parent-child.

The operational principles of community child, youth, and family advocacy are integration, pluralism, coordination, and continuity. The principle of integration brings adults and youths together across existing structures in the community. Because they are mandated to serve all young people, the schools are central in providing both direction and facilities. Because communities must recognize children and youths as a constituency, local government must be involved in adapting community facilities and activities to their needs. Because they can provide both ideas and resources, voluntary organizations and churches also are essential participants. In essence, the fate of youth in a community is directly related to the overall integration and vitality of that community and the recognition of young people as a permanent part of the community.

The principle of pluralism recognizes that individual differences in talents, abilities, and interests dictate that a variety of options be available to the young, as they are to adults. No single program or approach will suffice. For example, simply opening a youth recreational center is not enough. One means of implementing the principle of pluralism is to adapt existing resources to youths. As examples, this can be done by making school facilities and programs available after school hours, forming police and fire department auxiliary groups for young people, organizing interest groups around library resources, and involving youths in planning and carrying out community activities and projects. An expression of pluralism is drawing upon youth-oriented organizations, such as scouting, church youth programs, Little Leagues, and the YMCA and YWCA. Another expression is by establishing recreational and athletic programs with both public and volunteer support and offering training and team participation in a variety of skills and sports.

The principle of coordination is particularly applicable to vulnerable young people who have been identified by educational, law enforcement, social service, and mental health agencies. In order to prevent these young people from developing more serious problems for themselves, their families, and their communities, the collaborative efforts of these agencies are needed at both general and specific case levels. All too frequently, the lack of coordination between these services results in inefficiency and ineffectiveness in serving troubled youths and their families.

The principle of continuity is vital, because interested parents and youths age rapidly and move on to other activities. It can be implemented by institutionalizing the advocacy process in an organizational structure with community-wide influence (Sandhu & Heaseley, 1981). An Advocacy Commission for Children, Youth, and Families consisting of politically influential adults with an interest in the young and of youths themselves with professional, parent, and youth advisory committees can unify the efforts of county, city, church, and private agencies by functioning as a nonprofit corporation funded by public and private sources.

In summary, child and youth advocacy offers a means of bringing the voice of the inarticulate young, both as individuals and as classes, into a society and communities planned and managed by adults. It is not a megaphone for the wishes of young people but is a means to determine and meet their authentic needs. A broad popular base for child advocacy can be tapped by calling public attention to the problems children and youth encounter at all levels of community life. Finding children at risk can be done by sensitizing people already on the scene. We do not require more research to know what young people need; our present knowledge can be more broadly disseminated, and professionals can be more effectively trained and deployed. To insure that services are available, those responsible for planning and developing human services can be sensitized to the needs of the young. Most importantly, advocacy knowledge and skills should be included in the training of professionals who deal with children and youth.

In the broadest sense, child advocacy extends to the conservation of the earth and the achievement of harmony in global relations for the next generation. More specifically, it is an endeavor that ranges from creating a society that fosters personal competence in parents and children to improving the life of a single child. Both individual and class advocacy can help the United States place a high priority on competent child rearing and avert future social and economic decline. Our society and our children depend upon us to make that commitment.

350

REFERENCES

Calhoun, J. A. (1987). *Making a Difference: Young People in Community Crime Prevention.* Washington, DC: National Crime Prevention Council.

Committee for Economic Development. (1987). *Children in Need: Investment Strategies for the Educationally Disadvantaged.* New York: Committee for Economic Development.

Downs, A. (1972). Up and down with ecology: The issue - attention cycle. *The Public Interest, Summer,* 39-50.

Haveman, R. H. (1988). *Starting Even: An Equal Opportunity Program to Combat the Nation's New Poverty.* New York: Simon & Schuster.

Mead, M. (1976). Society's problem with children. In J. C. Westman (Ed.), *Proceedings of the University of Wisconsin Conference on Child Advocacy.* Madison, WI: University of Wisconsin-Extension, Health Sciences Unit.

Melman, S. (1988). *Planning for Economic Conversion* (Waging Peace Series, No. 16). Santa Barbara, CA: Nuclear Age Peace Foundation.

National Crime Prevention Council. (1988). *Reaching Out: Youth as Resources in School - Based Programs.* Washington, DC: National Crime Prevention Council.

Rhodes, W. C. (1972). *Behavior Threat and Community Response.* New York: Behavioral Publications.

Sandhu, H. S., & Heaseley, C. W. (1981). *Improving Juvenile Justice: Power Advocacy, Diversion, Decriminalization, Deinstitutionalization, and Due Process.* New York: Human Sciences Press.

Smeeding, T., & Torrey, B. (1988). Poor children in rich countries. *Science, 242,* 873-877.

Teplitz, Z. (1979). Consumerism. In J. D. Noshpitz (Ed.), *Handbook of Child Psychiatry* (pp. 421-426). New York: Basic Books.

Thurow, L. C. (1987). A surge in inequality. *Scientific American, 256,* 30-37.

Westman, J. C. (1979). *Child Advocacy.* New York: Free Press.

Zelizer, V. A. (1985). *Pricing the Priceless Child.* New York: Basic Books.

AUTHOR INDEX

359

SUBJECT INDEX